The Tyndale Old Testament Commentaries

General Editor:
PROFESSOR D. J. WISEMAN, O.B.E., M.A., D.LIT., F.B.A., F.S.A.

DEUTERONOMY

DEUTERONOMY

AN INTRODUCTION AND COMMENTARY

by

J. A. THOMPSON, M.A., M.SC., B.D., B.ED., PH.D.
*formerly Reader in the Department of Middle Eastern Studies,
University of Melbourne*

INTER-VARSITY PRESS
LEICESTER, ENGLAND
DOWNERS GROVE, ILLINOIS, U.S.A.

Deuteronomy
Inter-Varsity Press
38 De Montfort Street, Leicester LE1 7GP, England
Box 1400, Downers Grove, Illinois 60515 U.S.A.

© *Inter-Varsity Press, London 1974*

uccf

*Inter-Varsity Press, England, is the publishing division of the Universities and
Colleges Christian Fellowship (formerly the Inter-Varsity Fellowship), a student
movement linking Christian Unions in universities and colleges throughout the United
Kingdom and the Republic of Ireland, and a member movement of the International
Fellowship of Evangelical Students. For information about local and national
activities write to UCCF, 38 De Montfort Street, Leicester, LE1 7GP.*

*InterVarsity Press, U.S.A., is the book-publishing division of Inter-Varsity
Christian Fellowship, a student movement active on campus at hundreds of
universities, colleges and schools of nursing. For information about local and regional
activities, write IVCF, 233 Langdon St., Madison, WI 53703.*

*Distributed in Canada through InterVarsity Press, 860 Denison St., Unit 3,
Markham, Ontario L3R 4H1, Canada.*

Text set in Great Britain
Printed in Great Britain at the Alden Press, Oxford

UK ISBN 0-85111-628-0 (hardback)
UK ISBN 0-85111-829-1 (paperback)
Library of Congress Catalog Card Number: 74-14303
USA ISBN 0-87784-882-3 (hardback)
USA ISBN 0-87784-255-8 (paperback)
USA ISBN 0-87784-880-7 (set of Tyndale Old Testament Commentaries, hardback)
USA ISBN 0-87784-280-9 (set of Tyndale Old Testament Commentaries, paperback)

21	20	19	18	17	16	15	14	13	12	11	10	9
96	95	94	93	92	91	90	89	88	87	86	85	

GENERAL PREFACE

THE aim of this series of *Tyndale Old Testament Commentaries*, as it was in the companion volumes on the New Testament, is to provide the student of the Bible with a handy, up-to-date commentary on each book, with the primary emphasis on exegesis. Major critical questions are discussed in the introductions and additional notes, while undue technicalities have been avoided.

In this series individual authors are, of course, free to make their own distinct contributions and express their own point of view on all controversial issues. Within the necessary limits of space they frequently draw attention to interpretations which they themselves do not hold but which represent the stated conclusions of sincere fellow Christians. This book of Deuteronomy has long been the subject of much discussion and debate, especially as to its authorship and date. Dr Thompson shows how many elements are obviously Mosaic and discusses others which may have been added subsequently. Devout scholars have proposed a date in the monarchy or later for the final compilation of this great influential book with its emphasis on law and history. The present author has given a fair account of the various possible solutions to this most vexed question. He combines this with a helpful and reverent exposition of the text and writes with the authority of one who is well versed in the many philological and archaeological findings which bear on this vital period in the divine revelation and in the history of God's people.

In the Old Testament in particular no single English translation is adequate to reflect the original text. The authors of these commentaries freely quote various versions, therefore, or give their own translation, in the endeavour to make the more difficult passages or words meaningful today. Where necessary, words from the Hebrew (and Aramaic) Text underlying their studies are transliterated. This will help the reader who may be unfamiliar with the Semitic languages to identify the word under discussion and thus to follow the argument. It is assumed throughout that the reader will have ready access to one, or more, reliable rendering of the Bible in English.

Interest in the meaning and message of the Old Testament continues undiminished and it is hoped that this series will thus

5

further the systematic study of the revelation of God and His will and ways as seen in these records. It is the prayer of the editor and publisher, as of the authors, that these books will help many to understand, and to respond to, the Word of God today.

D. J. Wiseman

CONTENTS

AUTHOR'S PREFACE

THE very considerable interest which the early Christians showed in the book of Deuteronomy provides some measure of its significance as a book of devotion and inspiration and a source of guidance for life. The sympathetic reader cannot fail to be challenged by the persistent demands throughout the book that he should acknowledge the complete and sole sovereignty of God in his life. Nor can he fail to be touched by the noble concept of God that underlies the whole book. Even though the great principles of Deuteronomy are expressed in terms which are at times strange to us in the twentieth century AD, we may grasp the principles and give them a present application. The results will be startling. Let the twentieth-century man place himself under the sovereignty of God in every area of his life and he will have begun to understand the import of the book of Deuteronomy.

There are many questions of a technical nature, such as historical background, literary form, language, *etc.*, on which commentators are not agreed. One can only explore the possibilities in each case and wait for more light. It is the strong opinion of the present commentator that the hand of Moses should be discerned throughout the book, even if it is not possible to decide the extent of editorial work.

It has seemed valuable to introduce the name *Yahweh*, the Hebrew name for Israel's God, in the course of the present exposition in the hope that readers might capture some of the majesty and wonder of that sacred Name. In English versions the expression *the Lord* seems to lack something of the character of the Hebrew name.

Acknowledgment is made of many helpful suggestions offered by Professor D. J. Wiseman, the General Editor of the series, and also by Dr G. J. Wenham of the Queen's University of Belfast. Special acknowledgment should be made of the help given by the author's wife in the preparation of the manuscript.

Such defects as remain are the author's own responsibility. It is his hope that this commentary will assist the reader of Deuteronomy to come to recognize the sovereignty of God in every area of his life.

JOHN A. THOMPSON

CHIEF ABBREVIATIONS

AASOR	*Annual of the American Schools of Oriental Research.*
ANEP	*The Ancient Near East in Pictures relating to the Old Testament* edited by J. B. Pritchard, 1954.
ANET	*Ancient Near Eastern Texts relating to the Old Testament*[2] edited by J. B. Pritchard, 1955.
AV	English Authorized Version (King James), 1611.
BA	*Biblical Archaeologist.*
BASOR	*Bulletin of the American Schools of Oriental Research.*
BJRL	*Bulletin of the John Rylands Library.*
BWANT	*Beiträge zur Wissenschaft vom Alten und Neuen Testament.*
BZ	*Biblische Zeitschrift* (new series).
CAH[2]	*Cambridge Ancient History* (second edition).
CBQ	*Catholic Biblical Quarterly.*
EQ	*Evangelical Quarterly.*
ET	English translation.
IB	*The Interpreter's Bible.*
IBD	*The Interpreter's Bible Dictionary.*
ICC	*International Critical Commentary.*
IEJ	*Israel Exploration Journal.*
ISBE	*International Standard Bible Encyclopedia.*
JAOS	*Journal of the American Oriental Society.*
JBL	*Journal of Biblical Literature.*
JCS	*Journal of Cuneiform Studies.*
JJS	*Journal of Jewish Studies.*
JPOS	*Journal of the Palestine Oriental Society.*
JPSA	Jewish Publication Society of America, 1962
JQR	*Jewish Quarterly Review.*
JSS	*Journal of Semitic Studies.*
LXX	The Septuagint (pre-Christian Greek version of the Old Testament).
MT	Massoretic Text.
NBD	*The New Bible Dictionary* edited by J. D. Douglas et al., 1962.
PEQ	*Palestine Exploration Fund Quarterly.*
RB	*Revue Biblique.*
RSV	American Revised Standard Version, 1952.
RTR	*The Reformed Theological Review.*
TB	*Tyndale Bulletin.*
VT	*Vetus Testamentum.*
ZAW	*Zeitschrift für die alttestamentliche Wissenschaft.*

SELECTED BIBLIOGRAPHY

I. COMMENTARIES

Blair, E. P. *Deuteronomy, Joshua (Layman's Bible Commentaries)*, 1964.

Buis, P. and Leclercq, J. *Le Deutéronome*, 1963.

Cunliffe-Jones, H. *Deuteronomy (Torch Bible Commentaries)*, 1951.

Driver, S. R. *A Critical and Exegetical Commentary on Deuteronomy (International Critical Commentary)*, 1902.

Henton Davies, G. 'Deuteronomy', *Peake's Commentary on the Bible*, Revised edition, 1962.

Keil, C. F. and Delitzsch, F. *Biblical Commentary on the Old Testament*, Vol. III, the Pentateuch, 1864.

Kline, Meredith G. *Treaty of the Great King*, 1963.

Smith, George Adam. *The Book of Deuteronomy (Cambridge Bible Series*, Revised Version), 1918.

von Rad, Gerhard. *Deuteronomy*, 1966.

Wright, G. E. *Deuteronomy (The Interpreter's Bible*, Vol. 2), 1953.

II. GENERAL

Bright, John. *A History of Israel*, 1960.

Brinker, R. *The Influence of Sanctuaries in Early Israel*, 1946.

Clements, R. E. *God's Chosen People*, 1968.

de Vaux, R. *Ancient Israel*, 1962.

Harrison, R. K. *Introduction to the Old Testament*, 1970.

Manley, G. T. *The Book of the Law*, 1957.

McCarthy, D. J. *Treaty and Covenant (Analecta Biblica*, 21), 1963.

Mendenhall, G. E. *Law and Covenant in Israel and the Ancient Near East*, 1955.

Nicholson, E. W. *Deuteronomy and Tradition*, 1967.

Pritchard, J. B. *Ancient Near Eastern Texts*,[2] 1955.

Review and Expositor, Vol. LXI, No. 4, 1962. Issue devoted to Deuteronomy.

Robertson, E. *The Old Testament Problem*, 1950.

von Rad, Gerhard. *Studies in Deuteronomy*, ET, 1953.

Weinfeld, Moshe. 'Deuteronomy', *Encyclopedia Judaica* (1971), Vol. V, Col. 1573–1583.

Weinfeld, Moshe. *Deuteronomy and the Deuteronomic School*, 1972.

Welch, Adam C. *The Code of Deuteronomy*, 1924.

Wiseman, D. J. *The Vassal Treaties of Esarhaddon (Iraq*, 20), 1958.

Wright, G. E. *The Old Testament and Theology*, 1965.

INTRODUCTION

THE narrative in the book of Numbers concludes with the children of Israel temporarily settled in the plains of Moab opposite Jericho, already at the threshold of the promised land (Nu. 33:48, 49; Dt. 1:5). The occupation of the lands on the east side of the river Jordan, which were to become part of Israel's territory in the coming centuries, was already completed. At this point in the story there was a pause while Moses expounded to Israel the character of their faith and nationhood. In the book of Deuteronomy the demands of Yahweh their God are recorded in many passages, but everywhere it is evident that Israel was challenged to a total unshared allegiance to Yahweh who had wrought mighty acts of deliverance on her behalf. *You must revere the Lord your God: only Him shall you worship, to Him you shall hold fast, . . . He is your God, who wrought for you those marvellous, awesome deeds that you saw with your own eyes. Your ancestors went down to Egypt seventy persons in all; and now the Lord your God has made you as numerous as the stars of heaven* (10:20–22, JPSA). The primary demand for Israel, which later became a primary demand for Christians also, was *You shall love the Lord your God with all your heart, and with all your soul, and with all your might* (6:5; *cf.* Mt. 22:37; Mk. 12:30; Lk. 10:27).

Deuteronomy is one of the greatest books of the Old Testament. Its influence on the domestic and personal religion of all ages has not been surpassed by any other book in the Bible. It is quoted over eighty times in the New Testament[1] and thus it belongs to a small group of four Old Testament books[2] to which the early Christians made frequent reference.

I. TITLE

The fifth book of the Torah was known to the Jews by a variety of names. One common term for it was *ēlleh haddᵉḇarîm* (these are the words), since these were the first words in the book. An abbreviated form of this title was simply *dᵉḇarîm* (words).

---

[1] References occur in all but six books of the New Testament, namely John, Colossians, 1 Thessalonians, 2 Timothy, and 1 and 2 Peter.
[2] Genesis, Deuteronomy, Psalms and Isaiah.

Another name which was familiar to the Jews was *mišneh hattôrâ*, or simply *mišneh* derived from 17:18. A third title was *sēp̄er tôḵāhôṯ* or 'book of admonitions'.

The name Deuteronomy derives from the Greek rendering of a phrase in 17:18 where the king who is to rule over Israel is commanded to prepare *a copy of this law*. The LXX rendered this phrase mistakenly as *to deuteronomion touto*, lit. 'this second (or, repeated) law'. Subsequently the Vulgate rendered the Greek noun *deuteronomium*. The contents of the book were thus regarded as a second law. The first had been given on Mount Horeb (Sinai). The second was a repetition of the first on the plains of Moab. Despite a mistaken translation of the Hebrew *mišnêh hattôrâ hazzō'ṯ* the name of the LXX translators is not entirely inappropriate since Deuteronomy is, in some measure at least, a re-presentation of the law of Sinai, albeit in the form of an exposition of the Mosaic law.

II. DEUTERONOMY AND THE DIVINE TORAH

Quite apart from the complex problems of date and authorship (to which we shall return), Deuteronomy is marked throughout by a spirit of urgency. The book comes even to the modern reader in much the same way as a challenging sermon, for it is directed towards moving the minds and wills of the hearers to decision: *choose life, that you and your descendants may live* (30:19). The work as a whole was evidently intended to give Israel instruction and education in her faith and to press home to her the demands of her faith. The book describes its own contents as *law* (*tôrâ*). It is described both as *this book of the law* (28:61; 29:21; 30:10; 31:26), and *this law* (1:5; 4:8; 17:18, 19; 27:3, 8, 26). More precisely 'law' is defined as *testimonies* (*'ēḏūṯ*), *statutes* (*mišpāṭîm*) and *ordinances* (*huqqîm*) (4:45; 6:20). Sometimes only two of these terms appear, *testimonies and statutes* (6:17), or *statutes and judgments* (AV)/*statutes and ordinances* (RSV) (4:1; 12:1). Normally, these are legal terms. However, the more comprehensive *tôrâ* seems to refer not so much to law in a juridical sense, as to religious teaching given by a priest, a prophet or a wise man.[1] Deuteronomy thus identifies legal enactments with religious instruction. In fact, careful study of Deuteronomy makes it clear that the book is not a juridical statement at all but rather an exposition of a faith. The book was evidently

---

[1] G. Ostborn, *Tora in the Old Testament; a Semantic Study* (1945).

never intended as a handbook for those in Israel who were charged to administer the law: kings, priests and judges. Even though blocks of law can be isolated,[1] whether these are apodictic[2] or casuistic,[3] they are interspersed with exposition and exhortation. Law in Deuteronomy is an expression of the will of God which must be obeyed. A people redeemed from slavery and bound to their God by a covenant needed some guidelines for a happy life in fellowship with God and with one another.

One reason for the presence of law in the book is that the Sinai covenant was cast in the shape of an ancient Near Eastern treaty[4] which listed the obligations laid on the vassal by the suzerain. These were a natural consequence of the suzerain's protection and care for his vassal. In like manner Yahweh had displayed on Israel's behalf mighty acts of deliverance and guidance not only during the exodus, but also during the wanderings in the wilderness. There was no reason why Yahweh, the God of Israel, should have acted in this way. Such activity on Israel's behalf flowed from His unmerited love. The only adequate response to such love was single-minded devotion and unshared allegiance. The tangible expression of such devotion and allegiance was obedience to the covenant stipulations. But even these were part of a total movement of grace, a fact that made law neither a burden to be borne nor a means of achieving merit before God. His laws were rather His gracious gift of guidance for a peaceful life in the new land. They thus provided guidelines for a happy life and a means by which Israel might demonstrate her loyalty to the God who had redeemed her.

The historical facts of Yahweh's redeeming activity are set out in some detail in the early part of the book in chapters 1–3. An exhortation to obey the law is given in chapter 4. The basic

---

[1] Gerhard von Rad, *Studies in Deuteronomy* (ET, 1953), pp. 11–24, isolates some of these.

[2] The term, as used by A. Alt in 'The origins of Israelite Law', *Essays on Old Testament History and Religion* (ET, 1966), refers to law that was given by proclamation and not as the result of judicial decisions. Apodictic law is generally couched in short, succinct statements, often of the form *Thou shalt* or *Thou shalt not*.

[3] Casuistic law is of the form 'if . . . then . . .'. It arose from the common law of the ancient Near East and similar laws were to be found in many codes.

[4] The nature of the ancient Near Eastern treaty and its significance for Deuteronomy are discussed below on pp. 17–21.

demands of Yahweh occur in chapters 5–11 in the form of great principles, while chapters 12–26 set out a great variety of day-to-day regulations to meet the practical demands of a nation living out its common life. These latter chapters demonstrate how such a nation might live according to the principles of chapters 5–11.

One other aspect of *tôrâ* in Deuteronomy is that it presents a picture of life within the covenant in which Israel would find fellowship with Yahweh her God and enjoy the blessings of the covenant.[1] Any other way of life was fraught with danger, *i.e.* a *curse*. In secular treaties rebellion brought punishment from the suzerain. So too with Yahweh's covenant. Rejection of His covenant, which was the outcome of His love, was the most heinous of all sins. It was, indeed, the essence of sin itself and would result in God's judgment on Israel.

In brief, therefore, Deuteronomy sets out in the divine *tôrâ* the whole body of teaching which showed the people of Israel the way to live in fellowship with Yahweh and with one another. That life would enable Israel to enjoy to the full all the blessings of the covenant. To live any other life was tantamount to a rejection of Yahweh's gracious intentions for His people.

III. THE STRUCTURE OF DEUTERONOMY

Even a cursory reading of Deuteronomy suggests that the book was arranged according to a definite plan. The most obvious feature of the structure is that it comprises three addresses of Moses to Israel. After an introduction (1:1–5) the first address commences at 1:6. It consists for the most part of a survey of the activity of Yahweh on Israel's behalf during their wanderings from Horeb (Mount Sinai) until their arrival at the Jordan river (1:6 – 3:29) and concludes with a hortatory section in which Moses appeals to Israel to give heed to the demands of Him who acted on their behalf (4:1–40). A brief appendix refers to the cities of refuge (4:41–43).

The second address, which is really the heart of the book, commences with chapter 5 after a brief introduction (4:44–49), and continues to the end of chapter 28. It seems at first sight that chapter 27 is a subsequent insertion into the main speech

---

[1] John Murray, *The Covenant of Grace* (1954), pp. 17–20.

(see commentary). We shall argue in the course of the present section that such a view is not necessary.

The third address, chapters 29 and 30, is really an appeal to Israel to accept the covenant. It concludes with the declaration of the choice before Israel, namely life or death (30:15-20). Chapters 31-34 appear at first sight to be appendices.

A closer examination of this structure will reveal that, whereas the second address is very long (chapters 5-28), the first (chapters 1-4) and the third (chapters 29, 30) are very brief. It would seem that 1:1-5 is an editorial introduction to the whole book since it refers to the fact that *Moses undertook to explain the law* (1:5). Then 4:44-49 seems to be the introduction to the second address.[1]

There have been a number of attempts in recent years to define the structure of Deuteronomy in a somewhat different way. Several of these will now be outlined.

Martin Noth has proposed[2] that chapters 1-4 should be regarded as an introduction to the great historical work which stretches from Joshua to 2 Kings, commonly called nowadays the Deuteronomic History of Israel. He regards chapters 1-3 as a brief résumé of the events which immediately preceded the conquest, from Horeb (Sinai) to the east bank of the Jordan river. The story is thereafter resumed at Joshua 1. Chapter 4 is seen as the conclusion to the historical survey, *i.e.* it is an appeal to Israel to obey Yahweh. Its introductory words 'and now' are commonly used in the Old Testament to introduce the conclusion to an argument.[3] Next, Noth regards 4:44-49 as the introduction to an older form of Deuteronomy which is concerned with Israel's faith and life, based on the Mosaic law. Chapters 5-11 constitute a problem. Apart from 5:6-21 (the decalogue) they are concerned more with exhortation than with statutes, commandments and ordinances. It is only with chapter 12 that these legal enactments commence and thereafter they continue till chapter 26.[4] Noth regards 4:44 - 30:20 as a book complete in itself with 1:1 - 4:43 and chapters 31-34 as belonging to some other literary context. Indeed he proposes that the editor of the great Deuteronomic

---

[1] See commentary. See also pp. 23-24 under 'Introductory phrases in Deuteronomy'.

[2] Martin Noth, *Überlieferungsgeschichte des Pentateuch* (1948).

[3] Ex. 19:5; Dt. 4:1; Jos. 24:14; 1 Sa. 8:9; 12:13, *etc.*

[4] See George Adam Smith, *The Book of Deuteronomy* (1918), pp. xlvii-xciv, for a detailed discussion of these.

History attached chapters 1–4 as an introduction to the history. The great prologue to the history was Deuteronomy 5–26 and 28 to which chapters 27, 29 and 30 were possibly already attached when the work was taken up. Chapters 31–34 were possibly added by the same editor although these too may have been already attached when he took them up.

Although there is clearly a good deal of speculation in Noth's theory it has been accepted by many Old Testament scholars as offering an explanation for the various chapters in Deuteronomy. But there are other theories.

Gerhard von Rad sees the book as a typical farewell speech,[1] other examples of which occur elsewhere in the Old Testament (*e.g.* Jos. 23; 1 Sa. 12; 1 Ch. 22 and 29). These speeches are in the form of the 'regular covenant formulary'. Just as in the secular realm the status of the new vassal had to be confirmed following the death of his predecessor, so in Israel the form of her relationship with Yahweh needed to be reaffirmed when a new leader took his place in the nation. Moses was laying down his office and Joshua was taking it up. Once again the 'basic principles' had to be stated (chapters 4–11), 'detailed stipulations' had to be set out (chapters 12–26), the covenant sanctions, *i.e.* the blessings and curses, had to be declared (chapters 27, 28), and the oath of allegiance had to be taken (chapter 29). For von Rad the *Sitz im Leben* demanded by this pattern was a cultic celebration, perhaps a feast of covenant renewal.[2] He argues that the book falls structurally into four sections:

1. Historical presentation of the events at Sinai and parenetic (advisory or hortatory) material connected with these events (Dt. 1–11).
2. The reading of the law (Dt. 12 – 26:15).
3. The sealing of the covenant (Dt. 26:16 19).
4. Blessings and curses (Dt. 27f.).

The strict form of the covenant formulary was, however, lost and the contents now appear in the form of a homiletic instruction for the laity. In this form the original cult setting is likewise abandoned and obscured. One of the great weaknesses of the theory is that in the Old Testament there is no evidence of the cultic celebration proposed by von Rad.

---

[1] Gerhard von Rad, *Deuteronomy* (1966), pp. 22, 23.
[2] Gerhard von Rad, *The Problem of the Hexateuch and Other Essays* (ET, 1966), pp. 27–33.

New light was thrown on the whole problem of the structure of Deuteronomy when G. E. Mendenhall published an important article in which he pointed out similarities between the Hittite treaties of the second millennium BC and the covenant of Israel with Yahweh.[1] Mendenhall's thesis was based on the work of V. Korošec (1931) who undertook a juristic analysis of the Hittite treaties.[2]

Subsequent discussion of the book of Deuteronomy has generally taken serious notice of Mendenhall's work.

The ancient Near Eastern treaty comprises the following elements:

1. The preamble in which the king is introduced.
2. The historical prologue in which past relations between the two parties are reviewed.
3. The treaty stipulations (a) General principles.
                     (b) Specific stipulations.
4. The treaty sanctions, curses and blessings.
5. The witnesses – gods who will guarantee the treaty.

G. E. Mendenhall included a sixth element in his original list, namely the provision for deposit of the treaty document in the temple and periodic public reading.

We will now refer to several recent attempts to relate the structure of Deuteronomy to the ancient Near Eastern treaty pattern.

Meredith G. Kline proposes[3] that Deuteronomy is a unity and holds it to be an authentic Mosaic document cast in the form of the ancient Near Eastern treaty. He interprets the book within the framework of the administration of God's redemptive covenant with Israel. He outlines the book as follows:[4]

1. Preamble: The covenant mediator, 1:1–5.
2. The historical prologue; covenant history, 1:6 – 4:49.
3. The covenant stipulations: covenant life.
    (a) The great commandment, 5:1 – 11:32.

---

[1] G. E. Mendenhall, *Law and Covenant in Israel and the Ancient Near East* (1955). This small but highly significant monograph is a reprint of two articles in *BA*, XVII, No. 2, May 1954, pp. 24–46, and XVII, No. 3, Sept. 1954, pp. 49–76.

[2] V. Korošec, *Hethitische Staatsvertraege* (1931).

[3] Meredith G. Kline, *Treaty of the Great King* (1963).

[4] *Ibid.*, pp. 7, 8.

    (b) Ancillary commandments, 12:1 – 26:19.

4. The covenant sanctions: covenant ratification, blessings and curses, covenant oath, 27:1 – 30:20.

5. Dynastic disposition: covenant continuity, 31:1 – 34:12.

D. J. McCarthy[1] investigated the relationship between the ancient Near Eastern treaty and the covenant in the Old Testament in a very detailed discussion. Apart from recognizing in Deuteronomy the basic structure of the ancient Near Eastern treaty he argued that Deuteronomy 1–3 should be set apart as a piece of historical writing which provides the background for the covenant that Moses was about to announce. Chapter 4 is a formal unit in itself which embraces basic elements of the covenant scheme. So also are chapters 29 and 30. This means that the kernel of Deuteronomy, chapters 5 to 28, is framed within two speeches in covenant form both of which end on a positive note and provide a framework of hope to counter the curses of chapter 28.

An important contribution to the discussion has recently been made by G. J. Wenham.[2] He argues that the Old Testament covenant form is a distinctive form that occurs only in the Old Testament. It bears some resemblance to both the 'law-code' form and the Middle Eastern treaty form. The former comprises a historical prologue, a block of laws and an epilogue.[3] In this form the epilogue contains a historical survey recapitulating some of the achievements of the king who promulgated the laws and mentioning the erection of the stele, a list of blessings on those who respect the laws and a list of curses on those who break the laws.

A study of Old Testament covenant forms such as those in Exodus 20ff., Deuteronomy, Joshua 24 and 1 Samuel 12 suggests a literary form comprising (1) a historical prologue; (2) covenant stipulations containing (a) basic principles; (b) detailed stipulations; (3) a document clause requiring the recording and sometimes the renewal of the covenant; (4) blessings; (5) curses; (6) recapitulation of the main covenant demand. Gordon Wenham sets out the comparison between the law codes, the Old Testament covenant and the Near Eastern treaties in tabular form as follows:

---

[1] D. J. McCarthy, *Treaty and Covenant* (*Analecta Biblica*, 21, 1963), pp. 131ff.

[2] In an unpublished thesis, *The Structure and Date of Deuteronomy*.

[3] Compare the Code of Hammurabi (*ANET*, pp. 163–180) with its prologue (pp. 164-165), the laws (pp. 166-177) and the epilogue (pp. 177-180).

Law Code	O.T. Covenant	N.E. Treaty
		1. Preamble
1. Prologue	1. Historical prologue	2. Historical prologue
2. Laws	2. Stipulations	3. Stipulations
	(a) basic	(a) basic
	(b) detailed	(b) detailed
3. Summary/Document clause	3. Document clause	4. Document clause
4. Blessing	4. Blessing	5. God list
5. Curse	5. Curse	6. Curses and blessings
	6. Recapitulation	

The item defined here as 'recapitulation' is peculiar to the Old Testament covenant.

If certain editorial headings are omitted the material in Deuteronomy 1–30 may be arranged as a typical Old Testament covenant form:

1:6 – 3:29	Historical prologue
4:1–40; 5:1 – 11:32	Basic stipulations
12:1 – 26:19	Detailed stipulations
27:1–26	Document clause
28:1–14	Blessings
28:15–68	Curses
29:1 – 30:20	Recapitulation

In that case it is not necessary to argue that chapters 1–3 were added later by the Deuteronomist. If we leave aside 4:41–49 which belongs with the headings scattered throughout the book, then 4:1–40 belongs with chapters 5–11. Some indication of the close link between chapters 4 and 5 may be seen if the section 4:34–40 is compared with 5:1–6 where the features mentioned in the first group of verses occur in the reversed order in the second group of verses. It seems as though 4:34–40 was linked originally to 5:1–6 and that chapter 4 may have formed part of the basic covenant principles. In the present text 4:41–49 is an interpolation.

The total picture of chapters 4 to 11 is then 4: 1–40 parenesis (exhortation or advice), 5:1 – 6:3 narrative, 6:4 – 8:20 parenesis, 9:1 – 10:11 narrative, 10:12 – 11:32 parenesis.[1]

Chapters 12:1 – 26:19 deal with the detailed stipulations. Then chapter 27 corresponds to the fourth section in V. Korošec's analysis,[2] the provision for deposit in the temple and

[1] N. Lohfink, *Das Hauptgebot: eine Untersuchung literarischer Einleitungsfragen zu Dt. 5–11* (*Analecta Biblica*, 20, 1963), pp. 66f.
[2] See above, p. 17.

periodic public reading and also to the document clause in the law code pattern.[1] Some commentators have removed 27 from its present position (see commentary), but following the outline of Deuteronomy suggested above (p. 19) it fits quite naturally precisely where it now appears in a typical Old Testament covenant pattern.

Then chapters 29-30 are a recapitulation of the covenant concluding with an appeal to Israel to be faithful in war (31:2–6). There is no need, therefore, to separate these chapters as an editorial addition made after chapters 1–28 were completed.

Chapters 31–34 do not belong to the covenant form as such but should be seen in the context of a covenant renewal. Joshua was to be Moses' successor and was charged with the responsibilities of being military commander and of dividing the promised land among the tribes (31:2–8). The Song of Moses (32:1–43) is woven into these chapters. It has close affinities with covenant ideas. The introduction to the song (31:24–29) takes up themes within the song and the whole idea of appointing Joshua links back to 1:37ff.; 3:21–28, providing editorial links between the early and later chapters in the whole book. Similarly chapter 33 is introduced by 32:48–52 which links back to 3:27f. where Moses is commanded to ascend Pisgah (*cf.* 34:1ff.). The land which Moses viewed is the theme of the blessings of 33:6–28. One gains the impression that the whole book is carefully designed by some editor who moulded all the material at his disposal according to his own plan.

Finally, reference should be made to the work of Moshe Weinfeld.[2] He has argued in common with other recent writers that the structure of Deuteronomy follows a literary tradition of covenant writing rather than imitating a periodical cultic ceremony (von Rad). While allowing that Deuteronomy preserves the motifs of the old covenant tradition he argues that these were re-worked and adapted to the covenant literary pattern by scribes/wise men of the Hezekiah–Josiah period. He sees many close parallels between Deuteronomy and the Assyrian treaties which, to him, are contemporary with Deuteronomy.

It is beyond question that the structure of Deuteronomy is

---

[1] See above, p. 19.
[2] Moshe Weinfeld, *Deuteronomy and the Deuteronomic School* (1972).

related in some way to the structure of the political treaties of the ancient Near East. Perhaps the Old Testament literary form is a special one which bears a close resemblance both to the treaties and to the law codes of the ancient Near East. Deuteronomy is, in any case, a carefully designed literary piece which owes much in its structure to ancient Near Eastern models.

IV. SOME LITERARY CHARACTERISTICS OF DEUTERONOMY

Deuteronomy is presented to us throughout in the style of speeches of Moses, two short ones, the first and the third, and one very long, the second. A careful analysis of the speeches reveals a wide variety of literary units. In some ways the book conveys the impression of extraordinary discontinuity. It often moves rapidly from one theme to another with apparent interruptions in the flow of thought. Despite a good deal of repetition in the vocabulary there are many changes in style, one of the most striking being the great variation in the use of the singular 'thou' and the plural 'you'. The whole book conveys the impression of a remarkably complex mosaic of very varied pieces of traditional material which have been welded together to form a unity. A number of aspects of this literary question will now be discussed.

a. The 'thou' and 'you' sections

One unusual feature of Deuteronomy is that in many sections the verbs and pronouns are in the second singular, while in others the second plural is used. In both cases it is Israel that is addressed.

Various explanations have been offered for this phenomenon. The most important of these will now be mentioned briefly. As early as 1894 two German writers, W. S. Staerk[1] and C. Steuernagel,[2] had proposed that Deuteronomy should be analysed into two sources, one containing singular nouns and verbs, and the other containing plural nouns and verbs. Steuernagel argued that the plural sections were historical and that they were addressed by Moses to the generation of Israel that stood at Sinai. On the other hand the singular passages were addressed to the generation of Israel that undertook the conquest. Steuernagel believed it was necessary to follow his

---

[1] W. Staerk, *Beitrage zur Kritik des Deuteronomiums* (1894).
[2] C. Steuernagel, *Der Rahmen des Deuteronomiums* (1894).

two sources through the central chapters 12 to 26. One recent writer, J. H. Hospers (1947), has restricted the analysis to the introduction (chapters 1–11) and the conclusion (chapters 27–30) of Deuteronomy. He finds a primitive form of Deuteronomy in the *thou* sections in 5:6–21; 6:4 – 9:7a; 12–26; 28; 30:11 – 31:16. The *you* sections, 1:6 – 6:1; 9:7b – 10:11; 28:69 – 29:28, he regards as later as well as all the small *you* sections in the body of the *thou* sections. Finally the *thou* sections in the Introduction (chapters 1–4) and in 30:1–10 are later than the *you* sections.

The entry of Martin Noth into the field of Deuteronomic criticism[1] put a different complexion on earlier studies. He argued that Deuteronomy was the introduction to the great historical work Joshua to 2 Kings. In this view chapters 1–3 were the introduction, not to the Code of Laws, but to the great Deuteronomic history for which they state the necessary presuppositions. Chapters 31:1–13, 24–26a and 34 are the historical conclusion to the Mosaic period, preparing the way for the conquest under Joshua. On Noth's view there was no longer any reason to seek for two (or more) Deuteronomic redactors for the book was a single, original composition in the singular (*thou*) but touched up with later complements in the plural (*you*). The great Deuteronomic historian (Noth's *Dtr*) found the primitive Code (Noth's *Dt*, the *thou* sections) already with the *you* sections added, and after supplying his own introduction in chapters 1–3 added the whole to his great history.

More recently, in 1962, G. Minette de Tillesse has come to a slightly different conclusion. Starting from Noth's view that the earliest form of Deuteronomy was the singular passages in chapters 5–30 to which additions were made in the plural and to which finally the Deuteronomic historian added chapters 1–3, perhaps 4, and 31ff., this writer argues that it was the Deuteronomic historian (his *Dtist*) who added the plural passages in chapters 5 to 30.[2] While this writer admits[3] that change of number may not be an adequate criterion in itself, he argues that, because the theology of the plural passages is not the same as that of the singular passages, he may still claim some validity for his criterion. Despite his contention it can be

---

[1] M. Noth, *Überlieferungsgeschichtliche Studien I*[2] (1957).

[2] G. Minette de Tillesse, 'Sections "tu" et sections "vous" dans le Deuteronome', *VT*, XII.1, Jan. 1962, pp. 29–87.

[3] *Ibid.*, p. 34.

shown that in some passages the plural sections cannot be omitted without disturbing the sense.[1]

N. Lohfink has argued along quite different lines by maintaining that 'number-mixing' is a special stylistic device for emphasizing a particular point.[2] He claims that the change from singular to plural is more significant than the change from plural to singular. The singular to plural change usually occurs in the verb while the plural to singular usually occurs in the suffix. In the narrative the plural is normally used unless the context demands the singular. Thus the mixing of the numbers seems to be governed by the form.

It may well be, therefore, that although the variation between 'thou' and 'you' sections is a literary feature of Deuteronomy it does not necessarily point to a difference in authorship but rather to a difference in emphasis.

b. Introductory phrases in Deuteronomy

At various points in Deuteronomy we meet with introductory phrases which appear to interrupt the flow of the covenant form. Clearly a treaty would have a heading of some kind at the beginning. This will account for 1:1–5: *These are the words that Moses spoke to all Israel beyond the Jordan in the wilderness . . . Moses undertook to explain this law, saying.* But what is to be said of other sub-headings such as 5:1, 27:1, *etc.*?

Some writers have taken these to indicate the presence of different literary sources. But there may be another explanation.[3] They may represent a change in speaker as they do in other parts of the Old Testament, for example, in the dialogue between God and Moses in Exodus 34 or in the famous interchange between Joshua and the people in Joshua 24, or again in 1 Samuel 12 which records the dialogue between Samuel and the people. Elsewhere in the Old Testament the device is used when the speaker addresses a different person (1 Ch. 28:2; 29:1). It is evident that in Deuteronomy 27:1, 9, 11; 31:14, 24f. there are changes in the speaker. Another possibility is that at certain points in a treaty document there was a pause where the recipients of the treaty made a response

---

[1] *Ibid.*, p. 36. *Cf.* E. W. Nicholson, *Deuteronomy and Tradition* (1967), pp. 33f.
[2] N. Lohfink, *Das Hauptgebot: eine Untersuchung literarischer Einleitungsfragen zu Dt. 5–11* (*Analecta Biblica*, 20, 1963), pp. 239ff.
[3] *Cf.* G. J. Wenham, *The Structure and Date of Deuteronomy* (unpublished thesis), pp. 210–213.

declaring acceptance of the treaty stipulations. For example, in Joshua 24 the people responded at several points (verses 16–18, 21, 22, 24). These responses are interspersed between the words of Joshua.[1] Such a practice may account for the headings in Deuteronomy 27:1, 9, 11; 29:1f.; 31:1f. It would seem from Exodus 19, Joshua 24 and 1 Samuel 12 that Israel made a response of acceptance after the reading of the covenant stipulations. This seems to be implied also by a comparison of Deuteronomy 26:16 and 26:17. It may be conjectured that there was a response also after 27:9, 10. It is a reasonable conjecture to propose responses after 26:19; 27:8; 27:10; 29:1; 30:20. In each case Moses is pictured as continuing the address preparatory to another response. Similarly the heading at 4:44–46 may follow a response from Israel after the historical introduction of chapters 1–3 and the setting forth of the basic principles in chapter 4; the chapter closes with the appeal of 4:40 to obey the commandments after which the narrative continues. Alternatively this latter passage may represent a second heading such as occurs in the treaty of Esarhaddon[2] or in the Sefiré Inscriptions.[3]

That oral responses were made during treaty ceremonies is clear from Deuteronomy 27:15–26 and also by implication in some of the non-biblical treaties. The responses were oral and were not written into the treaty document.

It is evident that a variety of alternative explanations may be offered for these introductory phrases.

c. The characteristic manner of presentation in Deuteronomy

Even the casual reader of Deuteronomy will be impressed with the remarkable way in which, in some sections, particular laws are first stated in a simple form and are then followed by exhortation, warning, promise. This supplementary material was designed, it would seem, to drive home the import of each law to the conscience of the hearer. Clearly, Deuteronomy is not codified law, but preaching about the law of Yahweh. Commandments are interspersed with hortatory material (parenesis) in a manner which is thoroughly characteristic of Deuteronomy. In recent years G. von Rad has given a good

[1] *Cf.* Ex. 19:8 in response to verses 4–6; 1 Sa. 12:4, 5b in response to verses 1–3 and 5a.
[2] D. J. Wiseman, 'The Vassal Treaties of Esarhaddon', *Iraq*, 20, 1958, pp. 1–99. See lines 1–12 and 41–45.
[3] J. A. Fitzmyer, *The Aramaic Inscriptions of Sefiré* (1967), face 1A:1–6, face B:1–6.

deal of attention to this characteristic of Deuteronomy. According to him[1] the passage 15:1–11, for example, commences with the ancient law: *At the end of every seven years you shall grant a release* (verse 1). The exact meaning of this requirement is then described in precise legal terminology: *And this is the manner of the release . . .* (verse 2). What follows in verses 3–11 is preaching. It lacks the conciseness of legal formulation and was clearly designed to make a strong personal appeal to the hearer to apply the law in a generous fashion.[2]

Another example occurs in 14:22–27. The ancient law reads: *You shall tithe all the yield of your seed, which comes forth from the field year by year* (verse 22). The remaining verses 23–27 are exposition. Again, in 15:12–18 the old law is stated as a conditional law (casuistic) in verse 12. The remaining verses 13–18 likewise make a strong appeal to the hearer to interpret the law in the most generous fashion.

The same procedure is adopted with all kinds of law, apodictic, casuistic, or even in cases where a law is merely implied.

d. The types of legal material in Deuteronomy

Some consideration should be given to the kinds of legal material occurring in Deuteronomy since chapters 12 to 26, which make up over half the book, are basically an exposition of individual laws.

First of all there are apodictic laws, *e.g.* 14:22; 15:1, 19; 16:18, *etc.* Some of these are collected together into short series, *e.g.* 16:21, 22; 17:1 (three); 16:19 (three); 22:5a, 5b, 9, 10, 11 (five); 22:30; 23:1, 2, 3, 7a, 7b (six).

Then there are casuistic or conditional laws expressed in a personalized form, 'if a man . . . then . . .'; sometimes with slight homiletical touches, *e.g.* 22:6, 7; 22:8; 23:21–23, 24, 25; 24:10–12; 24:19, *etc.* These casuistic laws are not normally treated in the same extended homiletical fashion as the apodictic laws, perhaps because they are trivial or rare, so that there was not the same need to press home to the conscience their observance. An exception is 15:12–18 (*cf.* Ex. 21:2–11). But pure conditional laws in the manner of the ancient Near Eastern law codes without any homiletical material or

---

[1] Gerhard von Rad, *Deuteronomy* (1966), pp. 105–107; *Studies in Deuteronomy* (1953), pp. 15, 16.

[2] Other problems relating to this and other passages are discussed in the commentary.

personalizing touches occur in such passages as 21:15–17, 18–23; 22:13–29; 24:1–4; 25:1–3; 25:5–10. By and large these casuistic laws occur towards the end of Deuteronomy while the great homiletical passages occur early in the book.

In addition to these two easily classified groups of legal material there are other types which are difficult to classify. Some of these deal with broad issues like the prophet (13:1–3; 18:9–22), the king (17:14–20), idolatry (13:6–18), the cities of refuge (19:1–13). Behind such passages there does not seem to be a formal law, apodictic or casuistic, although in the treatment of the themes are found the same sermon-like characteristics we have already mentioned. Two of these passages are actually couched in casuistic form although no underlying law is quoted (13:1–5, 6–18).

An important group of passages deals with the Holy War. There are regulations about the conduct of a war (20:1–9), the investment of cities (20:10–18, 19, 20), female prisoners (21:10–14), camp hygiene (23:10–14), exemptions for newly-married men (24:5), the treatment of the Amalekites (25:17–19).

Yet other regulations deal with the offering of the first-fruits (26:1–11) and procedures in the case of an unsolved murder (21:1–9).

Then there is a wide variety of material dealing with the law of feasts (chapter 16), the priests (18:1–8), the sanctuary (12:1–28), clean and unclean food (14:3–21), *etc.*

This brief review makes it clear that there is a very considerable variety of legal and traditional material in Deuteronomy which is presented under a variety of literary forms. Modern form-critical analysis has contributed considerably to the isolation of these various elements.[1]

e. Deuteronomy, the Book of the Covenant and the decalogue

Even a cursory glance at the contents of these three blocks of literature makes the reader aware of a number of close resemblances as well as a number of differences between them. Thus a significant number of the laws in the Book of the Covenant (Ex. 20:22 – 23:19) have a parallel in Deuteronomy as the following table will show:[2]

---

[1] Gerhard von Rad in his various writings has led the field in this respect, notably in *Studies in Deuteronomy* (1953); *Deuteronomy* (1966); *IBD*, I (1963), pp. 831–838.

[2] The table is from Gerhard von Rad, *Deuteronomy* (1966), p. 13. *Cf.* G. J. Wenham, 'Legal Forms in the Book of the Covenant', *TB*, 22, 1971, pp. 95–102.

Ex. 21:1–11	Dt. 15:12–18
Ex. 21:12–14	Dt. 19:1–13
Ex. 21:16	Dt. 24:7
Ex. 22:16f.	Dt. 22:28, 29
Ex. 22:21–24	Dt. 24:17–22
Ex. 22:25	Dt. 23:19–20
Ex. 22:26f.	Dt. 24:10–13
Ex. 22:29f.	Dt. 15:19–23
Ex. 22:31	Dt. 15:19–23
Ex. 22:31	Dt. 14:3–21
Ex. 23:1	Dt. 19:16–21
Ex. 23:2f., 6–8	Dt. 16:18–20
Ex. 23:4f.	Dt. 22:1–4
Ex. 23:9	Dt. 24:17f.
Ex. 23:10 f.	Dt. 15:1–11
Ex. 23:12	Dt. 5:13–15
Ex. 23:13	Dt. 6:13
Ex. 23:14–17	Dt. 16:1–17
Ex. 23:19a	Dt. 26:2–10
Ex. 23:19b	Dt. 14:21b

The exact number of parallels between the two blocks of legal material is difficult to decide. A similar list drawn up by G. T. Manley varies slightly in content.[1] But there is sufficient agreement between the various commentators to make it clear that the two blocks of legal material have a good deal in common. On the other hand there are laws in the Book of the Covenant which do not appear in Deuteronomy.[2] Von Rad estimates that some fifty per cent of the Book of the Covenant has no parallel in Deuteronomy.[3] It could hardly be argued, therefore, that Deuteronomy is a substitute for the Book of the Covenant.

An important question is the extent to which Deuteronomy differs from the Book of the Covenant in laws which the two have in common. For example, the two passages Exodus 21:2–6 and Deuteronomy 15:12–18 deal with the case of the Hebrew man who becomes a slave. In both passages the instruction is given that he shall serve six years and in the seventh year he is to be freed·unless he elects to remain in the service of his master. A comparison of the two passages reveals

---

[1] G. T. Manley, *The Book of the Law* (1957), pp. 77, 85.
[2] *Ibid.*, pp. 79, 86.
[3] G. von Rad, *Deuteronomy* (1966), p. 13.

several differences (see commentary for details). While the two accounts refer to the same basic principle the Exodus narrative deals with a man and Deuteronomy deals with either a man or a woman. It may be argued that the Deuteronomy law is merely an enlargement of the Exodus law in order to make it clear that the same law applied to women as well as to men. On the other hand it has been argued that the law in Deuteronomy came from a time when women as well as men could voluntarily sell themselves into slavery, possibly for economic reasons or perhaps when certain ancient cultic ceremonies, such as affixing the ear to the doorpost of the sanctuary, had ceased to operate. This could have obtained at some period subsequent to Moses. The ancient Mosaic law was observed in principle but operated with a difference in detail.

The law of the year of release provides another comparison. In Exodus 23:10f. reference is made to the fallow period of the land every seventh year. The Hebrew verb *lie fallow* (root *š-m-ṭ*) appears in the noun *release* (*š^emiṭṭâ*) in Deuteronomy 15:1–11, but what is in view in Deuteronomy is the release of a creditor from his debt at the end of seven years, whereas in Exodus 23:10f. the reference is to the release of the land from the burden of producing crops. Both laws appear to be based on the same sabbatical principle.

According to von Rad, the general law is given in Deuteronomy 15:1: *at the end of every seven years you shall grant a release* (*š^emiṭṭâ*). The *manner of the release* is then explained in legal terms in verse 2. Here is an application which is different from that in Exodus 23:11. It may be accounted for on the assumption that a principle expressed in Exodus 23:11 was used for a different purpose in a different set of circumstances. Thus, in the case of a debt incurred when one man loaned something to his neighbour there was to be a year of release when every man was required to 'let drop' any dues he claimed from his neighbour, a requirement that did not apply to the foreigner (*nokrî*). Von Rad interprets Deuteronomy 15:2 as an extension of and a later application of the older Mosaic law in a day when, having settled in the land, a man of Israel might fall into debt and arrange a loan from a fellow Israelite.[1] One way to liquidate the loan might be to work on the creditor's farm. However, during the year of release no work of this kind

---

[1] *Ibid.*, p. 106.

was to be done. In that case the debt was to be cancelled. Perhaps this idea was inherent in the Exodus law but it has come to clear expression in Deuteronomy with somewhat different terms of reference.[1]

The two versions of the decalogue provide a third comparison. These are found in Exodus 20 and Deuteronomy 5. Of the twenty or more differences between the two versions, thirteen appear as additions in Deuteronomy over and beyond Exodus 20.[2] Seven of these are merely concerned with the addition of the conjunction 'and' so that they are not of great significance. But apart from these there are additional words in Deuteronomy in the law of the sabbath (12) and the law of parents (16). (See commentary.)

Again, there are three minor differences in the wording of the second commandment, two variations in the fourth commandment, one in the ninth commandment, and in the tenth commandment an important rearrangement of the elements of a man's possessions so as to separate his wife from all other items. In Deuteronomy a man's wife is placed first in the list with the verb *ḥāmaḏ*, while the other items are used with the verb *hiṯ'awwâ*. It would seem that the text of Deuteronomy has a different emphasis at this point. There are not lacking in the pages of the Bible examples where some principle which found expression in a particular context needed to be expressed differently in another context. The principle remained but the expression of it was modified. Compare for example the modifications of earlier laws by Jesus in Matthew 5:21–48. On the view that Moses was responsible for both forms of the decalogue it is not inconceivable that after nearly forty years he would restate some of his principles to suit a new set of circumstances. Alternatively, it has been argued that Mosaic principles set out in the Exodus decalogue were re-expressed at some undefined time after his death in slightly different terms.

Further examples of the changes in wording between the

---

[1] G. T. Manley, *op. cit.*, p. 102, in his table H which he calls 'Laws of Clemency' argues that the year of release is only one of a group of such laws 'the complete irrelevancy of which to Josiah's reform is a serious objection to Wellhausen's dating' and asks, 'What has bird-nesting to do with reform?' The reply is 'Nothing'. But if we were to argue for a date for the final editing of Deuteronomy somewhat later than Moses, say during the early days of the Monarchy, though not so late as the seventh century, it is possible that some of these archaic laws were still relevant.

[2] J. J. Stamm and M. E. Andrew, *The Ten Commandments in Recent Research* (1967), pp. 13–18.

laws in the Book of the Covenant and the laws in Deuteronomy will be discussed in the commentary. The question that arises is whether the variations in practice suggested by these changes in wording would have required only the period between Sinai and Moab, say a generation, or whether they reflect a longer period of development. The traditional view has been that the changes can be accounted for as due to Moses himself in the light of a generation of experience. But it is arguable that a much longer time would have been necessary. Such a view does not destroy the idea of an ultimate Mosaic authority for the practices that appear under his name in Deuteronomy. Principles, even if they were expressed in a precise way in the form of laws formulated by Moses for his age, would need to be adapted to a later age. The principle of adaptation is fundamental in all aspects of religious development.[1]

From the literary point of view, differences between the Book of the Covenant and the book of Deuteronomy are undeniable. Concerning the exact significance of these differences there is room for a variety of interpretations.

f. The distinctive Deuteronomic vocabulary and style

Even a cursory reading of Deuteronomy will persuade the reader that there is a certain homogeneity of style which is characteristic of the book as a whole. Even in chapters 1–4, 27, 29–31, which some scholars have assigned to different sources, the same style is evident. Thus not only is there structural unity in Deuteronomy but there is a strong stylistic unity also, distinguished by its simplicity, its lucidity, its phraseology and its rhetorical character. It is not that the words and phrases, the idioms and expressions are always unique. But what constitutes the novelty of the Deuteronomic style is the manner in which phrases are combined and the structure and rhythm of the sentences.[2] That similar language occurs elsewhere in the Old Testament, notably in editorial material in the historical books, has been explained by arguing that the writers of books such as Joshua, Judges, Samuel and Kings were influenced by the Deuteronomic style, or that both shared in the character-

---

[1] For example, the ultimate sanction for the Christian communion service goes back to the command of Jesus to His disciples in the upper room. But the exact practice has varied from time to time and from group to group. Yet all claim the authority of Christ for their practice.

[2] S. R. Driver, *A Critical and Exegetical Commentary on Deuteronomy* (*ICC*, 1902), pp. lxxvi–lxxviii.

istic prose style in use in Israel in the days of the monarchy. Whatever the explanation, the style is distinctive. S. R. Driver at the end of the nineteenth century attempted a description of the vocabulary and style of Deuteronomy. His description has remained standard for nearly a century and is perhaps the best and most complete list available today.[1] The more recent list of Moshe Weinfeld is an attempt to include references to this vocabulary in other areas of the Old Testament where the characteristic vocabulary is found[2] and also to organize it around a number of basic theological tenets, *viz.* the struggle against idolatry, centralization of worship, the exodus, the covenant and election, the monotheistic creed, the observance of the law and loyalty to the covenant, inheritance of the land, and retribution and material motivation.

We shall attempt a selective listing of some of the more important words and expressions which occur frequently in Deuteronomy.

First of all, in reference to the observance of the law and loyalty to the covenant the following may be noted:

1. *to love* The verb is used both for the love of Yahweh for His people (4:37; 7:8, 13; 10:15; 23:5) and for the proper response of Israel to Yahweh (6:5; 7:9; 10:12; 11:1, 13, 22; 13:3, *etc.*). It is of some interest that the same idea occurs in secular treaties where a vassal is called upon to 'love' his suzerain. There may thus be an ancient Near Eastern background to the concept although the biblical idea is charged with a greater range and depth of meaning.[3]

2. *to hear,* and the expression *Hear, O Israel* (4:1 (Heb.); 5:1; 6:4; 9:1; 20:3; 27:9, *etc.*). The parallel expression *to hearken to (obey) the voice of Yahweh* (4:30; 8:20; 9:23; 13:4, 18; 15:5; 26:14, 17; 27:10; 28:1, 2, 15, *etc.*) uses the same verb.

3. *to serve Yahweh* (6:13; 10:12, 20; 11:13; 13:4; 28:47, *etc.*).

4. *to fear Yahweh* (4:10; 5:29; 6:2, 13, 24: 8:6; 10:12, 20; 13:4; 14:23; 17:19; 28:58; 31:12f.) and related expressions *to learn to fear Yahweh* (4:10; 14:23; 17:19; 31:12f.), *to fear Yahweh all the days/as long as you live* (4:10; 6:2; 14:23; 31:13).

---

[1] *Ibid.*, pp. lxxviii–lxxxiv.

[2] Moshe Weinfeld, *Deuteronomy and the Deuteronomic School* (1972), pp. 320–365.

[3] W. L. Moran, 'The Ancient Near Eastern background of the Love of God in Deuteronomy', *CBQ*, XXV.1, 1963, pp. 77–87.

5. *to cleave to Yahweh* (4:4; 10:20; 11:22; 13:4; 30:20).

6. *to walk in the way/ways of Yahweh* and related expressions (5:33; 8:6; 10:12; 11:22; 19:9; 26:17; 28:9; 30:16).

7. *to do that which is right (good) in the eyes of Yahweh* (6:18; 12:25, 28; 13:18; 21:9).

8. *to keep/do the commandments/statutes/testimonies/judgments/the words of this law, etc.* Such expressions are extremely common (5:29; 6:25; 11:8, 22; 13:18; 15:5; 19:9; 26:18, *etc.*).

9. *statutes and ordinances* (4:1, 5, 8, 14; 5:1; 11:32; 12:1; 26:16) plus *commandments* (5:31; 6:1; 7:11; 26:17) plus *testimonies* (4:45; 6:20). There are various combinations of these four nouns as well as many references to the more comprehensive term *law* (*tôrâ*).

The strong link between this language and the language of the Near Eastern treaty is clear.

Another group of expressions refers to rebellion against Yahweh and the covenant.

1. *to do that which is evil in the eyes of Yahweh* (4:25; 9:18; 17:2; 31:29); *to act wickedly* (4:16, 25; 31:29).

2. *to turn away, to turn aside from the way* (9:12, 16; 11:16, 28; 31:29), *to turn right or left* (5:32; 17:11, 20; 28:14).

3. *to vex/provoke Yahweh* (4:25; 9:7, 18; 31:29).

Many expressions refer to the struggle against idolatry. There are numerous references to foreign gods, and to the *abominations*.

1. *to follow after (go after) foreign (other) gods* (6:14; 8:19; 11:28; 13:2; 28:14).

2. *to serve (worship) other gods* (7:4; 11:16; 13:2, 6, 13; 17:3; 28:14, 36, 64; 29:26; *cf.* 4:19; 8:19; 30:17). Some of these passages refer to the worship of astral deities – sun, moon, stars (4:19; 17:3).

3. Idolatry as *abomination* (*tôʿēbâ*) (7:25, 26; 13:14; 17:4; 18:9; 20:18).

4. *an abomination to Yahweh your God* (7:25; 12:31; 17:1; 18:12; 22:5; 23:18; 25:16; 27:15).

5. References to cultic practices of foreign people: *burning/passing through the fire sons/daughters* (12:31; 18:10); *man-made gods of wood/stone* (4:28; 27:15; 28:64; 31:29).

6. *to do that which is evil in the eyes of Yahweh* (4:25; 9:18; 17:2; 31:29).

There are a number of recurring expressions which refer to centralization of worship.

1. *the place that the Lord will choose* (12:5, 11, 14, 18, 21, 26; 14:23, 24, 25; 15:20; 16:2, 6, 7, 11, 15, 16; 17:8, 10; 18:6; 26:2; 31:11).

2. *the place where the Lord will make his name to dwell* (12:5, 11; 14:23; 16:2, 6, 11; 26:2); *to put his name there* (12:5, 21; 14:24).

Other characteristic expressions refer to the exodus and its mighty acts and to Yahweh's choice (election) of Israel and His covenant with them.

1. *to redeem (pāḏâ) from Egypt/from the house of bondage* (5:6; 6:12; 7:8; 8:14; 9:26; 13:5; 15:15; 21:8; 24:18).

2. *Remember you were a slave in the land of Egypt* (5:15; 15:15; 16:12; 24:18, 22).

3. *(Yahweh) chose (bâḥar) (Israel)* (4:37; 7:6, 7; 10:15; 14:2).

4. *to be a people for himself* (4:20; 7:6; 14:2; 26:18; 27:9); *to establish a people for himself* (28:9; 29:13); *to call Israel by his name* (28:10).

5. *a treasured people (seḡullâ)* (7:6; 14:2; 26:18).

6. *a holy people* (7:6; 14:2, 21; 26:19; 28:9).

7. *your people Israel* (21:8; 26:15); *a people of inheritance* (4:20; 9:26, 29).

8. *covenant* There are many occurrences of this term in reference both to the patriarchs and to Israel (4:13, 23, 31; 5:2, 3; 7:2, 9, 12; 8:18, *etc.*).

There is a good deal of emphasis on the inheritance of the land which was Yahweh's gift to Israel.

1. *The land which Yahweh your God is giving you as an inheritance (to possess)* (4:21; 15:4; 19:10; 20:16; 21:23; 24:4; 25:19; 26:1).

2. *The land whither you come in to possess it/to possess them (the nations)/to possess their land* (4:1, 5; 6:18; 7:1; 8:1; 9:1, 5; 11:8, 10, 29, 31; 12:29; 28:21, 63; 30:16).

3. *possession (yerussâ)* (2:5, 9, 12, 19; 3:20).

4. *to dispossess (cause to possess) the nations* (4:38; 7:1, 17; 9:3, 4, 5; 11:23; 18:14).

5. *swear,* used of Yahweh's oath to the patriarchs (1:8, 35; 4:31; 6:10, 18, 23; 7:8, 12, 13; 8:1; 9:5, *etc.*).

6. *The land/rest/towns, etc./which Yahweh thy (our, etc.) God is giving thee (us, etc.)* (1:20, 25; 2:29; 3:20; 4:1, 40; 11:17, 31; 12:9; 13:12; 15:7; 16:5, 18, 20; 17:2, 14; 18:9; 25:15; 26:2; 27:2, 3; 28:8).

Some characteristic phrases refer to the blessings which will follow loyalty to the covenant.

1. *that the Lord may bless thee* (14:29; 23:20; 24:19; *cf.* 12:7; 14:24; 15:4, 6, 10, 14; 16:10, 15; *cf.* also the emphasis on Yahweh's *blessing* in 1:11; 2:7; 7:13; 15:18; 28:8, 12, *etc.*).

2. *that you may prolong your days in the land* (4:26, 40; 5:16, 33; 11:9; 17:20; 30:18; 32:47).

3. *to bless the work (enterprise) of your hands* (2:7; 14:29; 15:10, 18; 16:15; 23:20; 24:19; 28:8, 12).

4. *so that it may be well with you* (4:40; 5:16, 33; 6:3, 18; 12:25, 28; 22:7).

5. *to rejoice before Yahweh your God* (12:12, 18; 16:11; 27:7; *cf.* 14:26; 26:11).

There are numerous references in Deuteronomy to *Yahweh, the God of thy (our, your, their) fathers* (1:11, 21; 4:1; 6:3; 12:1; 26:7; 27:3; 29:25). It is the name *par excellence* of Israel's covenant God, her sovereign Lord. As such He lays sovereign demands on Israel. The expression *which I am commanding thee this day* appears frequently in Deuteronomy (4:40; 6:6; 7:11; 8:1, 11; 13:18; 15:15; 19:9; 27:10; 28:1, 13, 15; 30:2; 8, 11, 16, *etc.*).

There are a number of other expressions which are frequently used in Deuteronomy.

1. *all Israel* (1:1; 5:1; 13:11; 21:21; 27:9; 29:2; 31:1, 7, 11; 32:45; 34:12).

2. *thy (your) gates, i.e. the cities of Israel* (12:12, 15, 17, 18, 21; 14:21, 27, 28, 29; 15:7, 22; 16:5, 11, 14, 18; 17:2, 8; 18:6; 23:16; 24:14; 26:12; 28:52, 55, 57; 31:12).

3. *Horeb* is always used for *Sinai* (1:2, 6, 19; 5:2; 18:16).

This list is only a sample of the numerous words and phrases which recur many times in Deuteronomy and may be said to characterize the vocabulary and style of the book.

It has often been pointed out that many of these phrases occur in the historical books from Joshua to 2 Kings (the so-called Deuteronomic History), suggesting that the final editor(s) of these books was influenced either by the language of Deuteronomy itself or by some kindred influence. There also appear to be many links between the language of the Jeremiah prose passages and that of Deuteronomy[1] although there are

---

[1] Je. 7:23; 18:10; 34:15; 38:20; 40:9; 42:6. See M. Weinfeld, *op. cit.*, pp. 359–361.

many differences as well. G. E. Wright has asked how it came about that there was a literary relationship between Deuteronomy, the Deuteronomic historian(s) and the prose passages of Jeremiah.[1] He concludes that there must have been a fairly widespread rhetorical style during the seventh and early sixth centuries in Judah of which all three are representative.[2] But Deuteronomy has affinities likewise with earlier material, Hosea from the eighth century, and the Pentateuchal document E traditionally dated also to the eighth century. G. E. Wright argues strongly that this latter affinity may be more significant than has been realized. It is an affinity which would have been much more evident in the past had not scholars obscured the fact by attributing it to the hand of a Deuteronomic redactor.[3] May it not be then that the roots of the Deuteronomic style run back further into the past than has been recognized hitherto? But whatever the origin of the Deuteronomic style it is sufficiently distinctive to be a recognizable feature in the total range of Old Testament literature.

V. DEUTERONOMY AND THE CENTRAL SANCTUARY

It has been assumed by scholars during the past century that the book of Deuteronomy demands the centralization of all worship at a single sanctuary. Since this was never realized till Josiah's day, it has been argued that the book comes from his century. The view has been challenged from time to time, for example by A. C. Welch and T. Oestreicher[4] and more recently by J. N. M. Wijngaards, who has argued that Deuteronomy does not envisage centralization of worship at Jerusalem but refers to a series of sanctuaries which served in turn as the central shrine of the old Israelite amphictyony.[5] He would date Deuteronomy 5–28 to some time between 1250 and 1050 BC.[6] While this proposal presents problems of its own it raises again the question of centralization in Deuteronomy.

In order to understand the problem better it is important to review evidence which suggests that there was from the earliest

---

[1] *Deuteronomy* (*IB*, Vol. 2, 1953), p. 319.
[2] *Ibid.*, p. 320.
[3] *Ibid.*, p. 320. Footnote 28 is important.
[4] See below, p. 54.
[5] J. N. M. Wijngaards, *The Dramatization of Salvific History in the Deuteronomic Schools* (*Oudtestamentische Studiën*, 16, 1969), pp. 23ff.
[6] *Ibid.*, pp. 109ff.

times one sanctuary which assumed prominence over all others for the reason that the Ark rested there.

The biblical picture is that in the days of Moses the Ark marked the central sanctuary for Israel and travelled with the people during the wilderness wanderings. Once Israel was settled in the land the Ark retained its significance and became a centre for pilgrimage. It was situated at a variety of places during the days of the judges. Thus it rested at Gilgal (Jos. 4:19; 5:9; 7:6), Shechem (Jos. 8:33; *cf.* 24:1) and Bethel (Jdg. 20:18, 26–28; 21:2) at various times. Whether all of these places could be regarded as sites for the central sanctuary is difficult to prove, although Martin Noth has argued that this was so[1] and in particular he holds that the first amphictyonic shrine was at Shechem. That the Ark rested at a variety of places for at least a time seems clear but it is not certain that each of these places was a site for a central sanctuary.[2] In the case of Shiloh the biblical evidence leaves no doubt. By the middle of the eleventh century BC Shiloh was a meeting-place of the tribes where the tent of reunion was set up (Jos. 18:1). Evidently a structure of some kind stood there, for there are references to a 'house of God' (Jdg. 18:31), a 'house of the Lord' (1 Sa. 1:7, 24; 3:15) and a 'temple' (*hêḵāl*, 1 Sa. 3:3) which had doors and posts (1 Sa. 1:9; 3:15). The tribes came to Shiloh for an annual festival (Jdg. 21:19; 1 Sa. 1:3, 21) and there was a continuing ministry there under the care of Eli and his two sons. Archaeological work has demonstrated the existence of a town, although perhaps not a big one, on the site of Seilun (the modern name of the ancient town) in the eleventh century BC, at the time the Ark was captured (1 Sa. 4).[3]

The town Gibeon seems to have been an important sanctuary site after the sack of Shiloh although it is not certain that it became the central sanctuary. During the days of Samuel the prophet and King Saul (2 Sa. 20:8) a 'great stone' stood at Gibeon,[4] while Solomon went there to offer sacrifice and to

---

[1] M. Noth, *The History of Israel* [2](1960).

[2] G. J. Wenham, 'Deuteronomy and the Central Sanctuary', *TB*, 22, 1971, pp. 105ff.

[3] The Danish Palestine Exploration excavations under A. Schmidt in 1926–1929, 1932. See *PEQ*, 1927; *JPOS*, X, 1930, art. by H. Kjaer, pp. 87–114; W. F. Albright, *BASOR*, 9, 1923, pp. 10f.; M. L. Buhl and S. Holm-Nielsen, *Shiloh: The Danish Excavations at Tall Sailūn, Palestine in 1926, 29, 32 and 63* (1969).

[4] Another possible reference to Gibeon occurs in 2 Sa. 21:6 where LXX has 'At Gibeon of Saul, the chosen of Yahweh'. The 'Gibeah' of the MT

receive a message from the Lord (1 Ki. 3:5). The place is described as 'the great high place' (1 Ki. 3:4). Passages in Chronicles suggest that 'the tabernacle of the Lord' (1 Ch. 16:39; 21:29; 2 Ch. 1:3) was at Gibeon.

In due course David brought the Ark to Jerusalem (2 Sa. 6) after its long rest at Kiriath-Jearim. His son Solomon built the Temple there and Jerusalem became the central sanctuary. But despite the prestige attaching to the sanctuary at Jerusalem, it is clear that throughout the period of the monarchy worship continued, apparently quite legally, at shrines other than Jerusalem. This was evidently a continuation of earlier practice. The books of Judges and Samuel suggest that there was a considerable degree of cultic activity independent of the sanctuary where the Ark rested (Jdg. 6:24; 13:19; 21:4; 1 Sa. 7:9; 9:12; 10:8; 11:15; 13:9). Some passages indicate that 'burnt offerings' ('ôlôṯ) and 'peace offerings' (šᵉlāmîm) were offered in these places (Jdg. 21:4; 1 Sa. 13:9). Thus altars were erected both at places where the Ark stood such as Shechem, Bethel, Shiloh, Jerusalem, and also in other places like Beer-sheba, Gibeon, Mount Carmel. These existed contemporaneously with the sanctuary where the Ark rested.[1]

The case of Jeroboam's altars at Bethel and Dan was different. Whereas earlier shrines were not so much rivals of the central sanctuary at Jerusalem as places for local worship, the shrines of Jeroboam were in direct opposition to the central sanctuary at Jerusalem and were part of Jeroboam's bid to ensure political stability in the north. These shrines at Bethel and Dan were inveighed against by the prophets Amos (5:4f.) and Hosea (8:5f., 11; 13:2). The narrative in 1 Kings 13:1ff. is an early prophetic protest against forsaking the central sanctuary in Jerusalem. It was Yahweh that Israel should seek and not Bethel (Am. 5:4f.). It was Jerusalem that would be rebuilt when all other sanctuaries were destroyed (Am. 9:11).

In discussing the question of centralization some attention should be given to the 'high places' (bāmôṯ, singular bāmâ). There are no references to high places in the books of Joshua and Judges but Samuel is reported as 'going up' to the high place (1 Sa. 9:13) at Ramah, while a band of musical prophets

---

is possibly a corruption for Gibeon and RSV translates with some emendation 'before the Lord at Gibeon on the mountain of the Lord'.

[1] *Cf.* the altars on Mount Carmel (1 Ki. 19:10, 14) which coexisted with the altar in Jerusalem.

is mentioned as 'coming down from the high place'. No criticism is made of these places, or of the worship that was conducted there, by the Deuteronomic editors of Joshua, Judges and Samuel, although strong criticism of them occurs in Kings and also in some of the prophets (Ho. 10:8; Am. 7:9; Je. 7:31; 19:5, *etc.*). Nor were the altars of Yahweh which Elijah found thrown down (1 Ki. 19:10) condemned by these editors. They were evidently used during the ninth century BC by pious Israelites who could not go up to the central sanctuary in Jerusalem to worship.

It was Hezekiah who first tried to centralize all worship in Jerusalem and make the Jerusalem Temple the sole central sanctuary (2 Ki. 18:1–5; *cf.* 2 Ch. 29–31). His policy did not succeed and Josiah his grandson reintroduced it (2 Ki. 22–23; *cf.* 2 Ch. 34) but with only temporary success. After his death worship flourished again at high places throughout the land. Only after the exile did Jerusalem become the sole sanctuary in the land.

Archaeological evidence of the existence of sanctuaries outside Jerusalem during the period of the monarchy is growing. Excavations at Arad in the Negeb not far from Beersheba have revealed a sanctuary from the days of Solomon where a large altar built of earth and small field stones was in use (*cf.* Ex. 20:25), two small stone altars with charred organic remains on their concave surface, and a raised paved area described as a 'high place' (*bāmâ*) by the excavators, were found.[1] This sanctuary and its various cult objects remained in use till the late eighth or early seventh century BC when the altars and high place were covered over. The building itself remained in use till the late seventh century when it was destroyed.

Evidence of another local sanctuary comes from Dan in the far north of Israel where a large *bāmâ* has been discovered dating back to the ninth century BC. This continued in use throughout and beyond the Israelite period.[2] Another structure at the entry to the main gate of the city, evidently a pedestal of some kind, may also have had some cultic significance,[3] possibly as the base on which the calf stood (1 Ki. 12:28–30; 2 Ki. 10:29; Am. 8:14). But this is by no means certain.

---

[1] Y. Aharoni, 'Arad: Its Inscriptions and Temple', *BA*, Feb. 1968.
[2] A. Biran, Archaeological notes on Tel Dan in *IEJ*, 22, 1972, pp. 164–166.
[3] *Ibid.*, p. 165.

Excavations at Tel Sheba on the outskirts of Beersheba have brought to light a walled city dating back to David's time. It was in use throughout the days of the monarchy. Here too there is evidence of some kind of sanctuary or cultic centre.

Further excavation of sites in the Holy Land may well extend our knowledge of sanctuaries from the days of the kings. There were clearly other centres of worship besides the central sanctuary in Jerusalem during these centuries. Some of these, at least, did not draw any words of disapproval from the Deuteronomic editors of Kings (*e.g.* 1 Ki. 19:10). On the other hand there were centres of worship which were official in the northern kingdom, but not approved in the south, *e.g.* Bethel and Dan established by Jeroboam (1 Ki. 12:29). No doubt Jeroboam intended these centres for the worship of Yahweh, the golden calves being merely symbols of Yahweh, albeit dangerous ones for they were likely to encourage syncretism. But despite the official centres of worship in Jerusalem, Dan and Bethel, people continued to frequent places of Yahweh worship whose origins went back to pre-monarchic times. The danger with such sanctuaries was that they readily became places where aberration and apostasy grew up. Alongside this was the continuing danger that undiscerning Israelites might frequent local centres of Baal worship. Sooner or later there would arise a need to purify the worship of the local sanctuaries.

It is an undoubted fact that in the course of the centuries there were several reformers such as Asa (1 Ki. 15:12–14), Jehoshaphat (1 Ki. 22:46), Hezekiah (2 Ki. 18:4) and Josiah, who suppressed cult prostitution and idol worship. But for much of the time the 'high places' were tolerated and even men like Asa, Jehoshaphat, Joash, Amaziah, and Uzziah, who earned a measure of approval from the Deuteronomic historian, continued to allow the high places to function (1 Ki. 15:12–14; 22:43; 2 Ki. 14:4; 15:4). It was not until the time of Hezekiah that the high places were removed (2 Ki. 18:4). Archaeological evidence for Hezekiah's destruction of the high places has come from Arad,[1] as we have seen. But even Hezekiah allowed some form of worship to continue at local sanctuaries, to judge from the fact that the Arad shrine without the altar and high place remained in use. The biblical record indicates that it was Josiah who abolished worship outside

[1] See p. 38, footnote 1.

Jerusalem, commanding the priests in Judah to come up to Jerusalem. Despite his instructions not all the priests of the 'high places' obeyed but *ate unleavened bread among their brethren* (2 Ki. 23:9). Yet it is beyond dispute that Josiah undertook a vast reform which was designed to purify the worship of Yahweh from unholy elements, and *to defile the high places where the priests had burned incense.*[1]

These facts seem to indicate (a) that the purity of the cult in Israel was a continuing concern down the centuries and that the nation was in possession of a tradition that demanded purity of worship; (b) that there was an equally strong tradition that, alongside the sanctuary where the Ark stood, there existed other sanctuaries where legitimate worship might be carried on; (c) that the central sanctuary was, nevertheless, the focal point for many important national festivals. It was, in any case, the place where the high priest officiated.

In the light of this material we may look at what Deuteronomy has to say about the questions that are raised. The Ark, which was the focal point of the central sanctuary, is hardly referred to in Deuteronomy.[2] The Ark is the place where the tablets of the law, those symbols of Yahweh's covenant with Israel, were kept (10:1–5), and as such it was housed at the central sanctuary. Was then *the place which the Lord your God shall choose* necessarily the central sanctuary or were there several such places? The expressions *in one (any) of your tribes* and *from all your tribes* do not settle the question of a single sanctuary (12:5, 14) since, of themselves, they may be understood either as referring to one or to a number of authorized places.

A closer examination of the context in which the associated expression *the place which Yahweh your God shall choose* is used reveals a similar ambiguity in some passages. Thus in chapter 12, although it is clear that Israel is to destroy Canaanite cult centres and to bring her own sacrifices to *the place which the Lord your God will choose out of all your tribes* (12:6, 11, 18), it is not clear whether a single sanctuary or a number of authorized sanctuaries is intended. Nor are the prescriptions about *tithing*

---

[1] The verb *qiṭṭēr* can also be translated *offer up sacrifices* and may indicate in 2 Ki. 23:8 and elsewhere that these priests actually offered up sacrifices at the high places.

[2] Dt. 10:1–5, 8; 31:26. G. von Rad, *Studies in Deuteronomy* (1953), p. 40, and R. E. Clements, *God and Temple* (1965), pp. 95f., regard this lack of reference to the Ark as an attempt to play down the significance of the Ark as such and to draw attention rather to the covenant.

in 14:22–29 and about *firstlings* in 15:19–23 entirely clear. The law concerning the three great festivals of passover, weeks and tabernacles in chapter 16 would suit a central sanctuary if *tents* in 16:7 is taken to refer to temporary dwellings of pilgrims. Likewise the reference to the trial of difficult cases before *the judge who is in office in those days* certainly suits a central sanctuary. So also does the law concerning the right of Levites to assist at *the place which the Lord will choose* (18:6–8), and the prescriptions about the bringing of the first-fruits *to the altar of Yahweh your God* (26:4). The assembly which was called every seven years was likewise to be held at *the place* which Yahweh would choose (31:10–13) which would very easily suit the idea of a central sanctuary. But scholars like Adam Welch have stressed the ambiguity of all these texts and have argued for several official sanctuaries. The phrases *to put his name there* and *to make his name dwell there* (sometimes used in the same contexts) simply denote ownership.[1] The narrative in Deuteronomy 27 does not necessarily refer to the Shechem region as the place of the central sanctuary since the ceremony held there was of a special character. Certainly in a later day Rehoboam was made king at Shechem when the central sanctuary was in Jerusalem (1 Ki. 12:1). And even in Joshua's day, the covenant was renewed at Shechem (Jos. 24:1ff.) while the central sanctuary was at Shiloh (Jos. 18:1; 22:12). Although the central intention of the book of Deuteronomy is to stress the fact of the central sanctuary, the reference to the altar and the sacrifices on Mount Ebal in Deuteronomy 27 must be understood as having fulfilled a very special purpose, namely, that it was part of a total covenant ceremony. (See commentary on chapter 27 for a fuller discussion.) Certainly Shechem is never called *the place* nor did the Ark or the Tent of Meeting ever rest at Shechem. But despite ambiguities there is no compelling reason why we should not regard the phrase *the place which Yahweh your God shall choose* in Deuteronomy as referring to the central sanctuary. The whole book presents the ideal, feasible and capable of operation in the days of Moses, impossible to maintain from the days of the conquest onwards though not forgotten by the reformers such as Asa, Hezekiah and Josiah, but never realized till post-exilic times. There was a central sanctuary in Moses' day in the first half of the thirteenth century BC. It can be identified clearly at Shiloh in the eleventh century BC, and it

[1] G. J. Wenham has collected useful bibliography in *TB*, 22, 1971, pp. 112–114.

became permanent at Jerusalem from the tenth century BC onwards. The part it was intended to play in Israel's national and religious life is set out in Deuteronomy.

VI. THE BASIC SOCIAL AND RELIGIOUS BACKGROUND OF DEUTERONOMY

It is widely argued today that a great deal in Deuteronomy is ancient, although the degree to which it is ancient is not always defined. It seems to be almost a refrain in a commentary such as that of Gerhard von Rad[1] that such and such a law is 'early' or 'earlier'. In his view Deuteronomy is firmly rooted in the sacral and cultic traditions of the old Israelite amphictyony of the pre-monarchical period although in its present form it represents a modification of ancient laws to suit a later stage in Israel's history. Adam Welch[2] argued that the cultic laws of chapters 12, 14, 16 and 27 all point to the primitive conditions of the age of settlement, or at the very latest, some time before the days of Amos, possibly the tenth century BC. The functions of the prophet, the priests, the judges and the other civil officers were not yet fully specialized. The rules for the cities of refuge belong to the period of emergence from nomadic to settled life. E. Robertson argued strenuously that Deuteronomy was drawn up under the guidance of Samuel as the standard law book both civil and religious for the emerging monarchy, and hence it arose during the eleventh century BC.[3] R. Brinker advanced a similar view.[4]

Some attempt should be made to portray the society for which much of Deuteronomy was relevant before arriving at conclusions about the origin of the materials which lie at the basis of the book. To be sure, a later editor could easily have given himself to 'archaizing' activities. But 'archaizing' is based on a knowledge of the past. It is proper to ask what elements of Israel's past are portrayed in Deuteronomy. In particular, attention should be paid to elements that might have been more meaningful in pre-monarchic years than in, say, the eighth to the sixth centuries BC. The following should be noted:

[1] G. von Rad, *Deuteronomy* (1966).
[2] Adam C. Welch, *The Code of Deuteronomy* (1924).
[3] E. Robertson, 'Investigations into the Old Testament Problem: The Results', *BJRL*, 32.1, Sept. 1949; *The Old Testament Problem* (1950).
[4] R. Brinker, *The Influence of Sanctuaries in Early Israel* (1946). Note pp. 189–212.

a. Israel and her neighbours

Israel was instructed to exterminate the Canaanites (7:1–5; 20:16ff.) and the Amalekites (25:17–19), and to regard the Ammonites and Moabites as permanent enemies (23:3 6).

b. Israel and war

There are several specific laws about the discharge of the Holy War (20:1–20; 21:10–14; 23:10–14; 24:5; 25:17–19).

c. Laws governing various aspects of daily life

There are close parallels between many of the laws of Deuteronomy and both the Book of the Covenant (Ex. 20:22 – 23:33) and the Code of Hammurabi.[1] Common to all three are laws about the release of slaves, manslaughter, man stealing and the *lex talionis*. Some laws are found in Deuteronomy and the Code of Hammurabi but not in the Book of the Covenant, *e.g.* laws concerning false witnesses, the rights of the first-born, incorrigible sons, slandered wives, adultery, rape and immodest actions (19:15–20; 21:15–17; 21:18–21; 22:13–21; 22:22–24; 22:25–27; 25:11f., corresponding in order to Hammurabi laws 1–4, 168–170, 186, 131, 129, 130, 48). Other laws occur in the Book of the Covenant and the Code of Hammurabi but not in Deuteronomy. Even though some fifty per cent of the ordinances in the Book of the Covenant are lacking in Deuteronomy, the fact that the three collections of legal material have so much in common points to some common source of ancient Semitic or Middle Eastern law lying behind all three. Deuteronomy is hardly to be regarded merely as an expansion of the Exodus code although in some cases it seems to present an expansion of an earlier law suitable to a more advanced economy (*cf.* Ex. 23:10f. and Dt. 15:1ff.). It would not be unreasonable to claim that many of the civil laws in Deuteronomy reflect a period before the institution of the monarchy and the appointment of magistrates by the king. Certainly the Book of the Covenant with which Deuteronomy has several parallels 'reflects an agricultural society of patriarchal type and simple mores'.[2]

d. Laws governing religious observances

Several of the laws referring to religious observances are

[1] G. T. Manley, *The Book of the Law* (1957), has several helpful tables in chapter 6, pp. 76–97.
[2] W. F. Albright, *The Biblical Period* (1963), p. 19.

common to the Book of the Covenant and Deuteronomy. Among these may be mentioned prohibition of seething a kid in its mother's milk (14:21b; Ex. 23:19b), consecration of firstlings (15:19, 20; Ex. 22:30), the three pilgrim feasts (16:1–17; Ex. 23:14–18), first-fruits (26:1, 2; Ex. 22:29a; 23:19a). Laws referring to sacrifices and offerings are not found in the Book of the Covenant but they occur in Deuteronomy, in H (Lv. 17–26) and in P (Ex. 25–40; Lv. 1–16, *etc.*). However, the fact that such items are not mentioned in the Book of the Covenant should not be thought to indicate that they were not in use in early times. The tithe, for example, was a very ancient offering. Moreover, it is clear from the cuneiform documents discovered at ancient Ugarit that such sacrifices as the *whole burnt offering* (*kll* = Heb. *kālîl*), the *peace offering* (*šlm* = Heb. *šelem*), the *compensation* or *guilt offering* ('*ṭm* = Heb. *'šām*), the *sacrifice* (*dbḥ* = Heb. *zebaḥ*) were part of the regular cult in Ugarit in the fourteenth century BC. Indeed we may add to this list a number of other items which have parallels in H and P as well as in Deuteronomy, the *burnt offering* (*šrp*), the *mnḥ* (reminiscent of Heb. *minḥâ*) which may have been a kind of gift offering, the *mtn* (Heb. *mattān*) which may have had a religious connotation at times, and the '*s* or '*st* (Heb. *'iššeh*), an offering that was burnt in the fire. Several verbs were used at Ugarit in connection with the sacrifices which have parallel use in Hebrew, *e.g.* *dbḥ* (Heb. *zābaḥ*), '*ly* (Heb. '*ālâ*), *šrp* (Heb. *śārap*).[1] In addition to these parallels a number of other nouns and verbs were used to describe aspects of a most complex cult. It seems extraordinary to deny to Israel in the thirteenth century BC a system of sacrifice such as that reflected in Deuteronomy, H and P, when the Canaanites had an extremely complex system in the same general area in the fourteenth century BC. Some words of W. F. Albright are apposite here.[2] In reference to the Priestly Code he writes: '. . . in it we have substantially the sacrificial and ritual practice of the Tabernacle as transmitted by tradition from the period before Solomon's Temple. . . . Just how much of this ritual goes back to Moses himself would be idle to conjecture in the present state of our knowledge; the spirit and much of the detail may be considered as antedating the Conquest of Canaan – in other words, as going back to Mosaic origins.'

[1] J. Gray, *The Legacy of Canaan*, Supp. to *VT*, V, 1957, pp. 192–217.
[2] W. F. Albright, *The Biblical Period* (1963), p. 19.

e. Absence of a reference to the Temple

Nowhere in Deuteronomy is there a reference to the Temple as such, but only to the *place where Yahweh will choose to place his name*, a reference to the central sanctuary, although in some circumstances it may refer to any approved sanctuary other than the central sanctuary.

f. The law of the king

See commentary on 17:14–20. There are many references in the Pentateuch to the kings of the nations round about Israel. There are also references to kings that will arise from among the descendants of the patriarchs in the patriarchal promises (Gn. 17:6, 16; 35:11). But nowhere else in the Pentateuch does one find a law for the king in Israel apart from Deuteronomy 17:14–20. On the view that Deuteronomy was not produced till the seventh century BC, these verses are taken to represent the state of affairs as they were at that time, whatever the origin of the law may have been. However, the idea of kingship was an old one in the ancient Near East and the picture in Deuteronomy is general enough to suit kings of the second half of the second millennium BC.[1] Apart from this one reference Deuteronomy is strangely silent about a king. There is an absence of any Davidic tradition in the book. There is no discussion about his functions. Professor Edward Robertson argues that the situation fits the time of Samuel.[2] In any case, it is arguable that even this section on the king need not necessarily reflect the days of Israel's kings. The apparent criticism of the kingly office could equally well be directed against Near Eastern kings in general.

It is not without good reason that many modern writers wish to push back the date of the earliest material in Deuteronomy at least to the pre-monarchic period. Martin Noth and Gerhard von Rad look to the old tribal confederacy of the days of the judges in the eleventh–twelfth century BC as the point of origin of much of the material. But having gone back to the eleventh–twelfth century BC one wonders why these writers will not go back the extra century to the time of Moses. The reason is that they are not persuaded that there was a tribal confederacy in the time of Moses in the thirteenth century BC, if indeed Moses was any more than a very shadowy

[1] I. Mendelsohn, 'Samuel's denunciation of Kingship in the light of the Akkadian documents of Ugarit', *BASOR*, 143, Oct. 1956, pp. 17–22.
[2] E. Robertson, *The Old Testament Problem* (1950), p. 44.

figure at all.[1] For these writers the entity 'Israel' only emerged in Canaan when a conglomerate of ancient traditions was welded together and given an 'all Israel' orientation. The shadowy figure of Moses became a point of focus for a wide variety of idealizing traditions.

When Moses is allowed to assume the stature which he has n Bible history, and when the Sinai event is allowed to assume a decisive role in the history of those tribal groups that formed the core of Israel,[2] the picture is entirely different from that of Noth and von Rad. Moses becomes the mediator of Yahweh's covenant with the tribal groups that made up the incipient 'Israel' and already in the days before the conquest there was a recognizable entity which was able to move into Canaan and undertake a real conquest.

What then was the nature of the people whom Yahweh called into covenant with Himself? Were they purely semi-nomads or was there something of the character of village people about them? It is entirely possible, granted the general historicity of the narrative in Exodus 1-12, that a sojourn of perhaps four hundred years in Egypt transformed an original semi-nomadic group into an essentially village people,[3] which is the picture in the Exodus narrative. They were thus already a village people by the time Moses led them out from Egypt and their nomadic or semi-nomadic existence was already far in the past. The Book of the Covenant and the earliest material in Deuteronomy may well reflect their community life in Egypt which was an adaptation of their earlier semi-settled life in Canaan. The period spent in the wilderness did not revive their semi-nomadic life, but rather allowed processes of consolidation to take place which issued in the covenant of Moab just prior to their entry into Canaan. We can postulate that during their period of waiting in the wilderness they were living a village type of life for most of the time. The biblical narrative suggests that they spent long periods in some places.

There are grounds then for thinking that behind the present Deuteronomy there lies an ancient and authentic pattern for national existence which goes back to Moses' time. What we have in the present Deuteronomy represents the end-point of

[1] Martin Noth, *The History of Israel*[2] (1960), pp. 127-138.
[2] The view of John Bright, *A History of Israel* (1960), pp. 125-126, seems to be closer to the biblical facts and is not lacking in supporting circumstantial evidence.
[3] Professor Francis I. Andersen proposed this view to the writer in March 1968 and has promised to develop it at a later date.

subsequent revisions both in language and in form. Such a view allows for an explanation of some of the phenomena that one meets in the study of Deuteronomy. On the one hand it preserves a vital link between Moses and Deuteronomy, and on the other hand it allows for the re-application of the great principles of the covenant at Sinai to the changing conditions of a new age, be it that of Samuel, or Solomon, or Hezekiah, or Josiah. What exactly was the nature of the material that left Moses' hands is not clear. But it reflected a simple village life, and it stressed Israel's character as a covenant people. There is no special reason why there should not have been some written document at an early date, since writing was common enough in Western Asia in his day, especially in Egypt. There are statements in Deuteronomy that 'Moses wrote'. But one does not need to commit oneself to the view that Moses wrote all or even a major part of Deuteronomy to argue that much in Deuteronomy goes back to the days of Moses. Some written material plus an adequate oral tradition would serve the purposes of preservation equally well.

VII. THE DATE AND AUTHORSHIP OF DEUTERONOMY

In Judaism and in early Christianity the Mosaic authorship of the entire Pentateuch was generally held. Ben Sira in Ecclesiasticus 24:23 affirms this. So do Philo and Josephus. A Mosaic authorship of the Pentateuch and, by implication, of Deuteronomy seems to be implied in the New Testament (Mt. 19:8; Mk. 12:26; Lk. 24:27, 44; Jn. 7:19, 23; Acts 13:39; 15:5; 28:23; 1 Cor. 9:9; 2 Cor. 3:15; Heb. 9:19; 10:28).[1] But there were other views. One of these, expressed in the apocryphal book 4 Ezra *c.* AD 90, was that the entire Old Testament had been lost and was then dictated under divine inspiration by Ezra to certain scribes. Some of the early Christian writers like Irenaeus, Clement of Alexandria and Tertullian knew of this view. In Judaism, too, there were those who raised questions about the traditional view from time to time.[2]

---

[1] Some of these references are ambiguous. They may refer merely to quotations from the roll called Moses, *i.e.* the Pentateuch; *e.g.* Mk. 12:26; Lk. 24:27, 44; 2 Cor. 3:15. Even such an expression as 'the law of Moses' is ambiguous.

[2] Useful reviews of the story of those who found difficulty with the Mosaic authorship of the entire Pentateuch may be found in R. H. Pfeiffer, *Introduction to the Old Testament* (1948), pp. 135f.; R. K. Harrison, *Introduction to the Old Testament* (1970), pp. 3–9.

However, the view that Deuteronomy was substantially Mosaic in origin was, with few exceptions, held by both Jews and Christians until the rise of the modern critical discussions in the late eighteenth and early nineteenth centuries AD. Certain European scholars denied the Mosaic authorship of Deuteronomy and ascribed it to an author or authors who lived approximately at the time of Josiah. Julius Wellhausen gave classic expression to this view which came to be widely accepted in the scholarly world. According to Wellhausen the author was not Moses but a writer, perhaps a prophet, who compiled the material of chapters 12 to 26 just before Josiah's reform of 621 BC. The view had been adumbrated as early as 1805 by W. M. L. de Wette, who proposed a seventh-century date for Deuteronomy believing it to have been the law book discovered in Josiah's day.[1]

Since Wellhausen's day variants of his view as well as a variety of other theories have been proposed. Dates ranging from the time of Moses to as late as 400 BC have been suggested. The debate goes on. There is still considerable uncertainty in the scholarly world about both the date and the authorship of Deuteronomy. One of the complicating factors in recent years is that scholars have been more willing than previously to allow that a great deal of Deuteronomy rests on ancient materials.[2]

Current views about the date and authorship of Deuteronomy may be classified into four groups. Within each group there are differences in detail and emphasis. These groups are:

a. A substantially Mosaic date and authorship. A certain range of post-Mosaic material is allowed.

b. The view that while Deuteronomy contains a great deal of material which goes back to the time of Moses the book was compiled some three or four hundred years later, perhaps in the days of Samuel or David or even during the early years after Solomon's death. A variety of editorial additions are allowed.

c. The view that Deuteronomy was written during the Hezekiah–Josiah period, that is during the seventh century BC. It is not denied that there may well be a considerable sub-

---

[1] The view will be discussed below. See p. 57.
[2] Representative modern writers are G. E. Wright, *Deuteronomy* (*IB*, Vol. 2, 1953), pp. 323–326; G. Henton Davies, 'Deuteronomy', *Peake's Commentary on the Bible* (revised ed., 1962), pp. 269f.; G. von Rad, *Deuteronomy* (1966), pp. 23–27; M. G. Kline, *Treaty of the Great King* (1963); Moshe Weinfeld, *Deuteronomy and the Deuteronomic School* (1972).

stratum of Mosaic material. But certainly Mosaic principles underlie much of the work.

d. The view that the book was a post-exilic work. Various dates from the time of Haggai and Zechariah up to *c.* 400 BC have been proposed.

We shall now undertake a brief discussion of each of these positions and endeavour to outline their implicit assumptions and their strengths and weaknesses.

a. An essentially Mosaic date and authorship

Probably no-one today would argue that Deuteronomy was entirely the work of Moses, although writers in former centuries attempted to show that Moses could have written of his own death by divine inspiration. The important question to be answered by scholars of this group is, What parts of the present book are demonstrably post-Mosaic? Opinions vary. We shall first of all present some of the most important reasons given for Mosaic authorship.

An argument that is regularly advanced by this school is that in Deuteronomy there are several references to Moses speaking (1:6, 9; 5:1; 27:1, 9; 29:2; 31:1, 30; 33:1, *etc.*) and at least two to his writing (31:9, 24). These latter passages are regarded as of particular importance. *And Moses wrote this law, and gave it to the priests the sons of Levi . . . When Moses had finished writing the words of this law in a book, to the very end, Moses commanded the Levites who carried the ark of the covenant of the Lord, 'Take this book of the law, and put it by the side of the ark of the covenant of the Lord your God, that it may be there for a witness against you.'* George L. Robinson writes, 'Now, these statements are either true or they are false. There is no escape. The authorship of no other book in the Old Testament is so explicitly emphasized.'[1]

It is not entirely certain what is meant by the phrase *this law* in 31:9 and 24. Opinions vary, but a widely-held view is that the reference is to the legislation itself in chapters 12 to 26.[2] The discourses and closing chapters were recorded and added later, although not much later than the period immediately following Moses' death.[3]

A further argument in support of Mosaic authorship is that

---

[1] *ISBE*, Vol. 2 (1943), p. 836.
[2] G. T. Manley in *NBD*, p. 308.
[3] *Ibid.*

Jesus appears to have accepted it. In Matthew 19:8 He referred to the law on divorce as something that Moses allowed, thus suggesting that the passage in Deuteronomy (24:1-4) had originated with Moses. Again, in His post-resurrection ministry He began with Moses and the prophets to interpret to them things concerning Himself (Lk. 24:27, 44). Paul too seems to have accepted Mosaic authorship, for he quotes Deuteronomy 25:4 in 1 Corinthians 9:9 as being a law of Moses. The writer to the Hebrews (10:28) likewise refers to a law of Moses, namely to Deuteronomy 17:2-6.

The difficulty with all these references is that the exact meaning of the term *Moses* is not clear. The Pentateuch as a single roll was known as *Moses*, just as the books of the Old Testament from Joshua to Kings plus all the prophets except Daniel are known as the *Prophets*, while all the other books are grouped together as *Writings*. Hence the use of the term *Moses* may not refer specifically to authorship in every passage but may merely refer to the Pentateuch as a roll called *Moses*. Incidentally the exact meaning of the term 'law' in such verses as Deuteronomy 31:9, 24 is also ambiguous, since the exact content of the 'law' which Moses wrote is not defined.

It is argued further that the laws of Deuteronomy refer to a simpler state of society than that which existed in the later centuries and that the Deuteronomic law fits better into the background of history and cultic practice at the close of the Mosaic age. In those days the Canaanites occupied the promised land. Their shrines were to be destroyed so as to remove temptation from Israel. The gifts and sacrifices of God's people were to be brought only to an authorized altar accompanied by proper rituals. The altar of God was not to be defiled by pagan fertility symbols (16:21f.) nor were Canaanite religious practices to be followed (12:29ff.). There was to be a central sanctuary at Shechem once Israel entered the land (27:1ff.), an idea that was meaningful in Moses' day and in the early years of the settlement. There is no reference whatever to Jerusalem as the central sanctuary. There is no king in Israel (17:14-17), although the nature of kingship was well understood from patterns of kingship known among the Canaanites. Many of the laws would have had meaning in the Mosaic period and shortly afterwards but would have been strange anachronisms in a later age.[1]

---

[1] G. T. Manley, *The Book of the Law* (1957), takes up many of these issues.

More recently another reason for a Mosaic date has been advanced by Meredith G. Kline.[1] In the light of recent discussions about the nature of ancient Near Eastern treaties between great kings and their vassals[2] Kline has emphasized the structural unity and integrity of Deuteronomy. When reviewed as a whole it exhibits on a large scale the complete treaty formulation of the ancient Near East. As such it can no longer be considered as the end-product of a series of redactions which reached a final form in the seventh century BC. It is basic to Kline's argument that the classical period of the Near Eastern treaty was the second millennium BC, when the complete range of elements including the historical prologue was included in the treaty document. When Kline wrote, the evidence seemed to point to the fact that the first-millennium treaties lacked the historical prologue. Now Deuteronomy has a historical prologue in 1:5 – 4:49 and thus qualifies for inclusion among the classical second-millennium treaties. He concludes his discussion with the words, 'Now that the form critical data compel the recognition of the antiquity not merely of this or that element within Deuteronomy but of the Deuteronomic treaty in its integrity any persistent insistence on a final edition of the book around the seventh century BC can be nothing more than a vestigial hypothesis, no longer performing a significant function in Old Testament criticism.'[3]

But the final word has not been said. The possibility must be allowed that Deuteronomy was cast in the shape of an ancient treaty by someone who wrote long after Moses' day. Alternatively, Kline's proposal that only in the second-millennium treaties does one find a historical prologue has been challenged more recently. The absence of a historical prologue on the Assyrian and Aramaic treaties[4] does not prove that the historical prologue was lacking. It may have been stated orally or have been assumed.[5] It may even have been present on the Sefiré Aramaic documents which are broken at the top. But in

---

[1] Meredith G. Kline, *Treaty of the Great King* (1963).
[2] See pp. 17–21 for a description of the ancient Near Eastern treaty.
[3] M. G. Kline, *op. cit.*, p. 44.
[4] D. J. Wiseman, 'The Vassal Treaties of Esarhaddon', *Iraq*, 20, 1958, pp. 29–30; A. Dupont-Sommer, *Les Inscriptions Araméennes de Sefiré* (1958).
[5] See J. A. Thompson, *The Ancient Near Eastern Treaties and the Old Testament* (1964), pp. 14, 15; D. J. Wiseman, *art. cit.*, p. 28. But *cf.* K. A. Kitchen, *Ancient Orient and Old Testament* (1966), pp. 94–102.

fact there is a seventh-century BC treaty where the historical prologue occurs.[1] Hence the fact that Deuteronomy has a historical introduction is not necessarily an argument for a date in the second millennium, although it may be.

Another argument used by contenders for a Mosaic origin, which is, however, double-edged, is that there are passages in the prophets that are reminiscent of Deuteronomy. Thus the law of the landmark (19:14) is known to Hosea (5:10); the need for a standard measure (25:13ff.) is known to Amos (8:5) and Micah (6:10f.); the triennial payment of the tithe (14:28) is known to Amos (4:4) and the authority of the priest (17:12; 24:6) is known to Hosea (4:4ff.). This argument is not conclusive, for these parallels do not necessarily prove that the eighth-century prophets knew Deuteronomy either in its developing form, or in its final form. Some scholars have argued that it is possible that Deuteronomy was based on the prophets. On the other hand it may be argued that the religious traditions enshrined in Deuteronomy (and elsewhere in the Pentateuch for that matter) had been perpetuated over many centuries – a state of affairs which obtained all over the ancient Near East where communities lived by ancient traditions regardless of written law codes.

Recent scholars who have contended for the Mosaic authorship of at least substantial parts of Deuteronomy, or even of the whole of it, include Meredith G. Kline,[2] R. K. Harrison[3] and M. H. Segal.[4] If a Mosaic authorship is accepted the question arises as to what place must then be allowed to post-Mosaic additions. Some of those who contend for a Mosaic authorship place these at a minimum. Clearly the account of the death of Moses in chapter 34 must be post-Mosaic. Some of the geographical expressions in the book are of particular interest from this point of view. Apparently the land of Canaan is viewed from outside. The expression 'beyond Jordan' has often been taken as a post-Mosaic expression because it appears to imply that the speaker is standing in Palestine. Contenders for a Mosaic authorship have argued that Moses may have known the geography of Canaan without having visited the land. But in fact the expression 'beyond Jordan' might mean 'in the

[1] A. F. Campbell, 'An historical prologue in a seventh century Treaty', *Biblica*, 50, 1969, pp. 534f.

[2] M. G. Kline, *op. cit.*

[3] R. K. Harrison, *Introduction to the Old Testament* (1970), pp. 635–662.

[4] *JQR*, 48, 1957–58.

region of Jordan'.[1] The expression is therefore often lacking in definition.

In a passage such as Deuteronomy 1:1 the places mentioned are difficult to identify today but may have had a basis in fact in Moses' day. The statement in 1:2 concerning an eleven-day journey from Horeb to Mount Seir seems to be a reliable estimate if Horeb is Jebel Musa.[2]

While various geographical data have been proposed as post-Mosaic from time to time, it is difficult to prove the case one way or the other. The possibility may be admitted that editorial touches occurred in the post-Mosaic period but it is not easy to prove which of those proposed are genuinely post-Mosaic.[3] Among those scholars who maintain an essentially Mosaic authorship opinions vary as to the precise extent of the post-Mosaica in Deuteronomy.

One very difficult question to answer is that of the *ipsissima verba* (*i.e.* the very words) of Moses. The problem is similar to that which occurs in the Gospels in the New Testament. Comparison of the words of Jesus in parallel Gospels shows that exact correspondence of words does not occur. Precisely how the words were transmitted by the early church is difficult for us today to say. It is just as difficult to decide what were the exact words (*ipsissima verba*) spoken by Jesus. There is no evidence that He wrote down His sayings. What then of Moses? The claim is certainly made that Moses spoke certain words and also that he wrote certain words. But it is extremely difficult to decide whether the words of Moses recorded in Deuteronomy are his *ipsissima verba* or whether they are the report of Moses' words after they have passed through the processes of transmission to some date after Moses' death.

b. A post-Mosaic, but pre-seventh-century date

Two main proposals have been made for a date of composition for Deuteronomy earlier than the widely held seventh-century date[4] but later than the time of Moses, namely the eleventh century, in the days of Samuel, and the tenth century, in the days of David.

[1] See commentary, p. 81, and the reference to an article by B. Gemser in *VT*, II, 1953, pp. 349ff.
[2] Y. Aharoni, *The Holy Land: Antiquity and Survival II*, 2–3 (1957), pp. 289f., 293, fig. 7. See commentary on 1:2.
[3] See R. K. Harrison, *op. cit.*, pp. 637–640; G. T. Manley, *The Book of the Law* (1957), chapter IV, pp. 48–64.
[4] This is the subject of section *c.* below.

The tenth-century date was proposed by Theodor Oestreicher in Germany in 1923,[1] and by Adam C. Welch in Scotland in 1924.[2] Oestreicher maintained that the story of Josiah's reform in 2 Kings 22f. is interested not in the centralization of the cult in Jerusalem but in purification from all heathen and especially Assyrian elements both in Jerusalem and elsewhere. Two of the terms he used have become famous. In his view the reform was concerned with *Kultreinheit* (cultic purity), not *Kulteinheit* (cultic unity). Josiah had begun his reformation on his own initiative (2 Ch. 34:3) several years before the 'law book', which was basically Deuteronomy, was discovered. What the finding of the 'law book' did was not to initiate the reform but to give a new impetus to a reform that had already begun.

A second point made by Oestreicher was that the original Deuteronomy did not demand an absolute centralization of the cult at Jerusalem but only a relative one at the larger sanctuaries. Deuteronomy 12:13f., which on the theory that Deuteronomy was produced in the seventh century was translated *Take heed that you do not offer your burnt offerings at every place that you see; but at* the *place which the Lord will choose in* one *of your tribes*, was translated by Oestreicher as follows: *Take heed that you do not offer your burnt offerings at* every *place that you see, but in* any *place which the Lord will choose in* any one *of your tribes*. On this view Deuteronomy 12:13f. was another way of expressing Exodus 20:24. The key sentence here is *in every place where I cause my name to be remembered I will come to you and bless you*.

Adam Welch came independently to the same conclusion that Deuteronomy did not demand absolute centralization of worship, although the scope of his investigation was narrower. He confined his study to Deuteronomy and did not discuss 2 Kings 22f. Welch argued that the only passage in all of Deuteronomy which taught centralization was 12:1–7, but he held this to be a later addition inserted at the beginning of the 'legal' section proper to ensure that the whole law should be read in its light. Omit this passage and the rest of the book may be read without centralization. He would translate the phrase the *place which Yahweh shall choose in* one *of your tribes*, that is, the reference is to any legitimate Yahweh sanctuary. Such a view according to Welch would eliminate the seemingly incredible command that the whole population of the country

[1] Theodor Oestreicher, *Das deuteronomische Grundgesetz* (1923).
[2] Adam C. Welch, *The Code of Deuteronomy* (1924).

should go to Jerusalem at the time of the harvest when an absence of everyone from the farms would be impossible. Instead, the people would go to the nearest Yahweh sanctuary. Thus the emphasis of the book was not on the *number* of places of worship but on the *character* of the places. Its burden was Yahwism against Baalism and it was designed to prevent both the indiscriminate use of heathen sanctuaries by Israel and also illegal private sanctuaries like that of Micah (Jdg. 17). From these presuppositions Welch concluded that Deuteronomy was basically the product of the religious movement in Benjamin and Ephraim which originated with Samuel and centred on Shiloh,[1] that is, it had its roots in northern Israel. Welch did not hold that the present book of Deuteronomy was written precisely in the days of Samuel. Indeed he held that some parts of it reflect the period of the Assyrian domination, *e.g.* the curses of chapter 28.[2] Other parts may be later still. The final editing of the materials was much later than Samuel's day. Nevertheless the work is certainly pre-Josiah and is based on ancient legal precepts far older than Josiah's day. One of Welch's conclusions which has had considerable appeal to more recent writers is that Deuteronomy probably originated in Northern Israel, for its closest relation was to the life of Ephraim and to the larger sanctuaries of Ephraim.[3]

The view of Welch and Oestreicher has been criticized on several grounds, particularly by those who hold to a late date for Deuteronomy. Welch's translation of Deuteronomy 12:13f. is held to be incorrect; it is argued that despite Welch's contrast between legitimate Yahweh and illegitimate heathen sanctuaries there is no specific indication that the Israelites were in the habit of going to heathen sanctuaries with their passover, tithes and firstlings. In particular there is no reference to a 'Baal sanctuary'. A further difficulty that is seen in Welch's view is his treatment of the passover which he held would be celebrated at *any Yahweh sanctuary* rather than specifically at Jerusalem.[4]

Despite the fact that the views of Adam Welch have not

---

[1] Adam C. Welch, *op. cit.*, p. 206.
[2] Adam C. Welch, *Deuteronomy, the Framework to the Code* (1932), pp. 129–139.
[3] Adam C. Welch, *The Code of Deuteronomy* (1924), pp. 38f., 74f., 113, 128f., 191f. *Cf.* remarks of G. E. Wright in *IB*, Vol. 2 (1953), pp. 324ff.; G. von Rad, *Deuteronomy* (1966), p. 26.
[4] Adam C. Welch, *op. cit.*, p. 66.

been accepted *in toto*, his insistence on the early historical background for many of Deuteronomy's laws gave support to those scholars who had made more conservative estimates of the age of these laws, often in the face of strong opposition. Other facets of his work provided a stimulus for further consideration of the nature of Deuteronomy against entrenched critical theories.

The second theory of a post-Mosaic but pre-seventh-century date for Deuteronomy was that of E. Robertson, first proposed in a series of lectures[1] and then concisely expressed in a book.[2] His view was in some respects like that of Welch although he maintained that the book of Deuteronomy was largely the work of Samuel who had undertaken a codification of ancient divine law and had also prepared fresh legislation of a civil nature.[3] He saw Samuel as a great statesman who yielded to the clamour of the people for a king and established the monarchy under Saul. Such a movement away from priestly control towards the civil power represented by the king would require a re-orientation of national life. In Deuteronomy for the first time the king appears and the high priest disappears. But a political union of the tribes under one king made centralization of worship both desirable and possible. A return to centralization of worship from the decentralization thrust upon Israel by the nature of the conquest was natural and ultimately inevitable. The site of the new capital which was also to be the central sanctuary had to be carefully chosen.[4]

The views of Robertson were underlined and extended somewhat by R. Brinker.[5] He too was concerned to refute the arguments for a date of Deuteronomy in the days of Josiah and argued that the legislation formulated in Deuteronomy was basically Mosaic but had been supplemented by decisions made by priests and judges given at different sanctuaries.[6]

---

[1] 'Temple and Torah', *BJRL*, 26.1, 1941; 'The Riddle of the Torah', *BJRL*, 27.2, 1943; 'The Pentateuch Problem', *BJRL*, 29.1, 1945; 'Investigations into the Old Testament Problem: The Results', *BJRL*, 32.1, 1949.

[2] E. Robertson, *The Old Testament Problem* (1950).

[3] In his essay 'Investigations into the Old Testament problem: The Results', *BJRL*, 32.1, 1949, p. 12, he refers to 2 Ch. 19:11, where a distinction is made between two categories of law, religious and civil. *Cf.* his discussion in *The Old Testament Problem* (1950).

[4] 'Investigations into the Old Testament Problem: The Results', *BJRL*, 32.1, 1949, p. 12.

[5] R. Brinker, *The Influence of Sanctuaries in Early Israel* (1946).

[6] R. Brinker, *op. cit.*, pp. 189–212.

Following the suggestion of Robertson[1] Brinker regarded this formulation by a council of priests under the supervision of Samuel[2] as an expansion of the Mosaic Book of the Covenant. One serious difficulty in the view is that the books of Samuel do not even hint at a gathering of priests and scribes who might have undertaken such a task. Nor do the books contain the word *law (tôrâ)*. Moreover the leader appointed by Samuel according to these books was a *nāḡîḏ* or *military leader* (1 Sa. 9:16; 10:1; 13:14; 25:30; 2 Sa. 6:21; 7:8) and not the *king (melek)* envisaged in Deuteronomy 17:14ff.[3]

Like Robertson, Welch and Oestreicher, Brinker insisted that the guiding principle of Deuteronomy was not centralization of worship but the protection of Israel from the threat of Canaanite idolatry in a day of national crisis.

What is particularly valuable about the work of Robertson and Brinker, despite the speculative character of their proposals, is their emphasis on the fact that authentic Mosaic material had been carefully preserved at the sanctuaries of Israel during the centuries since Moses, from say *c.* 1250 to 1050 BC, that is, for a period of approximately two hundred years.

c. A seventh-century date

While there are competent scholars who do not accept a seventh-century date for Deuteronomy, the majority of modern scholars accept a date some time in the seventh century, either earlier or later, for the publication of the book.

This view dates back in its essentials to the appearance of a dissertation by the German scholar W. M. L. de Wette in 1805, in which he held that the law book used by Josiah in his religious reforms was Deuteronomy which had only recently been written. The thesis was developed, amplified and firmly established by Julius Wellhausen in 1876 and subsequently passed on by succeeding generations of scholars with modifications.

There are several basic presuppositions in this theory among which the following should be noted:[4]

[1] *The Old Testament Problem*, pp. 60ff.
[2] R. Brinker, *op. cit.*, pp. 223f.
[3] The fact that *melek* is used of Saul in these books can be regarded as the work of later editors. What is more significant is the preservation of the term *nāḡîḏ*.
[4] J. Dahl, 'The case for the currently accepted date of Deuteronomy' in

1. Deuteronomy in whole or in part was compiled at some time in the century preceding the reforms described in 2 Kings 22f. as carried through by Josiah in 621 BC.[1]

2. This document furnished the immediate inspiration for Josiah's reforms and served as his programme for them.

3. Deuteronomy was essentially a prophetic work and not a priestly document.

4. The book is not to be regarded as a formal code but as an ideal programme. The lack of penalties in some areas, for example for failure to attend feasts, is seen as evidence that the book was not a legal code as such.

5. The chief formal demand of the book is for centralization of the cult at the Temple in Jerusalem which involved the abolition of the local sanctuaries scattered throughout the land.

6. Even so, the book of Deuteronomy contains a good deal of ancient material. It contains laws that go back to the Book of the Covenant, and from here to a remoter antiquity. These are recorded alongside later additions. Some writers allow that subsequent to Josiah's time and even after the fall of Jerusalem in 586 BC further additions were made.

In the defence of these propositions the proponents of the seventh-century date advanced three lines of argument, the literary, the religious and the historical.

The *literary* argument was twofold, being based partly on evidence drawn from literary relationships with other codes and partly on style and vocabulary.

It was argued that Deuteronomy is closely related to the Book of the Covenant (Ex. 20:22 – 23:19) although it reflects a more advanced and complicated community life.[2] It has few parallels with the Holiness Code (H) in Leviticus 17–26, and still less with the Priestly Code (P). In fact, the order of these legal documents is JE, D, H, P. The same result follows for historical sections where D is dependent on JE.

In reference to other books in the Old Testament it was

---

a Symposium on the Problem of Deuteronomy, *JBL*, XLVII, 1928, pp. 358–379.

[1] Opinions vary between scholars as to the extent of the original work. Wellhausen limited the original book to chapters 12–26; S. R. Driver in *A Critical and Exegetical Commentary on Deuteronomy* (*ICC*, 1902), p. lxxii, inclines to chapters 1–3, 5–26, 28; George Adam Smith, *The Book of Deuteronomy* (1918), pp. xcivff., thinks that the original work was chapters 12–26 in the main plus some form of the discourses now in chapters 1–11, 28–30. There are numerous variations of these views.

[2] See above, pp. 26ff.

argued that there is no trace of Deuteronomy in the eighth-century prophets. Apparent references in these books to Deuteronomic thinking were held not to be genuine utterances of the prophets. On the other hand a strong relationship was seen with the prophets Jeremiah and Ezekiel, while Joshua, Judges, Samuel and Kings were held to be the result of Deuteronomic redactions of earlier historical material.

Further, the style and vocabulary of Deuteronomy were held to mark the transition to later tendencies and to be of a piece with other writings of the seventh century.

The *religious* argument was based on the contention that in its religious ideas Deuteronomy followed closely after the great social prophets of the eighth century with the social passion of Amos, the national devotion of Isaiah, and the strong emphasis of Hosea on love. Moreover the theism of the book was said to reflect an advanced stage of religious thought far removed from the primitive concepts of the period of Saul and David and the crude monolatry of Elijah. The false religions referred to were those of the days of Manasseh (2 Ki. 21:1ff.).

The *historical* argument centres around the finding of the book of the law in the Jerusalem Temple (2 Ki. 22; 23) and the reforms of Josiah. It was argued that no other group of laws in the Old Testament corresponds so closely point for point with the measures carried out in these reforms as does Deuteronomy.

While it may be claimed that a seventh-century date for the final composition of Deuteronomy is still held by the majority of scholars, the arguments advanced by the early proponents of this view have all been challenged and modified.

Some brief reference will now be made to several recent writers who still hold to a seventh-century date but with considerable modifications of the classical arguments. Writers like S. R. Driver[1] and George Adam Smith[2] follow rather more closely the classical line and will not be discussed.

A key figure in modern discussions is Gerhard von Rad.[3] In his various writings on Deuteronomy von Rad takes up a number of important issues. His analysis of the structure of Deuteronomy has already been discussed.[4] At the time of his

---

[1] *A Critical and Exegetical Commentary on Deuteronomy (ICC*, 1902).
[2] *The Book of Deuteronomy* (1918).
[3] *Studies in Deuteronomy* (ET, 1953); 'Deuteronomy', in *IBD*, I (1963), pp. 831–838; *Deuteronomy* (1966).
[4] See above, p. 16.

earlier writings, prior to 1956, the structure of the ancient
Near Eastern treaty pattern was not fully understood. He proposed then that the structure of Deuteronomy ran back to its
Sitz im Leben in a cultic celebration, perhaps a feast of covenant
renewal.[1] He has also isolated a variety of ancient blocks of law
including material from the Book of the Covenant (Ex. 21–23).[2]
Further, he has proposed that the book of Deuteronomy had
its origin in the Northern Kingdom where the Levites preserved ancient covenant traditions and laws. One of the
important features of his work is the detailed analysis of the
literary method of Deuteronomy in which law, parenesis and
historical recital are closely linked.[3] This method is not unknown elsewhere in the Old Testament. It occurs, for example,
in the E tradition in Exodus 19ff. with which Deuteronomy
has many links. In his view, older units of tradition were all
subordinated to the structure of the cultic celebration which he
believes was associated with the feast of tabernacles (Dt.
31:10b). References to Shechem in Deuteronomy provide him
with a link with Joshua 24, where a covenant renewal ceremony is described.

How then does von Rad date Deuteronomy to the seventh
century BC? He regards the book as the work of Levites who
took up the old amphictyonic traditions which had been preserved in Levitical circles over the centuries and re-interpreted
and adapted these ancient laws for later circumstances.[4] He
points out that Deuteronomy represents the law as having been
given by Moses and not directly by God as in Exodus 20–23,
and 25–31. In its present form the book is presented as preaching about the law. In von Rad's view it owes this shape to the
Levites.[5] The special circumstance under which this was done
was the revival of the old Israelite militia in Judah.[6] He argues
that the many references to the Holy War in Deuteronomy
point to such a revival. It was the *people of the land* (*'am hā'āreṣ*)
who had preserved a pure form of Yahwism.[7] They were
offended by the syncretism they found in Jerusalem and set

---

[1] *Ibid.*
[2] See *Studies in Deuteronomy* (1953), pp. 60–69.
[3] *Ibid.*, pp. 11–36.
[4] *Ibid.*, p. 61.
[5] *Ibid.*, p. 14.
[6] *Ibid.*, p. 62.
[7] That the *'am hā'āreṣ* were the prosperous land-owning class in Judah
has not been accepted by all writers. See E. de Vaux, *Ancient Israel* (1962),
pp. 70ff.; E. W. Nicholson, *Deuteronomy and Tradition* (1967), pp. 86f.

out to reform the cultus there, but it was the Levites who acted as the spokesmen for this movement and were the real authors of Deuteronomy. The origin of the traditions was in the Northern Kingdom.[1] For that reason the concept of a central sanctuary based on the ancient model at Shechem is prominent. As evidence that Deuteronomy was written late and not in the days of the amphictyony von Rad points out differences between Deuteronomy and the earlier Book of the Covenant.[2] Further evidence for a date much later than Moses comes from the law of the king (17:14–20) and the references to siege techniques (20:20), both of which are too like later parallels to fit the age of the amphictyony.

Von Rad's contribution to the discussion has a number of valuable aspects. His recognition of a unified structure to Deuteronomy based on the pattern of a covenant renewal ceremony points the way to a reconsideration of the unity of Deuteronomy. His view that amphictyonic institutions, laws and concepts are preserved in the book, even if in a modified form, is also valuable. One of his proposals which has not met with general agreement is that it was the Levites who wrote Deuteronomy in connection with a revival movement during the seventh century. In order to avoid the conclusion that the very idea of centralization would have destroyed the importance of the Levites he argues that the centralization passages are late, or perhaps that the Levites were not cult personnel.[3] There is, in fact, no evidence of a reform movement promoted by the *people of the land* ('*am hā'āreṣ*), nor of any popular demand for Josiah to reform Judah's cultus. Rather, Josiah is pictured as conducting his own reform with the help, perhaps, of a few advisers.

Another modern writer who holds to a modified form of the seventh-century date for Deuteronomy is G. E. Wright.[4] He argues that Josiah's reform was not without a precedent. It was similar in many ways to that of Hezekiah at the end of the eighth century. Behind both reforms lay ancient traditions, Mosaic traditions indeed. He claims that 'Any investigation

---

[1] *Studies in Deuteronomy* (1953), p. 67.

[2] See his discussion on the law of slaves and the year of release, *Deuteronomy* (1966), p. 14.

[3] Moshe Weinfeld, 'Deuteronomy – the present state of the enquiry', *JBL*, LXXXVI, Part III, 1967, pp. 252f., has given his own strong criticism of this view. See also his *Deuteronomy and the Deuteronomic School* (1972).

[4] See *Deuteronomy* (*IB*, Vol. 2, 1953), Introduction, pp. 311–330, especially pp. 320–326.

into the origin of Deuteronomy, however, will lead ultimately to the figure of Moses himself'.[1] He argues that Deuteronomy is best understood as an exposition of the ancient faith of Israel, first taught by Moses but here revived by those who regarded it as the normative faith of Israel. But who were these people and when did they produce Deuteronomy? Wright points to various tell-tale facts. The movement towards centralization of the sanctuary as seen in the reforms of Hezekiah and Josiah seems to point to Deuteronomy 12. The relationship in style between Jeremiah and Deuteronomy is suggestive. The protest in Israel against foreign cultic practices, a protest which began with Elijah in the ninth century and continued here and there in Israel until Josiah's day, is seen to be significant. The references to the *host of heaven* (4:19; 17:3) are thought to point to the period of Assyrian domination because it was in this period that Assyrian influences were strong (*cf.* 2 Ki. 21:3–5; 23:11). This would point to the century between 740 and 640 BC as the period when the book was written. But G. E. Wright recognizes that behind any final composition lay a long interpretative tradition and appears to accept with approval the view of von Rad that it was the Levites of Northern Israel who preserved the Mosaic traditions, which stemmed ultimately from the Shechem sanctuary. His general conclusion is that 'all Old Testament law is fixed within the Mosaic era, and Deuteronomy must be considered as an exposition of the Mosaic faith by those who were vitally concerned in seeing its revival as the normative faith of the state. Yet like so much of the biblical writing, Deuteronomy is actually an anonymous production. All credit is given to Moses the founder of the faith, and to the God whose servant he was.'[2]

A third representative modern writer who adheres to a seventh-century date for Deuteronomy is E. W. Nicholson.[3] He has proposed an original book consisting for the most part of the singular passages in chapters 5 to 26 together with some of chapter 28 (which was expanded after the fall of Jerusalem in 586 BC and chapter 30 added to it). Then the Deuteronomistic historian incorporated this material into his history but added the plural passages in chapters 6 to 26 plus the framework of chapters 1 to 3, and parts of chapters 31 and 34. Later still chapters 32 and 33 were added.

In his view the book arose not among the Levites but among

---

[1] *Ibid.*, p. 326.   [2] *Ibid.*

[3] E. W. Nicholson, *Deuteronomy and Tradition* (1967).

the prophetic party of the Northern Kingdom. This group fled south to Judah after the fall of Samaria in 721 BC and there drew up their programme of reform and revival with Jerusalem as its political and cultic centre. The precise period in which Deuteronomy was composed was very probably during the dark days of Manasseh's reign which followed the bright hopes of Hezekiah's day. When Hezekiah's reforms failed the prophetic group drew up their own plans for reform in the shape of Deuteronomy. In order to have it accepted they made certain concessions to the Jerusalem traditions by demanding the centralization of the cult. This was the book that was found in Josiah's day in the Temple, where it had been deposited by its authors. It was accepted by the Jerusalem authorities and provided reinforcement for the reforms which Josiah had already commenced. When Deuteronomy was thus accorded a place in Judah, the Deuteronomic circle once more sprang to life and gave rise to the Deuteronomistic history contained in Deuteronomy to 2 Kings.

Nicholson's idea that the origin of Deuteronomy is to be sought among a prophetic group is reminiscent of earlier views that it is a development of the preaching of the eighth-century prophets. However, Nicholson allows that ancient traditions were preserved by this group. But the idea is speculative and merely shifts the problem of origin from the Levites to a prophetic group – for neither of which is there unambiguous evidence.

The fourth recent writer is Ronald Clements.[1] Like others he allows that Deuteronomy is based on northern traditions which found their way into the south and were accepted by the Judaean authorities and enforced. He too holds that the authors of Deuteronomy came south after the fall of Samaria in 721 BC and composed their work in Jerusalem, hoping to bring about a reform in the Jerusalem cult. They attempted this reform in a variety of ways. They endeavoured to reform the Jerusalem attitude to the Ark by proposing that it was not the throne of the invisibly-present Yahweh whose dwelling-place was Mount Zion, but merely the container of the tables of the law.[2] Further, they not merely agreed with the old claim of

[1] R. E. Clements, *God's Chosen People, A Theological Interpretation of the Book of Deuteronomy* (1968); *Prophecy and Covenant* (1965); 'Deuteronomy and the Jerusalem Cult Tradition', *VT*, XV, 1965.

[2] R. E. Clements, 'Deuteronomy and the Jerusalem Cult Tradition', *VT*, XV, 1965, pp. 300–312.

Jerusalem to a place of primacy but extended that claim, modifying the grounds for it. It was not, they argued, that Yahweh dwelt there, but that His *name* dwelt there. Moreover, the uniqueness of the sanctuary was independent of any political claims associated with the Davidic monarchy.[1] Again, stress was laid rather on the election of Israel than on the election of David, to counterbalance the claims of the Jerusalem kingship theology.[2] And finally the authors laid stress on the idea of Yahweh's land which He had given to His people as a counter to the doctrine that Mount Zion was especially the symbol of Yahweh's holy land.

Clements' views have been criticized by several writers who adhere to the seventh-century date.[3] These argue that it is not at all clear that the aim of Deuteronomy was to reform the Jerusalem cult tradition, but more probably that the aim of the writers of Deuteronomy was rather to save the whole nation and revive it in the face of political disintegration at the time when Israel's existence as Yahweh's covenant people was threatened before the Assyrian menace. Samaria had fallen in 721 BC and Judah had to be saved. Working in Jerusalem the reformers formulated their traditions into a reformation programme which they hoped the Judaean authorities might accept and carry out.

Another recent writer who adheres to a seventh-century date is Moshe Weinfeld, who assumes that it was a literary circle familiar with ancient treaty forms that composed the book of Deuteronomy, namely, the scribes of the period Hezekiah–Josiah.[4] This period has been recognized as one of religious revival all over the Near East.[5] In Judah, however, the scribes in the courts of Hezekiah and Josiah achieved a religio-national ideology which was inspired by a new emphasis on Wisdom themes. The book of Deuteronomy preserves the motifs of the old covenant tradition, but these were reworked and adapted to the covenant type prevalent in the eighth and seventh century BC. Indeed Deuteronomy as we now have it represents a transition from the narrow statutory corpus of law to the humanistic outlook. One reason why Weinfeld regards

[1] *Ibid.*, pp. 303–305.
[2] *Ibid.*, pp. 305–307.
[3] *E.g.* E. W. Nicholson, *Deuteronomy and Tradition* (1967), pp. 104–106.
[4] Moshe Weinfeld, 'Deuteronomy – the present state of the inquiry', *JBL*, LXXXVI, Part III, 1967; *Deuteronomy and the Deuteronomic School* (1972).
[5] W. F. Albright, *From the Stone Age to Christianity* (2nd ed. 1957), pp. 314–319.

Deuteronomy as coming from wise men is that prophets, priests and wise men are distinguished as separate groups in the late seventh and early sixth centuries (Je. 18:18; Ezk. 7:26). Jeremiah speaks specifically of the scribes – wise men who said *How can you say, 'We are wise, and the law of the Lord is with us'?* (Je. 8:8).

Finally, reference should be made to the work of N. Lohfink, who has given fresh consideration to the narrative in 2 Kings 22 to 23 referring to the finding of the law book. In this section chapters 22:3 – 23:3, 21–23 refer to the discovery of the book while 23:4–20 refers to reforms probably carried out over a period. In the material referring to the discovery of the book strong emphasis is placed on the role of the king. The story is concerned with a covenant renewal ceremony in which the king hears the law, repents and is forgiven (22:3–20), renews the covenant (23:1–3) and celebrates the passover (23:21–23).[1] Lohfink proposes that this narrative may have been composed at the king's direction and placed in the royal archives. But the point is that the narrative is not concerned chiefly with the law book as many have assumed, but with a king who was devoted to the covenant. It is precisely the *book of the covenant (sēper habbᵉrît)* that is referred to (23:2, 21). Hints are given that the book contained stipulations against the worship of other gods (22:16f.), that it was binding on the *fathers* (22:13), that it contained curses (22:13, 17), that it referred to the passover which was at least as old as the days of the judges (23:21f.); that is, that the book was a covenant document. Indeed it was probably the old covenant document of the Jerusalem Temple. The tenor of the narrative suggests that the document was recognized as genuine (2 Ki. 22:13; 23:21) and old. There is some evidence to suggest that the book was Deuteronomy, either the whole or part.[2] Lohfink proposes that Josiah's book was approximately Deuteronomy chapters 5 to 28 and points out that the equation of Deuteronomy with the Jerusalem covenant document has important implications. It is not likely to have grown out of the preaching of Levites in Northern Israel. It is more likely that the kings of Judah, especially David, made every effort to incorporate the old amphictyonic institutions

---

[1] N. Lohfink, 'Die Bundesurkunde des Königs Josias', *Biblica*, 44, 1963, pp. 261–288, 461–498.

[2] *Cf.* 23:3 with common Deuteronomic expressions 'cut a covenant', 'walk after', 'commandments, testimonies and statutes', 'all his heart and all his soul' and note Dt. 16:1 where the passover is enjoined.

into the Jerusalem royal cult. Thus David brought the Ark to Jerusalem, which became the religious centre. Lohfink argues that there was a line of legal continuity between the original covenant document going back as far as David in Jerusalem or even to Shiloh, and the Deuteronomy of Josiah's day. No doubt there had been revisions by authorized persons although the extent of this is not certain.

It might be argued in extension of Lohfink's view that the complete covenant form would require a historical introduction, a document clause and a recapitulation section[1] and hence would not be complete without such chapters as 1 to 3, 27 and 29 to 30, that is, the document found in Josiah's day comprised chapters 1 to 30. To what extent this represented an expansion of an original document we cannot determine.

d. A post-exilic date

Two representative modern writers who propose a post-exilic date for Deuteronomy are the German G. Hölscher[2] and the English R. H. Kennett.[3]

In 1922 Hölscher proposed that the impracticable demands of Deuteronomy such as the demand for a single sanctuary would have been mere idealism in pre-exilic times. He asked, for example, whether it could be seriously entertained that the entire population of the country should journey to Jerusalem for a whole week at festival time, leaving farm animals to fend for themselves. But this objection is not insurmountable, since something like this was done in New Testament times.

Hölscher quoted many examples from all areas of Deuteronomy to demonstrate how impracticable its laws were for the days of Josiah. He proposed, therefore, that Deuteronomy was not a programme for reform but the wishful thinking of unrealistic post-exilic dreamers. He sought to show that Deuteronomy was written by priests about 500 BC. He found support in the fact that there was little contact between Haggai and Zechariah 1–8 and Deuteronomy but many references to Deuteronomy in Malachi.[4] The language of Nehemiah 13:25–27 is also Deuteronomic. In fact, Deuteronomy was a private document for Levitical priests in Jerusalem, not

---

[1] See pp. 19f.

[2] 'Komposition und Ursprung des Deuteronomiums', *ZAW*, XL, 1922, pp. 161–255.

[3] R. H. Kennett, *Deuteronomy and the Decalogue* (1920).

[4] 1:2, 6, 8; 2:1, 2f., 4, 5, 8; 3:1, 3.

the programme for Josiah's reform but a product of it. Hölscher thus took a position of complete opposition to the views of Wellhausen by regarding Deuteronomy as fundamentally priestly rather than prophetic. It was idealistic in character, written in a day when the Judaean kingdom no longer existed and the people were subservient to a foreign power. It was written *c.* 500 BC and not in Josiah's day.

The English scholar R. H. Kennett had anticipated Hölscher's views two years earlier and had argued that Deuteronomy was compiled by priestly circles in Palestine during the sixth century BC, that is, during the exilic period. It reflected the interests of the Levites predominantly. One weakness of the theory is its failure to produce evidence for the presence of such influential priestly groups in Judah during the exilic period.

What then are we to say about the origin and date of Deuteronomy? There is clearly no agreement among the scholars. It is widely recognized that much of the book is ancient, stemming perhaps from the days of the judges when Israel's political structure was rather like that of an amphictyonic league. Some modern writers would hold the view that any investigation of the origin of Deuteronomy will lead ultimately to the figure of Moses himself.[1] Granted the historicity of Moses and of his significant part in the emergence of Israel as a nation, it seems altogether likely that he would have given some guidance to those recently escaped from Egypt about the organization of life in the new land. But even if the essence and spirit of Deuteronomy is Mosaic, the significant question arises as to how close we can draw to Moses himself in the detailed content. A great deal of the material in the book is compatible with a composition at almost any era of Israel's history, particularly in view of the fact that Israel guarded her ancient traditions carefully and sought after continuity in many areas of her life, social, legal, cultic. When Jeremiah spoke of the *ancient paths* (Je. 6:16), he had in mind the ways of the ancient covenant between Yahweh and Israel which were good ways that needed to be set before Israel in every age and which were applicable to every new situation.

The present writer finds it difficult to decide on the date at which Deuteronomy reached its final form and feels that there

---

[1] See above, p. 62, n. 1.

is something to be said for the view that, while Moses himself provided Israel with the heart of Deuteronomy, it became necessary in new situations to re-present the words of Moses and to show their relevance to the new day. One thinks of key points in Israel's history when this might have happened: in the days when the Kingdom was newly established under Saul or David or Solomon; or again in the critical period following the break-up of the Kingdom on Solomon's death; or again at a number of points during the critical centuries that followed.

In the present state of our knowledge some things are clear. The book is based firmly on the historical figure of Moses and in some way or other enshrines words which he spoke to Israel in Moab. On the other hand editorial processes have brought the book to its present form. What the exact form of the addresses of Moses may have been it is impossible to say. Nor is it possible to give a precise date to the final composition of the book. The viewpoint adopted in the present commentary is that a substantial portion of Deuteronomy comes from a period well before the seventh century BC. Indeed it may have assumed somewhat of its present form in the general period of the United Monarchy. This would give a date of the eleventh to tenth century BC, some two to three centuries after Moses.[1]

VIII. THE THEOLOGY OF DEUTERONOMY

Both the literary shape of Deuteronomy and its underlying central concept provide an important clue to the basic theology of the book. Yahweh, the God of Israel, appears in a strong covenantal setting. He is the great King, the Lord of the covenant. From this central concept Israel's finest theological ideas derived.[2] G. E. Mendenhall's study, *Law and Covenant in Israel and the Ancient Near East* (1955)[3] made clear that the

---

[1] *Cf.* G. J. Wenham, 'Deuteronomy and the Central Sanctuary', *TB*, 22, 1971, pp. 116–118. The view is here expressed that Deuteronomy would have been a suitable document to be used by Rehoboam when he came to Shechem to be made king after Solomon's death (1 Ki. 12:1). This would suggest a composition some time in the period of the united monarchy.

[2] Already in 1935 Ludwig Koehler in his *Old Testament Theology*, before the days of our understanding of the significance of the ancient Near Eastern treaties for biblical study, had declared that 'the one fundamental statement in the theology of the Old Testament is this: God is the Ruling Lord'. See ET (1957), p. 30.

[3] First published as two articles in *BA*, XVII, No. 2, May 1954, pp. 24–46, and No. 3, September 1954, pp. 45–76.

historical forms and language of the treaties were adapted to express Israel's view of God. The Mosaic covenant portrayed God as the great King who entered into a treaty (covenant) with Israel so that He became their God and they His people. Much of the covenant language of the Old Testament is either etymologically or semantically parallel to the language of the secular treaties. Yahweh is pictured as King, Lord, Judge, Warrior, while Israel is pictured as servant whose obligation is to 'hearken, obey' (*šāmaʿ*) and to 'serve' (*ʿābaḏ*).

Against this background we may now undertake a study of the central theological ideas of Deuteronomy.

a. *Yahweh the Lord of the covenant*

Secular treaties commenced with a preamble in which a reference would be made to 'So and so the *great king*'.[1] Various epithets were then used to describe the king: *powerful, favourite of the gods, valiant* and the like.

It is not possible to identify a detailed preamble as such in Deuteronomy. In structure, the first clear element of the covenant pattern is the historical introduction.[2] Nevertheless there are many epithets throughout the book which might well have been taken up into a preamble. There is no unequivocal reference to Yahweh as *King* (*meleḵ*).[3] The use of the term *King* for Yahweh is comparatively rare in the Old Testament. This may have been because of the ambiguity of the term, which was used by the petty kings of the small city-states in the land to which Israel came after the exodus. The royalty of Yahweh, the Lord of Israel, was the antithesis of their petty sovereignty, for Yahweh's sovereignty was cosmic in scope. *To Yahweh belong heaven and the heaven of heavens* (10:14), and He is *God of gods and Lord of lords* (10:17). As such He is unique. *There is no other besides him* (4:35). Israel's understanding of Yahweh is succinctly stated in the words *Yahweh our God, Yahweh is one* (or alone) (6:4).[4]

---

[1] *ANET*, pp. 202, 203.

[2] Meredith G. Kline, *Treaty of the Great King* (1963), pp. 7f., regards 1:1–5 as the preamble which introduces the covenant mediator. Perhaps the brief expression in 1:6, *Yahweh our God*, may be regarded as a preamble. But it is very brief indeed.

[3] The translation of 33:5 in RSV *Yahweh became king* is not necessary. See commentary.

[4] Or however this enigmatic four-word sentence is to be translated. See commentary.

As sovereign Lord over all, Yahweh demanded undivided allegiance from His people. He was a *devouring fire, a jealous God* (4:24). The adjective 'jealous', or 'zealous' (*qannâ'*) does not have the connotation of the English word but represents rather the active zealousness of Yahweh to maintain His own uniqueness and holiness. He will not share His sovereignty with any other deity. Idolatry or divided allegiance merits His judgment.[1]

It was as sovereign Lord that Yahweh made a covenant (*kārat bᵉrit*) with Israel (4:23, 31; 5:2, 3; 9:9; 29:1, 12). He would remember this covenant and keep it (7:9, 12). He displayed 'covenant faithfulness' or 'steadfast loyalty' (*hesed*, 5:10; 7:9, 12). He was *just* (*saddîq*) and *upright* (*yāšār*), a *God of faithfulness* (*ēl 'ᵉmûnâ*), *without iniquity* (32:4), *Father* (32:6) and *Rock* (*sûr*, 32:15, 18, 30, 31).

The range of sovereignty suggested by these epithets is vast. Israel's Lord was the Lord of the whole universe who had a sovereign claim not merely upon His people Israel but on the whole world.

b. *Yahweh the God of history*
An important feature of the ancient Near Eastern treaty was the historical prologue which reviewed the past relationships between the great king and the vassal and laid down patterns for future relations between the two countries.[2] It was usual to trace the history some little distance into the past where possible, and then to stress the kindness of the overlord towards his vassal. There was point in this. The vassal owed an obligation of perpetual gratitude toward the great king because of the kindness and favour which he and his forefathers had already received. The vassal was exchanging *future* obedience to specific commands for *past* benefits he had received without any real right to them.[3] This kind of thinking is evident in Israel too. Thus in the classic passage in Exodus 19:4–6 the record runs *You have seen what I did to the Egyptians, and how I bore you on eagles' wings and brought you to myself. Now therefore, if you will obey my voice and keep my covenant, you shall be my own possession*

[1] Compare the injunction of Muršiliš the great Hittite king to Duppi-Teššub of Amurru: *Do not turn your eyes to anyone else. Your fathers presented tribute to Egypt, you shall not do that. ANET*, p. 204, end of para. 8.

[2] See *ANET*, pp. 203f.

[3] See G. E. Mendenhall, *Law and Covenant in Israel and the Ancient Near East* (1955), p. 32.

among all peoples. . . . It was against a background of great redemptive, delivering acts that Yahweh could appeal to Israel to accept His suzerainty. The pattern is clear in Deuteronomy. Chapters 1 to 3 set out the saving activity of Yahweh from Sinai to the threshold of the promised land. Then comes the appeal in 4:1 *And now (weʿattâ) give heed to the statutes and the ordinances.* The saving acts of Yahweh when He delivered Israel from Egypt are not forgotten and are the background to this appeal (4:34; 5:6; 6:21–23; 7:8, 18, 19; 9:26; 26:8; 29:2, 3; 34:11, 12, *etc.*).

There is a well-recognized vocabulary used for the redemptive activity of Yahweh in the Old Testament. In reference to the exodus the verb 'act', 'do' (ʿāsâ) is often used (4:34; 7:18; 29:2; 34:12) but it is a general verb and lacks something of the thrust of other verbs such as *save (hôšîʿa)* and *redeem (pādâ)* which have a metaphorical use.

How did Yahweh act on behalf of His people? He *redeemed* them. Here Deuteronomy has several occurrences of the verb *pādâ*, the root of which in other Semitic languages is used to describe the act of liberating someone from the possession of another by the giving of a ransom.[1] The verb thus has strong metaphorical associations. It is used in 7:8; 9:26; 15:15 and 24:18 in reference to the redemption of Israel from Egypt and in 21:8 in a more general sense.

In other passages the verb *save (hôšîʿa)* occurs where the picture is of the bringing forth of those who were under restraint into a broad place. Thus Yahweh is described in 20:4 as saving His people when their enemies did battle with them after their escape from Egypt, while in 33:29 Israel is described as a people *saved by Yahweh*, the shield that guards them and their glorious sword. In 32:15 Yahweh is named the rock of their salvation (yešûâ).

In yet other passages the work of Yahweh is described as *bringing* Israel *out* of Egypt (hôṣîʾ, 1:27; 4:20, 37; 5:6, 15; 6:12, 21, 23; 7:8, 19; 8:14; 9:12, 26; 16:1) or *bringing* them *into* the promised land (4:38; 6:23; 8:7; 9:4, 28; 26:9; 30:5; 31:20). The saving work of Yahweh in bringing Israel out of Egypt is described in very vivid anthropomorphic metaphors. It was out of an iron furnace that Israel came (4:20) and it was by the agency of Yahweh's outstretched arm (4:34; 5:15; 7:19) and by testings and signs and wonders, and war and terrors

---

[1] As in Arabic, Akkadian and Ugaritic.

(4:34; 6:22; 7:19). Such language gave clear expression to the powerful character of Yahweh's redemptive acts.

Deuteronomy teaches that Yahweh's rescue of Israel from Egypt and her safe conduct during the wilderness wanderings was all with a view to fulfilment of His promise to the fathers. Yahweh the sovereign Lord of the universe was also the Lord of history and He would direct the course of history to His own ends. His promise to the fathers that their descendants would be many and that they would dwell in a land that He would give them is writ large in the patriarchal narratives (Gn. 12:1–7; 13:14–17; 15:5, 18–21, *etc.*). The point is made time and again in Deuteronomy that Yahweh *swore* (*nišbaʻ*) to give the land to the fathers (1:35; 8:1; 9:5; 10:11; 11:9, 21; 19:8; 26:3, 15; 28:11; 30:20; 31:7, 20, 21, 23; 34:4). Hence there is a strong emphasis on the fact that the land was a gift from Yahweh (1:20, 25; 2:29; 3:20; 4:40; 5:16, *etc.*).[1] Israel possessed no natural right to the land and even needed Yahweh's assistance to enter into possession of her inheritance. It is in this connection that the concept of the Holy War[2] has to be considered.

The suzerain of the ancient Near East went forth to war for two purposes – to protect his vassals from their foes, and to do battle against those who stood in the way of his sovereignty, whether these were erring vassals or neighbouring states who hindered the progress of his plans. Yahweh, as the Suzerain supreme, also undertook wars for both redemptive and judgmental ends. He was, indeed, *God the Warrior*. Since it was in the purposes of Yahweh to give Israel the land, the conquest of the land would be assured if it were under His direction and with His help. In herself Israel was *the fewest of all peoples* (7:7). But the conquest of Canaan would be by Yahweh's conquest. The point is made in other parts of the Old Testament.[3] The conquest of the promised land was Yahweh's gracious activity on behalf of those who had been oppressed and outcast. But it was also an act of judgment on the people of the land. Because of their corruption the divine government decreed the end of their rule. Deuteronomy 9:4–7 is especially important in this latter connection. Israel was the agent in God's over-all

---

[1] There are some twenty-five references to the fact in Deuteronomy.

[2] See G. von Rad, *Studies in Deuteronomy* (1953), pp. 45–59; G. E. Wright, *Deuteronomy* (*IB*, Vol. 2, 1953), pp. 327, 328.

[3] Am. 2:9; Pss. 78:53–55; 80:8–11; *cf.* Acts 13:16–19 in the New Testament.

purposes. As the Lord of history He was bringing judgment on the Canaanites. At the same time the overthrow of the Canaanites fulfilled the promises to the fathers (Gn. 12:1–3; 15:12–21; 17:1–8) and rounded out the work of redemption which began with deliverance from Pharaoh's oppression in Egypt.

It is against this background that such passages as Deuteronomy chapters 7 and 8; 9:1–6; 11:1–25; 31:3–8 should be read. It was none other than Yahweh who removed the powerful opposing nations from before Israel (7:1, 2; 9:3; 11:2–4; 31:3–6). Since the victory was assured, Israel was called upon to trust in Yahweh and not to be fearful in the presence of apparently superior foes, despite her apparent weakness. In the hour of victory all that would normally be regarded as booty, including the inhabitants of the land, was to be 'devoted' to Yahweh. Thus would every harmful thing be 'burned out' (RSV 'purged out') (17:7, 12; 19:13; 21:9, 21; 22:21, 22, 24; 24:7) and the land purified. Although the concept of the Holy War[1] may seem a strange one to the enlightened Christian conscience, it nevertheless has positive values. Its context is that of the universal divine Monarch whose concern is to maintain universal order. In such a context the picture of the divine Warrior finds its place. He works by mediate means through agents who act as is appropriate in the immediate situation in which they find themselves. At times, Israel is His agent. But Assyria, Babylon, Persia might serve His purpose also. Positively, the concepts of God the Warrior and the Holy War stress the fact that there is a power in the universe set against the forces of evil. In the warfare He pursues He will not be defeated. The end will be judgment on wicked men and redemption for those who acknowledge His sovereignty.[2]

There is another aspect of the activity of God in history which is concerned with the operation of the blessings and the curses. This is a facet of the broader truth that God exercises both redemption and judgment in history. The picture in Deuteronomy is based on the Near Eastern treaty pattern in which curses and blessings feature as the covenant sanctions. In general, the view expressed in Deuteronomy is that obedience to God and His covenant leads to 'blessing', while disobedience leads to 'cursing'. The primary requirement of

[1] See above, p. 26, for laws relating to the Holy War.
[2] A valuable discussion on the concept of God the Warrior occurs in G. Ernest Wright, *The Old Testament and Theology* (1965), pp. 121–150.

the covenant was complete obedience to the covenant obligations as expressed in the law. In the wake of obedience followed
'blessing', prosperity, security, continued possession of the
land, *etc*. Israel was bidden *to walk in his* (God's) *ways . . . that it
may go well with you* and *that the Lord may bless you* (4:40; 5:16;
6:3, 18; 12:28, *etc*.). But these 'blessings' were conditional upon
obedience. God's law was to be kept in order that there should
be no evil among the people. Sin among the people defiled the
land and as a result nature failed to yield her abundance among
the crops, the flocks and the herds (28:16–18, 38–42; *cf*.
Am. 4:6–9, *etc*.). Moreover the land, which was the gift of
Yahweh and upon which Israel had no claim, might be taken
away and Israel exiled (28:25, 47–52, 62–67).

This view, sometimes called the Deuteronomic view of
history, is basic in the books from Joshua to 2 Kings. Later
historians were able to prove from the whole range of Israel's
history from the conquest to the fall of Jerusalem in 586 BC
that obedience to the covenant resulted in national blessing
for Israel, while disobedience resulted in judgment.

The consequences of obedience and disobedience are set out
in challenging words in the stirring peroration at the end of the
second address of Moses in chapter 28 (*cf*. also 11:26–28;
30:15–20). The issue was one of life and death and it demanded
radical decision on Israel's part. *I have set before you this day life
and good, death and evil* (30:15). Or again, *I have set before you life
and death, blessing and curse; therefore choose life, that you and your
descendants may live, loving the Lord your God, obeying his voice, and
cleaving to him; for that means life to you and length of days, that you
may dwell in the land which the Lord swore to your fathers, to Abraham,
to Isaac, and to Jacob, to give them* (30:19, 20).

c. Israel the people of the covenant

Israel was the vassal of Yahweh the universal Suzerain. The
relationship between God and Israel was given this concrete
form early in Israel's life, at least as early as Moses. There was
a certain inscrutability about the reason for Yahweh's choice
of Israel to be His vassal and to act as His agent; she lacked any
special merit that would make such a choice inevitable (7:6–8).
The comparatively rare word *sᵉḡullâ*, meaning 'specially
prized', 'specially treasured', is used to describe Israel (7:6;
14:2; 26:18; *cf*. Ex. 19:5).[1] Another descriptive term used of

[1] The English word 'peculiar' in AV derives from Latin *peculiaris*, itself
derived from the noun *peculium*, a technical term denoting the private

Israel is *holy* (*qādôš*), which denotes something set apart, in this case for Yahweh (7:6). For Israel all power was centred in the great Suzerain and all other powers in the world held authority from Him, or else rebelled against His rule. The injunction *You shall have no other gods before me* can be understood to declare that the world was a political monocracy. Israel was set apart in total allegiance to this great Sovereign. This meant she was under obligation to keep the covenant stipulations.

There were first of all important general principles to be observed. She was required to *walk in his* (*Yahweh's*) *ways* (8:6; 10:12; 11:22, *etc.*). Out of gratitude to Yahweh for all His benefits it was her duty to *fear* Him (4:10; 6:2, 13, 24; 8:6, *etc.*), *i.e.* to reverence Him; to *love* Him (6:5; 10:12; 11:1, 13, 22; 13:3, *etc.*); to *hold fast* (AV *cleave*) to Him (10:20; 11:22; 13:4, *etc.*); and to *serve* Him (6:13; 11:13, *etc.*). Her allegiance was to be complete and unshared (6:14, 15; 7:4; 8:19, 20; 11:16, 17, 28; 30:17, 18).

But such whole-hearted devotion to Yahweh would issue in a life which was a practical expression of Israel's holiness. It was not that by living such a life she was to become holy. She was holy already in view of the fact that Yahweh had set her apart for Himself. But by such a life she was to give expression to her holiness. And this had meaning in every part of her life: social, political, religious. This demand was both a national and an individual concern. It was this wide applicability of holiness to daily living that gave the idea of holiness a strong ethical colouring.

Israel's daily life, then, was to be lived according to the specific stipulations of the covenant. Even a cursory glance at the wide range of laws set out in chapters 12–26 will show how comprehensive were the demands of holiness for they touched such widely different areas as worship, food, criminal law, hygiene, the duties of officials and judges, king, priest and prophets, the treatment of captives in war, inheritance, theft, false witnesses, welfare of animals and birds, *etc.* Strong prohibitions were made against many of the practices of the Canaanites in religion and in daily life. Participation in such practices merited the most severe penalties (6:14; 7:1ff., 25f.; 8:19f.; 13:1ff., *etc.*).

---

property which a child or slave was allowed to possess. A similar term occurs in ancient non-biblical literature. Thus at Alalakh the king was described as the *sikiltu* or 'treasured possession' of the god. There are other examples.

In a sense all these laws were addressed to the whole nation. Yet finally, obedience to any one law was individual and personal. For this reason the many exhortations are directed to the hearts and wills of the individual hearers. Obedience to Yahweh's commands has a peculiarly personal application in the last resort. The core of the divine command was the decalogue (chapter 5), comprising in the first four commandments a man's obligations to God and in the remaining six his obligations to his fellows. It was with God Himself that Israel as a nation and as a collection of responsible individuals had to do. Above all the laws was the *Shema* of 6:4, 5 commanding Israel to love Yahweh with the whole being (6:6–9). All other laws found their basis in this inward motivation. Love of one's fellows, love of resident aliens, love of animals, concern for the underprivileged in society were all the outward expression of one's love of God. Where every individual loved God and kept His covenant stipulations, a society might emerge which enjoyed the totality of well-being, *i.e. peace (šālôm).*

d. *The worship of the God of the covenant*

Clearly, if Israel's whole life was to be lived in the awareness of Yahweh's character and activity, an important feature of her life would need to be the worship of Yahweh her God. This was all the more important in the light of Yahweh's election of Israel above all the nations of the earth, and in view of His mighty acts on her behalf.

How then was Yahweh to be worshipped? Certainly not at a Canaanite shrine, nor according to Canaanite rites. He was to be worshipped at the place where He would choose to place His name. But worship offered there was only part of the worship of a whole life. The personal and spiritual character of worship is strongly emphasized in Deuteronomy. Attitude of heart is more important than external acts. The inward dispositions of love and gratitude are basic.

The demand that Israel should *love* Yahweh is writ large in the book. On the formal level it has been observed that even in some ancient Near Eastern vassal treaties the vassal was commanded to love his royal superior.[1] But in Israel's case

---

[1] W. L. Moran, 'The ancient Near Eastern background of the Love of God in Deuteronomy', *CBQ*, 25, 1963, pp. 77–87; *cf.* N. Lohfink, 'Hate and love in Osee 9:15', *CBQ*, 25, 1963, p. 417; D. J. McCarthy, 'Notes on the love of God in Deuteronomy and the Father–Son relationship between Yahweh and Israel', *CBQ*, 27, 1965, pp. 144–147, and *Treaty and Covenant* (1963), pp. 118f.

something more was required than a love that was commanded. Rather did Yahweh seek for a deep and warm personal response. This attitude was to characterize the whole of the people's life.

The second basic disposition of gratitude is likewise stressed throughout Deuteronomy. Israel was called upon to *remember* Yahweh and all His acts of deliverance (5:15; 7:18; 8:2; 9:7; 15:15; 16:3, 12, *etc.*). The deliverance from Egypt was to be recalled at every observance of the feast of unleavened bread (16:2, 3). The motivating significance of that deliverance is stated in connection with several laws (15:15; 16:12; 24:18, 22). The verb *zāḵar*, 'remember', occurs no less than sixteen times in Deuteronomy with particular reference to the deliverance from Egypt (7:18; 8:2, 14; 9:7; 16:12; 24:9, *etc.*). This active recall, not merely by those who had participated in the exodus, but by all the future members of Israel, was designed to enable the continuing Israel to participate in the great acts of redemption wrought by Yahweh in the course of their own history. Such a recollection and identification in memory and by faith would stimulate both gratitude and love in the Israelite of every age.[1]

Israel's cult played an important part in bringing these facts before the people. Her feasts and festivals, her psalms and no doubt her prayers too, made frequent reference to the theme of redemption from Egypt. The exodus events were woven into the warp and woof of the whole of her religious life. The prophets also made frequent mention of the exodus. It was through the knowledge of her past that Israel would come to understand her election and would continually be made aware of her privileged status and hence of her continuing debt of gratitude to God. As she brought her sacrifices and gifts to the sanctuary she was reminded that these were offered *that you may learn to fear (reverence) Yahweh your God always* (14:23). It was not so much the gifts and sacrifices that mattered as the attitude of the offerer. The cult was an aid to worship but was not the essence of worship, for true worship lies hidden in the recesses of the human heart and flows out to God as a result of the worshipper's love, gratitude and reverence.

---

[1] The Christian worshipper will recall at once the Lord's Supper, which provides an opportunity to 'remember' the Lord's death. Such an act of remembrance leads to an identification with Christ and a response of faith, love and gratitude.

ANALYSIS

A. FIRST ADDRESS OF MOSES: WHAT GOD HAS DONE (1:1 – 4:43)

I. GENERAL INTRODUCTION: MOSES SPEAKS TO ALL ISRAEL (1:1–5)

II. HISTORICAL RETROSPECT: GOD'S MIGHTY ACTS BETWEEN HOREB AND BETH-PEOR (1:6 – 3:29)
   a. The first attempt at conquest: from Horeb to Hormah (1:6–46)
   b. The journey through Transjordan (2:1–25)
   c. The conquest of Transjordan (2:26 – 3:11)
   d. The distribution of the conquered land (3:12–17)
   e. Preparations for the invasion of Western Palestine (3:18–29)

III. THE PRACTICAL CONSEQUENCES FOR ISRAEL OF GOD'S DELIVERING ACTS (4:1–40)
   a. The appeal to hearken and obey (4:1–8)
   b. God's appearance at Mount Horeb (4:9–14)
   c. The dangers of idolatry (4:15–31)
   d. Israel the chosen people (4:32–40)

IV. CITIES OF REFUGE SET APART (4:41–43)

B. SECOND ADDRESS OF MOSES: THE LAW OF GOD (4:44 – 28:68)

I. INTRODUCTION TO THE SECOND ADDRESS OF MOSES (4:44–49)

II. THE NATURE OF THE COVENANT FAITH: THE FUNDAMENTAL DEMAND FOR TOTAL ALLEGIANCE TO YAHWEH (5:1 – 11:32)
   a. The heart of the covenant faith (5:1 – 6:3)
   b. Yahweh is our God, Yahweh is One (6:4–9)
   c. The importance of remembering (6:10–25)
   d. The conquest of Canaan: an aspect of the Holy War (7:1–26)

COMMENTARY

A. First address of Moses: what God has done (1:1 – 4:43)

I. GENERAL INTRODUCTION: MOSES SPEAKS TO ALL ISRAEL (1:1–5)

These verses are typical of editorial paragraphs which occur at the beginning of several sections in Deuteronomy and also at the beginning of other Old Testament books, *e.g.* Amos 1:1; Ezekiel 1:1–3, *etc.*

1. The first verse of the book explains the nature of the whole book, which consists of *the words that Moses spoke to all Israel*. The expression *all Israel* is very common (indeed, one might say, characteristic) in Deuteronomy, although the alternative expression *children of Israel*, which occurs elsewhere in the Pentateuch, does occur in 4:44 (*cf.* 1:3; 32:51; 34:8 where the phrase 'people of Israel' occurs). The words were intended to apply to the whole nation. There are indications elsewhere in the book that 'all Israel' included the forefathers, the present Israel and even those who were yet to be (*cf.* 5:3), *i.e.* God's word through Moses had permanent significance for Israel. In a later verse Moses' words are defined as his undertaking to *explain the law* (5). The book is thus not set forth specifically as the utterance of God but rather as an exposition of what God had already spoken. Only in a few passages in the book is God represented as speaking in the first person (7:4; 11:13, 14; 17:3; 29:6). Nevertheless, Moses as the covenant mediator might be thought of as bringing God's word to the people.

The scene of the exposition was *beyond the Jordan in the wilderness*. The specific place is difficult to identify. The phrase 'beyond Jordan' might be translated 'in the region of Jordan'.[1] The term *Arabah* is used of the area of the great Jordan rift valley both north and south of the Dead Sea. It would seem likely that here the area to the north is meant (see verse 7).

2. If Mount Horeb be identified with one of the mountains

---

[1] B. Gemser, '*Be'ēber hajjordēn*: In Jordan's Borderland', *VT*, II.4, 1953, pp. 349–355. Also R. K. Harrison, *Introduction to the Old Testament* (1970), pp. 637f.

in the Sinai peninsula, the estimate of an *eleven days' journey* on foot from Mount Horeb (Sinai) to Kadesh-barnea by way of Mount Seir (Edom) is approximately correct. However, the significance of this verse in its present position is not easy to determine. Perhaps a contrast was intended. Whereas it was a mere eleven days from Horeb to Kadesh-barnea, a whole generation elapsed before Israel entered the land of promise. The exact location of Mount Sinai is the subject of controversy. Some scholars have identified it with Jebel Ḥalal, some twenty-two miles west of Kadesh-barnea. Most scholars, however, locate it in the southern part of the Sinai peninsula, because both geographical indications and the biblical narrative make this area the most probable.[1] The name *Horeb* is normal for Sinai in Deuteronomy except in 33:2. Elsewhere Horeb is used only in Exodus 3:1; 17:6; 33:6; 1 Kings 19:8; Psalm 106:19; Malachi 4:4. Horeb (lit. 'desolation', *cf.* Je. 44:2) is an apt name, since the area round Sinai is barren and uninviting.

3. Rebellion had delayed the realization of the promise till the *fortieth year*, *i.e.* from the exodus. The entry was now to be from the east instead of from the south. Just prior to the crossing of the Jordan from the plains of Moab, Moses brought God's commandment to the people. The only date in the whole book is given here, *the fortieth year, the eleventh month, the first day*.

4. A historical orientation is added. The address of Moses was given after the defeat of the Amorite kings (Nu. 21:21–35). The Amorites were ancient dwellers in this area, being attested as early as *c.* 1900 BC in some Egyptian documents known as the Execration Texts.[2]

5. The meaning of *beyond Jordan* is here defined as *in the land of Moab*. The expression is not necessarily an indication that the writer of the narrative lived to the west of the Jordan, since the phrase is too general (1:1). If such a decision is made it depends on other evidence. That this identification suits verse 1 gains support from the fact that the term 'wilderness' or 'Arabah' is used also for areas north of the Dead Sea in the Jordan rift (1:7; 11:30; 1 Sa. 23:24, *etc.*). The expository

---

[1] See Y. Aharoni, *The Land of the Bible* (1968), pp. 181, 182, 188.

[2] Egyptian rulers sought to control their enemies by writing their names and accompanying curses on bowls or small clay figurines which were then smashed in some temple ritual so as to release the curses. Two such groups of texts from *c.* 1900 BC refer to Amorites in the Galilee area. See *ANET*, pp. 328f.

character of Deuteronomy, which will be pointed out many times in the pages of this commentary, is foreshadowed by the verb *explain* (Heb. *bē'ēr*, 'expound', 'make clear').[1] It is characteristic of Deuteronomy that a law is first stated and then explained with accompanying hortatory material, thus pressing home the obligation which is laid upon the hearer.

II. HISTORICAL RETROSPECT: GOD'S MIGHTY ACTS BETWEEN HOREB AND BETH-PEOR (1:6 – 3:29)

The acts of God on behalf of Israel are set forth as the ground on which He made His appeal to Israel to enter into covenant with Him, much in the manner of the historical prologue in the Near Eastern treaty. For Israel, God became known, not through mythological, mystical or philosophical argument, but through His word and through specific historical acts. Both of these were later expounded by His servants the prophets and by other inspired interpreters. The same is true of the word Jesus spoke about His death and resurrection. His word and the subsequent fulfilment of that word lay at the basis of the subsequent theological interpretation of the acts of God in Christ.

The present historical survey consists of a series of short scenes each centred around a discourse in which Yahweh and Israel participate. Moses as narrator draws Israel's attention to incidents during her long journey when she failed to co-operate with Yahweh in the execution of the Holy War.

Many parallels in expression between this passage and passages in Exodus and Numbers have been noted.[2]

a. The first attempt at conquest: from Horeb to Hormah (1:6-46)

The first act in the drama is presented in the form of several brief discourses which are arranged in a complicated literary

---

[1] The verb is rare. Basically it denotes 'dig' or 'hew', but it is used of writing on stone (27:8) or tablets (Hab. 2:2). Its use here in Dt. 1:5 is metaphorical.

[2] S. R. Driver, *Deuteronomy* (*ICC*, 1902), pp. iii–xix.

form.[1] In describing events at Horeb, Yahweh speaks (6–8), then Moses (9–13), then the people (14), then Moses (15–17). The next dialogue takes place at Kadesh-barnea. Moses speaks first (20–21), then the people (22), the spies (25), the people (27–28), Moses (29–31), and finally Yahweh (35–36). The section closes with a discourse in which Yahweh speaks first (37), then the people (41), and finally Yahweh (42).[2] The whole is enclosed within the broader framework of Moses' first speech, which was evidently arranged with considerable care since the discourses within it contain a number of parallel expressions and key words which are repeated: *mountain, land, go up, conquer, etc.* There may have been a didactic purpose in this repetition. Israel was unwilling to obey God at His first command but had to be exhorted to *go up, conquer, etc.*, more than once. The repetition of the words thus stressed the magnitude of Israel's rebellion. *Cf.* a similar technique in Jonah.

i. At Horeb (1:6–8). The covenant name for Israel's God, Yahweh, is here introduced in the expression *the Lord our God*, lit. Yahweh our God. The name occurs frequently in Deuteronomy and will be used from time to time in the pages that follow. He is described as *our God*, emphasizing the close, personal relationship existing between God and His covenant people. The great covenant correlate 'your God . . . my people' occurs many times in Deuteronomy. It was Yahweh, the divine Leader of the conquering nation, who now gave the command to His hosts to move forward to the specific objective before them, *the hill country of the Amorites* (7), *i.e.* the mountainous region which was later to be occupied by the two kingdoms, Judah and Israel, and *to all their neighbours*. The Amorites of the mountain area (Jos. 10:5) were remnants of the great Amorite movement that swept into Western Asia in the closing years of the third millennium BC. But the population in Western Palestine was a mixed one, as we learn from names on a variety of baked clay tablets such as the Amarna documents[3] (*cf.* Nu. 13:29).

---

[1] The form is a *chiasmus*. A number of ideas are referred to in a particular order up to a central point, after which the order is reversed, *e.g.* A, B, C, D, E, D[1], C[1], B[1], A[1].

[2] The three patterns are: At Horeb: Yahweh, Moses, people, Moses; at Kadesh-barnea: Moses, people, spies, people, Moses, Yahweh; and finally: Yahweh, people, Yahweh.

[3] Found at Tell el-Amarna in Egypt in 1887 dating to the early four-

The *Arabah* seems to refer to areas north of the Dead Sea (*cf.* 4:49; 11:30; Jos. 8:14; 12:1, 3; 1 Sa. 23:24). The *lowland* (*šᵉp̄ēlâ*) comprised the foothills along the Mediterranean area (Jos. 15:33, 34). The *Negeb* was the southern part of the land between the hills and the desert, the area in which Beer-sheba and Kadesh-barnea lay. *The seacoast, the land of the Canaanites* extended well north, perhaps as far as Tyre. Indeed, the ideal limits of the land stretched out as far as the Euphrates. Probably only in David's time was the ideal even approximately realized (2 Sa. 8:3; *cf.* Gn. 15:18). A more practical picture is given in Numbers 34:7–11.

This then was the land promised *to Abraham, to Isaac, and to Jacob* (Gn. 12:1–7; 13:14–17; 15:18, *etc.*), but now to be possessed. The twin promises of a seed and a land were basic in Israel's thinking and feature prominently in Deuteronomy (1:35; 6:10, 18, 23; 7:13; 8:1; 9:5; 10:11, *etc.*). It was something to which Yahweh had *sworn*.

ii. Organization of the people (1:9–18). The outworking of God's promise to Abraham resulted in the multiplication of Abraham's seed till they were as *the stars of heaven for multitude*. This latte ᐟ expression, like so many in the Old Testament, is a vivid figure of speech. It means, simply, a great number. The whole passage deals with organizational arrangements which became necessary in order to govern such a people. Some commentators regard verses 9–18 as a parenthesis or digression provoked by the mention of God's promise to Abraham. Its fulfilment in the great number of Israelites leads on to a discussion of the appointment of judges. The main story is resumed at verse 19.

9. *At that time.* The reference is to the appointment of judicial assistants to Moses (Ex. 18:24). The expression used here occurs in Numbers 11:14, where it refers to Moses' complaint to the seventy elders.

12, 13. Moses envisaged increasing trouble and *strife* (*rîb̠*). This latter term normally connotes a lawsuit of some kind. Clearly, as the population grew, there would need to be some delegation of responsibility such as had been suggested by Jethro, Moses' father-in-law (Ex. 18:13–27; *cf.* Nu. 11:14).

teenth century BC. It is possible that the term Amorite may include other pre-Israelite inhabitants; *cf.* the term Canaanite in other parts of the Pentateuch, *e.g.* Gn. 12:6; 24:3, 37; 50:11; Ex. 13:11; Nu. 13:29.

Now, wise men, men of discernment and experience, were taken from all tribes as leaders.

14, 15. The plan was accepted by the people and Moses appointed men to exercise authority of various kinds, military, judicial, *etc.* The terms *thousands, hundreds, fifties* denote military groupings, not numerical statistics. They occur several times in this sense in Deuteronomy. The *officers* (*šôṭēr*)[1] were subordinate officials whose exact task is not defined, but they were used in the administration of justice, in the maintenance of civil order, and in military discipline. Perhaps their task was to enforce the instructions of their superiors in various fields.

16, 17. Important principles of justice are now declared. Judges were to judge impartially. Justice was to be extended to the resident alien (*gēr*), who was a free man although not admitted to all the privileges of Israel. In general, Israel was forbidden to enter into alliances with pagans. Presumably these *aliens* accepted Israel's faith and way of life and were thus spared the strictures of 7:1–5. Elsewhere in Deuteronomy, as well as in other parts of the Old Testament, Israel is commanded to guard carefully the rights of resident aliens (10:19; 24:17; 27:19; *cf.* Lv. 23:22; Je. 7:6; Ezk. 22:7, *etc.*).

The reason for such impartial justice was that Israel was a theocracy where justice was the concern of God as Sovereign. Difficult cases were to be referred to Moses, God's faithful mediator (*cf.* 1 Ki. 3:16–28). It was common practice in the ancient Near East to refer difficult cases to the monarch. In Israel God was the Monarch, but acted through His representative.

iii. From Horeb to Kadesh-barnea (1:19–46). The section provides a summary of events narrated in Numbers 13 and 14. Everything had been done on the part of God and Moses to bring Israel speedily and safely to the land of promise. But Israel was compelled to remain outside the land for forty years because of her rebellion and her resistance to the commandments of God. Israel's discontent with God's guidance was evident from the very beginning (*cf.* Nu. 11; 12). Thereafter their rebellion was displayed time and again.

19. The journey through the wilderness was evidently a gruelling experience, for it is described both here and elsewhere in vivid language (8:15; 32:10). It was a journey of

---

[1] The term may be related to Akk. *šaṭāru*, 'to write'. The officials were chosen to ease Moses' burden of writing down decisions.

over 100 miles across the forbidding desert of et-Tih. But the Lord had spoken and the people must go forward. Their immediate destination was the oasis of Ain-Kadesh from which they would enter the land.

20, 21. Moses gave the order to take possession of the land (*cf.* 1:7, 8). Since the Lord had set the land before them in accordance with His promise to the fathers, Israel should not fear. It is one of the motifs of Deuteronomy that Yahweh, who is the God of history, would bring His word to pass.

22–25. The sending of the spies. The decision to carry out a reconnaissance would have been quite normal practice (*cf.* Jos. 2:1; 7:2), but the sequel showed either weak faith or lack of faith. At the time this was not apparent and Moses approved the plan to send out spies. One representative of each tribe was sent (Nu. 13:1–16). Only the beautiful *Valley of Eshcol* (lit. 'bunch of grapes') with its magnificent grapes is noted here.[1] But this in itself was encouragement enough for the man of faith. The spies reported, *It is a good land which Yahweh our God gives us.* God had not deceived the people. The evidence lay before their eyes. They may well trust Him.

26–33. Israel's lack of faith. There were two other aspects of the report of the spies, the imposing stature of the Anakim who lived in the land and the walled cities scattered here and there. These in themselves need not have been an obstacle in the Holy War[2] for, with Yahweh leading the hosts of Israel, victory was assured. But to refuse to go forward with their Ruler was rebellion against His command (26), and this found an outlet in murmuring in which wrong motives were attributed to Yahweh (27). He intended to lead them into a glorious victory, but they supposed that He intended their

---

[1] Comparison with Nu. 13:22, 23 has generally been taken to suggest that the Valley of Eshcol was near Hebron. The passage may not require this. See F. M. Abel, *Géographie de la Palestine* (3rd ed., 1967), pp. 401f.

[2] The expression Holy War used here and elsewhere in this commentary (*e.g.* 9:1–6; 20:1–20; 21:10–14, *etc.*) refers to those wars in early Israel in which Israel, acting under the direction of Yahweh, the Lord of history, took possession of Canaan in fulfilment of God's purposes and because of the wickedness of the nations that occupied Canaan. Not every war was part of the Holy War, however. See exegesis on 9:1–6; 20:1–20; 21:10–14. The idea of the Holy War has been popularized in recent years by G. von Rad in *Studies in Deuteronomy* (1953), pp. 45–59. See further in the Introduction, p. 72.

defeat and murmured in their tents (27), which was a sign of demobilization rather than of attack. What a reversal of the procedures of the Holy War!

28. The contemplation of the tall Anakim and their walled cities caused the heart of the people to melt.[1] It might have been the reverse. Fear of Israel might have caused the hearts of their enemies to melt (Jos. 2:11; 5:1; *cf.* Dt. 2:25). But the end result for Israel now was to be defeat rather than victory, and a vitiated interpretation of God's mighty acts of deliverance at the exodus as evidence of His hatred for Israel (27) rather than of His love (4:37; 7:8, *etc.*).

29-31. In the face of such cowardice Moses encouraged the people in terms they understood. *Do not be . . . afraid* (3:2, 22; 7:18; 20:1; Jos. 8:1, *etc.*), *Yahweh . . . will himself fight for you* (3:22; 20:4; Jos. 10:14, 42; 11:5f.). The evidence of the exodus and the wilderness was enough to prove his point. In fact, in the days of the exodus the people had believed God (Ex. 14:31).

32, 33. Despite Moses' appeal, and despite the evidence of past years, the people *did not believe*. The most subtle danger for Israel was the possibility that they might doubt the gracious guidance of God and His willingness to fulfil His promises. It was to become the besetting sin of Israel that they doubted the active and providential sovereignty of Yahweh in every crisis.

34-40. God's judgment on the people. In the face of such rebellion Yahweh, Israel's God and their Leader in the Holy War, visited the rebels in judgment.

35, 36. The judgment is expressed in the form of an oath[2] declaring that not one of the present generation of rebels would survive to see the land of promise. Only Caleb and Joshua, who were not party to the acts of unbelief, were to be exempted.

37. Moses himself bore the same punishment as the people, perhaps because he did not insist on the attack. *Cf.* comment on 3:26, 27 and footnote.

38. *To stand before* someone in Hebrew idiom is to attend upon a superior (1 Ki. 10:8). Joshua is referred to in several places as Moses' 'minister' or 'servant' (Ex. 24:13; 33:11; Nu.

---

[1] See exegesis on 2:10-12.

[2] In Hebrew verse 35 with *'im* meaning 'if' and we infer that some such expression as 'May such and such happen *if*' was in mind. This is the normal way to introduce an oath expressing denial.

11:28; Jos. 1:1). The disqualification of Moses necessitated the appointment of Joshua to lead the people into the land.

39. The promise to the fathers would be fulfilled in the next generation, and the children, for whose safety the rebels had expressed fear (Nu. 14:3), would in fact inherit the promise, for they had been innocent in the matter of the rebellion, having *no knowledge of good or evil*.

40. At God's command Moses and the people turned back to the wilderness towards the Red Sea and the area of Edom (*cf.* 2:1).

41-46. From Horeb to Kadesh-barnea. The present incident was an act of presumption on Israel's part and demonstrated the fact that not every war in which Israel was engaged was a valid part of the Holy War (*cf.* p. 87, footnote 2 and Introduction, p. 72).

41, 42. It is not always possible or permissible to recoup an opportunity lost by unbelief. It was, indeed, a further act of presumption for Israel to undertake a belated attack on Canaan in the face of Yahweh's prohibition. It is clearly the responsibility of God's people to obey without delay and to 'redeem the time' while the opportunity is open (*cf.* Eph. 5:15-17; Col. 4:5). God would not be in the midst of such people and defeat was inevitable.

43, 44. Bent on disobedience, the people went up to the hill-country against the Amorites only to be driven back and defeated. The presumptuous attack, far from turning aside God's verdict against them, only aggravated their case. Details of the defeat are not given, but the Amorites chased them and they fled like men before a swarm of bees and were defeated near Hormah in the land of Seir. The reference is probably to a place near the western borders of the Edomite territory which extended to the west of the Arabah. The name *Hormah* is related to the Hebrew word *ḥērem*, meaning 'ban', 'destruction'. There was a touch of irony in the fact that a defeated Israel fled to a place whose name suggested annihilation.

45, 46. Tears avail little in the face of wanton disobedience. The victory which once lay within their grasp was denied to them and Israel then spent long years in the region of Kadesh (lit. 'many days according to the days that you remained there'). It is easy to connect this with 2:1: 'So, after you had remained in Kadesh all that length of time, we marched back into the wilderness toward the Red Sea (lit. the Sea of Reeds).'

b. The journey through Transjordan (2:1-25)

The journey through Transjordan was the approach march to the victories which placed the area to the east of the Jordan river in Israel's hands. This chapter recounts a number of acts of obedience, but no impulsive acts of disobedience. There is no dialogue here as in chapter 1 but rather the alternation of divine commands with the obedience of Israel (3 and 8; 13a and 13b; *cf.* 3:2 and 3). The divine commands were not uniformly instructions to go forward or to fight. Israel was to conquer some areas and by-pass others. In this way the precise extent of the land to be occupied was defined by God and selfish human ambitions were restrained.

The account of the journey through Transjordan contains several formulae which occur more than once, *Rise up* (13, 24), *do not contend* (5, 19), *we turned* (8b; 3:1). While the narrative resembles that in Numbers 20 and 21 in some respects, it differs in others, as we shall see. It probably represents a different selection of the available facts.

1-3. Israel turns back toward the Red Sea. For some time Israel travelled around the hill-country of Seir. The region must have been on the western outskirts of Edomite territory.

2, 3. Uncertainty about the exact location of the area in question makes it difficult to trace the movement of Israel at this point. The instruction to turn north poses a question. Was Israel at the time somewhere near the southern end of Edom, so that in turning north she passed around the eastern borders of Edom to travel north in the direction of Moab? Or was she on the western edge of Edom, so that in turning north she moved up the Arabah and skirted the plateau of Edom on the west until she reached the Wadi Zered and then turned east up the wadi until she finally turned north again to skirt Moab? (*Cf.* verse 8.)

4-8. Israel skirts Edom. Israel did not pass through Edom proper, *i.e.* through the high plateau region which lay to the east of the Arabah. In Numbers 20:14ff. we learn of Edom's refusal to allow Israel to pass through her land. Edom's fear of a band of wandering nomads is understandable. According to Judges 11:17 Edom's refusal was given while Israel was still at Kadesh. It was not, in any case, Yahweh's intention to allow Israel to possess Edom at that time (*cf.* Dt. 23:7, 8). Both traditions are preserved in Deuteronomy even if they are somewhat telescoped.

6. *Cf.* Numbers 20:14–21. Israel was prepared to pay for food and water.

7. One reason why Yahweh forbad Israel to seize Edom was that He had made abundant provision for His people throughout their journeys so that they lacked nothing. Contentment with God's provision should have prevented them from turning aside to covet areas of which they had no need. Here is a salutary lesson for any age.

8. The exact meaning of *we went on, away from our brethren the sons of Esau who lived in Seir, away from the Arabah road from Elath and Ezion-geber. And we turned and went in the direction of Moab* is not clear. Alternative suggestions have already been made (see comments on verses 2, 3). In either case the passage of Israel along roads which lay beyond her immediate boundaries was no particular problem. A passage along the King's Highway which traversed the plateau would, however, have been a cause for concern.

9. Israel and Moab. Israel was likewise forbidden to harass Moab. There were ancient kinship links between Israel and Moab. Lot, the nephew of Abraham, was one of the Moabite ancestors. The location of *Ar*, which lay on the borders of Moab, is not known with certainty. Two sites have been suggested, Khirbet el-Medeiyineh in the Arnon Valley (*cf.* Nu. 21:15, 28; 22:36), or El-Miṣna' further south in central Moab.

The affirmation that it was Yahweh who gave to Edom and Moab their territories is a declaration of monotheism. To Yahweh alone belonged the prerogative of distributing to the peoples of the earth their homelands (5, 9; *cf.* 32:8f.; Am. 1; 2; 9:7).

10–12. An archaeological note. Reference is here made to the earlier inhabitants of Moab, the *Emim*, said to be *a people great and many, and tall as the Anakim*. The origin of such a note is impossible to discover. The name Anak was an ancient one. It is known on the Egyptian execration texts[1] of the twentieth and nineteenth centuries BC (*cf.* 1:28; Nu. 13:22, 33;

---

[1] See comment on 1:4.

Jos. 11:21, 22; 15:14). An alternative name was *Rephaim* (Gn.
14:5; Jos. 12:4; 13:12, *etc.*). In Genesis 14:5 the Rephaim are
mentioned as one of the pre-Israelite groups in Palestine who
were defeated by the invader Chedorlaomer. They are also
listed among the inhabitants of the promised land (Gn. 15:20).
In Transjordan they were known under different names. In
Moab they were called Emim. In Ammon they were known
as Zamzummim (20, 21). They are described as *tall as the
Anakim* or *as giants*. Perhaps the nouns *rāpâ* and *rāpā'* in 2
Samuel 21:16, 18, 20, 22 and 1 Chronicles 20:6, 8 are variant
forms of the same word, that is, *giants*. Outside the Bible, however, the name is unknown in an ethnic sense.

The noun *rᵉpā'îm* occurs in Psalm 88:10 (11, Heb.); Proverbs 2:18; 9:18; 21:16; Job 26:5; Isaiah 14:9; 26:14, 19 in the
sense of the shades of the dead in Sheol. It is possible that the
Israelites might have applied the term to the early inhabitants
of the land as persons long since dead.[1]

12. The nature of the *Horites* is not clear. The biblical
people of this name are confined to the area of Edom, a region
for which we have no independent evidence that the Hurrians
of West Asiatic history ever lived there. The names of the
Hurrians in Genesis 36 are all Semitic and attempts to equate
the Horites and the Hurrians have recently been questioned.[2]
The issue is, perhaps, not yet clear. It is certain that the
Hurrians were widespread in Western Asia early in the second
millennium BC. The historical note here tells us that the
Edomites dispossessed the original Horites in Mount Seir. An
interesting comparison is made with the activities of Israel in
the phrase *as Israel did to the land of their possession, which the
Lord gave to them*. Just as the Edomites dispossessed the Horites,
so Israel dispossessed other peoples to occupy the land Yahweh
had given them. It was Yahweh's prerogative to dispose of
lands as He would. Israel's land was not merely the land to the
west of Jordan; areas to the east of Jordan were occupied by
the two and a half tribes (3:12; Nu. 32). The term *Israel* in this
expression may refer to all or part of Israel.

13. The story which began at verse 9 and was interrupted
by the archaeological note in 10–12 is now resumed. Israel was
commanded to cross the Wadi Zered. The phrase *go over* could

---

[1] See article 'Rephaim' in *NBD*, pp. 1084f.
[2] R. de Vaux, 'Les Hurrites de l'histoire et les Horites de la Bible', *RB*,
October 1967, pp. 481–503.

be translated 'pass along', which is a possible rendering of the Hebrew verb.

14, 15. Another interpolation recalling the judgment that fell on the first generation (1:35, 40). Thirty-eight years had elapsed since Israel's departure from Kadesh.

16. The death of the defeatists who trembled at the report of the spies and would not enter the land now made possible the resumption of the journey and the fulfilment of God's promise.

17–19. Israel and Ammon. Near Ar (9) Israel crossed the area which bordered Moab, probably somewhere in the upper reaches of the Wadi Arnon. This would bring them near to the borders of Ammon. Again Israel was forbidden to harass a people to whom Yahweh had given its own land. There were ancient kinship links between Israel and Ammon (Gn. 19:36–38).

20–23. Another archaeological note. The area of Ammon, like Moab (10–12), had formerly been occupied by a tall people like the Anakim, known to the Ammonites as the Zamzummim. Once again we learn that Yahweh, the Lord of nations, dispossessed this people and gave the land to Ammon. The Israelites called these people the Rephaim (*cf.* 11), because there was something mysterious about them. Incidentally, says the writer, a similar dispossession had occurred on the coastal region at Gaza (Jos. 13:3), where the Caphtorim overcame the Avvim. In the latter case, the disposition of the land was not attributed to Yahweh as in the case of Moab, Edom and Ammon. The exact location of *Caphtor* is not known but it was possibly Crete.[1] Elsewhere in the Old Testament (Je. 47:4; Am. 9:7) it seems to refer to the sea coasts and islands of the Aegean Sea. The Philistines were part of the Sea Peoples who invaded the eastern Mediterranean coastlands in the thirteenth century BC under the pressure of the Dorian invasions.

24, 25. After several interpolations the narrative proceeds to the conquest of Transjordan. There was a new divine command directed against the Amorite king Sihon, *Begin to take possession, and contend with him in battle*. The command was supported by

[1] See article 'Caphtor' in *NBD*, p. 199.

a promise, *This day I will begin to put the dread and fear of you upon the peoples.* The Amorites had possessed these lands since the early years of the second millennium. Yahweh would now spread panic among His enemies, a common motif of the Holy War.[1] Interesting theological questions arise here. It may be asked whether this early injunction to Israel can be taken as an authority for the modern Christian to go to war in a righteous cause. No doubt the principle remains that God's people are to be engaged in the fight to overthrow evil and to advance the cause of Christ, but there would be wide disagreement among Christians in regard to whether a particular war were righteous or not. Nor would all feel that guidance in the modern situation can come from such a passage as this. Great principles vary in their application and what was a valid application in a former age may not be valid today, although the principle remains. In the days of the conquest of Canaan God commanded His people to contend with an enemy in battle (24). But in the Old Testament economy He commanded a variety of things which He did not command in the fuller light of the New Testament (*cf.* Mt. 5:43-48).

c. **The conquest of Transjordan** (2:26 – 3:11)

A brief account of the main victories which led to the possession of the whole of Transjordan is now given (*cf.* Nu. 21:21-35). Two Amorite kingdoms occupied these areas, that of Sihon from the Wadi Arnon to the Wadi Jabbok, and that of Og in Northern Gilead and Bashan. Sihon's kingdom was separated from Ammon by the upper reaches of the Wadi Jabbok which turns south after its eastward extension and then runs approximately north-south.

The question is raised as to whether Transjordan was in fact part of the promised land. If it was not, we can understand why Israel was instructed here to make peace with Sihon (20:10-18), whereas in areas to the west of the Jordan her enemies had to be exterminated (7:1-5). But compare verses 34, 35 of the present chapter. The problem is complex. Certainly, in later centuries Israel fought many wars to retain these lands in Transjordan which she evidently regarded as hers. Perhaps at the outset Israel conquered territory which was no real part of the land of promise defined in Genesis 12 and 15:18-20. Once conquered, however, areas in Transjordan were regarded as

[1] G. von Rad, *Studies in Deuteronomy* (1953), pp. 47f.

Israelite territory and were allotted to the two and a half tribes.[1]

26-37. The defeat of Sihon. 26. The campaign began with a diplomatic representation. Messengers *with words of peace* sought transit through the lands of Sihon. The expression *words of peace* may indicate that Moses was offering to make a treaty with Sihon. Ancient Near Eastern treaties are sometimes referred to as 'the words of the agreement', and the phrase 'to establish peace' generally meant 'to make a treaty' (Jos. 9:15; Jdg. 4:17; 1 Sa. 7:14; 2 Sa. 3:12f.; 1 Ki. 5:12). At the time the Israelites were at *Kedemoth*, which may be represented today by ez-Za'ferān some ten miles north of the Arnon.[2]

27, 28. The terms of the proposed agreement are now given. They are reminiscent of terms proposed to Edom (Nu. 20:14-21; *cf.* Nu. 21:21-23).

29. While both Edom and Moab opposed the transit of Israel through the heart of their territories along the King's Highway, they made no attempt to prevent their passage around the outskirts of these lands or through areas under their 'protection' (2:2-8).

30, 31. From his capital at *Heshbon*, which still exists today as an impressive mound eight miles north of Madeba and which has recently become the subject of archaeological investigation, Sihon sent his refusal to enter into a treaty. The reason is given that *the Lord your God hardened his spirit and made his heart obstinate* (*cf.* Ex. 7:3; 9:12; 10:1, 20, 27; 11:10; 14:4, 8, 17). The other side of this picture is that Sihon hardened his own heart (*cf.* Ex. 8:15, 32; 9:34). If we compare Sihon's case with that of Pharaoh in Exodus there are many parallels. In either case the hardening of the man's heart was quite as much by his own act as by the decree of God, for both Pharaoh and Sihon were unaffected by the demands of God which came through God's servants. Neither would bend his will to the will of God and each refusal produced a further hardening of the heart. Thus the demands of God, once rejected, became a hardening influence on Sihon's heart, so that he was unable to respond favourably to Israel's request.[3] The purposes of

[1] See Y. Kaufmann, *The Biblical Account of the Conquest of Palestine* (1953), pp. 46-56.
[2] F. M. Abel, *Géographie de la Palestine* (1938), p. 69.
[3] Note the useful discussion on the hardening of the heart in C. F. Keil and F. Delitzsch, *Commentary on the Pentateuch* (1864), pp. 453ff. This commentary has recently been re-published by Wm. B. Eerdmans.

Yahweh for Israel could not be frustrated and already He had *begun to give Sihon and his land over to* Israel.

32. It was when Sihon forsook the protection of his line of fortified posts and advanced out into open country that Israel defeated him in battle. Modern archaeological investigation[1] has shown that these ancient kingdoms were probably ringed by many small fortified posts. But now, driven on by a strange stubbornness, Sihon threw away his one chance of survival. The identification of *Jahaz* is uncertain, but it may have been either the modern Jalul or Khirbet et-Teim near Madeba. Both suit the geographical and topographical requirements fairly well. The town is mentioned in the ninth century in the Moabite Stone left by King Mesha of Moab.[2]

33. Israel's first victory, which marked the beginning of the dispossession of the Amorites, is ascribed to Yahweh who *gave him over to us; and we defeated him and his sons and all his people*. Yahweh was Israel's leader in the Holy War. (See Introduction, p. 72.)

34, 35. Victory was complete. The details of these verses are in accord with the laws for the Holy War (20:10–18). One aspect of the Holy War was the total destruction of all the booty. This was the law of *ḥērem*. Towns, people, flocks, *etc.* were dedicated to Yahweh for destruction, and were thus removed from the use of men (*cf.* Jos. 6:21; 7:20, 21). In some cases the destruction was only partial and certain items were reserved for the use of the people. Once Israel crossed the Jordan the law was rigidly applied, at least in the early days of the conquest (7:24–26; 13:16, 17; Jos. 6:17–19).

The practice of the law of *ḥērem* raises theological issues about the character of God. As so often, we must distinguish between principle and practice. The principle here is that Yahweh was to be Israel's only sovereign. All that opposed His purposes or His sovereignty over Israel was to be removed. Further, His holiness was offended by the wickedness of the nations of Canaan. We ought not to dismiss this practice lightly as nothing more than fanaticism. It affirms the Lordship of Yahweh over Israel and over His purposes for her in history, but also His judgment on wicked nations. In the Holy

---

[1] Nelson Glueck, *AASOR*, Vols. 18, 19, pp. 204ff.; *The Other Side of the Jordan* (1940), pp. 139f. The excavation of Heshbon has already been commenced. See Siegfried H. Horn, 'The 1968 Heshbon Expedition', *BA*, XXXII, No. 2, May 1968, pp. 26–46.

[2] See *ANET*, p. 320. The site is referred to at line 20.

War Yahweh accomplished purposes both of redemption and of judgment. The law of *ḥērem* gave expression to both these. The Christian will still accept the principles of divine redemption and divine judgment in history and also the total sovereignty of God over his whole life. However, the application of the principle in the Christian age is very different.[1]

36. The area conquered on this occasion stretched from the mountains of Gilead to the north bank of the Arnon river. The site of *Aroer* is known today and excavations were undertaken here in 1965.[2] It was one of the border fortresses of Moab. The description of its setting *on the edge of the valley of the Arnon* is both graphic and accurate. The gorge of the Arnon falls away 2,000 feet below this little fortress. A significant observation is that in all this area *there was not a city too high for us*. The reference is to walled fortresses which formed the heart of most cities in Palestine for many centuries. Again, the victory is ascribed to Yahweh.

37. In obedience to Yahweh's command Israel did not encroach on the land of the Ammonites, avoiding even the banks of the Wadi Jabbok. This was an example of obedience to the commands of Yahweh that Israel would have done well to follow in later generations.

3:1–11. The defeat of Og. 1–3. These verses are almost exactly a repetition of Numbers 21:33–35, the only difference being that the pronoun here is 'we' in contrast with 'they' in Numbers. *Bashan* was the area to the north and north-east of Galilee, an area rich in forests and renowned for its pastures and its high hills, inhabited today by the Druze people.

4, 5. The presence of walled cities argues for urban occupation. This area, in common with the whole of Transjordan, was devastated by the Amorites early in the second millennium BC. The story of the recovery of this area is complex. In the course of the following centuries the Amorites probably settled and urban life was gradually restored. Evidently, Amorites such as Sihon and Og were descendants of the earlier invaders.[3] The location of *Argob* can only be conjectured, but the account here suggests that it was a region where there were

[1] See G. E. Wright, *Deuteronomy* (*IB*, Vol. 2, 1953), pp. 327f.
[2] E. Olávarri, 'Sondages à 'Arô'er sur l'Arnon', *RB*, January 1965, pp. 77–94, and 'Fouilles à 'Arô'er sur l'Arnon. Les niveaux du Bronze Intermédiaire', *RB*, April 1969, pp. 229–259.
[3] See K. M. Kenyon, *Amorites and Canaanites* (1966), p. 64.

many towns, some of which were fortified and others open and undefended (*cf.* 1 Ki. 4:13).

6, 7. As in the case of Sihon and his capital Heshbon, Israel applied the law of *ḥērem* (*cf.* 2:34, 35) to Og and his towns. In this case the animals and booty from the towns were spared.

8–10. These verses provide a summarizing statement of the extent of the Israelite conquest. Alternative names for Mount Hermon are given. *Sirion* was the Sidonian or Canaanite name. In the Old Testament this name is used poetically in Psalm 29:6. The Amorite name *Senir* occurs in 1 Chronicles 5:23; Canticles 4:8; Ezekiel 27:5. The first two references make it clear that Hermon and Senir were distinct in one sense. Probably Hermon referred to the high snow-capped peak and Senir to the Anti-Lebanon range to the north. In the total campaign cities were conquered on *the tableland* (*mîšōr*), *i.e.* the Moabite plateau which became the territory of Reuben (Jos. 13:9, 16, 17, 21; Je. 48:8, 21), and in *all Gilead and all Bashan*.

11. An interesting detail is here preserved about Og. He was the last of the Rephaim (*cf.* 2:10–12), so that, strictly speaking, he was a descendant of the original inhabitants of the land and not an Amorite (*cf.* 2:11, 20). On his death he was buried in a massive sarcophagus (lit. *bedstead*, 'resting place') made of basalt, called *iron* here because of its colour. Similar large sarcophagi have been found in Phoenicia, *e.g.* those of Ahiram and Eshmunzar. According to the record here the sarcophagus could be seen in Rabbah Ammon (the modern Amman) at the time Deuteronomy was committed to writing. Its dimensions are given as *nine cubits* by *four cubits*, *i.e.* 13 or 14 feet by 6 feet measured by the *common cubit* (lit. 'cubit of a man').

d. The distribution of the conquered land (3:12–17)

Moses was allowed to witness the start of the conquest and he supervised the first distribution of the land (*cf.* Nu. 32; Jos. 13). The tribes of Reuben and Gad were allotted the kingdom of Sihon between the Wadis Arnon and Jabbok, while the half-tribe of Manasseh, in which the chief clan was Machir, received the lands to the north of Jabbok. There may have been a certain idealization of the picture, and no doubt much land needed to be possessed after the initial conquest.[1]

[1] For the question of whether Transjordan was part of the promised land see comment on 2:26 – 3:11.

12. For the expression *Aroer, which is on the edge of the valley of the Arnon*, see comment on 2:36. That the Gadites were still a recognizable group in the ninth century is clear from the Moabite stone, an important record left by Mesha king of Moab (2 Ki. 3:4).[1] Gilead comprised two areas, southern Gilead from Heshbon to the Wadi Jabbok, and northern Gilead between the Wadis Jabbok and Yarmuk.

13–15. Northern Gilead and all Bashan, *i.e.* the territory of Og, or otherwise *the region of Argob*, was given to the half-tribe of Manasseh. It was, in fact, *Jair*, one of the sub-tribes of Manasseh, which occupied this area while *Machir*, another of the sub-tribes, received Gilead, dispossessing the Amorites there (Nu. 32:39).

16. Reuben and Gad occupied the more southerly areas, bounded on the south by the bottom of the Arnon gorge and on the east by the north–south section of the Jabbok, some 25 or 30 miles east of the Jordan.

17. This passage seems to be a definition of the whole western boundary of Transjordan, which comprised the Arabah from the Salt Sea (Dead Sea) to the town of *Chinnereth*, on the western shore of the Sea of Galilee, which gave its name to the sea. For the term *Arabah* see comments on 1:1, 5, 7. The Dead Sea is described as lying *under the slopes of Pisgah* (*cf.* 4:49; 34:1; Nu. 21:20; 23:14), the point from which Moses viewed the regions west of Jordan (3:27). An alternative interpretation of verse 17 is that it denotes the area occupied by Gad (*cf.* 12, 16, 17; Jos. 13:24–28). There is some difficulty in correlating the various passages in Numbers, Deuteronomy and Joshua in the matter of tribal boundaries, but this may be due to our failure to understand the import of the relevant texts.

e. Preparations for the invasion of Western Palestine (3:18–29)

The men of the two and a half tribes were required to assist their brethren in the conquest of lands to the west of the Jordan before settling down. God had given them their possession, but there was to be no selfish enjoyment of it until the whole nation had rest. In all respects the nation had to act as a group, in community, under the leadership of Yahweh, an important aspect of biblical thinking.

---

[1] See *ANET*, pp. 320, 321. The Gadites are mentioned in line 11.

18–20. All the men of valour who crossed the Jordan with their brethren left their wives and families, flocks and herds behind them (Nu. 32). If it be asked whether harm might befall their families and their possessions in their absence, the answer lies partly in the fact that certain groups of men were left behind, those under twenty years of age, and presumably those over an upper age limit. There may have been other limitations too (20:5–8). On the other hand the Amorites had been so recently defeated that they were not likely to prove a trouble for some time. The main thrust of these verses is, however, a religious one, in which the solidarity of the people is taught. We have no means of telling how completely the command of Moses was carried out. It was a fine concept in theory.

21, 22. On an earlier occasion *Joshua* had given good leadership in battle (Ex. 17:9–13). He was now reminded of Yahweh's deliverance in Transjordan and was promised the divine aid on the other side of the Jordan. Not fear but faith was to characterize the venture, since Yahweh, their Leader in the Holy War, would fight for His people.

23–29. The prayer of Moses. In a moving dialogue Moses addresses Yahweh as *O Lord God*, 'My Lord Yahweh' (*cf.* Je. 1:6) and pleads with Him to be allowed to enter the land. Moses takes his place with Samuel as one of the two great intercessors of the Old Testament (*cf.* Je. 15:1).

23–25. The verb *besought* is a strong one, meaning 'entreat', 'implore favour', 'make supplication'. There is deep pathos here. Moses had just begun to see the greatness and the power of Yahweh bringing to pass His promises to His people. No god in heaven or on earth could perform such deeds as His. With a deep longing in his heart Moses sought permission to cross over the Jordan and witness the end of the great pilgrimage which had begun under his leadership (Ex. 3:10). It was not to be. Like Jeremiah and others Moses was asked to accept the outworking of God's purposes in faith.

26, 27. The expression in rsv, *on your account* ($l^e ma'an^e kem$), calls for some comment. Some commentators have taken this to mean that in some sense Moses died outside the promised land as a substitute for the people, *i.e.* he suffered vicariously for them.[1] While it may be true that Moses suffered in his own

---

[1] G. von Rad, *Deuteronomy* (1966), p. 45; G. E. Wright, *Deuteronomy* (*IB*, Vol. 2, 1953), pp. 349f.

heart because of Israel's rebellion, it is also true that he himself
had sinned against Yahweh (32:51; Nu. 20:12). No doubt he
was provoked by Israel, but he was responsible for those
actions for which he was judged by Yahweh and as leader he
suffered for his own sins. In fact, the rebels died in the wilderness and bore their own sins, so Moses did *not* die 'instead of
them'. The preposition *lᵉmaᶜan* is variously translated 'because
of', 'for the sake of', 'on account of' when used as a preposition.
It is difficult to argue that it is unambiguously used in the
sense of 'instead of'. It is certainly used frequently to mean
'because of'. Hence in the present passage the expression is
best understood as meaning that Moses was judged because
what Israel did led him also into sin. How great is the responsibility of leaders in every age to act in integrity and according
to God's law despite what others do, even when their actions
are provocative. God's reply to his plea was *Let it suffice you;
speak no more to me of this matter.* Even so, Moses would have the
consolation of seeing the land from the summit of Pisgah.

Through the humble prayer of Moses and the firm reply of
Yahweh we discern a deep fellowship between God and a man
such as is rarely seen in all the Bible except perhaps between
Jeremiah and God. Jesus, of course, showed this supremely.
It is a unity of purpose which leads to the utterance of such
words as 'If thou art willing, remove this cup from me;
nevertheless not my will, but thine, be done' (Lk. 22:42). It is
only out of the experience of deep fellowship with God that
one may speak so.

In fact, Moses' death is not recorded until chapter 34, so
that the whole book of Deuteronomy is framed between the
announcement of Moses' impending death and the announcement of his actual death. The book is thus, in a sense, the
spiritual testament of Moses, Israel's great Lawgiver.

28. The impending death of Moses became the occasion for
the appointment of Joshua as his successor. Israel would conquer in the Name of Yahweh, but Joshua would lead them,
strong in the confidence that Yahweh, who had begun a good
work, would finish it (21, 28; *cf.* 1:38; 31:7f., 14, 23; Nu.
27:18–23).

29. The reference to *Beth-peor* identifies the scene of these
final acts of Moses (*cf.* 4:46). It was a site near Mount Pisgah,
not identifiable today with certainty, but it seems to have lain
in one of the ravines leading down to the Jordan plain (Nu.
22:1).

III. THE PRACTICAL CONSEQUENCES FOR ISRAEL OF GOD'S DELIVERING ACTS (4:1-40)

The first address of Moses reaches its climax in this chapter. The parallel between the literary structure of this chapter and that of the Near Eastern treaty is noteworthy. The author of the treaty is named (1, 2, 5, 10), reference is made to the preceding historical acts, the treaty stipulations are mentioned, the appeal is made for Israel to obey, the treaty sanctions, blessing and cursing, are referred to, witnesses are mentioned (26), and the obligation to transmit the knowledge of the treaty to the next generation is stated (10). While these elements of the Near Eastern treaty are not set out in a rigid legal form, but are woven into a speech without regard for strict formality, they can be clearly discerned.

a. The appeal to hearken and obey (4:1-8)

The introductory word *And now* (*we'attâ*) refers back to the previous recitation. It is preparatory to the appeal to obey, as though one might say 'And now, in the light of God's acts of deliverance, you should obey His commandments' (*cf.* Ex. 19:5; Dt. 10:12; Jos. 24:14, *etc.*).

1. Moses instructed the people in the statutes and the commandments of God and urged them to give heed to them and do them. Obedience would result in blessing which meant life and the possession of the land. Life in this context probably refers simply to physical life, in contrast to death and destruction which would follow on disobedience. The principle here stated has become known as the Deuteronomic principle. It is stated many times in Deuteronomy, but it is also found elsewhere in the Old Testament, either directly or by inference.

2. In keeping with the Near Eastern treaties and law codes the covenant was not to be altered in any way. (*Cf.* Mt. 23:16-26; Mk. 7:9-13.)

3, 4. A vivid illustration of the fact that disobedience to God's law brings destruction and death is now given. At *Baal-peor* (Beth-peor, 3:29) Israel became involved in the idolatry of the Baal of Peor (Nu. 25:1-9). When certain Israelite men went with Moabite women to their homes, they joined in idolatrous rites and worshipped the god Baal. The judgment that followed was understood to be the consequence of that idolatrous worship. Those who remained faithful in the face of that temptation were spared the plague and were alive at the time of Moses' address.

5, 6. The significance of this event was that Israel was thereby taught that the only way to survive in the new land was by being faithful to Yahweh's covenant and obeying the statutes and ordinances of Yahweh which Moses had given them. The way of wisdom was the way of the covenant. Indeed, national existence was at stake, for Yahweh, who brought the nation into being and gave it a land to live in, would destroy it if it rejected His complete Lordship.

An interesting corollary is added. When the nations round about heard that Yahweh had committed His laws to His people, they would recognize in Israel special qualities of wisdom and understanding. Therein lay Israel's unique claim to recognition among the nations.

7, 8. Moses made two deductions: first, the fact that God had given His law to Israel pointed to an intimacy of relationship between Him and Israel that existed in no other religion; secondly, the law of Yahweh, which surpassed all other laws in righteousness, should be the pride of Israel (*cf.* Pss. 119; 147:19, *etc.*). The superiority of Israel's law could be demonstrated both on the ground of comparison with the other law codes of the ancient world, and also on the ground that any law which came from Yahweh rested on the righteousness of God Himself, of whom the law was but a reflection.

b. God's appearance at Mount Horeb (4:9-14)

A second event from the past is recalled. The reference to statutes and ordinances (8) recalled the experience of God's people at Mount Horeb (Sinai) recorded in Exodus 19:16-19; 20:18, 19. Two central features of that experience are here underlined: first, God made known His *words* to them; secondly, Israel learnt that, although God was present at Sinai and spoke from the midst of the clouds, He did not reveal Himself in physical form. Israel was thereby instructed that no physical representation of God was necessary for her worship. In this she differed radically from her idolatrous neighbours (Ex. 20:3-6). It was a fact that Israel was not to forget.

9. The two injunctions *take heed* and *keep your soul diligently* are prefaced by a strong particle *only* (*raq*), which normally has a restrictive significance. The phrase *take heed*, or 'take heed to thyself', occurs in many contexts in Deuteronomy. The verb form is basically reflexive in meaning,[1] so that the injunction is directed to Israel in a personal sense. In several passages, as here, Israel is told to take heed not to forget what God has done for her (*cf.* 6:12; 8:11). Elsewhere she is warned to take heed to avoid pagan practices (12:30), not to offer burnt offerings at unauthorized places (12:13), not to begrudge the Levite or one's brother what is his due (12:19; 15:9), *etc.* Such breaches of the covenant were an offence to the Lord and would be attended by His judgment. The great events of Horeb were to be guarded carefully lest they be forgotten. Moreover, the faithful transmission of the story to the children was obligatory for Israel (*cf.* 6:20; Ex. 13:8, 14). The appeal to Israel 'to remember and not to forget' God's saving acts is made again and again in Deuteronomy, for they were the foundation to Israel's claim to be God's people and the basis on which God challenged Israel to enter into His covenant. The same principle applies in the New Testament, where the acts of God in Christ are absolutely fundamental for the church and lie at the basis of God's appeal to men to enter into a new relationship with Himself. They too are to be taught to the children of believers.

10. The *words* referred to were the *ten words, i.e.* the ten commandments (4:13; 5:22). At Horeb, more was involved than the mere hearing of words. The saving acts of God made known in the exodus and the subsequent declaration of His covenant stipulations were intended to evoke a response of obedience in Israel. The only adequate response for Israel was to *fear* God, *i.e.* to reverence Him, by acknowledging His sovereignty. Reverence would express itself in worship and in obedience. There was a close connection between worship and life. Conversely the way of irreverence was the way of death (30:15–20). The verb *fear* and the corresponding noun have a rich connotation in Deuteronomy and throughout the Old Testament. Both verb and noun can mean slavish fear and are used sometimes to describe those who have sinned (Gn. 3:10; Pr. 10:24; *cf.* Acts 24:25; Heb. 10:27, 31; Rev. 21:8). But very often the reference is to holy fear, or reverence, which results from the believer's apprehension of the living God. The 'fear of the Lord' is one of the dominating thoughts of the Old Testament. It is to be recognized as the proper response of a man to God. It is God-given and enables a man to reverence God's person, to obey His commandments and to hate evil

[1] The Niphal.

(Je. 32:40; Heb. 5:7). It is the beginning of wisdom (Ps. 111:10), the secret of uprightness (Pr. 8:13), the whole duty of man (Ec. 12:13). It is given as one of the characteristics of the Messiah (Is. 11:2, 3). God's people in every age were urged to cultivate the fear of the Lord and to walk in it (Ps. 34:11; Je. 2:19; Acts 9:31; 10:2; Eph. 5:21; Phil. 2:12). Gentile adherents of the synagogue were called 'God-fearers' (Acts 10:2; 13:16, 26). In Deuteronomy in particular the verb occurs at 4:10; 5:29; 6:2, 13; 8:6; 10:12, 20; 14:23; 17:19; 28:58; 31:12, 13, *etc.*[1]

11. Human words are quite inadequate to describe the glory and the awful majesty of God. The best we can do is to make use of symbolic expressions. The present passage may be translated alternatively, *The mountain was ablaze with flames to the very skies, dark with densest clouds* (JPSA).

12. When Yahweh revealed Himself the people *heard the sound of words, but saw no form.* Idolatry was thus rejected for all time. This was a central feature of Israel's faith in every age. It was, of course, in the Word incarnate that God spoke His final word (Jn. 1:1, 14; Heb. 1:1, 2).

13, 14. At Horeb, too, God offered His *covenant* to the people. There is a partial identification here of the covenant and the ten words. The covenant is, however, wider than the covenant stipulations. Nevertheless, the acceptance of the covenant involved Israel in obedience to the covenant stipulations. Part of the evidence that Israel had accepted the covenant was that she lived by Yahweh's commandments. In a later day James was to say, 'Show me your faith apart from your works, and I by my works will show you my faith' (Jas. 2:18).

The writing down of covenant stipulations on a covenant document was normal in secular treaties and, in so far as Moses saw in the covenant at Sinai a parallel to the secular treaty, he would record the covenant stipulations on a document or documents such as *tables of stone*. It was Moses' task to instruct the people in these covenant stipulations so that they might have a pattern for life in the new land. Undue emphasis on laws, however, could lead to an externalizing of the covenant as though all God asked was obedience to laws. He demanded this, to be sure, but the covenant was essentially a relationship. Laws need to be written inwardly on the heart, lest the gospel

[1] See article 'Fear' in *NBD*, pp. 419f.; J.-J. von Allmen, *Vocabulary of the Bible* (1958), pp. 113–119; Alan Richardson, *A Theological Word-book of the Bible* (1950), p. 81.

be lost in law (*cf.* Je. 31:31–34). The book of Deuteronomy as a whole does guard against this danger (*cf.* 6:4–9).

It has been proposed recently[1] that the parallel between the Sinai covenant and the Near Eastern treaty is preserved also in this detail of the *two tables of stone*. When a secular treaty was entered into, duplicates of the treaty document were made, one being retained by the vassal and one by the suzerain. One copy was lodged in the temple of one of the suzerain's deities and one in the temple of one of the vassal's deities. Because Yahweh was at once Israel's covenant Suzerain and the Guarantor of Israel's oath, only one sanctuary was necessary for the depositing of both treaty duplicates. An alternative view to that of M. G. Kline is that two tables were used in order to accommodate all the material that was to be recorded. Whatever the explanation, the two tables were deposited in the ark (Ex.25:16, 21; 40:20; Dt. 10:2).

c. The dangers of idolatry (4:15–31)

Since God did not reveal Himself in physical form, Israel was not to represent Him in physical form. To disobey God's commandment in this matter was to be in danger of divine judgment. It is of interest that this passage is a detailed commentary on the second commandment.[2]

16–19. Some of the possible objects that men might use in idolatrous worship are now given. Examples of most, if not all, of these could be found in the religion of the Canaanites, the Egyptians, the Hittites, *etc.* Astral deities, too, were recognized in many areas long before Moses' day, and certainly many centuries before the Assyrians from whom, according to certain scholars, they found their way into Israel. The Hittites regularly included astral deities among lists of deities who were invoked in their treaty documents to act as guarantors of the treaty.[3]

On the question of God's allotment of the peoples of the world to various areas, see comment on 32:8f. Presumably in the areas where they were distributed they worshipped various deities.

20. Israel's peculiar position is now defined. God had taken

---

[1] Meredith G. Kline, *Treaty of the Great King* (1963), pp. 13–26.
[2] W. Zimmerli, 'Das zweite Gebot', *A. Bertholet Festschrift* (1950).
[3] See, *e.g.*, *ANET*, pp. 205f., in a treaty of Šuppiluliumaš dating to the early fourteenth century BC.

her from the iron furnace of Egypt to be His very own inheritance. The expression *his own possession* occurs in other passages also (7:6; 14:2; 26:18; Ex. 19:5, *etc.*). The recognition of their high status in God's sight should have had profound consequences for their behaviour.

21, 22. The judgment that rested on Moses was a warning to Israel of the consequences of any compromise of their total allegiance to Yahweh. *Cf.* 1:37; 3:26.

23, 24. The possibility that Israel might have to bear her own judgment was a grim one. Yahweh was *a devouring fire, a jealous God* (*cf.* 5:9; 6:15; Ex. 34:14). The term *jealous* (*qannā'*) does not connote the same as the English word, but rather an active zealousness for righteousness which arose from Yahweh's holiness. Because of this Yahweh would not countenance Israel's allegiance to any other God. Thus idolatry in any form was forbidden.

25-28. There was a danger that prolonged enjoyment of the blessings of the land might result in forgetfulness of the demands of the covenant, so that after many years Israel might turn to idolatry and vex Yahweh. If that happened the curses of the covenant, here defined by national death (26), separation from the land (26) and scattering among the nations (27), would come into operation. The maledictions here are akin to those in chapter 28, although it is the breach of the second commandment that is in question rather than of the whole law. But that would have been symptomatic of the inward rejection of Yahweh's sovereignty. *Heaven and earth* were invited to witness Yahweh's declaration of these judgments (30:19; 31:28; *cf.* Mi. 6:1, 2). Should such judgments take place so that Israel went into exile, she would serve other gods in a strange land and substitute for the living God, who could act on her behalf, lifeless and insentient creations of men. In fact, on more than one occasion during Israel's history some of her people went into exile, but notably following the fall of Samaria (2 Ki. 17:6) and the fall of Jerusalem (2 Ki. 24:14f.; 25:10ff.). God's warning thus came to fulfilment.

29-31. Even in the predicament of exile God may be sought and found. One feature of Yahweh's covenant with Israel in contrast with the secular treaties was that a rebel might *return* ('repent') to Yahweh and be forgiven and thus have the prospect of beginning a new life of obedience. In the secular realm rebellion was seldom treated with mercy, even if there was a show of repentance. But then the nature of Yahweh was quite different from that of secular kings. He was a merciful God who was ever mindful of His covenant. After Israel's folly and judgment God would grant repentance, so that beyond the operation of the curses lay the possibility of restoration. The phrase *in the latter days* need not be interpreted eschatologically, but merely in the sense of 'in the future'. So Yahweh is a consuming God to the rebel (24), but a merciful God to the repentant.

There is no need to interpret these verses, as some commentators have, as a post-exilic addition to the text of Deuteronomy. The statement is perfectly general and ought to be understood against the widespread practice of taking captives in war. Canaanite captives are depicted on Egyptian monuments before Moses' day, for example. The possibility of such an eventuality would not have escaped the attention of Moses. Indeed, verses 29 to 31 provide an apt commentary on the latter part of the second commandment (5:8–10).

d. Israel the chosen people (4:32–40)

On what grounds may Israel hope for restoration? There were two: the mercy of God (31) and the fact that Israel was a favoured people. Both the verses 31 and 32 begin with the particle *for (kî)*, and both provide an answer to the question. In the light of these facts Israel should remain obedient and enjoy the blessings God intended for her.

32, 33. Moses asked the people whether any other nation beside Israel, since the creation of the world, had been given such clear and direct evidence of the existence of its God and survived. Direct contact with deity was fraught with grave danger. Yet, wonder of wonders, the gap between God's holiness and Israel's rebellion and sin was bridged. This was ever a cause for reverent wonder in Israel (Gn. 32:30; Ex. 3:6; 19:21; 20:19; 33:20; Jdg. 6:22, 23; 13:22). It is one of the most remarkable phenomena of history that the people of Israel have remained as an identifiable group, even though they have been scattered among the nations for well over two thousand years.

34. Again, Yahweh did what no other gods could do. He delivered His people from the hands of a mighty earthly ruler by confronting him with various testings and by displaying before him signs and wonders, performing mighty acts of deliverance before his very eyes. For Israel the proof of God's existence and of His grace came from what He had done for His people just as much as from any statement of the fact made by a prophet. The redemptive and saving acts of Yahweh were fundamental in Israel's faith.

35. The phrases *Yahweh is God* and *there is no other besides him* give expression to the simple fact that in Israel Yahweh alone was to be Sovereign (*cf.* verse 39). There was no other power in the universe which could determine the destinies of men on earth. If such a view is not a fully-developed monotheism, it is certainly a practical monotheism. But there is no reason to doubt that such a simple pragmatic view was very ancient in Israel.[1]

36–39. The two features of Yahweh's love for, and election of, Israel are here stressed. They are reiterated many times in Deuteronomy. The ability of Yahweh to instruct or discipline Israel (36), to love her fathers, to choose their descendants and to deliver them from Egypt (37), and to drive out the peoples of Canaan in order to give the land to Israel for an inheritance (38), leads to the conclusion that He is God in heaven and earth. No other has such powers.

40. Hence Israel ought to recognize Yahweh's sovereignty and obey His covenant stipulations. The result of such a response would be the enjoyment of God's blessing on the present Israel and on her descendants for ever. The miraculous mercies of the past and the prospect of future blessings could be urged as a ground for serious reckoning with the claims of Yahweh's ultimate sovereignty over the whole earth.

IV. CITIES OF REFUGE SET APART (4:41–43)

Because Moses is not represented here as speaking, but is reported in the third person, these verses are sometimes regarded as an appendix. Comparison with Numbers 35:1–14 suggests that Moses is here shown to be carrying out a divine injunction. Three cities were appointed in Transjordan, one in each of the sectors, southern, central and northern, to provide asylum for the man who committed manslaughter inadvertently (*cf.* 19:1–13). In nomadic societies the possibility of blood revenge acted as a restraint upon men. In settled societies, however, there were proper legal procedures for the

[1] W. F. Albright, *From the Stone Age to Christianity*[2] (1957), pp. 271f.

trial of such persons. Until these processes were established, some such provision as is envisaged here would be necessary. There seems no reason to doubt that such a practice was ancient and that it was the kind of provision Moses might have made.

B. Second address of Moses: the law of God (4:44 – 28:68)

This lengthy section of Deuteronomy is really the core of the book. It sets out the covenant stipulations (see Introduction, p. 14), first in the form of general principles (chapters 5–11) and then in the form of detailed, specific requirements. Such a method bears a close resemblance to what is found in the Near Eastern treaties where, following the historical prologue, the fundamental demand for a vassal's total allegiance to the suzerain is expressed first in general terms and then in the specific treaty stipulations. In a similar way Moses confronted Israel with the primary demand for total allegiance to Yahweh, first of all in general terms and then in more specific terms.

I. INTRODUCTION TO THE SECOND ADDRESS OF MOSES (4:44-49)

These verses serve a similar purpose to 1:4, 5, namely, to summarize the historical events which preceded the covenant demand that was to follow. It is as though Moses returned to his task of addressing Israel after a break and resumed with a brief summary of the preceding historical events which were the basis for Yahweh's demand.[1]

44, 45. Each of the terms *law* (*tôrâ*), *testimonies* (*ʿēḏûṯ*), *statutes* (*ḥôq*), and *ordinances* or judicial decisions (*mišpāṭ*), has its own connotation, although detailed definition is not necessarily intended here. *Law* denoted 'teaching' in a very general sense. *Testimonies* denoted covenant stipulations. *Statutes* were laws that were written down or inscribed on some suitable medium. *Ordinances* were the decisions of a judge.

46. For the phrase *beyond the Jordan* see comments on 1:1; 2:26 – 3:11.

47, 48. See chapter 3. An alternative name is given for Mount Hermon, *Siʾōn*, probably the same as Sirion in 3:9 and Psalm 29:6. It is otherwise unknown.

---

[1] See Introduction, p. 70.

II. THE NATURE OF THE COVENANT FAITH: THE FUNDAMENTAL DEMAND FOR TOTAL ALLEGIANCE TO YAHWEH (5:1 – 11:32)

In seven chapters the nature of Yahweh's demand is now set out in the form of great principles. The deliverance of past days is the ground on which Moses appeals to Israel to hear what Yahweh requires of them.

One of the questions that arises in this section concerns the use of both singular and plural pronouns 'thou' and 'thee', 'you' and 'ye'. This usage is obscured in the RSV but is preserved in the AV. (*Cf.* 6:4 with 6:5; 6:13 with 6:14; and 6:16, 17 with 6:18, 19.) Literary critics have approached this variation in singular and plural in a variety of ways. A few have argued that it points to independent sources. Many have suggested that the singular passages are original and the plural passages are later additions. A careful study of the text shows that this latter proposal involves the breaking up of sentences at critical points.[1] It may be that the solution to the problem lies in the fact that we are dealing here with a feature of Semitic style which occurs in ancient Near Eastern treaties and other literature.[2] What purpose was served by such a device is not clear, but it may have been that by such 'number-mixing' attention could be drawn to particular points.[3] For a more complete discussion of the issues see Introduction, pp. 21ff.

a. The heart of the covenant faith (5:1 – 6:3)

At the heart of Israel's covenant faith lay the Sinai covenant and the decalogue. It must be insisted that the covenant was more than a list of covenant stipulations. It was fundamentally a relationship between Yahweh and Israel (*cf.* 4:13, 14). But the covenant stipulations were important because they defined the basic demands of the covenant. As so often in Deuteronomy, the section 5:6–21 contains a number of aspects of the Near Eastern treaty pattern.

[1] E. W. Nicholson, *Deuteronomy and Tradition* (1967), pp. 33f.; G. Minette de Tillesse, *VT*, XII.1, Jan. 1962, pp. 29–87.
[2] K. A. Kitchen, *Ancient Orient and Old Testament* (1966), p. 129.
[3] N. Lohfink, *Das Hauptgebot: Eine Untersuchung literarischer Einleitungsfragen zu Dt. 5–11* (*Analecta Biblica*, 20, 1963), pp. 66f.

i. The ten commandments (decalogue) (5:1-21). 1. The decalogue, the most basic expression of the general demands of the covenant, is now introduced. The first verse contains four injunctions, *hear, learn, be careful* and *do* (*cf.* 32, 33). The solemn formula *Hear, O Israel* occurs elsewhere in Deuteronomy at the commencement of important sections (6:4; 9:1; 20:3; 27:9).

2, 3. The original covenant at Horeb is first recalled (*cf.* Ex. 20). The fact is emphasized that the Horeb event was not simply an event of the past which concerned Israel's ancestors only, but was the concern of Israel in every age. The original Israel held within it all later Israelites. It was the responsibility of every Israelite in every age to identify himself with his ancestors and to participate in memory and in faith in their experience of God's deliverance. In fact, it was already a later generation that entered the land and inherited the promises, for the older members of the generation that stood at Sinai had died. Only those who were children at Sinai survived to enter the promised land.

The expression *made a covenant* (lit. 'cut a covenant') is an interesting one. Its origin is not entirely clear, but it may have arisen from the fact that in many covenant-making ceremonies beasts were slain and cut in two and the parties to the covenant passed between the pieces (Gn. 15:9, 10, 17; Je. 34:17, 18). From some covenant documents it is clear that the parties called down on themselves a curse and expressed the wish that they might become as the slain beasts of the covenant ceremony should they reject the covenant. However the fact was expressed or symbolized, the dire consequences of covenant breach were made clear in all ancient covenants. Conversely, blessings would attend the man who kept his covenant. The covenant of Yahweh with His people Israel, at least in its formal elements, had many parallels with secular covenants. (See Introduction, p. 17.)

4. The expression *The Lord spoke with you face to face* does not imply that Israel saw God (*cf.* 4:12; 34:10), but suggests that the covenant was made in the area of personal relationship rather than in purely legalistic areas. (*Cf.* Ex. 33:11; Nu. 14:14 where *face to face* seems to mean 'in person', that is, in the immediacy of personal contact.)

5. Both at Sinai and in several subsequent situations Moses was a mediator between God and Israel. Moses' function was all the more necessary because of Israel's fear of the fiery theophany (*cf.* 4:12; Ex. 19:16–25). Some passages suggest that Israel heard the voice of Yahweh at Sinai, but perhaps this was through the voice of Moses the mediator (4:12; Ex. 19:9).

6–21. In these verses the ten covenant 'words', the so-called ten commandments or the decalogue, are introduced (*cf.* Ex. 20:1–17). These have been normative for both Israel and the Christian church through the ages. Their importance for Israel is attested by many references in prophets, psalmists and rabbis over the centuries. Jesus referred to them on various occasions (Mt. 5:21, 27, 33; Mk. 12:29–31; Lk. 10:27; 18:20) and they lie behind many statements in the Epistles (Rom. 2:21, 22; Gal. 5:19f.; Eph. 4:28; 5:3; Heb. 4:9; Jas. 2:11, *etc.*).

Basically, the ten commandments assert that God's people have two great areas of obligation – to God and to their fellows. The careful observance of both is essential to wholesome living. The violation of any one of them is a violation of one's relationship with God Himself (Jas. 2:10). It is therefore obligatory for God's people to respect the integrity both of the Lord Himself and of their fellow believers. The first four commandments lay stress on the sovereign rights of God whose identity, nature, name and day are to be fully acknowledged. The following six commandments have to do with obligations to parents and with the life, person, property and reputation of one's fellows.

In the New Testament stress is often laid on the fact that salvation is not to be found in the law, but only in God who saves men by His sovereign grace. Nevertheless, the Christian man was not to be antinomian, *i.e.* opposed to the keeping of the law. To offend in one point was to be guilty of all (Jas. 2:10, 11). The observance of the ten commandments was a natural outcome of the new life in Christ, the result of having the law written on the fleshy tables of the heart (Je. 31:33; Heb. 10:16, 17).

6. The phrase *I am Yahweh your God* announces the originator of the covenant and corresponds to the preamble of the Near Eastern treaty. The rest of the verse corresponds to the historical prologue of the treaty. God is not defined in an abstract sense, but in terms of the saving acts He has performed on Israel's behalf.

7. The first commandment is a clear statement of a broad general principle. In common with most of the other commandments it is presented in negative form. It gives clear expression to the principle of total allegiance to Yahweh.

Whether or not the people of Israel, or even some of them, allowed the existence of other gods, they were required to acknowledge that for them Yahweh alone was sovereign Lord. In that confession lay the roots of monotheism. Yahweh could not tolerate rivals. The phrase *before me* ('*al pānay*), which could be translated in a variety of ways, *e.g.* 'near by me', 'at my side', 'against me', 'in defiance of me', 'to my detriment',[1] gives expression to this fact. For Israel, Yahweh stood alone. The same principle of divine sovereignty in everything found application in the food laws (14:3–21), the sanctions against idolatry (chapter 13), the injunction to destroy pagan sanctuaries (7:5; 12:3), the laws of separation (7:3, 4), *etc.*

8. The second commandment of the decalogue is almost identical with the form in Exodus 20:4–6. It may have been directed originally, not so much against pagan gods, as against a false idea of the worship of Yahweh which might lead Israel to represent Him by an image, in the manner of the pagans (4:15–19). Israel is forbidden to make images of the whole range of created things in the sky, on the earth and in the waters.

9a. The prostration of Israel before any image, or the service of any god thus represented, is forbidden. The verb *bow down* suggests an attitude of submission such as would be adopted by a vassal before his suzerain.[2] The other verb, *serve*, likewise denotes an attitude of submission. Since the 'service' of God, and the act of prostration before God, are both responses of worship, these verbs are used at times to mean worship. In days when the idea of worship has lost a good deal of its true meaning, these verbs remind us that one of the most important aspects of worship is that the worshipper displays an attitude of submission to God. In that attitude he is stripped of all his self-will and surrenders himself to God who is his sovereign Lord.

9b, 10. The formula in these verses is part of a well-known liturgical expression which occurs in Exodus 34:6, 7 in a fuller form. Yahweh is again defined as *jealous, i.e.* actively engaged in the establishment of His own sovereignty, who will not tolerate idolatry in any form since this amounts to divided

---

[1] J. J. Stamm and M. E. Andrew, *The Ten Commandments in Recent Research* (1967), p. 79.

[2] The Hebrew verb *hištaḥ{}^{a}wâ* derives from a root *ḥ-w-y* which in Ugaritic forms a *hišt-* stem meaning 'bow oneself down', 'stoop'. See G. R. Driver, *Canaanite Myths and Legends* (1956), p. 139.

allegiance (*cf.* 4:15–31). Such zeal in the assertion of His own sovereignty might be manifested either in judgment or in blessing even to future generations. It would be shown as judgment on those Israelites who rejected His total sovereignty and attempted to share allegiance with other gods, while it would be displayed as steadfast love (*ḥeseḏ*) for those who loved Him and kept His commandments.

Similar thinking is found in the Near Eastern treaties, where loyal vassals and their families were promised the blessing of the great king, but disloyal vassals could expect judgment both on themselves and on their children.[1] If the phraseology is that of a liturgical confession it may still owe something to its secular parallel. Religious expressions are very often metaphors drawn from secular life.

11a. The third commandment is a prohibition of the careless use of *the name* Yahweh in the taking of oaths or in the uttering of curses and blessings in formulae of various kinds. In the ancient world and in the thought of Israel the *name* was held to be part of the one who bore it and its use in the case of a deity was thought to bring the power of the deity to bear on a particular situation. Clearly a believing man might invoke the name of Yahweh, but the careless use of His name was forbidden.

11b. This is in the nature of a cursing formula, and expresses the judgment that would befall one who offended in the law expressed in 11a.

12–15. The fourth commandment is expressed in a positive form rather than negatively. There are differences between the law here and that in Exodus 20:8 11. In verse 12a *observe* replaces 'remember', and in 12b the words *as the Lord your God commanded you* are an addition. In 14 *your ox, your ass* and *any* are additions. None of these changes is particularly important. The term *gates* (14) denotes 'cities'. The whole passage reflects the typical Israelite society with its three strata, the native Israelite, the resident alien or sojourner, and the slave (*cf.* 14:21).

The reason given in verse 15 for keeping the sabbath is different from that in Exodus 20:11. Here it is said to be in memory of the deliverance from Egypt. If Israel gave thought to her own days of servitude, she would be encouraged to treat mercifully every man, woman or beast that was engaged in daily toil. (*Cf.* 15:15; 16:12; 24:18, 22.) In Exodus the reason given is that the sabbath has been a holy day since creation

[1] *ANET*, p. 205.

(Ex. 20:11; *cf.* Gn. 2:2, 3). There were thus two good reasons for observing the sabbath. This commandment has posed many problems for the Christian. Jesus' statements (Mk. 2:27, 28) that the sabbath was made for man, not man for the sabbath, and that He, the Son of man, was Lord of the sabbath, removed the law for ever from the unwholesome restrictions of the rabbis. The Christian observance of Sunday is, of course, not an observance of the seventh day but of the first day, and hence is in the nature of a new commandment based on a new covenant. It is nevertheless the 'fulfilment' of the old. The first day provides opportunity to commemorate the resurrection of Christ which made possible deliverance from the bondage of sin (*cf.* verse 12), and the renewal of life by way of a new creation (*cf.* Ex. 20:10, 11).

16. With the fifth commandment begins the statement of the obligations of the man of Israel to his fellows, that is, his obligations to society at large. The first of these concerns a man's behaviour inside the basic unit of society, the family. The law is stated positively (*cf.* 27:16 and Ex. 21:17, where it is stated negatively). The observance of this law was so important that blessings were promised to those who observed it. The form in Deuteronomy is longer than that in Exodus 20:12 and adds another blessing. This is another example of the strong tendency in Deuteronomy to elaborate on the Exodus material (*cf.* Pr. 19:26; Mk. 7:9-13).

17-20. The last five commandments cover fundamental requirements for life in society; respect for life (17), respect for the sanctity of marriage and the marital rights of one's fellows (18), respect for the property of another (19), respect for another's reputation (20), and finally the rejection of covetousness (21). The first four of these are expressed in a very brief form, possibly the original form of all ten of the commandments of the decalogue.[1] The prohibition of murder in the Old Testament as in other ancient societies has reference to private killing (*rāṣaḥ*). In Israel the law did not concern such areas as the Holy War, nor did it exclude the death of idolaters, murderers and various other law-breakers which is commanded in a number of passages in Deuteronomy (13:5, 9; 17:6, 7; 21:22, *etc.*). The attempt to invoke this law as an argument for pacifism or for the abolition of the death penalty is based on a misunderstanding of verse 17. Justification for these questions would need to be sought in other Scriptures

[1] J. J. Stamm and M. E. Andrew, *op. cit.*, pp. 18-22.

and argued on other grounds. Adultery and theft were regarded as social evils in other ancient societies.[1] False witness, too, was subject to severe penalties.[2] In these respects Israel followed her contemporaries, although Yahweh placed His imprimatur on these laws in Israel. The laws are here stated in apodictic form, whereas in the Code of Hammurabi they are in casuistic form.

It is worth reflecting that these last five commandments, which occur so widely in ancient Near Eastern law codes, reflect certain fundamental requirements for all societies. We may believe that they are woven into the very warp and woof of human law and that they owe their origin to the Creator of the universe. That they should form part of the decalogue is only an indication of their divine origin. Men have turned aside from these laws repeatedly in many societies and in many ages.

21. The last law in the decalogue, referring to covetousness, calls for some special comments. It deals with inward motivation. The wording differs from that in Exodus 20:17 where a man's house (possibly 'household') is mentioned before his wife and is set apart in a separate sentence with the verb *ḥāmaḏ*, while the other items are all grouped together with the wife under the same verb.[3] In Deuteronomy the wife is placed first with the verb *ḥāmaḏ*, while all the other items are grouped together with a different verb (*hiṯ'awwâ*). The passage in Deuteronomy suggests a different attitude to women from that in Exodus. There are other examples of this sensitive attitude to women in Deuteronomy, *e.g.* 21:10–14; 22:13–19; 24:1–5.[4]

ii. Israel's reaction: fear and devotion (5:22–27). The importance of God's revelation in the ten words is stressed and reference is made to the fear engendered in Israel in the presence of the Sinai theophany and of their promise to obey Yahweh.

22. A brief description of the theophany of Exodus 19:16–20

---

[1] The attitude of Egyptian society is reflected in The Book of the Dead, *ANET*, pp. 34, 35, B 19; B 2, 4, 8; for killing see A 14, 15; B 5.

[2] See Hammurabi's Code, Law I, *ANET*, pp. 163–177; The Book of the Dead, Law B 9, *ANET*, p. 35.

[3] It may be that 'house' is a summarizing term denoting all that belonged to a man, so that the second phrase is a detailed list. This kind of thing is common in Deuteronomy and expresses the idea, 'I mean to say'.

[4] See Introduction, p. 29.

is now given with an insistence that these laws came from Yahweh Himself. One way of expressing this belief was to state that *he wrote them upon two tables of stone*. Whereas the decalogue came from Yahweh, the rest of the law came through the mediation of Moses. The expression *and he added no more* is unusual and may indicate that these commandments were such a complete summary of the fundamental requirements of the covenant that no other law needed to be added. All other law was a mere interpretation and expansion of these basic principles. Alternatively, the expression may refer to a particular occasion when the Lord made known precisely these ten laws. Other laws must have been given on other occasions, since the total volume of law known in Israel and originating from God was considerable. The meaning of the sentence *And he wrote them upon two tables of stone* is not clear. *Cf.* Exodus 31:18; 32:15, 16. But God sometimes used agents to accomplish His purpose and undertook His work by the hands of men (Is. 10:5, 6; 44:28; Je. 43:10–13, *etc.*). When the first tables were broken and a second set was prepared, the writing was attributed to Moses (Ex. 34:28). It is not unreasonable to suggest that what happened on the second occasion was what happened on the first, and that in both cases Moses was God's amanuensis. In any case we have here a good example of anthropomorphism, *i.e.* the attributing of human actions to God. But God is a Spirit and has no physical form. Anthropomorphism is a literary device for stating in limited human terms that God is personal and may be known in personal terms.

23–27. It was the representatives of Israel, the heads of the tribes and the elders, moved by deep fear in the divine presence, who asked that in future they should be represented before God by Moses, who would act as their mediator. The present narrative deals with the covenant made in Moab (1:1; 4:45, 46; 29:1) and stresses the continuity of the two covenants of Moab and Sinai. Moses' right to act as mediator in Moab went back to his action at Horeb-Sinai. Israel, despite her fear, recognized Yahweh as her God and committed herself to obey Him (27).

iii. Yahweh's acceptance of a Mediator (5:28–31).

28–30. The Lord approved Israel's promise to hear and obey and expressed the hope that the reverent devotion inspired by the Sinai theophany might continue always as characteristic of Israel's attitude to Him. In the keeping of His command-ments lay their welfare.

31. After the dismissal of the people to their tents Moses remained with God on the mountain and received the com-mandments, the statutes and the ordinances which he was to teach the people. These would be their guide for life in the land of promise.

iv. The benefits of keeping God's law (5:32 – 6:3). The concluding section of this narrative is an exhortation to the people to be obedient to the law of God without deviation. These verses represent mature hortatory and homiletical comment. All Israel was one with the forefathers who had stood at Sinai and was bound to keep the law of Yahweh her sovereign Lord. There could be no questioning that obligation if she were to continue in her proper relationship with Yahweh. But there were side benefits. When Yahweh was obeyed Israel would enjoy the blessing of life itself, but also her life would be happy and long and would be perpetuated in offspring (5:33; 6:3).

32, 33. The homiletical and hortatory emphasis is particu-larly clear in these verses. The link between obedience to Yahweh's covenant and national and individual blessing is made clear by the use of the expression 'in order that', 'to the end that' (*lemaʿan*).

6:1–3. The injunction of 5:32, 33 is now expressed with a new emphasis. The expression *the statutes and the ordinances*, which occurs elsewhere (5:1; 12:1), is here preceded by the word *commandment* in the singular (*miṣwâ*; *cf.* AV, which is mistakenly in the plural). The term should probably be trans-lated as 'charge'. In detail the charge is represented by *statutes and commandments*, although these are not formally given till chapters 12 to 26. At this point the main concern is to express general principles. Israel is exhorted to *do* and to *keep* Yahweh's laws and to *fear* (reverence) Him. Any blessings that followed would be the outworking of the patriarchal promise (Gn. 12:1–7). The descriptive phrase, *a land flowing with milk and honey* (3), is not merely an idealistic picture such as would be painted in a nomadic setting. A similar expression is used to describe northern Palestine in the ancient Egyptian Tale of Sinuhe,[1] while one of the Canaanite texts from Ras Shamra (ancient Ugarit) contains the words,

[1] *ANET*, pp. 18–25, lines 80 to 90.

'The skies will rain down milk
And the valleys will flow honey.'[1]

The same expression is met four times in Exodus (3:8, 17;
13:5; 33:3), once in Leviticus (20:24), four times in Numbers
(13:27; 14:8; 16:13, 14), and five more times in Deuteronomy
(11:9; 26:9, 15; 27:3; 31:20). It was evidently a well-known
literary motif widely used in the lands of the Levant.

b. Yahweh is our God, Yahweh is One (6:4–9)

This great book now moves on to give expression to what was
the heart of Israel's confession, namely that Yahweh was not a
pantheon of gods, but *One*. He was, therefore, to be the sole
object of Israel's faith and obedience. Nor was she to forget
Yahweh or attempt to share her allegiance with other gods in
days of prosperity. Moreover, she was to ensure continuity of
this allegiance and this covenant faith by diligently teaching
her children.

4. *Hear, O Israel.* Israel is invited to respond to Yahweh with
the same fullness of love that Yahweh displayed towards His
people. In the New Testament verse 5 is described by Jesus as
the first and great commandment (Mt. 22:36–38. *Cf.* Mk.
12:29–34; Lk. 10:27, 28). This small section (4–9) has been
known to the Jews for many centuries as the *Shema* (Heb.,
Hear) and has been recited along with 11:13–21 and Numbers
15:37–41 as a daily prayer. The reference to the binding of
God's laws on one's forehead is discussed under 6:8. The
prescription of verse 4 has sometimes been regarded as the
positive way of expressing the negative commands of the first
two commandments of the decalogue (5:7–10). This central
confession of faith consists of only four words, *Yahweh, our God,
Yahweh, One.*[2] The expression has been variously understood.
Possible translations are 'Yahweh our God, Yahweh is one',
'Yahweh is our God, Yahweh is one'. 'Yahweh is our God,
Yahweh alone'. Whatever translation is chosen the essential
meaning is clear. Yahweh was to be the sole object of Israel's
worship, allegiance and affection. The word 'one' or 'alone'
implies monotheism, even if it does not state it with all the

---

[1] 'Poems about Baal and Anat', *ANET*, p. 140, part of Text I, AB, iii
to iv, lines 6 and 7.

[2] The Christian doctrine of the Trinity does not contradict this text,
although it involves a different understanding of the concept of trinity in the
Godhead.

subtleties of theological formulation. Biblical monotheism was given a practical and existential expression which would lead to the abandonment of such views as monolatry. Even if some in Israel acknowledged the existence of other gods, the affirmation that Yahweh alone was Sovereign and the sole object of Israel's obedience sounded the death-knell to all views lesser than monotheism.

5. *You shall love Yahweh your God.* Israel's obedience was not to spring from a barren legalism based on necessity and duty. It was to arise from a relationship based on love. It is of interest that in some of the Near Eastern treaties a similar word is used to express the relationship between a vassal and his suzerain.[1] The Hebrew equivalent of this use of the word 'love' occurs in 1 Kings 5:1, 'Hiram always loved David'. Even in secular treaties the need was felt for a deeper relationship than a merely legalistic one. However, the biblical term 'love' has a much deeper connotation. Hosea uses the verb to express the affection of Yahweh for Israel, making use of strong metaphors drawn from family life, husband and wife (Ho. 3:1), father and son (Ho. 11:1). The extent of a man's love for God was to be total. Israel was to love God with her whole being. The expression *with all your heart, and with all your soul, and with all your might* is a favourite one in Deuteronomy (4:29; 10:12; 11:13; 13:3; 26:16; 30:2, 6, 10) and gives some insight into ancient Hebrew psychology. The *heart* was regarded as the seat of the mind and will as well as of a wide range of emotions. The term *soul* is difficult to define, but it seems to refer to the source of life and vitality, or even of one's 'being'. In Genesis 2:7 and 19 man and animals are described as living 'beings'. The two terms *heart* and *soul* between them indicate that a man is to love God with unreserved devotion. To give more weight to the demand a third expression is added, *with all your might, i.e.* 'with all your strength'.[2]

6. The necessity to have the law of God *upon your heart* rather than on tables of stone is here declared (*cf.* 11:18; Je. 31:33). Comparison with the New Testament is interesting. The test of a man's love for the Lord Jesus Christ is that he keeps His commandments; 'he who has my commandments and keeps them, he it is who loves me' (Jn. 14:21; *cf.* 1 Jn. 5:2).

[1] W. L. Moran, 'The Ancient Near Eastern background of the love of God in Deuteronomy', *CBQ*, XXV, I, 1963, pp. 77–87.
[2] The New Testament adds yet another phrase, 'with all your mind' (Mk. 12:30; Lk. 10:27).

These passages show that obedience to the commandments is an outgrowth of love. If it is objected that love cannot be commanded (5) but must be spontaneous, the reply must be that love flows out of gratitude and devotion. It is an expression of loyalty. The man who loves gladly loves with his whole being. The present injunction was given to make clear to Israel what was to be the character of her relationship to Yahweh her Lord. Anything less than whole-hearted devotion and allegiance would lead to a shared allegiance, which would have been impossible. The command to love cannot be interpreted as an evidence that love is anything other than spontaneous, but rather evidence that only a love that is undivided can be called love in its truest sense.

7–9. When any man loves God in a total way he gladly obeys His 'words' which are inscribed on the heart. The demand of love towards God implies all other demands, and the disposition to love God implies the disposition both to obey His commandments and to impart these to the children of the following generations, so as to maintain an attitude of love and obedience among the people of God from age to age (7a, 20ff.). The book of Deuteronomy attaches a special importance to this task of teaching the family (4:9b; 6:20–25; 11:19). But the demands of Yahweh's covenant are to be the subject of conversation at all times in the home, by the way, by night and by day. Israel is to *teach them diligently, talk of them* constantly, *bind them as a sign* on various parts of the body, and *write them*. God's love and His covenant demands were to be the central and absorbing interest of a man's whole life.

8, 9. What was given originally as a metaphor became for later Jews a literal injunction. The present passage, along with 11:13–21, Exodus 13:1–10, 11–16, was written on small scrolls, placed in small leather containers and bound on the forehead and the left arm when the *Shema* was recited. The origin of the phylacteries (*teṗillîn; cf.* Mt. 23:5) lies in this literalism. The phylacteries were worn by every male Jew during the time of morning prayer except on the sabbath and on festival days, which were signs in themselves. A further practice developed, that of enclosing these four passages in a small container for attaching to the doorpost of one's house (the *mezûzâ*). Ancient copies of these documents have been found in the Qumran caves and elsewhere.[1] Clearly such a practice might well have

[1] D. Barthélemy and J. T. Milik, *Qumran Cave I* (1953), pp. 72–76. See also *NBD*, p. 995.

had deep significance for some people. The small passages of Scripture were 'signs' standing for the whole body of the law which was to be observed and taught. But where the practice descended into one of legalism, it destroyed the whole spirit of the ancient injunction. It was love toward God and the remembrance of all His past mercies that moved men to obedience. These were *signs* enough, apart from any physical reminders. The recollection of the saving acts of God and the declaration of His covenant demands would suffice to keep faith and allegiance alive.

c. The importance of remembering (6:10-25)

In biblical faith the remembrance of God's past mercies and delivering acts is fundamental. In the hour of prosperity, or at times when all goes well, men forget God and may even turn aside from allegiance to Yahweh. Two aspects of the importance of remembering are now taken up. In the first place there is a negative statement: men are exhorted not to forget (10-19). In the second place, Israel is charged to transmit to the children the great facts of the deliverance from Egypt.

i. The danger of forgetting (6:10-19). 10-13. In several places in Deuteronomy the fact is stressed that an established agrarian civilization awaited Israel on their arrival in the land of promise. All this would become theirs without any effort on their part. In a poorly watered land which has a long dry season, reserves of water are essential for life. But Israel found cisterns dug, vineyards and olive trees flourishing, cities and houses built, all waiting for their possession (*cf.* 8:7-11; 11:13-17; 26:10; 32:14). It was a severe temptation for the people of Israel to devote themselves to these earthly treasures and to forget that they were the gift of God's love and the fulfilment of His promise to the patriarchs (10). Hence Israel ought not to forget Yahweh and His great acts of deliverance which liberated their forefathers from slavery in Egypt (12). Rather should their lives be characterized by holy fear or reverence, which is the root of obedience and the basis of proper attitudes in life, by loyal service which arose out of their reverence, and by making Yahweh the guarantor of their integrity and honesty in every undertaking as they took oaths in His name alone. The later history of Israel is replete with instances of a people who failed to heed this warning. For

example, during the prosperous years of the eighth century BC God was honoured only by external observances; the weightier matters of His law were forgotten (Am. 5:4, 5, 14; 6:1, 4-6; Ho. 2:5, 8; Is. 1:4, 21-23). Numerous other examples could be gathered from the history of Israel and from the history of the Christian church. In our own day the nominalism of the church in our affluent Western world bears loud testimony to the fact that in its prosperity the church has forgotten God.

14. The tragedy of forgetfulness was that Israel would turn to the gods of the peoples round about which were, in fact, no gods. These were gods of nature and fertility, whose normal moral requirements were not to be compared with the stern ethical demands of Yahweh.

15. The deliberate neglect of Yahweh was equivalent to defiance of the great sovereign Lord of all life. In the secular realm a rebellious vassal was punished by his overlord. In the realm where Yahweh reigned 'curses' likewise fell on the covenant-breaker. Yahweh, who was *a jealous God (cf.* 5:9), would visit His own people with judgment. The presence of Yahweh among His people was an encouragement to good conduct and provided a strong incentive for Israel to walk in His ways.

16. The incident at *Massah* (Ex. 17:1-7), in which Israel *put God to the test*, is now recalled as another warning. To *test* God is to impose conditions on Him and to make His response to the people's demand in the hour of crisis the condition of their continuing to follow Him. In the wilderness when the people needed water they proposed the production of water by Moses as a test to determine whether Yahweh was among them or not (Ex. 17:7). But such an act is an impertinence and contrary to faith, for it refuses the signs offered by God and proposes to substitute others which are acceptable to man. By doubting God's sovereignty in the hour of need or crisis, the people sought to gain the initiative and to compel God to prove Himself to them by spectacular deeds which they themselves had proposed (*cf.* 1:19-46). In His day Jesus refused to offer signs to the scribes and Pharisees (Mt. 12:38, 39; 16:1-4; Mk. 8:11, 12; Lk. 11:16, 29, 30; *cf.* 1 Cor. 1:22).

17-19. Once again Israel is exhorted to keep the covenant stipulations diligently, and to do what is right in Yahweh's eyes (17, 18a). And again the blessings that follow obedience are mentioned; prosperity, occupancy of the land and the overthrow of all her enemies (18b, 19; *cf.* Ex. 23:27-32).

ii. Teaching the covenant faith (6:20–25). 20. Children are bound to enquire sooner or later why it is that their parents live a certain kind of life in contrast with the life of those about them. Anticipating the future, Moses urged the people to have their answer ready when the children asked why they kept the covenant stipulations (*testimonies*), *statutes*, and judicial decisions (RSV *ordinances*; AV *judgments*) which Yahweh had given to Israel.

21–25. A recitation of God's redemptive activity in delivering their forefathers from Egypt and in leading them to the land of promise was the appropriate answer to the children. Israel's belief in God was thus expressed not in terms of an abstract formulation, but in terms of God's dynamic activity. Even a child could understand a story. The content of that story was simple: slavery in Egypt (21a), the wondrous acts of God against Pharaoh and the Egyptians by which Israel was freed (21b, 22), the safe conduct from Egypt to the land of promise (23), and the final arrival in the land Yahweh had sworn to give the fathers. This recital bears a close resemblance to other confessions of faith in the Old Testament (26:5–9; Jos. 24:2–13).[1] No doubt the constant recital of these facts eventually gave rise to a liturgical formulation. It was in the light of these acts of deliverance that Yahweh could invite Israel to enter into His covenant and lay upon them, for their good, the covenant obligations which Israel now observed and which marked them off from their neighbours. All this would be the subject of enquiry from succeeding generations of Israel's sons. The commandments were designed, not as a burden to be borne, but as the gracious provision by a beneficent Sovereign of a guide for good living. Thus would Yahweh preserve Israel alive. Obedience to His law would be *righteousness* (*ṣeḏāqâ*) for Israel. This latter word is difficult to define. In some Old Testament passages it denotes the norm in a given area. In the plural it denotes 'saving acts' (Jdg. 5:11; 1 Sa. 12:7; Ps. 103:6; Mi. 6:5, *etc.*). In other passages it refers

[1] This recital has been called by Gerhard von Rad and others a 'Cultic Credo' and has been used to argue that the Sinai event, which does not appear in Dt. 26:5–9, was no part of Israel's original faith. But the fact that one element of a credo is omitted is no argument that it did not once exist. Another well-known literary form which appears especially in Exodus links the exodus event very closely with the Sinai event in the manner in which the Near Eastern treaty links the historical background to a treaty with the treaty stipulations. The full truth about Israel's beliefs is discovered only by a combination of several different 'credos'. See on 26:4.

to a right attitude towards, or relationship with, Yahweh (see commentary on 9:4a). When Abraham believed God this was a proper attitude for him to adopt and it brought him into a proper relationship with God. In the present context the standard proposed is conformity to God's covenant. This would result in the enjoyment of the blessing of the covenant. It was a kind of thinking which was understood in the secular world in reference to the treaties of the day, when loyal and faithful vassals enjoyed the favour of their overlords. Compare Psalm 24:3–5, where the man who keeps the law of God receives blessing from the Lord and vindication or 'righteousness' (*ṣᵉḏāqâ*) from his saving God (God of his salvation). Alternatively the term might denote 'deliverance' or 'salvation', as in several Old Testament passages (Is. 41:10; 46:13; 51:1, 5, *etc.*).

d. The conquest of Canaan: an aspect of the Holy War (7:1–26)

Once the sovereignty of Yahweh had been established and acknowledged, the Holy War could proceed and the conquest could begin. (See Introduction, p. 70.) Chapters 5 and 6 set out the fundamental requirements of the covenant faith and stress the sovereignty of Yahweh and the need for absolute obedience. That being understood, some instructions about the attitude Israel should adopt towards the people of Canaan and towards their places of worship and cult objects followed. Israel might well ask what dangers would confront her and what prospects she had of success as she stood on the threshold of the promised land. In what light should she view herself as she faced this new experience? To these questions Israel's attention is now directed.

i. Israel's attitude to the people of the land and to their shrines and cult objects (7:1–5). 1. The seven nations listed did not acknowledge the sovereignty of Yahweh. Moreover they occupied the land which He had given to His people. Further, they were devotees of other gods whom Yahweh could not tolerate in His presence. They were, therefore, proper subjects for the Holy War. While seven of Israel's enemies are listed here, the number varies from three to ten in other parts of the Old Testament (*cf.* Gn. 15:19–22; Ex. 34:11; Nu. 13:28, 29; Jdg. 3:5). The Perizzites, Hivites and Jebusites

do not appear to be known outside the Bible. The *Jebusites* were evidently a Canaanite group which lived in the hill country near Jerusalem. The *Perizzites* seem to have lived in unwalled villages both east and west of Jordan (the Hebrew text of 3:5 may have a reference to the Perizzites). The *Girgashites* are mentioned several times in the Old Testament (Gn. 10:16; 15:21; Dt. 7:1; Jos. 3:10; 24:11; 1 Ch. 1:14; Ne. 9:8). They seem to be mentioned in Egyptian texts as allies of the Hittites. The *Hivites* (or Horites) may be the same people as the Hurrians (see commentary on 2:12). The exact connotation of the name *Hittites* is not clear. The term Hatti was used very loosely by the Assyrians and Babylonians at a later period for Syria-Palestine. It may well be that the reference here is to the same group which we meet in Genesis 10:15, where in the table of the nations the name Heth appears as a descendant of Canaan so that the Hittites, or children of Heth as they might be called, were really a Canaanite group who had been in Palestine for centuries past.[1] In any case these too would be overthrown by the Lord.

The terms *Amorites* and *Canaanites* are also difficult to define, since they were not always used precisely in the Old Testament. However, uncertainty about the identification of these peoples does not detract from the fact that when Israel entered the land she was confronted with groups of people which were greater and more powerful than she was. The declaration of this fact was designed to enhance the power of Yahweh. No power was beyond His control as He undertook to fulfil His promises to Israel.

2, 3. In the Holy War Yahweh led His people out to battle and the enemy was overwhelmed. After the battle the people surrendered to Yahweh, as the Victor, the fruits of the victory. Sometimes this spoil included men, women, children, cattle and possessions (Jos. 6:17f.; 1 Sa. 15:3). Sometimes these were all destroyed. At other times the women, the children and the beasts were spared. But the obligation was on Israel to surrender everything to Yahweh in recognition of the fact that the victory was His and that He had exclusive rights over the spoil, either to save it or to destroy it. Spoil offered to Yahweh for destruction was known as *ḥērem*. Unless otherwise decreed, all the spoil, including human beings, was banned from human use and destroyed. The verb translated *utterly destroy* is derived

[1] H. A. Hoffner, 'Some contributions of Hittitology to Old Testament Study', *TB*, 20, 1969, pp. 28–37.

from the noun *ḥērem*. Presumably the entire enemy was not slain during the Holy War, because further instructions forbid Israel to enter into a covenant with the inhabitants of the land or to undertake marriage arrangements with them, lest they weaken the allegiance of Israel to Yahweh. For other aspects of the Holy War see Introduction (p. 73), where some attempt is made to understand this divinely-ordered genocide as the outcome of God's action to accomplish both His judgment on wicked nations and His purposes of redemption for His people.[1] The books of Joshua and Judges give evidence of the practice of devoting cities and their inhabitants as a *ḥērem* to Yahweh (Jos. 6:21; Jdg. 1:17; 20:48; *cf.* Jdg. 1:25; 1 Sa. 15).

4. The danger of compromising alliances is here alluded to. The outcome would be divine judgment because of the broken covenant.

5. This verse, along with verse 3, suggests that in the case of those Canaanites who had not been overcome, Israel's separation from them could be expressed either by refusing to enter into marriages with them or by the destruction of their sanctuaries (*cf.* Ex. 34:13–16). Some commentators have suggested that the injunction of verse 2 was an ideal, not always carried into effect, but remaining as a divine command in order to provide a vivid picture of how completely Israel ought to reject all compromise. See commentary on verses 2, 3. For Israel, separation from those who did not acknowledge Yahweh was a matter of life or death, for her own faith contrasted so greatly with that of her neighbours that any risk of having it watered down in any way was to be avoided. Israel herself was set apart for Yahweh's exclusive use.

The *Asherim* were cult items which are thought to have been wooden poles representing the goddess Asherah. They stood at Canaanite places of worship (Ex. 34:13) alongside the altar of Baal (Jdg. 6:25, 28). Some support for this picture comes from archaeological work at such places as Hazor, Megiddo, Lachish, Arad and Bethshean, where temples, altars and cult objects of various kinds have been discovered. For example at Megiddo the excavators discovered a large altar dating to about 1900 BC, some 6 feet high and some 29 feet in diameter, with stone steps leading up to the top of it. Beside it stood a stone pillar (perhaps the symbol for Baal) and nearby was a post-hole in which it is conjectured a wooden pillar once stood. Other examples are to be found in archaeological literature.

[1] See also J. W. Wenham, *The Goodness of God* (1974), chapter 8.

ii. The character of Israel (7:6–16). Why should Israel act in this way? The verses that follow give the reason. She was a *holy* or 'separated' people, chosen by God and called into a covenant with Him. That fact set her apart from all peoples. A surrender of her privileged position by compromise was, therefore, unthinkable.

6. The word *for* (*kî*) introduces the reason why Yahweh's demands were so uncompromising. Israel was *a people holy* (*qāḏôš*) *to Yahweh*, and *a people for his own possession* (*seḡullâ*). These phrases are reminiscent of, and no doubt based on, Exodus 19:5, 6.[1] Basically, holiness is an attribute of God which sets Him apart from everything else in creation. Whatever the meaning of the idea behind the root *q-d-š*, the term gave expression to the unique qualities of deity. Something of this quality may be conferred by God on people or things set apart exclusively for His use, so that 'holy' comes to mean in a secondary sense 'set apart', *i.e.* for God. In this sense Israel was different from all other peoples of her day. She was Yahweh's *seḡullâ* (special treasure), *chosen* by Him out of all other peoples. The verb 'choose' is common in Deuteronomy in reference particularly to Israel, but the idea is an ancient one (Gn. 12:1–3; Nu. 23:19–24). Already in the patriarch Abraham, Israel had been chosen.

7, 8. Why was Israel chosen by Yahweh? That was inscrutable. She was a small group of people without great culture or prestige. She possessed no special personal qualities which would warrant such a choice. The election was the act of God alone (*cf.* Jn. 15:16). The ultimate cause for that choice lay in the mystery of divine love. Yet the fact is that God *did* love Israel and *did* choose her, thereby honouring His promise to the fathers. He came to this poor oppressed group in bondage to the pharaoh of Egypt and in a series of great saving acts He liberated them. The verb *redeem* (*pāḏâ*) is often used in a secular sense for 'ransom'. But we ought not to press the metaphor so far as to ask what was the price paid. The emphasis is rather on the result, the liberation of the people. What then was the character of Israel? She was a people whose fathers had received the gracious promises of Yahweh. She had been chosen in virtue of Yahweh's love for her. She had been liberated from slavery in Egypt by a display of Yahweh's power. Let her once grasp these great facts and she would

[1] See discussion on 'Israel the people of the covenant' in the Introduction, p. 74.

realize that she was indeed a holy and a specially treasured people. Any tendency on her part, therefore, to surrender such a noble status was reprehensible in the extreme.

It is worthy of comment that something of this thinking is carried over into the New Testament. The Christian believer is also chosen by God (Jn. 15:16) as a sheer act of grace on His part. God, in Christ, came to men who were in the bondage of sin and liberated them from the power of darkness and transferred them into the kingdom of His beloved Son (Col. 1:13, 14).

9, 10. Expressions similar to these occur in other places in the Old Testament (*cf.* Ex. 20:6; 34:6, 7) and have the appearance of liturgical formulae or phrases from ancient confessions of faith. Just when they took on their final shape we shall probably never know. It is not inconceivable that Moses described Yahweh in noble terms and the liturgical formula given here may represent a polished and expanded version of something Moses once said. As the formula now stands it is full of significance. Yahweh is described as *the faithful God* (*ne'emān*), *i.e.* He is reliable and trustworthy, abiding by His promise. He is, moreover, one who *keeps covenant* and displays *steadfast love* (*ḥesed*). This latter term occurs some 245 times in the Old Testament and normally connotes an inner aspect of character which promotes God or man, quite apart from the constraint of law, to show kindness, magnanimity and faithfulness to another, particularly in areas where there are mutual responsibilities such as one finds in agreements or covenants.[1]

When men are in a relationship of *love* with Yahweh, they discover that Yahweh is faithful to His covenant relationship and loyal to His promises. The wonderful fact about Him is that, although by reason of Israel's neglect and breach of covenant He might have been released from His obligations to Israel, yet He continued faithful. Conversely, where there is no relationship of love, but rather one of hate in which men reject Yahweh and become so disloyal to Him as to disregard Him and defy Him, then for their breach of covenant and for their base ingratitude they taste the judgments that attend the man who breaks His covenant. Yahweh is a jealous God who will tolerate no challenge to His sovereignty (6:10–15).

[1] See for detailed study of this term N. H. Snaith, *The Distinctive Ideas of the Old Testament* (1944), pp. 94–130; Nelson Glueck, *Ḥesed in the Bible*, ET (1967).

11. In the light of all these factors Israel is urged to fulfil her covenant obligations fully.

12-15. God bestows the blessings of His covenant, His faithfulness and His love, on those who are obedient. His blessings will extend to all that belongs to them so that Israel will multiply as a people, while her crops, herds and flocks will yield abundance. Barrenness will be unknown among the people and their animals. Diseases like those that plagued the Egyptians will be removed from them and transferred to their enemies.

In this passage, as in many others in the Old Testament, a close relationship between the people and the land is envisaged. An obedient people enjoy the blessing of Yahweh on their land, while those who are disobedient discover that the curse touches their crops and flocks. Comparison of this short list of curses and blessings with those in 27:11 – 28:68 and Leviticus 26 is instructive. The curses and blessings mentioned in these passages are reminiscent of those in similar lists in the ancient Near Eastern treaties for the period 2500 to 650 BC.[1]

16. The last of the blessings is the promise that Israel will overthrow her foes in the new land (*cf.* verses 1, 2). This verse summarizes the concept of holiness or separation and underlines again the need for Israel to be Yahweh's obedient agent in the overthrow of those who worship other gods.

iii. The difficulties of the Holy War and the need for faith (7:17-26).

At first sight the enemies listed in the opening verse of this chapter appear formidable and irresistible (17). Only the memory of God's past deliverance from Egypt and of all the wondrous deeds He performed then and since could serve to arm the people for the coming ordeal.

17-19. The cure for fear of the enemy is to *remember what the Lord your God did to Pharaoh and to all Egypt*. The remembrance of God's saving acts is a constant theme in both the Old and the New Testaments. It lifts man from his own inner thoughts and fears to something objective. For Israel, in the Holy War upon which they were to embark, the victory was already assured because Yahweh was their Captain. In any case, He would fulfil His own purposes.

20. The *hornets* which God would send represented some powerful agency which He would use in the overthrow of

---

[1] *ANET*, pp. 205, 206.

Israel's enemies (*cf.* Ex. 23:28; Jos. 24:12). The exact connotation of the term is disputed. The phrase may be intended in a fairly literal sense and refer to swarms of stinging insects that might assist the people of Israel in their attacks on the enemy. Some interpreters see in the term a reference to the invasions of the Egyptians over the years preceding the Israelite conquest, since some Egyptian pharaohs included a species of hornet in their insignia. Alternatively, the term may be used in a symbolic sense. Just as the hornet stings, so God will provide agencies to sting the inhabitants of the land at the time of Israel's arrival.

21, 23. One aspect of the Holy War was that terror sent by Yahweh would come upon the enemy. A numinous panic would spread among the foes of Israel, who would act blindly and accomplish their own destruction (23; Jos. 10:10; Jdg. 4:15; 1 Sa. 5:9; 7:10, *etc.*). This is why the numbers engaged in the Holy War were irrelevant, for God could save by many or by few (Jdg. 7:2f.; 1 Sa. 13:15f.; 14:6, *etc.*). Yahweh was a great God and one to be feared (21).

22. This verse is really a parenthesis looking beyond the Holy War. The enemies of Yahweh would be driven out only gradually, so that the wild beasts might be kept under control. Practical reasons would modify the speed with which Israel could separate herself from the Canaanites. Although she was separated from the 'world' in status, she could not live outside her world. The conquest would take time. But disobedience to Yahweh and His covenant would also slow down the conquest, as we learn from Judges 2:20–23. Sometimes Israel's enemies acted as a test whether Israel would really walk in the ways of Yahweh (Jdg. 2:22).

24–26. In the Holy War it was necessary for Israel to put away everything, whether man or inanimate object, that would turn her away from total allegiance to Yahweh. This injunction applied particularly to the kings who were the leaders of Israel's enemies. Even their memory was to be wiped out. Similarly, the personal possessions and cult objects of the people of the land were to be placed under the ban and be regarded as a *ḥērem*. (See Introduction, p. 73, and commentary on 7:2, 3.) None of these things was to be taken into the homes of God's people lest they partook of their character and became liable themselves for 'sacred extermination' (*ḥērem*). This is the meaning of the expression *become accursed like it* (26). A telling illustration of what would happen if the forbidden thing was

kept in one's private possession is provided in the story of
Achan at Ai (Jos. 7).

e. Lessons from the past: the dangers of prosperity (8:1 – 10:11)

Two important lessons from the past are now referred to.
First, the experience of God's care in the wilderness period,
when the people of Israel were unable to help themselves,
taught them the lesson of humility through the Lord's providential discipline. The memory of that experience should keep
them from pride in their own achievements amid the security
and prosperity of the new land (8:1–20). Secondly, any success
they might enjoy in the coming conquest was not to be interpreted as a mark of divine approval for their own righteousness
(9:1–6). In fact, both in the incident of the golden calf (9:7–21)
and in a number of other incidents (9:22, 23), Israel had proved
herself stubborn and rebellious. She was delivered only after
the intercession of Moses (9:24–29). Past experience should
remind the people that they needed discipline for their
rebellious ways. Yet through all their recalcitrance Yahweh
remained faithful, even to the extent of granting them two
more tables of stone when the first ones were broken (10:1–11;
cf. Ex. 32:19; 34:1–4). All the experiences of the past would
underline the fact that Israel was dependent on Yahweh for
divine care, provision, protection and forgiveness. To forget
these facts was to display base ingratitude and self-deifying
pride.

i. The discipline of the wilderness and its lessons (8:1–10). 1.

Israel is commanded to heed the charge which
Moses was setting before them. The singular word *commandment* seems to be a collective which denotes the body of
commandments or perhaps the charge. Only by giving heed
to this charge could Israel enjoy the blessing of the covenant
succinctly summarized here in terms of life, descendants and a
land.

2. The remembrance of God's acts of deliverance and of
judgment would provide motivation for the future. The recollection of hardships suffered in the wilderness would lead to a
humbling of Israel's spirit. Already during the forty years of
wandering God had taught Israel utter dependence on Him
for water and food. Hunger and thirst could not be satisfied by

human aid but only by God. The need for such divine provision in the hour of their extremity could not but humiliate the people. It was, indeed, God's intention to humble them and to test them in order to discover their real motives, *i.e. what was in your heart*.

3. A good illustration of the point made in verse 2 was readily available. The people having been allowed to hunger in the wilderness were then fed on strange food, *manna* (*hammān*; Ex. 16; Nu. 11), of which they had had no experience hitherto. The manna may have been the sweet substance that collects on tamarisk trees and bushes in the Sinai area in early summer. It is thought that it is exuded by small insects which suck up the sap of the tree, extract what they need and exude the rest.[1] Some of the sap of the tree itself may ooze from the bark and collect on the limbs of the tree. According to Joshua 5:12 the provision of manna ceased once Israel had crossed the Jordan and entered the land of Canaan. The provision of food, which Israel did not know previously, made plain the lesson that it is not mere food that gives life. Without the divine word the food itself may not be available. It is not *by bread alone* that a man lives, but *by everything that proceeds out of the mouth of the Lord*, *i.e.* at His command. Material sustenance is important and essential to life. But life is more than food. At each step of the way the people were fed by Yahweh, on whom they depended. Nothing was possible without Him, and even to eat they had to await His pleasure. The deeper lesson to be learnt from the concrete illustration of bread for the body was that there are deeper dimensions to life than physical hunger. The manna was given to Israel as a test (Ex. 16:4; Nu. 11:6; 21:4, 5), in which the venture of faith was contrasted with human security (Ex. 16:3; Nu. 11:5).

This passage was quoted by Jesus on the occasion of His temptation. His reply to the Devil when tempted to command stones to become loaves of bread was to quote these words as something that was *written* (see Mt. 4:4; Lk. 4:4). Evidently for Him what was written provided an adequate reply to the Tempter. The book of Deuteronomy is frequently quoted in the New Testament in the Gospels, in Paul's letters, in Acts and in Hebrews. It clearly carried great weight in the early church.

4. A further illustration of the care of Yahweh for Israel is couched in vivid symbolic language, which means simply that

[1] F. S. Bodenheimer, 'The Manna of Sinai', *BA*, X, 1947, pp. 2–6; Winifred Walker, *All the Plants of the Bible* (1957), p. 126.

God supplied their every need (see 29:5; Ne. 9:21 and *cf.* Mt. 6:25ff.).

5. The purpose of these experiences was educational. Often in the Old Testament God is shown as sending suffering to humble and to discipline His servants so that they might learn lessons they would otherwise miss, *e.g.* the testing of Abraham, Job, Joseph, Jeremiah. God's methods have not changed over the centuries. The family of God still learns lessons through suffering.

6. The new generation is urged to keep Yahweh's commandments, to walk in His ways and to fear (reverence) Him. The formula is used frequently in Deuteronomy. It serves to introduce the argument already outlined in 6:10–15.

7–9a. A contrast is at once presented. The Lord is bringing His people to a good land of which the agricultural resources would excite the imagination of those who had been living a nomadic existence. There were natural reserves of water, brooks, springs and deep sources which gush forth in valleys and hills. These resources of water would guarantee crops of grain and fruit.

9b. The reference to *iron* and *copper* in the hills is remarkably exact. Ancient copper mines and smelters have been discovered in recent years in the Arabah below the Dead Sea,[1] and geological survey has demonstrated the presence of ores of copper and iron in the nearby hills.

10. Such abundant provision should call forth continuous praise to Yahweh for His goodness. Clearly it was God's intention that His people should enjoy His good gifts. It is no part of biblical faith to espouse a view of life which bans enjoyment and pleasure. It is, indeed, a misunderstanding of the facts of the case, that those who live according to God's laws are unhappy people. The biblical view is not 'puritanical' in the commonly understood meaning of the word (*cf.* Pss. 42:4; 67:4; Is. 12:3; 61:3; Jn. 15:11; Phil. 4:4, *etc.*).

ii. Warning against pride and forgetfulness (8:11–20).

11. Israel is under deep obligation to obey Yahweh in the light of His great goodness.

12–17. In one of the longest sentences in Hebrew literature Israel is given a stern warning. When men have abundance of food and great possessions (12, 13) they tend to forget the pit

---

[1] Nelson Glueck, *The Other Side of the Jordan* (1940), pp. 50–88.

whence they were dug and the pathway by which they achieved their prosperity. For Israel there could have been no prosperity had not Yahweh brought them out from the slavery of Egypt and cared for them during the wanderings (14–16). There is always a danger that men's hearts might become lifted up with pride (14) and, forgetful of the facts of the case, declare, *My power and the might of my hand have gotten me this wealth* (17; Ps. 127:1; Pr. 30:9; Ho. 13:6). Such a claim is an arrogant elevation of self to the status of God.

18. Hence Israel was to remember that it was Yahweh alone who gave her the strength to acquire wealth. Moreover, every blessing she enjoyed was the result of His covenant with her and the outcome of His promise to her forefathers. This lesson for Israel has wide implications for all mankind. Wealth and prosperity can never be regarded as a natural right. They are the gift of God. Since the majority of people in the world lack wealth, those who are wealthy need to beware lest pride in their own achievements possess them and bring about their ruin.

19, 20. The section closes on a solemn note. Israel needed to learn that, if she as a nation dishonoured her covenant with Yahweh, she would cease to have a claim upon Him and when judgment came at last she need only look to her disobedience and forgetfulness for the reason. Each new generation of Israel needed to grasp this fact and to decide for themselves to be obedient to Yahweh who loved them and had chosen them for His own inscrutable purposes. Life and death hung upon that decision (*cf.* 30:15–20).

iii. Conquest, the outcome of Yahweh's will not of Israel's righteousness (9:1–6).

In the brief section before us two points are emphasized: first, that in the Holy War of conquest the real victor would be Yahweh and Israel was only His agent; secondly, since it would be Yahweh who gave the victory Israel ought not to claim that she was led to victory because of some inherent virtue or righteousness she possessed. Only Yahweh possessed righteousness. Alternatively, there was the fact of the unrighteousness of the peoples of Canaan. But Israel did not feature in any comparison, as though Yahweh would give the victory to the more righteous of two contending parties. Comparative righteousness is, in any case, hard to assess.

1, 2. There is a grand optimism in the call to Israel (*cf.*

1:28–30; 20:2–5). The greatness of the opposition is here described in typical hyperbolic terms. The nations are *greater and mightier* than Israel. Their cities are *great and fortified up to heaven*. The only group of enemies mentioned is the most redoubtable of all, the *Anakim*, of whom legend said that they were giants of whom people asked, *Who can stand before the sons of Anak?* Such heightened language served to enhance the prestige of Yahweh who was able to overcome even such foes as these (*cf.* 2:10).

3. Yahweh is now presented as *a devouring fire* who would overthrow these foes and drive them out. There are no provisos here, such as occur in 7:22. The urgent call to immediate battle leaves no time for detailed discussion of the length of time the task will take. Clearly, if Yahweh had promised a land to the patriarchs and that land was occupied by other peoples, there would need to be a conquest which involved a Holy War.

4a. How would Israel interpret such a victory? She might argue that, although the victory was Yahweh's alone, it was yet a victory which belonged to Israel by right. The great word *righteousness* is now introduced. As we have seen (6:21–25) the term connotes what is 'right', 'standard', 'normal'. There are things that are 'right' for God and things that are 'right' for man. In courts of law the innocent man was declared to be 'in the right' (*ṣaddîq*), and the guilty man was declared to be 'in the wrong' (*rāšā'*). On the world-scale Yahweh was engaged in establishing what was 'right' from His viewpoint. In the present instance it was 'right' that Yahweh should assist His people to possess the land, for this was the divine promise. It was occupied by people who were 'in the wrong'. In the active prosecution of His purpose to make things 'right' Yahweh led Israel in the Holy War. When Israel finally occupied the land, it was not for her to argue that she must have been 'in the right' herself and that Yahweh was therefore bound to give her the land as a reward for her 'righteousness'. In fact she was far from being 'in the right' (*cf.* verse 6). Her 'rights' in the matter were never under discussion. God had His own purposes to work out. In working these out He would display His own *righteousness*. He was 'in the right' by nature, and He would actively establish 'right' in His world. To do this, He, as the righteous Lord, might call and use human agents such as Israel to bring under judgment those who were 'wicked' or 'in the wrong'. It was a facet of His righteousness to display such elements as 'wrath', 'jealousy' and 'anger'. In the Holy War Yahweh was actively and righteously at work.

4b, 5. Two factors operated, the righteousness of Yahweh and the unrighteousness of the people of Canaan. What the future might hold for Israel was in God's hands. Since she had been chosen to fulfil Yahweh's purpose, the fulfilment of His purpose would require a victory. However, Yahweh was sovereign and He might choose even the ungodly nations to fulfil His purposes at times (*cf.* Assyria in Is. 10:5, 13, 15; Babylon, Je. 25:9; 27:6; Persia, Is. 44:28; 45:1–6). The two reasons given here for the conquest of Canaan are the *wickedness of these nations* (*cf.* Gn. 15:16), and *that he may confirm the word which the Lord swore to your fathers*.

6. Indeed, Israel's claim to righteousness is expressly rejected. Far from being righteous Israel is declared to be *stubborn* (lit. 'hard of neck'). That Yahweh should have persisted with such a nation was only because of His great love (*cf.* 7:6–8; *cf.* Rom. 5:6–8).

iv. The stubbornness of Israel (9:7–29).

The fact of Israel's stubbornness is now illustrated by glimpses into her past experiences. The main incident alluded to is that of the golden calf (8–21). Others are alluded to briefly (22, 23). There are many parallels between the narrative here and that in Exodus 24:12–18 and Exodus 32 and 34, including some direct quotations. In fact the present narrative may be regarded as a free re-telling of the Exodus story.[1]

In retrospect, the intercession of Moses (18–20, 25–29) is set over against the rebellion of Israel (7–17, 21–24). In this way the love and mercy of Yahweh for Israel are underlined.

7, 8. Memory and forgetfulness stand in sharp contrast once again. The double imperative, one stated positively and one negatively, adds weight to what follows, namely, that Israel had *provoked* Yahweh *to wrath* (or judgment) from the day they came out of Egypt. This was a stern reminder to Israel that any claim to righteousness was mere pretence. The supreme example of Israel's rebellion took place *at Horeb* (Sinai) soon after she had willingly accepted the terms of the covenant (Ex. 32–34). The story is now retold in verses 9–21.

9–11. The *tables of stone* or *tables of the covenant* were the 'documents' on which the covenant was recorded. This was in

---

[1] See S. R. Driver, *Deuteronomy* (*ICC*, 1902), pp. 112–114, for direct parallels and divergences.

the manner of the Near Eastern treaties where the treaties were recorded on *tablets*. Perhaps the same term is intended here – hence translate 'tablets of stone'. (See 5:22; Ex. 31:18; *cf*. Ex. 32:15f.; 34:1.)

Several elements of this narrative sound strange to Western ears: lack of food and drink for forty days, the presentation of stone slabs to Moses by God, and the writing on stone slabs by the finger of God. Such language is common in the Old Testament and is typical of the East. It is open to ask the question, for example, whether the figure *forty* may perhaps denote something like 'for a considerable time' or even 'a solemn period of waiting or preparation' (*cf*. Gn. 7:4; 1 Ki. 19:8; Jon. 3:4; Mt. 4:2; Acts 1:3). The expression occurs in non-biblical literature in the Moabite Stone, line 8. Again, it is common in the Old Testament to ascribe events to the activity of God when, in fact, the events were performed by His agents, although the credit was given to Him. Thus the conquest of Canaan was His work, although it was undertaken by Israel. In this chapter Yahweh is described as 'thrusting out' the peoples of Canaan (4). Our Western minds seek too readily to give literalist and materialist explanations of such expressions. Might not the passage mean simply that, during a period of solemn preoccupation with a holy task and under the guidance of God, it was Moses who both selected the stones and wrote upon them? Yet he could claim that God gave him the stones and that his writing upon them was none other than God's writing. It is not unknown in our modern speech for men and women to use such expressions as 'The Lord opened the door for me', or 'The Lord obtained a visa for me', *etc*. Such anthropomorphisms are necessary in view of our human limitations if we are to apprehend, even in a limited way, the mystery of the person and work of God. (See commentary on 5:22.)

12–14. Hardly was the task completed when Moses was overwhelmed by a sense of urgency to return to the Israelite camp where the people whom he had brought from Egypt had made a *molten image* (Ex. 32:7–10, 15, 19, 20) and were engaged in activities which demonstrated clearly that they had broken their covenant and had given their allegiance to another. This would result in the operation of the curses of the covenant, two of which are mentioned here, destruction of persons and the blotting out of their names from the memory of men. In that setting Yahweh suggested that He could equally well fulfil His purposes through Moses and his descendants who were, of course, descendants of Abraham.

The nature of the golden calf calls for some comment. It was, in any case, a contravention of the second commandment (5:8). It has been suggested that this image is to be compared with images of beasts in other Near Eastern religions which acted as supporting pedestals for deities. Several excellent examples of these are extant today.[1] In particular the storm god of Canaan stood on the back of a bull. Other deities stood on other animals. The animal was not intended as an object of worship but as a symbol of the deity. In some examples in the ancient Near East animals appear alone, but the context suggests that they symbolize a deity.[2] The attempt to symbolize Yahweh's presence among His people by a golden calf could only lead to deep confusion, for it suggested idolatry even if the intention was to give encouragement to the faint-hearted in Israel by symbolizing Yahweh's presence among them.

15-17. When Moses came down from the mountain carrying the covenant document in his hands he discovered that the covenant had been broken already. He confirmed this breach of covenant by smashing the covenant document. That such a procedure was followed in the case of treaty breaches in the ancient Near East is attested in a number of extant documents.[3] If the covenant were subsequently renewed a new document was required.

18, 19. The motif of the *forty days and forty nights* appears again, this time denoting a lengthy period of intercession by Moses. Through her breach of the covenant Israel made herself liable to the curses of the covenant (19). The fear of such consequences led Moses to intercede with Yahweh on behalf of the people. The content of the prayer is given in verses 25-29. The other verses in this section (20-24) are really a parenthesis.

20. Moses' intercession for Aaron is not mentioned in Exodus. This is surprising, because it was Aaron who made the golden calf (Ex. 32:1-6) and one would expect judgment to fall on him. But even Israel's High Priest had to be snatched from judgment, according to Deuteronomy. How completely

---

[1] *ANEP*, pictures 470-474, 500, 501, 522, 534, 537.
[2] O. R. Gurney, *The Hittites* (1964), pp. 134, 149.
[3] E. F. Weidner, 'Politische Dokumente aus Kleinasien', *Boghazkoi Studien*, 1923, vols. 8, 9. See Treaty of Šuppiluliumaš and Šunaššura, IV, lines 25f.; Treaty of Hattušiliš III and Bentešina, lines 24f.

devoid of merit, therefore, and how dependent on the mercy of God was a people whose very High Priest had to be saved from death. The incident is mentioned here not necessarily in chronological order but because of the point that it makes in the context of a discussion on Israel's rebellion.

21. Moses' action in smashing *the sinful thing* provides a strong illustration of the proper line of action to be followed in such cases. There are numerous injunctions throughout Deuteronomy to destroy all cult objects (*cf.* 7:5, 25; 12:3, *etc.*).

22-24. The Horeb incident did not stand alone. There were the incidents at *Taberah* (Nu. 11:1-3) where the people complained, at *Massah* where God was put to the test when the people lacked water (6:16; Ex. 17:1-7; Nu. 20:10-13), at *Kibroth-hattaavah* where the people complained about manna (Nu. 11:31-34), and at *Kadesh-barnea* where gross unbelief was displayed when the spies brought back their report (1:21-36; Nu. 13; 14). In every case Israel questioned God's plan for her life. They neither believed His promises nor obeyed His commands.

25-29. After the topical digressions, the story returns to Moses' mediatorial and intercessory prayer. Had it not been for Moses' intercession and God's forbearance Israel would have perished at Horeb. She was spared only to rebel again and again. The incident of Horeb should have revealed her stubborn character, and the prevailing prayer of Moses and the mercy of Yahweh should have encouraged her to show proper loyalty to her sovereign Lord. Alas, her character was refractory. She needed the continuing forbearance of God and the repeated intercession of Moses to preserve her. Moses fulfilled a multiple function. He was Israel's charismatic leader, her mediator to stand between her and God (5:23-29), her intercessor (Ex. 32:11-14, 31, 32; 33:12-16; Nu. 14:13-19) and even the one who suffered because of Israel's sin (1:37; 3:23-29; *cf.* Ex. 32:32). See commentary on 3:23-29. The details of Moses' prayer are significant. He reminded God that this was the people He had *redeemed* (*pāḍâ*) from Egypt *with a mighty hand* (26). Moreover, from this same people had come those who were obedient, Abraham, Isaac, Jacob. Further, if destruction befell this people the Egyptians would mock and say that He who took them from Egypt was not able to lead them to the land of promise (28). Therefore, in spite of the stubborn wickedness of this people (27), and out of regard both for His own prestige and authority among the nations, and for the sake of His promise to the fathers, God was implored to stay His hand of judgment. If He now destroyed Israel, even though such an action would be but the outcome of a broken covenant, and even if He later fulfilled His promises to the fathers in another way, His action would be misunderstood. For the exodus was at once a judgment on sinful Egypt and the redemption of His own oppressed people, His heritage. If He did not bring His redemption to completion by delivering His people to the land of promise, men would lose their fear of Him, thinking that His powers were limited. The covenant sanctions of cursing and blessing would be held in contempt.

Moses' role as intercessor stands out strongly here (*cf.* Ex. 32:11-14, 31, 32; 33:12-16; 34:9; Nu. 14:13-19). While his total work for Israel was extraordinarily many-sided, his work as an intercessor was outstanding. Indeed, the biblical picture is that, had it not been for Moses' selfless intercession and God's merciful forbearance, the nation would have been destroyed. Moses takes his place with those of whom it is said in James 5:16, 'The prayer of a righteous man has great power in its effects.' (*Cf.* Abraham in Gn. 18:23-32; Samuel in 1 Sa. 8:6-9, 21, 22; 12:7, 17f.; Elijah in 1 Ki. 18:36-39; Daniel in Dn. 6:10; the Christians in Acts 4:23-31.) The example of many in Old Testament and New Testament alike and the call to intercessory prayer (1 Thes. 5:17; 1 Tim. 2:8, *etc.*) remain with the modern believer. 'More things are wrought by prayer than this world dreams of' (Tennyson). God's merciful forbearance towards sinful men is closely linked with consistent intercession.

v. Covenant renewal (10:1-11). In the secular realm the renewal of a covenant after its breach involved the preparation of new treaty documents and the taking of a new oath of allegiance. So it was with Israel (Ex. 34:1-4). In the following verses we have a very condensed account of the incident without special attention to exact chronology. It was sufficient to draw attention to some of the more important features of those events which presumably everyone knew about. Moses wished to move on to the conclusion of the argument and the important question, 'And now what does Yahweh require of you?' (12).

1-4. In these verses the account of the construction of the ark as the lodging-place of the stone tablets is interwoven with the account of the preparation and engraving of the tablets which were later to be deposited there. The section has a summarizing purpose and is designed to state in a comprehensive and general way that God in His mercy had renewed the covenant with His rebellious people. The ark is mentioned as being the place where the covenant document was lodged. Things which belonged together are here linked together without strict attention to chronological order or the lapse of time. In fact, the whole procedure took some time, for the documents had to be prepared, the ark had to be made, and the tabernacle prepared. Details are given in Exodus 35:30ff.; 36:2; 37:1; 40:20, 21. For the expressions *I will write on the tables the words that were on the first tables* . . . (2) and *he wrote on the tables, as at the first writing* (4), see commentary on 9:9–11.

The requirement that the covenant document was to be housed in the ark is a reflection of secular practice in the ancient Near East. It was normal to lodge copies of the treaty document in the sanctuaries of the contracting parties, where they were under the surveillance of the deities who would guarantee the treaty, and, in case of a breach of treaty, would visit the offending party with judgment. Incidentally, references to the ark are rare in Deuteronomy. It is referred to only here and in 31:26, which is surprising, since it seems to have played an important role in the life of Israel.[1] But this may be because the book of Deuteronomy is more concerned with the covenant itself than with details about the construction of the ark or the rituals associated with the central sanctuary. These rituals were, in any case, only an expression of allegiance and reverence to Yahweh, the God of the covenant. It is to be noted that the new tables were to be identical with the first ones which Moses broke, *i.e.* it was the same covenant that was renewed after Yahweh had granted forgiveness to the people (verse 4 presupposes 9:19 and 10:10). Yahweh had but one covenant with His people, which arose out of the same mighty acts of deliverance and made the same demands upon them. Even in the great day of renewal envisaged by Jeremiah (Je. 31:31–34) it is the same law that is to be written on the heart, the eternal law of God. The sense in which the law would be new in that day would be that it would be differently administered, it would have a different mediator, and it would be written on the heart, but it would be fundamentally the same covenant. The great theme in Moses' day was 'I will be

[1] See R. de Vaux, *Ancient Israel* (1962), pp. 297–302 for a helpful discussion on 'the Ark of the Covenant'.

your God, and you will be my people' (Lv. 26:12), and 'I will take you for my people, and I will be your God' (Ex. 6:7). The same formula is taken up in apostolic days (2 Cor. 6:16) and in the Apocalypse (Rev. 21:3). However, while the formula remains the same, it becomes filled with fresh meaning as the centuries unfold until it acquires such deep significance that the old covenant can hardly be recognized in it, so that it is called a 'new covenant'.

5. A further series of events which took place over a period of time is reported in a very condensed sentence.

6, 7. This small fragment is reported in the third person as a parenthesis in the main argument. If Deuteronomy assumed its final shape some time after Moses, then these two verses may be regarded as a fragment of an old itinerary quoted from an unknown source and preserved here. Its origin is not known, nor, indeed, the reason for inserting it here. The sites *Beeroth Bene-jaakan* (the wells of Bene Ja'akan) and *Moserah* are known in Numbers 33:30-32, where they are in the reverse order. Variant lists of places visited during the journey evidently existed. The Old Testament is not always interested in exact order or in exact chronology (*cf.* the order of the temptations in Matthew 4 and Luke 4 in the New Testament). The wells of Bene Ja'akan are possibly the modern El Birein, some 12 miles north of Kadesh-barnea (Ain Kadesh), while Moserah is possibly to be sought about 10 miles to the east at 'Abde or Wadi Harouniyyeh.

Deuteronomy records the death of Aaron at this point. Elsewhere it is said to have taken place at Mount Hor, 'on the border of the land of Edom' (32:50; Nu. 20:22-29). The two areas are approximately the same. An interesting conjecture was made a century ago[1] that Numbers 33:36b-41a once stood after verse 30a and that the original order of the stations was: Wilderness of Zin (Kadesh), Mount Hor, Moseroth, Bene Ja'akan, Hor-haggidgad, Jotbathah, Abronah, Ezion Geber, Zalmonah, *etc.* In that case Moserah was close to Mount Hor. The note, *and his son Eleazar ministered as priest in his stead*, indicates that not only did God restore the covenant but He also restored the priesthood of Aaron, and despite Aaron's sin at Sinai, invested his son with his high office on his death. This was grace and mercy indeed.

8. After the parenthesis of verses 6 and 7 we are referred

[1] By H. Ewald. See S. R. Driver, *Deuteronomy* (*ICC*, 1902), p. 119.

back to events at Horeb (5). Details are given in Exodus 32:25-29, where the consecration of the tribe of Levi is mentioned. Levi was set apart for the sacred duties of the tabernacle because of zeal on Yahweh's behalf. While the high-priestly duties at the central sanctuary were confined to Aaron's family, the task of guarding the law and the ark where the covenant documents were housed was committed to the Levites. Compare Numbers 3 and 4 for details about the consecration of the Levites. Through the centuries that followed, the Levites, scattered throughout the land, must have undertaken a great deal of faithful ministry. It is not at all unlikely that groups of faithful Levites preserved the true covenant faith in days of apostasy. Three principal functions of the Levites are here outlined: a. *to carry the ark* (Nu. 3:31; 4:15), the special task of the Kohathites, a non-priestly family of the Levites. The ark is more fully described as *the ark of the covenant of Yahweh*, *i.e.* the ark containing the covenant document, the tables of the law; b. *to stand before Yahweh to minister to him, etc.* The phrase *stand before* is an idiom meaning 'wait upon', 'serve'. It is used of many kinds of service in the Old Testament, a vassal and his overlord, a prophet and God, a priest and God (17:12; Jdg. 20:28; 1 Ki. 10:8; 12:8; 17:1; 18:15; Je. 52:12; Ezk. 44:15). This task is here confined to the priestly Levites (18:5; 21:5; Nu. 6:23f.). The non-priestly Levites, however, assisted them (18:7); c. *to bless in his name*, a duty confined to the priestly Levites (21:5; Lv. 9:22; Nu. 6:23). On rare occasions this duty was also performed by kings (2 Sa. 6:18; 1 Ki. 8:14, 55). For a fuller discussion on the place of the Levites see commentary on 18:1-8.

9. Because of these responsibilities the tribe of Levi had no inheritance in the land, *i.e.* no areas of land were allotted to them from which they might gain their support. Rather the tribe of Levi was maintained by sacred dues and other offerings made to the Lord by the people. This is the meaning of the expression *Yahweh is his inheritance* (*cf.* 12:12b; 14:27b, 29; 18:1). Despite the expression *as Yahweh your God said to him*, there is no record in the Pentateuch of such an utterance having been addressed to the whole tribe of Levi. In Numbers 18:20 the phrase is addressed to Aaron but this, no doubt, was taken to refer to the whole tribe, as the following verses 21-24 suggest.

10, 11. The results of Moses' intercession are summed up (9:18, 25). Once again Yahweh withheld His hand of judgment (*that time also*; *cf.* 9:19). Instead, Moses was commanded to resume the journey at the head of the people.

f. A call to commitment: what does the Lord your God require of you? (10:12 – 11:32)

The expression, *And now*, is common in contexts where, after a recital of what God has done, the people needed to be brought to a point of personal decision on the issue (*cf.* 4:1; Ex. 19:5; Jos. 24:14, *etc.*). This amounted to a choice between the blessing and the curse (11:26–32). It was none other than Yahweh their God who was calling them to obedience. He was the Judge of the whole earth, whose impartial judgment had already been known in Egypt and in the wilderness (11:1–7) and would yet be known in Canaan (11:8–25). What, then, did Yahweh, Israel's God, require of His people? In brief, total allegiance to Him and obedience to His covenant demands.

i. What does the Lord your God require of you? (10:12–22).
12, 13. The rhetorical question *And now, Israel, what does Yahweh your God require of you?* should be compared with Micah 6:8. God's total requirement is summarized under five demands, *fear* (reverence) him, *walk in all his ways*, *love him*, *serve* him with one's whole being, and *keep* his *commandments and statutes*. The verbs *fear* (reverence), *walk*, *love*, *serve* and *keep* recur many times in Deuteronomy (*e.g.* 6:13f.; 10:12, 20; 11:22; 13:4, *etc.*). They represent interrelated attitudes. Basic to all obedience are reverence for and love of God (6:4–19). Men in whom these attitudes are found will *walk* in God's ways, *serve* Him and *keep* His laws. The man who loves God will serve Him and observe His laws, for no man can claim to love God while neglecting to keep His law. Worship and life are inseparable. The further point is made that God's law is not a burden to be borne, but God's gracious provision for Israel's *good* (13). To live well means to obey God's law, and to obey presupposes a reverent love for Him who gave the law (*cf.* 11:1–25).

14, 15. Why should Israel respond to Yahweh her God with such complete allegiance? The depths are plumbed in the answer that follows. It was not merely because of His saving acts or because Israel's good was bound up with such obedience.

The real reason was more profound. Israel was to love God because God first loved her. Here is a magnificent picture of the grandeur of God to whom belong the heavens and the earth. The contrast with insignificant Israel is striking. Yet Yahweh loved her. The terms in which God's complete independence is described are superlatives. The phrase *the heaven of heavens*, *i.e.* the highest heaven, exhausts the idea of heaven. To God belongs not merely heaven but the highest heaven. The earth and all that is in it are His also. God would seem to be beyond every personal need. Were He to seek for the companionship of men we might expect Him to choose great and powerful nations. But He who inhabits eternity (Is. 57:15), to whom belong the cattle on a thousand hills (Ps. 50:10), and before whom the nations are as a drop from a bucket (Is. 40:15), loved Israel above all others. Here is deep mystery. It is for this reason basically that Israel should respond to Him in reverence and in love. Yahweh set His love upon the fathers and chose their descendants after them. In particular, He chose those who stood there that day (*cf.* 7:6–11). This point is made grammatically by the sharp disjunctive and restrictive adverb *yet*, or 'only' (*raq*), which makes a vivid contrast between the whole universe and this one small group of people of whom it is said that *Yahweh set his heart in love upon* them. The verb denotes 'be attached to', 'have pleasure or delight in'. Why He should desire to love specifically the patriarchs remains a mystery hidden in the divine mind.

The Christian is reminded at once of the many statements in the New Testament about God's love towards His children. In particular the love of Christ for those whom He has redeemed is stressed again and again (Jn. 3:16; 13:1; Gal. 2:20; Eph. 2:4; 5:2, 25; 2 Thes. 2:16; 1 Jn. 4:10, 11; Rev. 1:5). It is important for a Christian to realize that in the New Testament the Christian church (Gk. *ekklēsia*) is regarded as the true people of God (Jas. 1:1; 1 Pet. 2:5, 9, 10). Christians are the true 'Jews' (Rom. 2:29; *cf.* Rev. 2:9), Israel (Rom. 9:6), Israel after the Spirit (Rom. 8:1–11), the seed of Abraham (Gal. 3:29), the Israel of God (Gal. 6:16), the circumcision (Phil. 3:3; Col. 2:11), the peculiar people (Tit. 2:14; 1 Pet. 2:9f.; *cf.* Ex. 19:5). The early church did not regard itself as a sect within the larger 'Israel' of Judaism, or as a new or different people of God. In Paul's imagery of the olive tree in Romans 11, he sees only one Israel into which the Gentiles are grafted so that there is no difference between the church and Israel.

The true Israel was constituted through a faith relationship and not merely on the basis of physical descent.[1]

16. The metaphor of circumcision is now employed in reference to the heart. An uncircumcised heart is one which is, as it were, closed in and impervious to God's incoming, just as an uncircumcised ear (Je. 6:10) is one which hears imperfectly being covered over, and uncircumcised lips (Ex. 6:12, 30) are lips which speak incoherently because they are sealed wholly or in part. If that which hinders is cut away (the parallel with physical circumcision is obvious), then the circumcised heart becomes open and, being freed from hindering obstructions, it can become pliable and amenable to the direction of God. The result of such a circumcision will be submission to the will of God and the end of stubbornness. Nothing less befits the inscrutable, electing love of Yahweh. Indeed, without circumcision of the heart true fear of God and true love of God are both impossible. Paul was to declare in a later day, 'We are the true circumcision, who worship God in spirit, and glory in Christ Jesus, and put no confidence in the flesh' (Phil. 3:3; *cf.* Rom. 2:25–29). See the closing paragraph of the comments on verses 14, 15, above.

17, 18. The majesty of Yahweh and His awful justice provided a further motive for obedience. Clearly, this is the God with whom Christians also have to do. In the presence of such an one we are exhorted in the words of Hebrews 12:28f.: 'Let us offer to God acceptable worship, with reverence and awe; for our God is a consuming fire.' It is of particular interest that much of Hebrews is concerned, like Deuteronomy, with the exodus and the wilderness wandering. The writer of Hebrews, some 1,400 years after those original events, was still moved with deep reverence and awe.

The remarkable accumulation of titles for God in verse 17 was designed, no doubt, to emphasize the uniqueness, absolute supremacy and total sovereignty of Yahweh over every other power in the universe. Yahweh is *God of gods* and *Lord of lords, i.e.* supreme God and supreme Lord, the unrestricted Ruler over all powers in heaven and earth (Ps. 95:3). These were not merely honorific titles such as might be used in a polytheistic religion, but were basically an affirmation of monotheism. Once it is accepted that no other gods or lords have power or significance beside Yahweh and that He alone is worthy of worship and devotion, polytheism is ruled out. The further

[1] See E. Earle Ellis, *Paul's Use of the Old Testament* (1957), pp. 136–139.

statement, that Yahweh is *great*, *mighty*, and to be feared (*terrible*), would remind Israel of the mighty acts of deliverance which He wrought in the days of the exodus. The adjective *mighty* (*gibbōr*) is commonly used of a warrior, and seems to have overtones of the Holy War in which Yahweh as leader in battle displayed the qualities of a warrior (Ps. 24:8; Is. 9:6; 10:21; 42:13; Je. 20:11). Overtones both of reverence and of fear may also be suspected in the use of this adjective. A God who could visit the refractory pharaoh of Egypt with such varied and effective judgments was certainly both to be feared and reverenced. Again, Yahweh was impartial (lit. 'he does not lift up faces'). He pays no respect to individuals. Before His bar of justice all men stand equal. With Him there will be no miscarriage of justice through bribery.

On the positive and active side, and as another aspect of His 'righteousness', He is concerned to establish justice for those who are weak and defenceless, the *fatherless*, the *widow*, and the *sojourner*, or resident alien (*gēr*).[1] Of the latter it is said that Yahweh 'loves' him and provides for him. The group of resident aliens is always in danger of oppression, whether in ancient Israel or in modern society. Both in Deuteronomy and in other parts of the Old Testament Israel is urged to show kindness to such people (1:16; 10:19; 24:14, 17; 27:19; Ex. 23:9). In many passages he is included, as here, with the fatherless and the widow as an object of care (14:29; 24:17–22; 26:11–13). In other passages he is included with the Israelite as enjoying the benefits of the covenant, so that he too was expected to observe the festivals and to keep the law (16:11, 14; 26:11; 29:10, 11; 31:12). Clearly the Christian is no different from Israel in this respect and the emphasis of this verse on social concern is equally applicable. The New Testament has much to say about the responsibility of Christians in this regard, either directly or by implication (Rom. 12:13; 1 Cor. 16:1f.; 2 Cor. 8:1–6; Jas. 1:27; 2:1–7).

19. One reason for loving the resident alien is to be inferred from the above discussion: he is to be loved because God loves him. Another reason is now given. Israel had known what it was to be a resident alien in Egypt and could appreciate the importance of such loving concern (5:15; 15:15; 16:12; 24:18–22). The injunction 'Thou shalt love thy neighbour as thyself', though not stated formally in Deuteronomy, is clearly

[1] This claim is not unique. Mesopotamian literature has examples of kings who expressed concern for the welfare of widows and orphans.

presented in principle. Such an injunction was evidently known in Israel, to judge from Leviticus 19:18.

20. *Cf.* verses 12, 13.

21, 22. Yahweh is described finally in two ways. *He is your praise, i.e.* He is to be the object of Israel's praise. And again, *He is your God,* the One who carried out mighty deeds of deliverance. Israel had been witness of these acts of God, not specifically the people who were present on the plains of Moab (1:5; 29:1), but Israel as a nation. In fact, the older generation of those who were physically present at the exodus died in the wilderness. According to Numbers 14:29, 30 none of those who were twenty years old and upward at the time of the rejection of the advice of Joshua and Caleb, following the report of the spies, would enter the promised land. Presumably, therefore, those under twenty had the possibility of entering. But it was still true of the nation at any time that, as a nation, she had witnessed those acts of divine omnipotence which had filled men with fear and trembling. Not the least of His marvellous acts was that Yahweh had transformed a tiny group of seventy individuals (Ex. 1:5) into a nation of some size. The expression *as the stars of heaven for multitude* is a typical piece of Eastern hyperbole (1:10; 28:62). This fact in itself constituted a reason for Yahweh's claim on Israel for her gratitude and loyalty.

ii. An appeal to the past. The relation of obedience to blessing (11:1–9). With chapter 11 the discussion of the broad principles that were to govern the life of Israel is drawn to a close. The chapter is to be understood as a re-emphasis of these principles before the detailed laws of the so-called Deuteronomic Code (12:1 – 26:19) are presented. The logic of the argument in chapters 5 to 11 may be presented as follows: general introduction centring around the ten commandments (chapter 5); statement and discussion of general principles (chapters 6 and 7); important lessons from history (chapters 8 – 10:11); the divine demand (10:12–22); concluding peroration (chapter 11).

Broadly, chapter 11 deals with the importance of the choice which lies before Israel – obedience or disobedience. Israel is exhorted to obey God in full recognition of the fact that disobedience leads to unhappy consequences (1–9). There is a close link between obedience and the successful development of the land of promise (10–17, 22–25). Children should be taught these important facts (18–21). The final choice before

Israel was obedience or disobedience, blessing or cursing (26-32).

1. This verse links back to the section 10:12-22, where the second singular pronoun is used. The use of the second singular may make the appeal more personal. Comparison with 8:1 is instructive (although 8:1 is plural). In each case a generalized call to obedience is given followed by an appeal to the experience of the past. Here the twin command is *love Yahweh your God* and *keep his charge*. The two are closely interrelated, as we have seen. The word *charge* (*mišmeret*) occurs only here in Deuteronomy. Elsewhere in the Old Testament it refers to Yahweh's demands in regard to religious observances (Lv. 8:35; 18:30; 22:9; Nu. 9:19, 23), or more generally to any demand Yahweh may make (Gn. 26:5; Jos. 22:3; 1 Ki. 2:3).

2-4. The audience addressed on the plains of Moab was very different from that which had witnessed God's mighty acts in the days of the exodus. All the older generation had died in the wilderness and of those who had escaped from Egypt, only the younger generation under twenty years of age at the time remained (Nu. 14:29. *Cf.* commentary on 10:21, 22). To these were now added all those who had been born during the wilderness wandering. The people then assembled at Moab had known something of God's wonderful activity, either directly or by hearsay. Moses addressed them all and urged them to consider the *discipline* (*mûsār*) of the Lord, *i.e.* His instruction. A series of nouns in the accusative case now follows, as though these constituted the instruction – *his greatness, his mighty hand and his outstretched arm, his signs and his deeds which he did in Egypt to Pharaoh.* The range of terms used here occurs elsewhere in the Old Testament and seems to represent a standardized form of expression (3:24; 4:34; 6:22; 7:8, 19; 9:26). Each has reference to the divine judgment on Egypt. There was instruction here for the discerning man of Israel.

5-7. Attention is directed to incidents during the wilderness wanderings. In particular the episode of *Dathan and Abiram* is mentioned (Nu. 16). These men rebelled against the authority of Moses, Yahweh's chosen leader, and were destroyed with their families and possessions when the earth swallowed them up. The narrative in Deuteronomy does not refer to Korah. The lesson was, of course, that refusal to acknowledge the man whom God appointed leader was equivalent to rejection of God Himself. The rejection of God's chosen leader is not confined to this story alone in the Old Testament. It was a common experience of prophets such as Amos (Am. 7:12–16), Jeremiah (Je. 1:18f., *etc.*), Ezekiel (Ezk. 3:4–9). The climax to such activity came with the rejection of the Lord Jesus Himself, as the Gospels testify again and again. But the tendency is universal and arises from man's unwillingness to accept the status of creature under divine sovereignty.

8, 9. The word *therefore* underlines the fact that Yahweh's claim to Israel's obedience rests on what He has done for them. The conjunction *in order that* (*l^ema^c an*) adds a strong contingency. The fulfilment of the divine promise was not automatic. If need be God could fulfil His promise through Moses alone and thereafter through his descendants (*cf.* 9:14). The promise rested not merely on physical descent but supremely on obedience.

iii. Yahweh's blessing in the land of promise only for obedient people (11:10–25).

A comparison is drawn between Egypt and the promised land. In Egypt the land yielded its crops in response to the efforts of men, who merely needed to irrigate their lands with the abundant waters of the Nile. In Canaan, where there was no irrigation, the people would have to depend on God for water. If Israel loved and served Yahweh in obedience to His commands, He would heap the blessings of nature upon her. Disobedience and rebellion, however, would result in lack of rain and consequent lack of agricultural yields.

10. The Israelites during the period of oppression in Egypt had been engaged in all manner of service in the field and had thus become acquainted with Egyptian methods of agriculture (Ex. 1:14). The Nile, fed by the snows of Central Africa, provided abundant water which was conveyed to the farmlands along canals and channels. The water was lifted from the river by a simple arrangement of a container at the end of a balanced pole, the *shaduf*, and poured into larger channels from whence it ran into a complex of smaller and smaller channels. As various areas received sufficient water the small channel was closed off by pushing earth across it with the *feet*. Subsequently, water could be admitted to the same channel by kicking away the small blockage of earth. Egypt was *like a garden of vegetables* (green plants), which required constant care but yielded magnificent crops. The continuous expenditure of human effort would tend to create the impression that the high productivity of the land was due entirely to human industry.

11, 12. The new land Canaan was a rugged land without the natural advantages of Egypt with its constant supply of water, so that it owed any prosperity it had to the rain which Yahweh Himself sent. It was a test of faith to depend on Yahweh alone. Hence the land of promise became a land of religious significance for Israel.

13-15. If Israel loved and served Yahweh with her whole being (*heart* and *soul*), Yahweh would grant her the regular sequence of rains in their season, *the early rain* (*yôreh*), which came as heavy downpours in October–November, and *the later rain* (*malqôš*), which appeared as storms in March–April. The autumn rains in October–November broke the summer drought and made ploughing possible. The spring rains in March–April were the last before the summer and brought a green coat to the whole land. Between these two periods there was other rain in normal seasons. Indeed, the rain that fell between the two kinds of rain described here was, in some ways, the most important and it came in storms and showers during the whole rainy period.[1] The later rain was indispensable for fruit trees and for settling the harvest. But granted this, the farmers gathered in their grain, grapes and olives to provide food for the people. The rains also ensured pastures for the beasts and flocks.

16, 17. If Israel attributed these blessings to other gods, such as Baal, Hadad, *etc.* (*cf.* Ho. 2:7–14), Yahweh would withdraw them from His people, for that would be tantamount to breach of covenant and would result in the operation of the curses of the covenant. Lack of rain, failure of the crops, and the destruction of life were standard curses all over the ancient Near East and are written into many of the treaties which have been preserved for us. These verses give expression to the belief, which is found in many areas of the Old Testament, that there was a close connection between loyalty and obedience to Yahweh and material blessing (*cf.* Am. 4:6–10). God was sovereign over both nature and history and could make the weather and other natural phenomena serve historical ends (Gn. 6–9; 1 Ki. 17:1; Joel 2:11; Am. 4:7; Hg. 2:17; *cf.* 1 Cor. 11:29f.; Jas. 5:17f.). This is a difficult doctrine to interpret in particular cases, and is of a piece with the view that suffering is the result of sin (*e.g.* Job). It often happens that men prosper despite great sin, and a land often enjoys great natural productivity even while its people reject the sovereignty of God. The

[1] See article 'Rain', *NBD*, pp. 1074f.

doctrine does, however, give expression to a deeper truth, namely, that nature itself is under God's sovereignty and the phenomena of nature are, in some way, an expression of His will. If a faithful people could learn by means of this doctrine to give thanks to God for every bountiful harvest, and allow every natural misfortune to become an occasion for heart searching and repentance for any evil thing in their lives, then the doctrine, despite its difficulties, is not merely one that gives light on God as Judge, but is also of considerable practical importance. It enables God's people to hold firmly to such views as that nature is not independent of God, that a rich productivity in flock and field is a cause for gratitude and praise to God, and that seasons of drought and low agricultural yield are powerful stimuli to forsake all known evil. In any case, there is always need for repentance in some area of life. If prosperity makes men forgetful, ungrateful and complacent, while the lack of natural and material blessings leads men to repentance, then these latter are a blessing in disguise.

18–21. Since obedience to Yahweh was fundamental for Israel's well-being, the commandments of Moses needed to be laid up in the heart of the present generation and carefully transmitted to future generations.

18–20. These verses are a repetition of 6:6–9 with slight variations. See commentary above.

21. Loyalty to the covenant would result in Israel's permanent possession of the promised land. The expression *as long as the heavens are above the earth* is a vivid way of saying 'for ever'. The divine promise sworn to the fathers would never fail for men who obeyed God. But, conversely, Israel would lose her land if she proved unfaithful.

22. It appears that there is a contingency in the fulfilment of the divine promise for any particular individual or generation. If God, in His purposes, intends to fulfil His promise ultimately, He is not bound to fulfil His promise in the case of a disobedient people. Hence Israel must take great care (Hebrew uses the so-called infinitive absolute to add emphasis to the verb) to do what God had commanded through Moses. But it is not mere formal legalistic obedience that God asks, but obedience based on love and close attachment to Yahweh.

23. See commentary on 7:1, 2; 9:1–6.

24. The extent of the land of promise vaguely outlined in 1:7 and here in 24a as *every place on which the sole of your foot treads* (*cf.* 2:5; Jos. 1:3; 14:9) is now defined in terms of the ideal limits *from the wilderness to*[1] *Lebanon*, *i.e.* from the Sinai area and the Negeb to the mountains of Lebanon from north to south, *and from the River, the river Euphrates, to the western sea* (the Mediterranean) from east to west. In fact, only in the days of David did Israel ever control anything like this area (*cf.* Gn. 15:18).

25. In the prosecution of the Holy War of conquest Yahweh would strike terror into the hearts of the foe (2:25; 7:21-24. *Cf.* Ex. 23:27).

iv. The call for decision and choice (11:26-32). The general principles which were to characterize Israel's approach to life have been carefully expounded in chapters 5 to 11. It is time to call for decision (*cf.* 30:15-20). Two ways present themselves – the way of obedience which will lead to blessing, and the way of disobedience which will lead to cursing. Neutrality on the issue is excluded. Israel is called to committal.

26. Some of the secular vassal treaties refer to both curses and blessings in the same document.[2] When a vassal accepted the treaty he accepted both. Which of the two was realized depended only on the vassal's behaviour toward his overlord.

27, 28. The attitude of Israel to the covenant stipulations of Yahweh was crucial. These verses draw attention to the fact that Israel could give her allegiance either to Yahweh or to *other gods which you have not known*. There may be some stress on the verb *know*, which often connotes a more intimate relationship than mere intellectual acquaintance (9:24; Gn. 4:17, 25; 19:5, 8; Ho. 8:2; 13:4; Am. 3:2; Na. 1:7; Pss. 36:10; 144:3, *etc.*). And, of course, it was Yahweh who had created Israel and nurtured her, not these other gods who were powerless to act. At the deepest level of her life it was Yahweh who *knew* Israel and who may be *known* by Israel.

29-32. These facts were to be of permanent significance for

[1] There is probably a scribal error here. The passage is defining the limits south–north and east–west. Hebrew has 'from the wilderness and Lebanon', but the sense is that these define the northern and southern limits. The second part of the text reads 'from . . . to . . .'. The translation here allows for the English sense.

[2] The secular vassal treaties are not consistent in this regard. Hittite treaties often have both (*ANET*, p. 205, in the treaty between Muršiliš and Duppi-Teššub; p. 206 in the treaty between Šuppiluliumaš and Mattiwaza). The Assyrian treaties publish the curses only (see D. J. Wiseman, 'The Vassal Treaties of Esarhaddon', *Iraq*, 20, 1958).

Israel, so that from time to time she should renew her covenant and hear again of the curses and the blessings. The covenant which was first entered into at Sinai (Ex. 19:1–8), and now renewed on the plains of Moab (29:1), would need to be renewed once Israel crossed the Jordan. That such a ceremony was eventually carried out is clear from Joshua 8:30–35. There is a parallel between the demand here and the requirements of the secular treaties. With the death of the former vassal, who was really the national leader of the vassal state, the new leader was required to renew his father's treaty. Israel, too, on the death of Moses and on the accession of Joshua, must renew her covenant with Yahweh. The parallel goes further. It was not uncommon for a king, some time before his death, to require his vassals to swear allegiance to his successor.[1] If Moses, the regent and representative of the great King, was soon to be succeeded by Joshua, then the covenant renewal at Moab might be seen as guaranteeing the succession of Joshua after Moses' death. Yahweh would, of course, remain King, but His sovereignty would be guaranteed in the change of leadership from Moses to Joshua if the covenant were renewed just prior to Moses' death. It would be renewed again when the land was finally occupied under Joshua's leadership (Jos. 24).

29. This topic is taken up in some detail in chapter 27. See commentary at that point. *Mount Gerizim* lies to the south and *Mount Ebal* to the north of the valley through which the road passes on the way from Shechem to Samaria. Shechem lay on the shoulder between the two, hence its name (Heb. *šekem* means 'shoulder'). The expression *set the blessing on Mount Gerizim and the curse on Mount Ebal* means, in the first instance, to proclaim them from these points. But there may have been some symbolic meaning too. Shechem and the two mountains lay at the very heart of the new land and there, at the focal point of the promised land, were the two silent witnesses to Yahweh's demand for Israel to choose where her allegiance would be placed. Gerizim being on the south, or on the right hand as one looked east, was on the side of favour and, there-fore, of blessing (Gn. 35:18, RSV mg.; Mt. 25:33). The relative positions of these two mountains should be identified on a map.[2]

---

[1] As in Esarhaddon's treaties with his vassals before his death. See D. J. Wiseman, *op. cit.*

[2] See *NBD*, map 4.

30. Some attempt is here made to define the position of Gerizim and Ebal more exactly. But the verse, which is in the form of a question, is obscure for us today, however lucid it may have been for those who first heard it. Four identifying features are given: a. *beyond the Jordan, i.e.* to the west of the Jordan from the viewpoint of Moab; b. *west of the road, toward the going down of the sun* (lit. 'behind the way of the going of the sun'), a difficult phrase. *Behind the way* denotes 'to the west of' or 'beyond' some particular road, perhaps the north–south trunk road which traverses western Palestine, so that the expression may mean simply 'beyond the western road'. The LXX reads 'behind, towards the sunset'. c. The third definition is that these mountains were *in the land of the Canaanites who live in the Arabah.* The Arabah here denotes the Jordan Valley (1:7; 3:17; 4:49; Jos. 8:14; 1 Sa. 23:24, *etc.*) where the Canaanites dwelt. The Canaanites were, however, more widely distributed than the Jordan Valley. The whole of western Palestine is at times called the land of Canaan (Nu. 13:29; Jos. 5:1; 13:4, *etc.*). d. Finally, these mountains were *over against* ('opposite', 'in front of') *Gilgal, beside the oak of Moreh.* This latter phrase is also difficult. The name carries an article 'The Gilgal' (or the round circle of stones, the cromlech), suggesting a place of prominence, which seems to rule out the Gilgal near to Gerizim and Ebal. Alternatively, the preposition 'opposite' or 'facing' may mean 'beyond', *i.e.* the two mountains were 'beyond Gilgal', the first stopping-place after Israel crossed the Jordan. Another proposal is to link the phrases 'in the land of the Canaanites who live in the Arabah' and 'western road', so that the text is read as defining the point of departure of the track which led from the point where the Jordan was crossed to Shechem. The verse might then be paraphrased: 'The mountains, you know, are beyond Jordan, at the end of the western road in the country of the Canaanites who live in the neighbourhood of Gilgal, near to the oaks of Moreh.' The *oaks of Moreh* were situated near Shechem (Gn. 12:6; 35:4; Jos. 24:26; Jdg. 9:6).[1]

31, 32. The lengthy section which began at 5:1 now comes to a close. Israel is about to cross the Jordan to take possession of the land of promise (4:1; 5:32; 9:1). Since, in the final analysis, success in the undertaking will depend on obedience, the closing exhortation to Israel is to be careful to carry out

---

[1] JPSA translates: 'Both are on the west side of Jordan, toward the setting sun, in the land of the Canaanites who dwell in the Arabah, near Gilgal, by the terebinths of Moreh.'

the statutes and the ordinances which Moses had set before the people.

III. THE LAW OF GOD: THE DETAILED COVENANT STIPULATIONS (12:1 – 26:19)

These chapters consist partly of laws which had reference to circumstances not contemplated by the laws given at Sinai (Ex. 20:1 – 23:19) and partly of laws which were already known. As a whole they were already designed to regulate the religious, civil and domestic life of Israel in the land of Canaan in harmony with her calling to be a holy nation. It is clear that there was intended to be a timelessness about the laws of Sinai. They came to each new generation as though they were newly delivered. The appeal was, therefore, not merely of historical interest, but it also had a present application. 'Not with our fathers did Yahweh make this covenant, but with us, who are all of us here alive this day' (5:3). Such a statement would be pertinent at any time after the Sinai event. It was certainly so on the plains of Moab. But it was no less applicable in the days when Deuteronomy reached its final form. (See Introduction.) And today, over 3,000 years later, the great central demands of Deuteronomy still come to the reader with divine authority, although the immediate setting has changed and some of the details are no longer relevant.

There is an interesting literary link between chapters 11 and 12. At the conclusion of chapters 5 to 11, which we have regarded as comprising the general stipulations, there is a section 11:26–32, which may be analysed into a. blessing and curse (26, 27), b. Gerizim and Ebal (29, 30) and c. the command to obey the commandments (31, 32). The following chapters 12 to 28 present these elements in reverse: c[1]. the commandments (12:1 – 26:16), b[1]. Gerizim and Ebal (27:1–8, 11–26) and a[1]. blessings and curses (28:1–68).[1] This use of the literary technique of *chiasmus* has been noted elsewhere in Deuteronomy.[2]

The literary method followed in many passages in the following chapters is, first, to state the basic law or principle,

[1] Note that 27:9–10 is really an introductory phrase. See Introduction, p. 27. G. J. Wenham in his unpublished PhD thesis, *The Structure and Date of Deuteronomy*, has given another illustration at the junction between chapters 4 and 5, if 4:41–49 be omitted as an introductory phrase. (P.T.O.)

then to give an interpretation of it, and finally to stress its contemporary significance by exhortation, warning and promise. It was evidently hoped that in this way the new, living Israel might respond in obedience and commitment in the same way as the Israel that once stood at Sinai.

It has been customary to refer to the material in 12:1 – 26:19 as the Code of Deuteronomy, or the Deuteronomic Code. The expression may be used providing it is understood that these chapters do not comprise a formal law code, but rather a re-statement of law in a homiletical and expository setting.

The inner spirit which was to characterize the members of God's covenant family has been broadly delineated in chapters 5–11. In line with the literary structure of the Near Eastern treaty, specific stipulations follow the statement of the general principles. Chapters 12–26 deal with the detailed application of the broad principles. The whole section is introduced by the words: *These are the statutes and ordinances which you shall be careful to do in the land which Yahweh, the God of your fathers, has given you to possess, all the days that you live upon the earth* (12:1).

In fact, these chapters do not present formal statutes and ordinances alone. A comparison with Exodus 20:22 – 23:19, the so-called 'book of the covenant', will show the difference between codified legal material and preaching about commandments. In the exposition of these earlier laws, homiletical elements are borrowed from chapters 5–11 and these are used again and again to motivate Israel to obedience. Thus there are numerous references to Yahweh's gift of the land, to His promise of blessing to an obedient people and curses to a disobedient people, and to His acts of deliverance both at the exodus and throughout Israel's history. Further, a variety of phrases originating in this ancient covenant tradition recurs in these chapters, *e.g. so you shall purge* ('burn out') *the evil from the*

4:34, 35	Exodus from Egypt	a
4:36	Revelation at Horeb	b
4:37–39	Covenant relationship	c
4:40	Statutes and Commandments	d
5:1	Statutes and Ordinances	d¹
5:2	Covenant	c¹
5:4–5	Revelation at Horeb	b¹
5:6	Exodus from Egypt	a¹

Similarly N. Lohfink (*Das Hauptgebot*, p. 67) has observed that there is an intricate bridge linking chapters 5 and 6. Such observations point to a unity of authorship.

[2] See commentary on 1:6–46.

midst of you (nine times), *you shall rejoice before Yahweh* (three times), *you shall remember that you were a slave in Egypt* (four times), etc.

It is not easy to discern any clear and logical arrangement of the laws in these chapters except in very broad outline. Four areas may be suggested: worship (12:1 – 16:17); the organization of the state (16:18 – 20:20); family law, to which a variety of other laws have been attached (21:1 – 23:1); laws of purity, to which various social laws have been attached (23:2 – 25:19). In 26:1–15 two rituals are added and finally a closing exhortation in 26:16–19.

It ought to be noted that the original laws of Deuteronomy were meant to give guidance to a small agrarian nation over 3,000 years ago, so that in many cases they do not apply to our modern situation. Nevertheless these laws were presented in a covenant setting, and the way in which the broad principles of the covenant were worked out in the affairs of the common life is of extreme interest to the modern interpreter. A wide variety of laws, some of which were taken from the common law of the ancient Near East, are here presented in a covenant[1] setting with the motivation of obedience to Yahweh, the sovereign Lord of Israel.

a. The worship of a holy people (12:1 – 16:17)

This first section represents about one-third of the so-called Code of Deuteronomy. It is thoroughly typical of the literary form of much of the book and provides many illustrations of the way in which older covenant laws were re-presented with a renewed challenge to commitment and obedience.

That this first block of material should be connected with worship is, no doubt, deliberate. Unless Israel were properly related to Yahweh, the divine Ruler of the nation, she would never realize her true nationhood. In her worship, Israel recognized the sovereignty of Yahweh and heard His law. Several important aspects of the worship of Yahweh are dealt with in this section: the central sanctuary (chapter 12); idolatry (chapter 13); prohibition of pagan mourning rites (14:1, 2); the diet of a holy people (14:3–21); tithing (14:22–29); the year of release (15:1–11); limitation of debt and slavery (15:12–18); offerings of flocks and herds (15:19–23); passover

[1] Several of the laws of Hammurabi, for example, have parallels in the Mosaic laws. See *ANET*, pp. 163–177.

(16:1–8); pentecost or harvest festival (16:9–12); feast of tabernacles (16:13–15); yearly pilgrimages (16:16, 17).

i. The worship of the central sanctuary[1] (12:1–28). After a summarizing sentence, which is really an introduction to the whole of the Deuteronomic Code, two questions are raised: Israel's attitude to non-Yahweh sanctuaries and the importance of *the place which Yahweh your God will choose*. Both of these were important in the days of the old tribal confederacy, when a central shrine was necessary to provide cohesion between the various tribal groups in much the same way as the central sanctuary of the Greek and Roman amphictyonies of the first millennium provided a focus for several city states.[2] After the rise of the kingdom an army and a civil service held the nation together. But in earlier times the sense of unity was provided partly by the great covenant renewal ceremonies at the central sanctuary and partly by the charismatic national leaders. It has been argued that in pre-monarchic times the central sanctuary moved from place to place, Shechem (Jos. 24:1), Bethel (Jdg. 20:18, 26, 27) and Shiloh (Jdg. 18:31; 1 Sa. 1:3, 21; 4:3, 4), and that each place became in turn *the place which Yahweh your God will choose*.[3] The frequent use of this latter expression in Deuteronomy probably points back to the ancient traditions of the tribal confederacy. To this place the tribes gathered for covenant renewal ceremonies, for certain other cultic ceremonies, and also in order to determine Yahweh's will when they wished to embark on some common enterprise.

The demand for a central sanctuary was thus not something new when Josiah sought to centralize Israel's worship at the temple in Jerusalem in the seventh century BC. By that time, however, the central sanctuary had lost something of its original character. No longer was it needed to give political unity, for that was provided by the machinery of state. Its main function now was religious. The ancient cultic ceremonies

---

[1] See discussion on 'Deuteronomy and the Central Sanctuary' in Introduction, pp. 35ff.

[2] Martin Noth, *The History of Israel*[2] (1960); 'Das System der zwölf Stamme Israels', *BWANT*, IV, 1930.

[3] This at least is the view of Martin Noth, although others have questioned the view. Thus the references to Shechem in Jos. 8:30ff. and Jos. 24 may refer merely to covenant renewal ceremonies. References to Bethel and Gilgal have likewise been questioned. There is no doubt, however, about Shiloh.

were observed there. *The place which Yahweh will choose to put his name* was, and had been since David's day, Jerusalem. But the idea of a central sanctuary was as old as Moses.

The really critical question about chapter 12 is whether it has to do primarily with centralization of worship or with purity of worship and the proper recognition of the sovereignty of Yahweh in Israel. One emphasis that cannot be avoided is that this chapter stresses that Israel must not use the numerous cult centres scattered throughout the land for the worship of Yahweh. Rather must she destroy all these and bring her burnt offerings, sacrifices, tithes and firstlings to 'the place' (12:6, 11). It is not entirely clear, however, whether a single sanctuary is intended or whether a multiplicity of Yahweh sanctuaries is allowed. Clearly the number of Yahweh sanctuaries were to be limited, since special allowance was made for those who lived a long way from the sanctuary. At first sight 12:1–7 seems to stress unity of worship at one altar. But it might be argued that this represents the final step in the revision of an ancient requirement, the main concern of which was something else. In fact, the bulk of Deuteronomy is concerned with ordinances which neither require nor mention the demand for centralization. Chapter 27 proves a difficult problem. A special ceremony on Mount Ebal involving the erection of an altar and the offering of burnt offerings is there commanded (see commentary *in loc.*). Was then Mount Ebal 'the place', or was it merely the place where the covenant was to be renewed, while 'the place where the Lord chose to put his name', that is, the central sanctuary, was elsewhere? In other words, what is commanded in chapter 12 is a 'central' sanctuary but not a 'sole' sanctuary. If that is so, then Deuteronomy may well date from a period before the days of Hezekiah and Josiah, who wanted to limit *all* worship to *one* sanctuary.

While it may be argued that a great deal of the book of Deuteronomy goes back ultimately both in spirit and content to Moses, but proximately to the days of the old tribal confederacy based on Shechem (*cf.* references to Ebal and Gerizim in 27:4–14), it must be recognized that great principles found a different expression in the course of time, so that some updating of these principles to suit later practice may well have taken place. It is precisely at this point that considerable disagreement has arisen among scholars, for while the possibility of revision may be recognized, it is not easy to decide categorically when such a revision was made. It is for this reason that dates have been given for Deuteronomy as widely apart as the days of Samuel, the days of Solomon, the days of Manasseh, the days of Josiah and even the post-exilic age.[1] What has to be understood, however, is that the concept of a central sanctuary, where Yahweh's sovereignty in Israel was acknowledged at regular intervals, goes back to pre-monarchic times in Israel. At the same time the evidence of the books of Joshua, Judges and Samuel is strong enough to demonstrate that this central shrine was not the only place of worship and sacrifice in Israel.

Broadly, chapter 12 falls into two parts: verses 1–12, where the second plural is used,[2] and verses 13–28, where the second singular is used.[3]

An alternative useful division of the chapter is into four sections: a. verses 2–7, b. verses 8–12, c. verses 13–19, and d. verses 20–28. The various requirements are presented in the form of a direct command *You shall* (2, 3, 5, 6, 7, 11, 12, 18, *etc.*), or of prohibition, *You shall not* (4, 8, 16, 17, 24). We have here, then, the apodictic type of legal formulation as distinct from the casuistic type.[4]

12:1–7. The law of the central sanctuary. 1. The opening sentence is a typical identifying title. There is no further title till 29:1, so that chapters 12–28 appear to represent a unity in their final form.

2–7. It is difficult to avoid the impression that the demand here is for one particular sanctuary at which burnt offerings, sacrifices, tithes and firstlings were to be offered, *i.e.* the central sanctuary. The sanctuaries of the people of the land were to be destroyed and Israel was to worship at an appointed place and there offer their sacrifices and offerings and enjoy their communal meals and times of rejoicing.

2, 3. The phrase *surely destroy* is an emphatic one in Hebrew, being achieved by the addition of a second verbal form before the finite verb.[5] The command to destroy pagan shrines with their emblems and instruments of idolatry presupposes that

---

[1] See Introduction, p. 42.

[2] Except in verse 5 where the MT has the singular. However, the Samaritan and the LXX have the second plural here.

[3] See Introduction, p. 21.

[4] See p. 25.

[5] The so-called *infinitive absolute*. We may capture some of the sense of this form by translating 'destroying, you will destroy'. Strictly the additional verbal form is a verbal noun and not an infinitive.

Israel will have the power to do this. Such a command could be only an ideal in the days of Moses, even if we allow that Israel was prepared to obey the divine injunction. Only in a later day, when Israel possessed this power, was the instruction realizable (*cf.* 7:5, 25; Ex. 23:24; 34:13). The custom of placing shrines on mountains and hills and under leafy trees is referred to elsewhere in the Old Testament as a common practice of the Canaanites. It was copied by Israel in times of apostasy (1 Ki. 14:23; 2 Ki. 16:4; 17:10; 2 Ch. 28:4; Is. 57:5; Je. 2:20; 3:6, 13), making reform necessary. When the Israelites stood in Transjordan with Moses still their leader, Canaanite shrines were studded all over the promised land. The Canaanite sacrificial system differed little from that of Israel at a superficial glance,[1] but it was addressed to other deities. It was thus quite natural for Moses to demand the destruction of these shrines. But it was not till a later day when Israel ruled the land that the ideal might become a possibility. In fact, when the possibility arose, the will was lacking and Israel tolerated other shrines in disobedience to Moses' injunction. Attempts were made at reform by Asa (1 Ki. 15:11–14), Hezekiah (2 Ki. 18:3, 4) and Josiah (2 Ki. 23:4–25; 2 Ch. 34:3–7). Only the latter achieved any great measure of success in areas under his control, but on his death pagan worship reappeared, as the prophecies of Jeremiah and Ezekiel clearly show.

Modern archaeological work has revealed the nature of some of the items referrred to in these verses. The *altars* were similar to that described in Exodus 20:25, 26.[2] The *pillars* (*maṣṣēbâ*) were large upright stones associated with the altars in the Canaanite shrines, possibly symbols of the god Baal,[3] while the *Asherim* (AV *groves*) were symbols of the mother goddess Asherah, evidently made of wood, for they could be cut down and burnt. Post-holes from which the wood has rotted away have been found in Canaanite sanctuaries in Palestine. The *graven images* (*pāsîl*) were probably in stone and could be hewn down. Once these cult symbols were destroyed the Canaanites could not make contact with the gods and in course of time these would be forgotten and their name would disappear from the place where they had been worshipped.

4. The meaning of the phrase *You* (plural) *shall not do so to*

---

[1] J. Gray, *The Legacy of Canaan*, Supp. to *VT*, V, 1965, pp. 194–199.
[2] *ANEP*, pictures 729, 730, 731, 734.
[3] G. E. Wright, *Shechem* (1965), pp. 82–87, figs. 36 39, 41, 42.

the Lord (Yahweh) *your God* is not entirely clear. It may mean simply that Yahweh was not bound to the ancient sanctuaries of other gods, but was free to decide His own place of worship, so that His worship differed both in place and manner from the cults of the Baalim (*cf.* 5, 30). Some commentators have seen here a protest against the worship of Yahweh in many places following the Canaanite practice, thus underlining the contrast of many sanctuaries with one sanctuary. Israel was thus commanded not to build altars and offer sacrifices to Yahweh in any place of their own choice but (verses 5ff.) only at the place which He chose for them. Whereas the Canaanites might seek and worship their nature gods in places where they thought they could discern the divine presence, Israel must go only to the place designated by the Lord.

5. A number of questions arise here for the interpreter. First of all there is a question about the text to be followed. The phrase translated in the AV *even unto his habitation* (*le šiknô*) seems to contain the noun *šēken*, 'habitation', but this word occurs only here in the Old Testament. The AV makes the phrase dependent on the verb *seek*: *unto his habitation shall ye seek*. On the other hand the RSV takes the verb *seek* as the main verb in the sentence and regards the consonants *lškn* as having been vocalized *le šakke nô*, *i.e.* as the infinitive of the verb *šikkēn* meaning 'to cause to dwell', *i.e.* 'to tabernacle'. The verb is so used in verse 11 and 26:2 and may have been used here originally. When the Israelites came to this place, the place of the *name*, they were before Yahweh (7, 12; 26:2, 5).

Yet another suggestion about the meaning of the phrase *to put his name* is that it is equivalent to an Akkadian expression *šakānum šumam*, which indicates a claim to sovereignty. This proposal avoids any suggestion that Yahweh was in any sense confined to the central sanctuary. As God of the whole earth He might make Himself known and accept the sacrifices and worship of His children wherever He chose to assert His sovereignty.

A kindred expression occurs in the Old Testament. In a number of passages where God claims ownership, possession or sovereignty in respect to a place, people or nations, the phrase *called by my* (thy) *name* is used (2 Sa. 12:28; 1 Ki. 8:43; 2 Ch. 7:14; Je. 7:10, 11, 14, 30; 34:15; Dn. 9:18, 19). The expression is used for God's sovereignty over His people (Dt. 28:10; 2 Ch. 7:14; Is. 63:19; Je. 14:9; Am. 9:12).

Where then was this place? Although it later became identified with Jerusalem, it was certainly not so in the days of the old tribal confederacy but, as we have seen,[1] it was to be identified with the central sanctuary which was situated in a variety of places. In a time of transition Yahweh might choose several places in turn until finally the precise and permanent site was chosen. This was Jerusalem from David's time onwards, although that could not have been envisaged in Moses' day. But whatever the place, it was the divine authority and the divine presence that gave significance to it.

6. The offerings to be presented at the place that Yahweh chose, in addition to those prescribed for the three annual pilgrimages, are now listed. These are the *burnt offerings* (*'ôlâ*), the *sacrifices* (*zeḇaḥ*), the *tithes* (*ma'aśēr*), the *offering that you present* (*t°rûmaṯ yaḏ*, lit. what is lifted up in the hand, AV 'heave offering'), *votive offerings* (*neḏer*), the *freewill offerings* (*n°ḏāḇâ*), and the *firstlings of herd and flock* (*b°ḵôrâ*), a comprehensive range of offerings.

The *burnt offerings* or holocausts (Lv. 1) were completely burnt. The individuals who brought them laid their hands on the beasts, thereby declaring that this sacrifice was their own and that the benefits of the sacrifice would be theirs. The *sacrifices* were offerings of thanksgiving to God which brought fellowship and union between a man and God. They might be termed more generally 'communion sacrifices'. They were of three kinds – sacrifices of praise and thanksgiving (*tôḏâ*, Lv. 7:12–15; 22:29, 30), the voluntary sacrifice (*n°ḏāḇâ*), *i.e.* one offered out of devotion to Yahweh (Lv. 7:16, 17; 22:18–23), and the votive sacrifice (*neḏer*), *i.e.* one offered by a person who bound himself with a vow (Lv. 7:16, 17; 22:18–23). In these, the beast when slain was shared, Yahweh's portion being burnt, the priest's portion being the breast and the right leg, and the portion of the offerer to be shared with his family and friends being the rest of the beast (Lv. 7 for details). We note the absence of expiatory sacrifices from this list (see Lv. 4:1 – 5:16). The *tithes* (see 14:22–29) comprised grain, wine, oil, and the firstlings of the herd and flock. The *offering that you present* (RSV) or the *heave offerings of your hand* (AV) represented a portion that was lifted up from the larger mass and set aside for the use of the priests (*cf.* 18:4; 26:2; Lv. 7:14, 32–34; Nu. 18:8, 9). The *freewill offerings* and the *votive offerings* or vows are elsewhere described as sacrifices (Lv. 7:16, 17; 22:18–23). The

---

[1] See Introduction, p. 35.

votive offerings represented promises made to God in an hour of crisis.[1]

7. All of these offerings had to be brought to the central sanctuary. In cases where they were eaten, as at the great annual festivals, the eating was thus *before the Lord*, *i.e.* in the Lord's presence. These were occasions of happy rejoicing and thanksgiving for God's blessing on all their undertakings (lit. 'the putting forth of your hand'). This injunction to *rejoice* on such occasions occurs elsewhere in Deuteronomy (14:26; 16:11, 14, 15; 26:11).

The reference to *households* raises a question. What is the extent of the household which was to share the feast with the offerer (*cf.* verse 18; 15:20)? It seems to have included sons, daughters, menservants, maidservants, and Levites. If whole households left their farms on such occasions there was a risk of theft. In view of the problems associated with such a wholesale migration it has sometimes been suggested that what is pictured here is an ideal which was, in fact, never realized. At best, representatives of the families attended the central sanctuary.

What then are we to conclude about the meaning of these verses? They are based on the concept of the central sanctuary (where the ark was kept), at which, ideally, all festivals were held and to which pilgrimage was made yearly. In the centuries following Moses, a multiplicity of high places and altars soon appeared. But the ideal remained, and in a day when faithful men in Israel realized that possibly the only cure for apostasy was actual centralization of worship, a re-application of the old Mosaic ideal became part of the platform of reform.

8–12. The implications of the law of the central sanctuary. The prescriptions of verses 5–7 are now re-stated in different words to emphasize the demands of the law of the central sanctuary. Even if this was only an ideal originally, it was a desirable ideal. The present section pictures a state of affairs in which *every man* (is) *doing whatever is right in his own eyes* (8). What was permissible in a time of transition, or of national weakness, could not be regarded as permanently allowable. The ideal law of the central sanctuary, that all

---

[1] It is interesting to note that the practice still persists in some areas of the world, *e.g.* among certain groups of Christians in West Azerbaijan, Iran.

sacrificial offerings and worship should be confined to an authorized place, was a basic requirement in Israel. Hence some change in customs currently observed was called for (8, 10, 11, 13, 14). Clearly such an instruction, though ancient, would come with great force to an apostate nation in a day when reforms were being undertaken, *e.g.* in the time of Josiah.

8–10. The people were commanded to give up the laxity that had hitherto characterized their practice. The expression *every man doing whatever is right in his own eyes* may denote licence (Jdg. 17:6; 21:25), or liberty. In a day of transition liberty was allowed to the people, although there was always the risk that it might become licence.

These verses refer to a state of affairs at some time in the future when Israel, having crossed the Jordan, had *rest from . . . enemies round about*. Two possible periods when this state of affairs obtained according to the biblical narrative were in the years following Joshua's campaigns (Jos. 22:4; 23:1), and in the years following David's campaigns (2 Sa. 7:1; 1 Ki. 5:3). It would seem that Israel failed to fulfil the command of Moses on either of these occasions. During the period from Judges to Saul there was great instability in the land and other sanctuaries are mentioned besides the central sanctuary (1 Sa. 9:12–14; 14:35; 2 Sa. 24:25). Likewise after the division of the kingdom, when the whole land was torn by war both internally and externally for several centuries, there were other sanctuaries, *e.g.* that at which Elijah sacrificed (1 Ki. 18:19–39).

11. The list of sacrifices here is nearly identical with that in verses 5 and 6, except that the phrase *all your votive offerings which you vow* replaces *your votive offerings, your freewill offerings, and the firstlings of your herd and of your flock*. The expression in the present verse is a summarizing one and may imply that the vow was something exceptional or that the sacrifice offered in fulfilment of the vow was superior.

12. Holy joy is to be a feature of the sacrificial feast (7, 18; 14:26; 16:11, 14, 15; 26:11; 27:7; Lv. 23:40). It is to be noted that the Levite is to be associated with the family festivities (*cf.* verse 19). The Levites were dependent on the generosity of the people (Nu. 18:21; 35:1ff.). The priests were cared for out of sacrifices (18:3–8), but *the Levite that is within your towns* (lit. 'gates') had no provision other than the charity of the people. Who were these Levites to whom such attention is paid in Deuteronomy? Originally they were members of the tribe of Levi. In early times special duties in connection with the tabernacle were allotted to sub-branches of the tribe, although only one family officiated at the altar. It would be inevitable that with the passage of the years large numbers of Levites could become superfluous. They may have fulfilled a teaching function in the villages (33:10; 2 Ch. 15:3; 17:8, 9; 30:22; 35:3; Ne. 8:7, 8). The view that the book of Deuteronomy in its final form arose out of the interpretative tradition of the Levites[1] has not been accepted by all scholars, but it may have some truth in it. The claim is made in 31:24 that Moses himself wrote this law in a document and gave this to the Levites to be put by the side of the ark (see commentary on 31:24-29). How close the words of this law (31:24) were to the book we now have is impossible to say. It is conceivable that in subsequent centuries the Levites undertook some interpretative comments.

13-19. The regular sanctuary and the question of meat for food. At this point there is a change to the second singular.[2] The discussion turns to the question of killing beasts for food. Did the ancient law of the central sanctuary, which required that sacrifices be slain only at the place which Yahweh had chosen, limit the eating of meat to festival occasions? It is here declared that slaughtering for secular use is permitted. The flesh of beasts not slain in the ritual ceremonies at the central sanctuary is placed on a par with that of wild animals, although the ritual regarding the blood had to be observed (16, 23f.).

13, 14. The law of the burnt offerings, which presumably applied to the other offerings, is again emphasized with the strong introductory imperative *Take heed*. These offerings are not to be presented at *every place that you see*, but only at the place which Yahweh approves in one of the tribes, *i.e.* the central sanctuary.

15, 16. It has sometimes been argued that the ancient Semites believed in the kinship of the tribe and its god with its animals, so that animals were too sacred to be slain except with solemn rites and in the presence and with the consent of the whole family, tribe or clan, who all partook of the flesh and set apart portions of the flesh and the blood for their god.[3]

[1] Gerhard von Rad, *Studies in Deuteronomy* (1953), pp. 60-69.
[2] Only in verse 16 is the plural used, but in the Samaritan this too is singular.
[3] W. Robertson Smith, *The Religion of the Semites* (1907), chapters viii and ix, pp. 269-352.

In Hebrew the same verb *zābaḥ* is used for both acts (Lv. 17:3-7; 1 Sa. 28:24; 1 Ki. 19:21). But if that were ever true, and it needs to be proved, there is no need to see in the present provision any such concept. The passage simply declares that the slaughter of animals for food is permitted, only the blood must be *poured out upon the earth like water*. It is equally important for ritual offerings and for slaughterings for food, to avoid the eating of blood. This prohibition provided a concrete recognition of the fact that God was the sole master of life, and since life belonged to Him, it was to be given back to Him. This was done ritually by pouring the blood beside or on an altar, on a stone (1 Sa. 14:32-35) or on the ground. 'You may kill and eat meat whenever you feel so inclined according to the means Yahweh has given you' (lit. 'according to the blessing of Yahweh your God'). This right could be exercised *within any of your towns* (lit. 'gates'). It was not confined to particular places, such as the central sanctuary or other approved places where sacrifices had to be offered. In that case, since the eating of meat at home was not associated with the sanctuary, distinctions between ritual cleanness and ritual uncleanness disappeared (*cf.* Lv. 7:20, 21).

17, 18. To avoid all ambiguity those items which belong in the realm of the sacred are again defined. Sacred meals, such as those set out here, are to be eaten at the central sanctuary and there alone. These are to be shared with the members of the family and with any Levite who may be in the town, in a spirit of happy rejoicing.

19. A special additional reminder is given not to forsake the Levite.

20-28. Sacred and ordinary meals. The previous instructions about eating meat are now repeated for emphasis. The people were permitted to slaughter a beast and to eat meat at home as often as they desired, in much the same way as they ate hunted game, provided the blood was not consumed. The true sacrificial meals were reserved for the sanctuary.

20-22. The provision here seems to be for those who were far from the central sanctuary and so did not participate in the ritual feasts. The simple statement of verse 15 is explained in more detail. The participation of the family in such a meal was not dependent on ceremonial cleanness and the kind of meat permissible included both that which was proper for sacrifice (*any of your herd or your flock*) as well as meat like game which was not used in sacrifice (*cf.* 15f.).

23–25. The only restriction on the eating of flesh was that the people were forbidden to consume blood (*cf.* 16; Gn. 9:4; Lv. 17:10ff.). Pouring blood on the ground would be a safe-guard against pouring it on a pagan altar and also against the appropriation of its 'life', which was God's alone (see commentary on 15, 16). The centralization of the slaughter of animals for sacrifice would avoid sacrifices on a pagan altar.

26, 27. A restriction is again placed on *the holy things, i.e.* the sacrificial offerings, tithes, vows, *etc.*

28. Obedience to God's commands in these matters is the principal prerequisite of blessing. This interspersing of exhortation with divine commands is quite characteristic of Deuteronomy. The comment is that it will go well with Israel and her descendants when she does what is good and right in the sight of Yahweh.

While there is no longer any specific application of the injunctions of chapter 12 for the Christian, there is a significant principle involved. The one centre for true worship is not a place but a Person (Jn. 4:19–26). In the Person of Jesus Christ the Christian finds the venue for true worship. The teaching of Deuteronomy on the one centre of true worship is limited, although the principle enunciated is correct.

ii. Idolatry, the paramount sin (12:29 – 13:18). The central issues of chapter 12 are introduced by verses 1–3 which are concerned with the prohibition of pagan rites. One purpose of confining sacrifices to the central sanctuary was to avoid contamination of the pure worship of Yahweh by idolatrous Canaanite practices (*cf.* 16:21 – 17:1). The point is taken up again in the following verses.

We sense the struggle to lift the worship of Israel from debasing elements. It was clear to Israel's best religious leaders that the mixing of pagan elements with the worship of Yahweh could never lead to a richer faith. Where alien practices were morally offensive they must be repudiated out of hand.

The grievousness of idolatry is best understood against the background of the demand for utter loyalty to Yahweh. Just as in the Near Eastern suzerainty treaties undivided allegiance was required of a vassal, so in the covenant between Yahweh and Israel the total allegiance of Israel was demanded. The worship of other gods was tantamount to an act of rebellion,

172

for it compromised the sovereign Lordship of Yahweh. A number of interesting parallels may be drawn between the covenant of Yahweh with Israel and the Near Eastern treaties between suzerains and their vassals. Vassals were warned against listening to evil words against their overlord. They were bound to report conspiracies or insulting words against the king, and were required to subdue rebels in their own domain by force of arms. And always, they were bound to maintain strict allegiance to their suzerain.[1] The secular parallel provides a fascinating background against which to view the present section.

29, 30. When Israel possessed the land of promise it was not sufficient merely to have a pure Yahweh sanctuary, but the manner of worship conducted there was to be free of all strange influences and elements.

31. While all pagan practices were excluded, the sacrifice of children is mentioned specially. This was one of the most ancient religious practices of Syria–Palestine. Already at the beginning of the second millennium BC it seems that infant sacrifice was practised in the land. The exact nature of the burnt skeletons of children found in large jars in excavations, *e.g.* at Gezer, is not clear, but child sacrifice seems to be suggested. The practice of passing children through the fire persisted into the days of the kings, *e.g.* Ahaz (2 Ki. 16:3; 17:17) and Manasseh (2 Ki. 21:6; *cf.* 2 Ki. 23:10). The priests (Lv. 18:21) and the prophets (Je. 7:31; 19:5; 32:35) both forbade the practice, but were unable to stamp it out.

32. In the Hebrew Bible chapter 13 begins with 12:32, which provides a suitable introduction to the case of the false prophet. Four cases of rebellion against Yahweh's Lordship are dealt with in Deuteronomy, three in chapter 13 and one in 17:2–7. The cases are presented in casuistic form, 'if . . . then . . .'.

13:1–5. The false prophet. The problem posed here was a delicate one. It was commonly acknowledged that prophets had the gift of interpreting dreams and of performing miraculous deeds. But what was Israel to do if one, while possessing these gifts, invited the people to be disloyal to Yahweh? The answer was simple. The people should refuse to listen to such prophets and should put them to death.

[1] An excellent example occurs in the vassal treaties of Esarhaddon the Assyrian. See D. J. Wiseman, 'The Vassal Treaties of Esarhaddon', *Iraq*, 20, 1958, lines 101–384.

1, 2. Not every dream or vision was a source of divine revelation, although God could and did use both at times (Gn. 20:3; 31:11; Nu. 12:6; Joel 2:28). Again, while the true prophet had the power to perform miracles (signs and wonders), others too exercised similar powers (Ex. 7:10–12). The man who possessed such gifts could not be Yahweh's prophet if he sought to destroy the allegiance of Yahweh's people. The covenant was irrevocable. Hence any prophet who advocated the worship and service of other gods was false and, as one who *taught rebellion against Yahweh* (5), was to be slain.

3–5. Faced with traitorous prophets, three lines of action were to be followed: a. Israel was not to listen. The people might recognize, in the attempt of the false prophet to turn them aside, a test of their loyalty. Clearly, God's purpose was not to destroy His own sovereignty. Hence, although He allowed the false prophets the use of prophetic gifts, their prostitution of these constituted for Israel a test of their own love of Yahweh. For if they loved Him with all their heart and with all their soul, nothing could persuade them to forsake Him. b. Faced with such a test, Israel should continue to walk after Yahweh, to reverence Him, to keep His commandments, to obey Him and to cling to Him (4). c. The false prophet should be put to death, because he had encouraged rebellion against Yahweh who had delivered Israel from Egypt.

It is not entirely clear whether the prophet who arose among the people was an Israelite or a foreigner. There is at least one recorded case in the Old Testament where false prophets, the prophets of Baal, were slain by Elijah (1 Ki. 18:40). However, although false prophets are frequently mentioned, references to their being punished are rare. This may be attributed to neglect of the law, but it may be an example of the fact that laws often pose a theoretical possibility and prescribe a severe penalty, not with the intention that this should be carried out, but in order to emphasize the heinousness of the crime. The threat of execution for such an offender was designed to prevent the spread of infection and purge out the evil from the midst of Israel (*cf.* 17:12; 19:11–13; 21:18–21; 22:21–24; 24:7). The question was: how could the corporate life of Israel be kept true to Yahweh? It is a perennial question. In a later day Paul advocated the expulsion of the man who took his father's wife (1 Cor. 5:1–13; note verse 13).

6–11. Seduction by near relatives. The second case is

also expressed in casuistic form. It concerns the attempt of one member of a family (or a close friend) to lead other members of the family astray from Yahweh by enticing them secretly, rather than openly, like the false prophet. The judgment is equally severe, death by stoning.

6, 7. The number of gods that might claim Israel's allegiance was considerable, *gods which neither you nor your fathers have known, some of the gods of the peoples that are round about you, whether near you or far off from you, from the one end of the earth to the other.* By means of this vivid language it was made plain to Israel that no god whatever was to take Yahweh's place (5:7).

8. Not even family ties, so significant elsewhere in Deuteronomy, would permit apostasy to be overlooked. The nature of God's covenant with Israel was such that loyalty and love to Him were more important than the love of one's family. The accumulation of prohibitions of a most severe kind serves to underline the gravity of the offence. We are reminded of Jesus' words in Luke 14:26, where a man is warned that he cannot be a disciple unless he hate father, mother, wife, children, brothers, sisters, and his own life. In both cases the completeness of the allegiance demanded is expressed in striking language.

9–11. The penalty prescribed was severe, stoning by the whole community with the family leading the way. It was more necessary for the family than for others to show that it neither had been nor wished to be a partaker in the evil deed. Until recently many societies in the Western world prescribed the death penalty in order to stress the serious nature of certain crimes. While, in practice, this penalty was not always carried out, it remained as a measure of the seriousness of the crime.

Whatever the origin of such a law, it served the purpose of making clear to a man who acted in this way that society disowned him, and that it would collectively destroy him. The procedures here accord well with the strong emphasis throughout Deuteronomy that society as a whole was involved in the national life. Conversely, each individual was required to play his part in the maintenance of the national life and the good order of society.

12–18. The apostate town. Sometimes the charge of leading people astray could be made against a whole town. Here too the statutory penalty was severe.

12, 13. The men of the city are called *base fellows* (RSV) or

175

children of Belial (AV). These expressions are both translations of the Hebrew *beliya'al*, 'without worth', which is God's estimate of such people despite their fine showing before the people of the town.

14. Since the penalty was so severe it was all the more necessary that it should be justly administered. A careful enquiry was to be undertaken to establish the facts (*cf.* 17:4). If the case was proven, the town was to be treated as a pagan town (*cf.* 20:10–18). The term *abominable thing* (*tô'ēḇâ*) is used in the Old Testament for something that is totally displeasing to God and denotes something impure, unclean and totally devoid of holiness (*cf.* 7:25, 26; 14:3; 17:1, 4; 18:9; 20:18).

15, 16. This penalty is to be compared with the treatment meted out to Canaanite Jericho (Jos. 6:17–21). The whole town, people, animals and property were submitted to 'sacred extermination' (*ḥērem*). The verb deriving from the same root is here translated *destroy utterly*. The sacrifice was to be like *a whole burnt offering*, *i.e.* it was to be total, since the whole population of the town was jointly responsible. Theirs was a corporate guilt and, as so often in the Old Testament, they were judged corporately. The town was then to be abandoned and left as *a heap* (lit. 'tell'). The term 'tell' is used in Arabic for any ruined site, *e.g.* ancient Jericho is called Tell es-Sulṭān. Compare the treatment of the Israelite town of Gibeah in the days of the judges (Jdg. 20:42–48).

17, 18. Nothing was to be excluded from the sacred extermination, so that no individual Israelite was to profit personally from the booty (*cf.* Achan, Jos. 7:20, 21). Only thus might the curses associated with the breach of covenant be stayed and Yahweh be persuaded to *turn from the fierceness of his anger, and show you mercy.* Justice done, Yahweh's blessings might continue to be enjoyed. Obedience to the commands of Yahweh is the only way for Israel to enjoy His blessing.

These latter verses 12 to 18 are an expression of the ancient concept of corporate punishment where there is corporate responsibility. Examples may be drawn from the days of the wilderness wanderings (Ex. 32:26–29; Nu. 25:4–9) and from the days of the conquest (Jos. 6:17–21; Jdg. 20:42–48). All that was unclean and was a violation of holiness was to be burnt out. Only so could the purity of the community be preserved or restored.

iii. Pagan mourning rites forbidden (14:1, 2). Israel is

carefully defined as *sons of Yahweh*, and *a people holy to Yahweh your God*. The two expressions *sons* and *holy people* are strongly emphasized in the Hebrew text by being placed first in the respective sentences, *Sons you are*, *A holy people you are*. The recognition of this fact should prepare Israel for the prohibition that follows. Clearly those who are Yahweh's children, the ones whom He has chosen to be *his own possession* (sᵉgullâ), ought not to become involved in the practices of their pagan neighbours. As children of Yahweh their divine Father, they were required to set aside customs unworthy of that relationship (*cf.* Is. 1:2–4; 30:1). The description of Israel in verse 2 is an exact reproduction of that in 7:6.

1b. The cutting of the body and the shaving of the head were common mourning rites in the ancient Near East and are referred to in numerous places in the Old Testament (Is. 3:24; 15:2; 22:12; Je. 16:6; 41:5; Ezk. 7:18; Am. 8:10; Mi. 1:16). The mutilation of the body persists still in some countries, *e.g.* in New Guinea, where a mourner, especially a woman, removes a joint of a finger, and in extreme cases more than one finger joint. Such practices were forbidden in Israel, both because they hinted at some conformity to pagan practices and also because Israel had a respect for the body as God's creation which was not to be disfigured or misused (*cf.* Lv. 19:27, 28).[1] That the law was not always observed in Israel is clear from Jeremiah 41:5; Ezekiel 7:18; Amos 8:10. A number of Israel's laws seem to have in mind the cult of the dead. Thus contact between the living and the dead through various media was forbidden (18:11), while physical contact with dead bodies led to ritual uncleanness (Nu. 19:11–18; 31:19). There might be here an underlying opposition to rites connected with the Canaanite god Mot (*cf.* 26:14; Ezk. 8:14). In any case, all such practices were forbidden to Israel.

iv. Clean and unclean foods (14:3–21). In the matter of food, a holy people must refrain from eating any abominable thing. The simple summarizing law *You* (sing.) *shall not eat any abominable thing* is probably an ancient apodictic law. A detailed list of clean and unclean animals gives an exact definition of the law.

It is not always possible to decide the grounds on which the

---

[1] Note the high regard for the perfect body implied in Lv. 21:17–21, and the requirement in Lv. 22:3–8 that a priest should guard against physical defilement.

creatures listed are declared to be clean or unclean. Hygienic explanations are possible in some cases, *e.g.* swine (8), and predatory birds that feast on carrion (12-18). It is possible that in some cases the creatures were linked in some way with pagan cult practices, *e.g.* the serpent was sacred to the fertility goddesses throughout the ancient Near East. The wild boar and the pig were sacred animals of Aliyan Baal at Ugarit and of Ishtar in Cyprus. The ibis and certain fish were venerated in Egypt. Superstition gave to the bat, which hid away in tombs and burial chambers, an aura of mystery. The practice of totemism may have endowed some animals with uncleanness in Israel's sight, *e.g.* the crow (raven, 14) was the totem of certain Arab clans. In some cases no clear reason for regarding an animal as unclean is obvious. But whatever the reason it was evidence of obedience in God's people that they made a distinction between clean and unclean food. Finally, it was not the observance of food laws that distinguished Israel as holy, but a total attitude of willing allegiance to Yahweh in love and obedience. Jesus enunciated the principle that it is not what goes into a man that defiles him, but what comes out of him (Mk. 7:15).[1]

3. See comment on 13:14 on *abominable thing*.

4-6. The list of animals that may be eaten is given first (*cf.* 1 Ki. 4:23). Note that a clean animal was required to possess both of the important characteristics, chewing the cud and parting the hoof.

7, 8. Categories of animals that were not to be eaten included those which showed only one of the two required characteristics. Among these are the camel, the hare, the rock badger, and the swine.

9, 10. Of creatures that lived in the waters only those that possessed both fins and scales were edible. Water creatures such as the eel, which had neither, resembled snakes. The list in Leviticus 11:9-12 is a little more detailed.

11-18a. A single word in Hebrew '*ôp* (lit. 'flying creature') is used to designate both birds and insects (20). The identifica-

---

[1] A recent discussion of the dietary and hygiene laws may be found in W. F. Albright, *Yahweh and the Gods of Canaan* (1968), pp. 152-157. He argues that the Israelite laws were more highly developed than the corresponding ancient Near Eastern lists of taboos. Many of the biblical laws have an empirical basis arising from observations that the eating of certain animals was a health hazard. But see J. Milgrom, *Interpretation*, 17, 1963, pp. 288-301.

tion of the birds in 12 to 18 is not always certain. They represent a wide variety of predatory birds.[1]

18b, 19. The *hoopoe* or mountain cock (*dûķîpet*), the bat and the winged insects are grouped together as unclean (*ṭāmē'*) and, therefore, not to be eaten (Lv. 11:19, 20).

20. Some insects were clean and might be eaten. These were the cricket, locust and grasshopper, creatures that had two strong back legs for leaping (Lv. 11:21, 22).

21a. The eating of the corpses of animals that had died naturally was forbidden, partly for hygienic purposes, and partly because their blood had not been released (12:23). In this verse there is an interesting description of the three main groups in the Israelite society: the Israelite who may not eat corpses, the resident *alien* (*gēr*) who might be given such food to eat, and the *foreigner* (*nokrî*) who might be sold a corpse for food (*cf.* Lv. 17:14–16). The reason why Israel should not eat animal corpses is that they are *a people holy to Yahweh your God.*

21b. The same law occurs in both Exodus 23:19 and 34:26. It may have in view a Canaanite rite described in an Ugaritic poem, where the injunction is given 'cook a kid in the milk, a lamb in the cream'.[2] The Israelite law is possibly a rejection of this custom and is the basis of the separation of meat and milk foods in later Judaism and among many Jews to this day.

v. Tithes (14:22–29). An annual tithe of the produce of the land was to be made to Yahweh in recognition of the fact that He was both the owner of the land and the one who bestowed life and fertility. It is clear from 12:6, 11 and 17 that Israel was commanded to bring to the central sanctuary tithes, firstlings (12:6, 17) and other offerings. In the present passage tithes (22) and firstlings (23) are again associated. They are to be brought to the place which Yahweh would choose, *i.e.* the central sanctuary. The question of when they were to be brought is not easy to answer. It has been argued that, in the days before the Temple, the kind of festival referred to in 1 Samuel 9:12; 20:29 was not an annual major festival, but a local and family celebration for which the tithe of grain, oil and wine and the firstlings of the flock might be used.[3] Many commentators argue, however, that the bringing of tithes to

[1] The unclean birds seem to have been birds of prey, *i.e.* carnivorous. See G. R. Driver, 'Birds in the Old Testament', *PEQ*, 87, 1955, pp. 5–20.
[2] Text 52, line 14. See Cyrus H. Gordon, *Ugaritic Handbook* (1965), p. 174.
[3] Adam C. Welch, *The Code of Deuteronomy* (1924), p. 38.

the central sanctuary was associated either with the harvest
festival or with the feast of weeks (pentecost), when offerings
were presented at the central sanctuary (15:19, 20; 16:16;
Ex. 23:17; 34:22, 23). There are several difficulties in this latter
suggestion. The fact that 26:1–15 mentions both the tithe and
the firstfruits in close proximity may be merely a literary
arrangement of two ancient liturgical formulae. But it may
also be argued that the basket of firstfruits was merely a symbolic portion of the tithe, while the command to 'rejoice in
all the good which Yahweh your God has given you' (26:11)
represents the joyful meal of 14:22–27. Again, since it seems
unlikely that a double tribute was expected, the firstfruits and
the tithe may have been identical, the tithe being a more
careful definition of the amount of the firstfruits. However, the
equation of the two seems difficult in the light of 18:4, where
the firstfruits are to be given to the priests.

We are probably not in possession of enough information to
give an entirely satisfactory answer to many of the questions
which arise in connection with Israel's ritual requirements.

In the present passage, irrespective of the time of the event,
Israel is instructed to bring tithes and firstlings to the place
which Yahweh had appointed (*cf.* commentary on 12:5). Here
the offerer, his household, and the Levite were to eat the sacred
meal. For those who lived far from the sanctuary provision was
made to exchange the tithe for money, which could then be
used to buy food for the feast at the central sanctuary (24–26).
Every third year, however, the tithe was to be stored in the
Israelite's own town or village to provide a charitable fund for
the needy, the Levites, the resident aliens, the widows, the
orphans, *etc.*

22. The idea of tithing was not peculiar to Israel. In some
lands tithes were regularly taken by kings as taxation. In a
time of crisis in Egypt the pharaoh authorized Joseph to take
as much as one-fifth (Gn. 41:34). Samuel's warning in
1 Samuel 8:15, 17 has this background, and Amos 5:11 may
allude to the practice of extorting tribute from poor people
who could ill afford to surrender such quantities of grain.
Religious tithing had its parallel in civil areas.

In the New Testament there are several references to
tithing. Jesus rebuked the scribes and Pharisees for observing
the law in this matter while neglecting 'the weightier matters
of the law' (Mt. 23:23; Lk. 11:42; 18:12), while the writer to
the Hebrews saw in the fact that Abraham gave a tithe to

Melchizedek a foreshadowing of a priesthood that was greater than the Aaronic priesthood which descended from Abraham (Heb. 7:1–10). The New Testament warns against the meticulous observance of every possible tithe as a substitute for weightier matters such as justice, mercy, and faith, and also against any sign of right living as a substitute for a humble, loving, generous and obedient heart (Lk. 18:9–14). At the same time the dedicated man will delight to give generously to the work of the Lord, perhaps even exceeding the tithe in love. 'God loves a cheerful giver' (2 Cor. 9:7). The Hebrew word for *tithe, maʿⁿśēr*, may be derived either from a root related to the number 'ten', or from a quite different root attested in Ugarit and South Arabic meaning more generally 'offering'.[1] The association of the word here with firstlings may suggest that the tithe was a kind of offering, namely the firstfruits of the field as a parallel to the firstlings of the flock. In any case, the tithe was an offering which represented an act of worship in honour of Yahweh the Lord of the earth and the sole Author of the harvest.

The law of tithing in its simplest form occurs in verse 22. Subsequent verses represent the exposition of the simple law in much the same way as the simple law of 15:1 is expounded in verses 2–11 and the simple law of 15:19 is expounded in verses 20–22. Such expositions are understood by G. von Rad[2] as later interpretations of basic laws so that they become relevant to the needs of a new age. Hence they are given a new form and adapted to new conditions. While such a view is possible, it is also possible that in any age a succinctly stated apodictic law would need some explanation, no less in the days of Moses or Joshua than in any subsequent century. The analysis of these passages into various elements is, however, very helpful. We are enabled thereby to grasp the basic demand. Whatever subsequent applications this might have, the heart of the demand remains.

Other forms of the law of tithing occur in Leviticus 27:30–33 and Numbers 18:21–32. Variations between Deuteronomy and these other expressions of the tithing law have been noted by commentators. Even if these exist, none of the variants is contrary to the spirit and intention of the ancient law, but merely a variation in detail.

[1] P. Buis and J. Leclercq, *Le Deutéronome* (1963), p. 117.
[2] G. von Rad, *Studies in Deuteronomy* (1953), pp. 15–17; *Deuteronomy* (1966), pp. 19, 106–108.

23. At first reading it would appear that the entire tithe was to be eaten at the central sanctuary, at the place where Yahweh chose to tabernacle His name. In that case the quantity to be eaten may have been considerable. Hence a question arises concerning how much of the tithe was taken to the central sanctuary. Perhaps, in fact, a portion only was taken for a communion feast at the sanctuary. At the end of the third year the entire tithe was to be stored up in the towns (28).

The agricultural tithe is here specified as a tithe of *grain*, *wine* (lit. 'unfermented grape juice') and *oil* (olive). The *firstlings* of the flock are mentioned, though not specified in detail (*cf.* 12:17; 15:19ff.). Possibly the details are taken for granted both here and in Numbers 18 (but *cf.* Lv. 27:30–33; 2 Ch. 31:6). The purpose of the present section is not so much to give a comprehensive and detailed statement of the law of tithing as to ensure that the tithe was reserved for the purpose intended by Yahweh. There was always a danger that Canaanite deities might be honoured at harvest time. To avoid this, insistence is here made that any religious ceremonies associated with the harvest and with tithing should be conducted at Yahweh's sanctuary and not at a pagan sanctuary. Thus would Israel *learn to fear Yahweh your God always*.

24–26. The provision made here has no parallel in the other Old Testament passages dealing with the tithe. It led to problems in a later day when there was a considerable traffic in the sale of animals in the Temple precincts (Jn. 2:13-17) and when the close link between the personal effort of the offerer and the sacred meal that he ate was lost.

The nature of the purchases that could be made as a substitute for the man's own tithe is summarized as *oxen, sheep, wine* and *strong drink*. The latter word, *šēkār*, and the corresponding verb refer to intoxicating drink. The law did not, of course, encourage over-indulgence, any more than does the use of wine in the Christian communion service encourage drunkenness. In any case, the Bible contains abundant material to encourage temperance (Pr. 20:1; 23:29–31; Is. 5:11, 22; Am. 4:1–3; Rom. 14:15, 20–23; 1 Cor. 8:9–12; Eph. 5:18; 1 Tim. 3:3; Tit. 1:7; 2:3; 1 Pet. 4:3).

We have here another example of the summarizing method used in Deuteronomy. A number of examples is given and then the summarizing phrase commencing with 'anything' (*kol*), or 'everything'. The present list concludes with the expression *whatever* (anything that) *your appetite craves* (translating *nepeš* as *appetite*).

27. The sacred meal was a joyous family meal to be eaten by the offerer and his household, but it was to be shared with any Levites who were in the town (*Levite* is collective). Comparison with other Old Testament passages reveals that the Levite had a claim on the tithe, although the exact nature of this claim is differently expressed. In Numbers 18:21-32 the Levites are given 'every tithe in Israel for an inheritance, in return for their service'. It appears from Numbers 18:20, 26 30 that one-tenth of the tithe was for the priests, *i.e.* for the Aaronites who officiated at the central sanctuary. There is no reference in Numbers to sharing the sacred meal with the Levites. The Deuteronomic law is either different or differently expressed, for it does not seem to allow the Levite exclusive rights to the tithe, but only a share in the family meal, although every third year his portion was probably greater. Another passage (Dt. 18:1-8) pictures the whole tribe of Levi, both those who exercised the ministry of priests (the priests the Levites) and those who were teachers and expositors (the clients who were classed with the poor), as being the recipients of the firstfruits of grain, wine and oil, and of the first fleece of the sheep (18:4).

How are these various views to be reconciled? Some exegetes, both Jewish and Christian, have argued that there was a second tithe to be taken after the first tithe which was brought according to the prescriptions of Numbers 18. There does not seem to be any ground for this in the text. In the present section (14:22-29) the tithe is not spoken of as something additional (*cf.* 18:3, 4). Other exegetes have proposed that the law of tithing in Numbers 18 represents a different stage in the development of the law from that in Deuteronomy 14. It might be asked, in that case, which one was earlier, the law in Numbers 18 in which the whole tithe was given to the Levites, or that in Deuteronomy where the tithe was used up partly at a sacred feast and partly in the relief of the poor? In both of these the Levites have a share. Some have argued that the law in Deuteronomy has the appearance of being the more primitive.[1] It is impossible to decide whether this is so or not. Against such a view it has been pointed out that it is difficult to see how so radically different an arrangement as

---

[1] S. R. Driver, *Deuteronomy* (*ICC*, 1902), p. 172.

that represented in Numbers 18 could develop out of that pictured in Deuteronomy 14. A compromise is made between these two views by proposing that Deuteronomy 14 represents the custom in northern Israel, while that in Numbers 18 represents the tithing law taught by the priests of Jerusalem for Judah (*cf.* Ne. 10:37).[1] Alternatively, it is proposed that the differences between the two are not as drastic as it appears. Neither Deuteronomy 14 nor Numbers 18 refers explicitly to an animal tithe. Only in Leviticus 27:30–33 is this so (*cf.* 2 Ch. 31:6). It is possible that the animal tithe was taken for granted in Deuteronomy and Numbers. Again, although according to Numbers 18:21 'every tithe' was to be given to the Levites, Deuteronomy 14 may mean simply that, notwithstanding this allocation, the offerer of the tithe might keep some for a communion feast at the sanctuary, except in the third year. A further modification is that other dependants were included along with the Levites in the use of the tithe in the third year. It is possible that the tithe had different uses. It was an offering which acknowledged God's ownership of the land and its fruits, a means to support the Levite and the needy, and an offering for the sake of charity.

There has been some discussion about where verse 27 should fit, whether with verse 26 or with verses 28, 29. The LXX omits *you shalt not forsake*, so that there is an easy flow on from verse 26, *you and your household and the Levite who is within your towns.* . . . On the other hand verse 27 may be taken with the following verses, so that the Levites are mentioned only in connection with the third-year tithe and are thus not seen as sharers in the family sacred meal.

28, 29. Every third year a different disposition of the tithe was prescribed. The whole of the tithe was to be stored in the village (*cf.* 26:12, which speaks of 'the third year, which is the year of tithing'), and not taken to the central sanctuary. It was to be used for the relief of local need. The confession to be used on that occasion is given in 26:13–15. As we have seen, this special tithe is not mentioned in Numbers 18 or Leviticus 27. The retention of the tithe in the villages in the third year would presumably have left the priests at the central sanctuary without sustenance. The harmonizing of the various procedures is thus not easy. Whatever the solution, the editor of Deuteronomy gives a reason for the practice, namely, *that*

---

[1] G. E. Wright, *Deuteronomy* (*IB*, Vol. 2, 1953), p. 425.

Yahweh your God may bless you in all the work of your hands that you do (29; *cf.* 15:4-6, 10, 11, 18). Further, this modification of the ancient law is thoroughly in keeping with biblical teaching both in the Old and New Testaments. The interests of the poor and needy are bound up with the interests of God Himself (24:15; Pr. 22:23). God prefers that they who bring offerings to Him should at the same time care for the poor (Is. 1:13-17; Ho. 6:6; Mt. 25:40; 1 Jn. 4:20, *etc.*).

vi. The year of release (15:1-11). It is one of the features of the Deuteronomic expression of Israelite law, although it may be seen elsewhere in the Old Testament, that there is a deep concern for the welfare of the individual member of society, whether rich or poor. Elsewhere in the ancient Near East men were treated in terms of their status in the community rather than as individuals. Members of the aristocracy, priests, landowners, rulers and military leaders always had the advantage. A study of the so-called Code of Hammurabi[1] will reveal that the slave and the underprivileged counted for less before the law. In Israel, however, the poor and needy were the special concern of God and the covenant family was expected to ensure the welfare of every member of the family. Hence Israelite law was framed to protect the underprivileged. Since Israel herself had once been enslaved in Egypt and had known the sorrow of oppression and the joy of redemption, she was bound to guarantee the freedom and welfare of individuals.

These principles are illustrated first of all in the regulation which deals with the year of release. In ancient times the *release* (*šᵉmiṭṭâ*, lit. 'letting go') referred to the practice of allowing the land to lie fallow every seventh year (Lv. 25:3f.).[2] This pointed to the belief that the land finally belonged to

---

[1] *ANET*, pp. 163-180. A study of the section from law 196 onwards will demonstrate the point. It has been argued in recent years that the so-called Code of Hammurabi was rather in the nature of a royal apologia to provide evidence for the people, for posterity, for future kings and for the gods that the king had executed his divinely ordained mandate to establish (social) justice (Akk. *mēšaram šakānu*) in the land and that he had been a just ruler according to the law. In the first instance the king proclaimed *mēšarum*, *i.e.* justice, equity, thereby declaring that he would put right the injustices and irregularities of past years. See D. J. Wiseman, 'The Laws of Hammurabi again', *JSS*, VII, 2, 1962, p. 163, n. 2; *JCS*, XV, 1961, pp. 162-168.

[2] There is something of a parallel between this practice and the *mēšarum*-acts of rulers in Mesopotamia who, in the first year of their reign, made a declaration that they intended to put right the injustices of the past. See previous footnote.

Yahweh (Lv. 25:23). A similar principle was to operate also in the case of a man who had incurred personal debts when the social and economic structure of Israel changed from that of a patriarchal peasant economy to the complex economy under the monarchy. In a later day, when a system of taxation developed, peasants were often unable to pay their dues and had to borrow money to meet obligations to the state. The annual yield of their fields was likely to be swallowed up in living and in paying their debt. At the end of six years, when the land was allowed to lie fallow, no claim was to be made against them by a creditor. The burden lay, of course, on the peasant, since the creditor could afford to live off the profits of previous years.

The literary form of the present section is significant and is characteristic of much of Deuteronomy. First of all there is an apodictic law *At the end of every seven years you shall grant a release* (1). In verse 2 there is an exact legal interpretation of the meaning, *this is the manner of the release*. Then in verses 3 to 11 there is an exposition and expansion of the basic law, so that the personal implications of the law for particular individuals are stressed.

1. The reference is to the sabbatical year which ended each seven-year period within a jubilee cycle. In the 'book of the covenant' (Ex. 23:10, 11) the year is referred to as one in which the land was to 'lie fallow, that the poor of your people may eat'. The root of the verb 'lie fallow' (*š-m-ṭ*) is also the root of the noun *release*. The law is expounded in more detail in Leviticus 25:1–7, where the year is called 'a sabbath of solemn rest for the land' (4). In Deuteronomy alone is the sabbatical year designated as a time when debts were to be remitted. Clearly the peasant could not pay debts from the produce of his land if the land was fallow. The year of jubilee in Leviticus 25:8–17, 25–55 is a related idea, but there it has reference to the land without mention of the problem of the debtor.

The idea of a *release* is not peculiar to Israel. Babylonian law recognized a similar practice and the expression 'to establish a (general) release' (*andurāram šakānum*) is related in meaning to the expression 'to establish (social) justice'. Indeed etymologically *andurārum* (Akk.) has the same root as Hebrew *deror*.[1]

---

[1] The term occurs in the sense of 'liberty' or 'release' in Lv. 25:10; Is. 61:1; Je. 34:8, 15, 17; Ezk. 46:17. See D. J. Wiseman, 'The Laws of Hammurabi again', *JSS*, VII, 2, 1962, p. 168; J. Lewy, *Eretz-Israel*, V, 1961, p. 28.

2. The manner (*dābār*) of the release is now given, since the bare apodictic law had to be interpreted. No doubt the explanation was clear to the people of that time, but the modern reader has difficulty with the Hebrew text and asks whether the *release* meant the total remission of the indebtedness or merely the suspension of it for that year. We may translate the Hebrew text in two ways: either *Let every creditor* (lit. 'owner of a loan from his hand') *drop* ('cancel') *that which he loaned to his friend*; or *Let every creditor* (lit. 'owner of a loan') *drop his hand in regard to what he has loaned to his friend*.

The first translation seems to suggest that the creditor dropped his claim completely. The RSV makes this sense clearer than the AV: *every creditor shall release what he has lent to his neighbour; he shall not exact it of his neighbour, his brother, because Yahweh's release has been proclaimed*. It is to be noted that one's *neighbour* is also one's *brother*, and the *release* is *Yahweh's release*. Israel was thus reminded of obligations to the whole people as though to a brother, and also of the redeeming and restoring grace of Yahweh.

The JPSA translation, on the other hand, suggests that it is only the rental or interest for that year that was remitted: *every creditor shall remit the due that he claims from his neighbour; he shall not dun his neighbour or kinsman, for the remission proclaimed is of the Lord*.

The following verses suggest that a total cancellation of the debt was intended, however strange this may appear to us today. The fact that the seventh year of release and the jubilee year of liberty together belonged to one symbolic unit suggests total cancellation of debts. In the jubilee sabbath the principle was extended to its limit in the restoration of personal freedom and the reversion of all lands to the original owners. Whenever the sabbatical release was applied it was a reminder of Yahweh's release of His people from the bondage of Egypt.

Whatever the exact sense of the passage may be, one point is clear: the man of Israel was to act with mercy towards a fellow Israelite who had fallen into debt through no fault of his own.

3. With this verse the more personal aspects of the law are raised. Israel is exhorted to deal with the poor always with generosity. The *foreigner* (*nokrî*) was different from the resident alien (*gēr*) who was absorbed into the Israelite community (*cf.* 14:21a). It was legal to require payment of debts from foreigners during the sabbatical year, for they were not included in the family circle of Israel. The law was designed to relieve poverty in Israel and to regulate relations between members of the covenant community.

4–6. While it seemed likely that Israel would always have poor people (11), yet the possibility that it might be otherwise should be envisaged. It is here affirmed, in keeping with the general view of Deuteronomy, that complete obedience to Yahweh and to His commandments would result in the bestowal of divine blessing. This would mean, among other things, that there would be no poor in the land (and hence the law of verse 2 would never need to be enforced), but also that Israel as a nation would never be in debt to other nations, but would rather lend to them. Nor would she ever be subdued by the nations, but would rule over them.

7–10. Here the writer passes from the exactness of legal expression to an urgent appeal to Israel to treat the poor at all times with an open hand and an open heart (7, 8, 10). While the law required that debtors should be released from their obligations every seventh year, love demanded nothing less than a continual attitude of generosity and mercy towards the poor. The letter killed, but the spirit gave life. The absence of compassion would lead men to the degrading reaction described in verse 9 and a law that was designed to protect the poor would become a reason for oppressing them. As the seventh year approached men of wealth would hesitate to make loans which would not be reimbursed. To lend a poor man something in the sixth year was practically to make him a gift. But it was precisely a gift of this kind that was being asked of Israel. Here was the affirmation of a great principle which found expression in other words in the New Testament centuries later (Mt. 5:43–48; Lk. 14:12–14; 2 Cor. 9:7). These verses anticipate the Sermon on the Mount because they penetrate behind the outward act to the motives and intents of the heart. Obedience towards God inevitably issues in generosity towards one's fellows. Indeed, in 1 John 3:17 hardness of heart is reckoned as a denial of every profession that the love of God abides in a man's heart. A mean and grudging spirit which provokes a cry of distress from a poor man is sinful in God's sight and merits divine condemnation. On the other hand, Yahweh never fails to respond in blessing to a happy and generous giver.

11. With unashamed realism the writer concludes that, in fact, there would always be poor in the land, because Israel would always be disobedient. Hence there would always be opportunities to display generosity towards the poor.

vii. The Hebrew slave (15:12–18). The second law designed to protect the poor is concerned with a Hebrew man or woman who entered into some contract of service because of debt. At the end of six years he was to be released and sent away with generous gifts which would help him to start a new life. In the faithful observance of this law Israel would recall her own time of slavery in Egypt and the abundant provision she enjoyed when her release came. A memory such as this would act as a powerful motivating force. If for some reason the man or woman in Israel desired of his own free will to remain in the service of the master, it was possible to do so for the rest of life. But even apart from that possibility, the release of a Hebrew slave was not to be counted loss, since six years of his service was equivalent to the cost of hiring a servant. Obedience to the law would guarantee the divine blessing and no loss would result to the master.

12. Here is a restatement of the law which occurs in Exodus 21:2–11. There are differences in the two statements. In Exodus 21 the female slave appears to have a lower status, whereas in Deuteronomy 15 male and female slaves appear to be equal. Again Deuteronomy 15:12 refers to both *a Hebrew man* and *a Hebrew woman*, whereas Exodus 21:2 refers only to a Hebrew slave. The verb in that case is in the third singular masculine. The woman in Exodus 21:2–11 is a concubine and not a free woman, although there may be a hint of a woman slave, so that what is implicit in Exodus becomes explicit in Deuteronomy. Further, the slave is described as a *brother* in Deuteronomy 15:12, but not in Exodus. While it seems that the two passages deal basically with the same issue, the version in Deuteronomy gives clearer definition.

The term *Hebrew* in both Exodus 21 and Deuteronomy 15 raises certain questions. Originally this term was widely used in the ancient Near East for people who occupied a particular social position. Generally the Hebrews (Habiru) were foreigners and were engaged in many types of hired service. The term in the Old Testament is not always complimentary. Indeed it is used more frequently of Israelites in a foreign or slave status than in a state of freedom. The Israelites in Egypt are often called *Hebrews* (Ex. 2:6, 11, 13; 3:18; 5:3; 7:16; 9:1, 13; 10:3, *etc.*). Again, in the days of the judges, when Israel was under Philistine domination, the Israelites were called *Hebrews* (1 Sa. 4:6, 9; 13:3; 14:11, 21, *etc.*). It is possible that in Deuteronomy 15 *Hebrew* denotes a Habiru (or Hapiru) slave and that the reference is to a foreigner normally engaged in various types of service but now fallen on bad times. It remains possible, especially in the light of Leviticus 25:39–55, that the reference is to an Israelite who has temporarily accepted a status which is virtually a slave status.

13, 14. The obligation to provide gifts for the man or woman who is at last freed does not appear in Exodus 21. By comparison Leviticus 25:39–55 states that a poor Israelite must not be treated as a slave, but only as a hired servant (especially verses 39–41). At the year of jubilee he and his family are to be freed together (*cf.* Ex. 21:4, where a master who provided a wife for a man was permitted to keep the wife and children. Evidently the wife was considered as almost equivalent to a concubine). The original law was applied in various ways, perhaps according to the time and place where it operated. In Jeremiah's day the law was disregarded (Je. 34:8–16). But despite certain limitations it gave expression to a genuine concern for slaves and showed a real attempt to legislate against the control of some individuals by others. The personal freedom of every member of the covenant family was at stake in this matter of slavery. Even though the provisions were designed to help only the people of Israel, they show a remarkable advance in social thinking.

The measure of the master's gifts to the slave who was freed was *As Yahweh your God has blessed you, you shall give to him*. The gifts were to include gifts from the flock, from the threshing-floor, *i.e.* from the grain gathered in, and from the wine that had been produced. These would enable a man to start afresh in life.

15. The erstwhile master was himself a member of a redeemed nation, although neither he nor his fellows had experienced the exodus deliverance. But, because of the corporate nature of Israel, any individual in any age could be regarded as one with those who had personally experienced the deliverance of the exodus and could in memory and by an act of identification enter into that ancient experience in faith. *You shall remember that you were a slave in the land of Egypt*. Hence any master of a slave in any age by freeing his own slave would be expressing gratitude to God for having liberated His own people (*cf.* 5:14, 15, where the same reason is given for the observance of the sabbath rest for slaves and masters alike). The argument was all the stronger when the slave was also a member of the redeemed Israel, although it carried some weight for other cases also.

16. As in the older law (Ex. 21:5, 6), provision was made for a man under contract of service (akin to slavery) to continue in that status for life. The slave may feel happy to live with his master permanently. Such a proposal was not as strange in a society that was still close to the nomadic state as it is to us. In such an economy the slave had an important place in the family (*cf.* Gn. 24:2ff., where Eliezer the servant was sent by Abraham to find a wife for Isaac).

17. The ceremony by which a slave was attached permanently to his master is similar to that in Exodus 21:6, although in Exodus 21 the ceremony was evidently a religious one. The master 'brought him to God', which probably indicates a ceremony at the sanctuary. The same procedure may have obtained in the law in Deuteronomy 15:16, although the specific statement that the master 'brought him to God' does not occur. It may therefore have taken place in the family circle as a symbolic rite. A man's ear, the symbol of obedience,[1] was affixed to the door of the master's house as a symbol that he was joined to his master's household.[2] The same procedure applied to both males and females.

18. Alas, laws which were originally designed to be helpful became burdensome. It might seem that a man to whom some debt was due would be unable to recoup his loss if he let the debtor go free. Against this one could set the promise of Yahweh's blessing for obedience. The term translated *double* in AV and *half* in RSV is Hebrew *mišneh*. It is probably a technical term meaning 'equivalent to'.[3] In other words the service of an Israelite was equivalent to what would be paid for a hired servant.

viii. The firstlings of flocks and herds (15:19–23). The same literary form is followed here as in the two preceding passages. The law is first stated in its simplest form and then

---

[1] *Cf.* Ps. 40:6; Hammurabi Law 282.

[2] A quaint modern application of this custom used to be in vogue in some English public schools, where boys who commenced Hebrew at a tender age were taken to the classroom by their fellows and pinned to the door by any sharp object. Such devotion to Hebrew was regarded as somewhat in the nature of a willing enslavement.

[3] D. J. Wiseman, art. 'Archaeology', *NBD*, p. 67, Section VIII. a.

expounded and explained. A distinction is drawn between first-born animals without blemish and those which are not perfect. The first group may be used as sacrificial animals and the second for ordinary secular purposes.

19a. The question of firstlings mentioned in 12:6, 7 and 14:23 is now resumed. Firstlings are to be set apart for Yahweh. The law is stated apodictically. Alternative forms of this law occur elsewhere in the Old Testament (Ex. 13:11–16; 22:29, 30; 34:19, 20; Lv. 27:26, 27; Nu. 18:15–18). All forms of the law are in basic agreement, although there are differences in detail. Thus in Numbers 18:17, 18 it appears that the firstlings belonged to Aaron, *i.e.* to the priests.

19b. Since the firstling was set apart for Yahweh it was not to be used for such secular tasks as working in the field, nor was the wool to be shorn from the flocks, *i.e.* these animals were withdrawn from all economic use.

20. The standard procedure for unblemished firstlings was to slay them at the sanctuary chosen by Yahweh and to eat their flesh in households. The procedure was to be an annual one.

21, 22. Blemished beasts were not acceptable as sacrifices. It was both an economic trick and an insult to God to offer them (*cf.* Mal. 1:7ff.). Lame, torn, blind and blemished firstlings had no sale-value in the market. They could be eaten in secular meals and treated like animals that were hunted as game, such as gazelles or harts (*cf.* 12:15, 22). The laws of ceremonial cleanness which applied in the case of purely religious meals did not apply.

23. Again, the prohibition of eating blood is made, as in 12:15, 16. This applied whether the animal was slaughtered for sacrifice or for a secular meal.

ix. The three annual pilgrimages (16:1–17). The lengthy section on the worship of the covenant people which began at 12:1 concludes with a brief outline of the laws for the three annual pilgrimages to the central sanctuary, the feast of passover and unleavened bread, the feast of weeks, and the feast of tabernacles. The Hebrew word for feast is *ḥaḡ*, reminding one of the Muslim annual pilgrimage to Mecca the *ḥaj*. Israel's three pilgrim feasts were to take place specifically at the central sanctuary (2, 6, 7, 11, 15, 16). The patterning of these feasts on a sabbatical scheme is in keeping with a variety of other sabbatical practices in Israel (*cf.* 15:1, 9, 12, 18, *etc.*). These three feasts in each case preserve something old and also introduce something new. It would seem that ancient agricultural festivals were invested with a new significance and became the occasion for historical commemoration, *i.e.* ancient festivals were historicized. While they were observed at the same time in the agricultural year, they pointed to events associated with the exodus, where Yahweh displayed His gracious saving activity in liberating His people from slavery in Egypt. The first of the three pilgrimages listed here is really a combination of two, namely the ancient feast of unleavened bread and the feast of passover.

1–8. The feast of passover and unleavened bread. 1. The legal maxim phrased apodictically reads *Observe the month* (new moon) *of Abib, and keep the passover to Yahweh your God.* The formulation is not unlike that in 5:12 referring to the sabbath. It is of interest that the month is named *Abib,* lit. 'the month of the green ears', following the older Canaanite system of naming months, that is, approximately March–April, in the spring. Later Israel changed to the Babylonian system when *Abib* became *Nisan.* The older terminology suggests that the present law goes back to a time when Canaanite terminology was in common use. The fact that Abib was in spring leads to the conclusion that the festival was a spring festival. And since it was in the month of Abib that Yahweh brought Israel out of Egypt, the historicizing of the festival in Israel was easy.

2. The original passover sacrifice was a lamb (Ex. 12:3ff.). In this verse Israel is commanded to *offer the passover* (*pesah*) *sacrifice from the flock or the herd.* Originally, passover was celebrated in family or kin groups (Ex. 12:1ff., 21). According to this legislation it had to be celebrated at the central sanctuary and so became a pilgrim feast. Comparison with the great passover ceremonies of Hezekiah (2 Ch. 30:13–27) and of Josiah (2 Ch. 35:1–19) suggests that it may have been a simultaneous feast celebrated at the central sanctuary as early as the days of the judges and then on into the days of the kings (2 Ki. 23:22; 2 Ch. 35:18). Many scholars think that there was an ancient tribal feast which was celebrated before the tribe set out for the spring pastures, in which an offering for the welfare of the flock was made.[1] Because the exodus corresponded in time to this event, and in the light of the whole

[1] See R. de Vaux, *Ancient Israel* (1962), pp. 489ff.

exodus story, the Israelites forgot the ancient ceremony and thereafter focused their attention only on the historical event of the exodus (Ex. 12).

Another question arises from a study of the passover ceremonies of Hezekiah and Josiah. The narratives suggest that the lamb was the normal beast to be slain (2 Ch. 30:15; 35:1). But other animals are mentioned also in connection with the general celebrations, passover offerings of lambs, kids and bulls (2 Ch. 35:7) in the case of Josiah, and bulls and sheep in the case of Hezekiah (2 Ch. 30:24). What was the nature of these additional animals? Were they to be used in the feast of unleavened bread that followed the feast of passover, or was it possible to offer beasts other than lambs? Certainly Deuteronomy 16:2 states that the passover sacrifice was *from the flock or the herd*. The verb used here, *offer the sacrifice* (*zābaḥ*), is generally used in a technical sense.

3. Another ancient feast, the feast of unleavened bread, seems to lie behind this verse. In a parallel passage in Exodus 23:14–17, where the three feasts are mentioned, the first is called the feast of unleavened bread (*maṣṣôṯ*), during which unleavened bread was to be eaten for seven days in the month of Abib (Ex. 23:14). From ancient times there was an agricultural feast celebrated at the time of barley harvest, which was also in spring. It is evident that the two festivals were combined, since they fell at the same period of the year. The feast of unleavened bread, lasting for seven days, followed directly on the passover (Lv. 23:5, 6; Ex. 12:14, 15). The passover was held on the fourteenth day of the month, and on the fifteenth day the feast of unleavened bread began and went on for seven days.

What proportion of those whom Moses addressed on the plains of Moab *came out of the land of Egypt in hurried flight* is impossible to say. The older generation had died in the wilderness and only those who were children at the time of the exodus survived. Still, they would have remembered those events very vividly and would have narrated them to their own children. However, although the audience was made up in considerable part of people who had been born since the days of the exodus, the injunction of verse 3 was still valid. Israel at all points in her history comprised a living whole which would remember for ever what God had done for the nation at the exodus. That memory formed the essence of the religious conscience of each individual in each generation. The value of the passover feast was to educate that conscience and to bring to life for each individual the great fact of national deliverance, compelling the children of each new generation to accept the obligations of a redeemed people. Basically, this is the thrust of the whole argument in Deuteronomy.

Unleavened bread, usual among the nomads (Gn. 19:3), became for Israel the symbol of its life in the desert. It also recalled to their minds the hasty exit from Egypt, when there was no time even to leaven the dough (Ex. 12:34). It was therefore *bread of affliction*, a reminder of the hardships of Egypt and the opposition of the pharaoh. Once the feast became the occasion for historical memory its agricultural associations were lost.

4. For the first part of this verse comparison should be made with Exodus 12:14-20; 13:3, 6, 7; 34:18; Leviticus 23:6. For the second part of the verse compare Exodus 12:10; 23:18b; 34:25b; Numbers 9:12.

5, 6. The transfer of the passover feast, from the home where it was observed in Egypt (Ex. 12:3-10) to the central sanctuary, is here enjoined on Israel. The time of eating was to be *in the evening at the going down of the sun*. It was the time when the exodus took place. By New Testament times the passover was once again a home festival. Thus Jesus ate the passover with His disciples in a specially prepared upper room (Mt. 26:17-19; Lk. 22:7-23).

7. The narrative in Exodus 12:8, 9 indicates that the flesh was to be roasted in the fire, but not eaten raw or boiled with water. The Deuteronomic law appears to authorize a change. The passover sacrifice was to be *boiled* (*cf.* the proceedings at the sanctuary of Shiloh, 1 Sa. 2:12ff.). This interpretation of the verb used here, *biššēl*, may not be the only possibility open. When the verb is followed by 'with water' (as in Ex. 12:9; 2 Ch. 35:13b) it clearly denotes *boil*. Also we may infer from the fact that at Shiloh, when one thrust a fork into the pan, kettle, cauldron or pot, the sacrifice was being boiled. But in 2 Chronicles 35:13a the verb is followed by the phrase 'with fire' and evidently means 'roast'. Incidentally in 2 Chronicles 35:13b the same verb is followed by the expression 'in pots, in cauldrons, and in pans', which shows in the same context two different uses. Perhaps, therefore, it means more generally 'to cook'.[1] In Deuteronomy 16:7 the verb is used without the

---

[1] The verb is used in Nu. 11:8 and 2 Sa. 13:8 for cooking cakes, almost certainly meaning 'bake' and not 'boil'. In Akkadian the verb *bašālu* means to cook by roasting or boiling.

defining clause, so that we cannot say with certainty what was intended.

On the morning following the passover feast the people were to *turn and go to your tents*. Such an instruction could be obeyed literally in a time when Israel was nomadic and lived in tents. In a later day conditions changed somewhat. It would be a case of pilgrims coming to the central sanctuary from afar, so that temporary accommodation would be necessary. According to the great Jewish-Christian scholar Alfred Edersheim,[1] in the days of Jesus some pilgrims were accommodated within the walls of the city, but many must have camped outside the city walls. In modern times the remnants of the Samaritan community camp in tents on Mount Gerizim at passover time.

8. The seventh day of the festival was a day of *solemn assembly* (*'aṣereṭ*). The term is used for the gathering of people for the celebration of public rites of some kind (2 Ki. 10:20; Is. 1:13; Joel 1:14; Am. 5:21), especially on the seventh day of passover week or on the eighth day of the festival of tabernacles.

9–12. The feast of weeks. The feast of weeks was an important feast in Israel over the centuries. Later it became known as pentecost, because it was celebrated on the fiftieth day from the sabbath beginning the passover. It has a variety of names in the Old Testament, 'the feast (pilgrimage) of weeks' (10; Ex. 34:22), 'the feast of harvest' (Ex. 23:16) and 'the day of the first fruits' (Nu. 28:26; *cf.* Ex. 23:16; 34:22). As the feast of harvest, or more correctly, the wheat harvest (*qāṣîr*), it was one of the main dates on the agricultural calendar of Palestine. In ancient times it was a feast for farmers who lived a settled life. In Deuteronomy it is not linked directly to Israel's salvation history.

9. The date of the harvest festival is here given as seven weeks after the sickle is first put to the standing grain (*cf.* Lv. 23:15, 16, fifty days), hence the name of the festival, the feast of weeks. The period of fifty days seems to have been the period between the beginning of the barley harvest and the end of the wheat harvest. It was long enough to allow for variation in harvest times throughout the land. In warmer parts of the land barley ripens in April and wheat somewhat later. In the hill country reaping may not commence till the end of May or

---

[1] A. Edersheim, *The Temple, its ministry and services at the time of Jesus Christ* (1874), p. 184.

early June.[1] Even so, the date of the feast must have been fixed only in general terms, for no date could accommodate all possible variations in harvest. The feast of unleavened bread (*maṣṣôt*) was a preparation for the second feast and the two together marked the beginning and the end of harvest time. The general spirit of joyful thanksgiving would not be spoiled if seasonal variations or geographical variations prevented exact coincidence of the harvest with the date of the feast prescribed at the central sanctuary. Arrangements could easily be made to offer the prescribed offerings (Lv. 23:16–21). The Christian feast of Pentecost has had from its very beginning a different meaning, for it is linked with the gift of the Holy Spirit (Acts 2). The fact that it coincided on that first occasion with the Jewish feast may be an indication that it pointed to the end of an old system and the commencement of a new, in which the promises of the old have come to fulfilment in the new.

10. The man of Israel was required to make a gift to Yahweh at this season commensurate with the measure of Yahweh's blessing on his crop (*cf.* verse 17).

11. The feast of weeks, like the other great annual festivals, was an occasion for joy as the worshippers shared a communion meal or a sacrificial feast *before Yahweh*, *i.e.* in God's presence (*cf.* 12:7; 14:26; 26:11). The present feast, like others, was ideally to be shared with the family, the servants, the Levites, the resident aliens, the fatherless and the widows. It was, after all, only a sharing in the bounty with which God had blessed the people. The particular interest of the book of Deuteronomy in the Levites is again to be noted here (*cf.* verse 14; 12:18, 19; 14:27, 29; 26:11, 12).

12. The recollection of the years of slavery in Egypt was to be a motive for a variety of actions in Israel, such as the kindly treatment of slaves (15:15), generosity and justice to the poor and needy (24:18, 22) and a warning against provoking Yahweh to anger (9:7).

13–15. The feast of tabernacles. The third feast of the year was in some ways the greatest of all. It is called in Leviticus 23:29 'the feast of Yahweh' and in Ezekiel 45:25 'the feast'. In the oldest calendars it is the feast of ingathering. It was to be celebrated *when you make your ingathering from your*

[1] The ancient Gezer calendar allowed a month for barley harvest and a month for wheat harvest. See *ANET*, p. 320, translation by W. F. Albright.

threshing floor and your wine press (13), *i.e.* at the harvest time during the autumn months of September and October. Thanksgiving for the harvest and festive joy were the keynotes of this festival also (14; Lv. 23:40). In the year of release at the time of the feast of booths the law was read to all Israel (31:9–13).

13. It is probable that this *feast of booths* (*sukkôt*) was also originally an agricultural feast celebrating the harvest of grapes and other fruits which ripen in the late summer and autumn. But it was historicized and became the occasion for remembering that at the time of the exodus the Israelites dwelt in booths (Lv. 23:40ff.). Like the feast of unleavened bread this feast lasted a week and according to Leviticus 23:36, 39 it lasted from the fifteenth to the twenty-first day of the seventh month, with a solemn assembly on the eighth day. Parallel passages which refer to this feast are Exodus 23:16; 34:22; Leviticus 23:33ff.; Numbers 29:12f.

14, 15. The joyful nature of the festival survived from the older agricultural festival, although the reason for the joy was now Yahweh's bountiful provision. This feast was also a shared feast and it took place at the central sanctuary. An important New Testament passage referring to events during the feast of tabernacles is John 7 and 8.

Joyfulness in worship is an important motif in Deuteronomy, but also generally in both the Old and New Testaments. Expressions of joy were made in many of the psalms that were sung in the Temple worship (Pss. 16:11; 27:6; 63:5; 66:1; 81:1, *etc.*). In God's presence, where the worshipper becomes aware of His past mercies, of His present forgiveness and of the prospect of His future blessing, the expression of deep joy seems to be natural and spontaneous. While it is important at times to be grieved over one's sins in God's presence, it is perhaps more normal to rejoice at all His gracious benefits.

16, 17. Summary of the yearly pilgrimages. The ancient requirement that the men of Israel should report to the central sanctuary three times a year has an interesting parallel in the Near Eastern treaty requirements. It was common practice for suzerains to require their vassals to report to them periodically, in some cases three times a year, in order to renew their allegiance and to bring tribute.

The three pilgrim feasts are now summarized as *the feast of unleavened bread, the feast of weeks* and *the feast of booths.* The passover, as such, is not mentioned. It is evidently subsumed under the feast of unleavened bread (*cf.* Ex. 23:14–17; 34:23). Whether these are regarded as national anniversaries or agricultural festivals or both, they provided Israel with the opportunity to affirm collectively her faith in Yahweh her Redeemer and the Lord of her land.

b. The character of Israel's leaders (16:18 – 18:22)

Following the lengthy section dealing with Israel's worship comes a shorter, but reasonably coherent, section on the character of Israel's leaders, judges (16:18–20), the court (17:8–13), kings (17:14–20), priests (18:1–8) and prophets (18:9–22). The short section 16:21 – 17:7 appears at first sight to be an intrusion which is unrelated to the context. It appears rather to belong to the laws of worship of the previous section. But there may have been a deliberate purpose in placing it here since it deals with the loyalty of the people to their covenant God. The erection of the cult symbols of other gods, the offering of blemished sacrifices, and the transgression of the covenant by acts of evil were all indications of a disloyal frame of mind. In Israel there was a unity between political-judicial righteousness and cultic holiness, since Yahweh was both king and God. Religious law and civil law were one. Both were embraced by the covenant stipulations. Although it may seem strange to us, with our tidy methods of Western logic, to insert among regulations concerned with Israel's officials a small section which deals with religious laws, this was evidently not the case with the people of Israel. Perhaps basically these verses stress the fact that Yahweh was the exclusive source of all authority, religious, political or social in Israel.

i. Judges (16:18–20). By piecing together a variety of references to judicial procedures in ancient Israel some idea of its main legal processes may be obtained.[1] Unfortunately, the information is limited. In early times it was the task of the priests to preserve the laws and to give authentic interpretations (Mal. 2:7). During the wilderness period Moses is pictured as Israel's chief judge, with assistant judges drawn from the tribes (1:12–18; Ex. 18:13–27). Probably these were the elders of the tribes. The present passage envisages two

[1] R. de Vaux, *Ancient Israel* (1962), pp. 143–163, gives a valuable presentation of the available information.

groups of officials, *judges* and *officers*, to be appointed, apparently *in all your towns*. Certain basic principles are then given for the guidance of these men.

18. It is not improbable that the *judges* (*šōp̄ēṭ*) were the leaders of the local councils of elders (*cf.* 19:12), perhaps local chiefs (*cf.* Jdg. 3:10; Ho. 13:10; Am. 2:3). The second group, the *officers* or officials (*šōṭēr*), were assistants of some kind. The root *š-ṭ-r* means 'write'. But these were not mere scribes (*cf.* 2 Ch. 34:13, where the two are distinguished). Perhaps they were 'clerks of court' attached to the judges (1 Ch. 23:4; 26:29). The same term is used elsewhere to denote officers in charge of forced labour (Ex. 5:6f.) and the administrative officers of the army (Dt. 20:5f.), both of whom were officials of state. It is at least open to question whether perhaps both of these groups were appointees of the state in later days. It was, in any case, the responsibility of the judges to judge the people with *righteous judgment* (lit. 'a judgment of righteousness)'. The term *righteousness* (*ṣeḏeq*) denotes 'what is right'. Every individual in Israel had rights according to God's law. It was the task of the judge to see that 'right' was restored to those who had been deprived of it, and, if need be, to punish offenders.

19. Three rules are stated apodictically. *You shall not pervert justice; you shall not show partiality; you shall not take a bribe.* Possibly these are quotations from an ancient corpus of apodictic law. The third of these is followed by a brief elucidation expressed in terms of an ancient proverb (*cf.* Ex. 23:1-3, 6-9). The expression *you shall not show partiality* is a vivid one, meaning literally 'Thou shalt not recognize (regard) faces', *i.e.* all citizens must be regarded as equal in law since all stand before Yahweh, the divine Judge, regardless of class.

20. Here is a homiletical observation arising out of the ancient law. The writer is not satisfied merely to quote the law but proceeds to press home the implications of that law. He says *Justice, and only justice, you shall follow*. The further point is made that the way to enjoy God's blessing is to obey His laws.

ii. Regulative principles in judicial procedures (16:21 – 17:7).

Because of the inter-relationship of cultic and civil processes, principles which applied in religious practice also applied in civil practice. Three principles are declared in these verses, the finality of Yahweh's authority, respect for Yahweh's name, and the need for careful investigation and substantiation of every offence before judgment was carried out. Two of these principles find support in three ancient apodictic laws, two of which are then quoted (16:21 – 17:1), while the third arises from the discussion of a case of apostasy (17:2–7).

16:21 – 17:1. Three apodictic laws referring to pagan worship are now stated in their barest form. *You shall not plant any tree as an Asherah beside the altar of Yahweh; you shall not set up a pillar (maṣṣēḇâ); you shall not sacrifice to Yahweh your God an ox or a sheep in which is a blemish.*

In their present form these laws are expanded slightly with interpretative comment.[1] The *Asherah* was a wooden post, the symbol of the goddess Asherah or Astarte, and the stone *pillar* symbolized the male deity Baal (*cf.* 12:3). These laws apply not only to the central sanctuary but to any altar of Yahweh, wherever it may be. Once the central sanctuary was recognized the laws applied with special significance to it, and in the days of the kings it was not unknown for such forbidden items to be found in the Temple (*e.g.* 2 Ki. 23:6).

The first two laws (16:21, 22) stressed the fact that Yahweh alone was Israel's God. This was a basic concept both for religion and for law. Hence in judicial processes, cases of extreme difficulty in Israel were decided by the priests at the central sanctuary in the presence of Yahweh, the ultimate authority in Israel.

The third law (17:1), with its emphasis on the honour of Yahweh, stressed a principle which is quite as important in judicial as in cultic matters. Where judges held Yahweh in honour they might be expected to give wise decisions.

2–7. The case of an apostate who transgressed the covenant by giving his allegiance to other gods is now treated. On dealing with such a serious matter (*cf.* chapter 13), an important principle of procedure, which was valid also in judicial matters, was followed. Guilt has to be proved by diligent search and on the evidence of two or three witnesses. Since the case is a capital offence the witnesses must initiate the death sentence by casting the first stones, thereby exposing themselves to blood revenge should their testimony prove false (*cf.* 19:15–21). The same principles were to apply in civil cases.

The reference to the worship of *the sun or the moon, or any of the host of heaven*, *i.e.* the stars, is sometimes regarded as indicating that the book of Deuteronomy was written in Assyrian

---

[1] Gerhard von Rad, *Deuteronomy* (1966), p. 115.

times. It should be noted, however, that the worship of the sun, moon and stars by polytheists was as old, and older, than Moses. Indeed it goes back to Sumerian times.

If the case of the apostate was proved after thorough investigation and on the basis of adequate evidence (4, 6), the man was to be stoned to death outside the camp (5; *cf.* Lv. 24:14; Nu. 15:36).

iii. The central tribunal (17:8-13). These verses comprise one of the sections in Deuteronomy which have the central sanctuary clearly in mind.[1]

The law here makes provision for the hearing, at the central sanctuary, of cases which were too difficult for the local tribunals. It was there that the highest tribunal of the land operated. The picture in Exodus 18:13ff. depicts Moses as the highest judicial authority, with a body of judges to assist him in less weighty matters. With the decentralization that arose after the settlement in the land, the 'lower courts' located in the town (lit. 'gates') could appeal to the higher tribunal at the central sanctuary. In particular, cases of homicide, civil law or assault were referable. The verdict of the central court was final, since it was regarded as an expression of the mind of God.

8. At times local courts might be called upon to give a legal decision[2] in a case that was *difficult* or *baffling* (JPSA). The verb 'be difficult' or 'be baffling' is related in its root to the noun *pele'*, which connotes something wonderful or miraculous, *e.g.* the mighty acts of God's deliverance in Egypt (Ex. 3:20; 15:11; 34:10). The case in question was, then, one that had some very unusual features. Three illustrations of the kind of case are given: a. different cases of homicide (lit. 'between blood and blood'), where it was difficult to decide between manslaughter and premeditated murder (*cf.* 19:1-13; Ex. 21:12-14); b. different cases of 'rights at law', where a decision about the rights of the two parties was difficult (*cf.* Ex. 22:1-15); c. different kinds of assault or personal injury (lit. 'between smiting and smiting'; *cf.* Ex. 21:12-34). A summarizing phrase that is common in Deuteronomy follows, (that is to

---

[1] Other passages concern the law of the altar in chapter 12, the law of tithing (14:22-29), the law of firstlings (15:19-23), the law of feasts (16:1-17), the law of the priests (18:1-8). If in practice these laws were not always observed in relation to the central sanctuary, the ideal remained.

[2] The term *mišpāṭ* used here means precisely 'legal decision'.

say) *any case within your towns*. All such cases were taken to the central sanctuary.

Some ambiguity arises as to who it was that made the appeal to the higher tribunal, whether the bench of judges referred to in 16:18–20, or the parties to the dispute. The present passage is not at all clear. However, reference to the precedent in Exodus 18:13ff., where the men appointed by Moses brought difficult cases to him, may suggest that it was the judges themselves who made the decision to *arise and go up to the place which Yahweh your God will choose*.

9. It would seem that the central judicature consisted of several priests and judges (*cf.* 19:17), each group having its leader, namely the High Priest, *i.e.* the chief of the Levitical priests, or *the* priest, and the chief judge, or *the* judge (12). Each of these is defined in this verse by the article. The procedure is an extension of that envisaged in Exodus 18:13ff. and is Mosaic in principle and in spirit. The 'higher' court would finally declare its judgment and how the sentence was to be carried out (lit. 'the manner of the sentence')[1] through its spokesman.

It is not without interest that 2 Chronicles 19:5–11 relates how Jehoshaphat, in the second quarter of the ninth century BC, set up a court not unlike that envisaged in this chapter. It was composed of Levites, priests and laymen with the High Priest as head of the court in religious matters, and a layman as Chief Judge in secular affairs (the king's matters). Note especially 2 Chronicles 19:11.

10, 11. The decision of the central tribunal was final. The minor judges must act according to the tenor (lit. 'mouth') of the sentence of the tribunal at the central sanctuary. There were two obvious reasons for this; first, that decision carried divine sanction, since it was given before the Lord (*cf.* Ex. 18:15, 16; 21:6; 22:8), and secondly, because the officials at the central sanctuary were men of wide experience and with a knowledge of legal decisions which was more than local. The final decision is described as *the instruction (verdict) which they teach you*. The term 'instruction' (*tôrâ*) and the verb 'teach' derive from the same root. Some body of instruction or a body of legal precedent may be in view. We may translate the passage, 'You must be careful to act according to the expert opinion which they shall teach you, and according to the

[1] The Hebrew word used for 'manner', *dābār*, is extremely flexible in meaning, *cf.* 'the manner of the release' in 15:2.

judicial decision they declare to you.'[1] There was no appeal, and there was to be no deviation from this decision.

12, 13. The authority of the central tribunal was such that the man who received the sentence and *acted presumptuously*[2] towards it was liable to a capital charge. He was a rebel against Yahweh. The death sentence for such a case would be a stern warning for other rebels (*cf.* 13:10, 11).

iv. The king (17:14-20).

It has often been argued that, because the picture of the king in these verses is so true to the behaviour of the kings of Israel and Judah, this passage is a reading back into the mind of Moses of a state of affairs that did not obtain till later centuries. It is possible, though, to take quite a different approach. There is no reason why Moses should not have been aware of the extremes to which human monarchs could go in the exercise of their autocratic rule, for he had the example of kings in Egypt and Canaan before him. Hence it is not unthinkable that he would warn Israel, who lived under a theocratic government, against the dangers of autocracy. On the other hand the possibility of a human monarch was not ruled out, providing that monarch exercised his authority under Yahweh and in conformity with the covenant stipulations He had made known to Israel, for finally Yahweh was Israel's King. The recognition of this fact does not, however, deny the possibility that in a day when the kings of Israel and Judah had become autocrats and neglected the covenant, some reformers wishing to bring Israel again under the sound of Moses' voice should have re-presented Moses' original words so as to demonstrate their particular relevance to a later age.

Originally Israel was a theocracy functioning through a tribal confederacy and bound together by common allegiance to Yahweh. Monarchy was secondary to the older tribal league. There were those in Israel in Samuel's day[3] who wanted 'a king to govern us like all the nations' (1 Sa. 8:5-9, 19, 20). Samuel was happy to give Israel a leader (RSV 'prince', *nāḡîḏ*) but was unhappy about giving them a king (*meleḵ*).[4] By draw-

---

[1] JPSA translates 'You shall act in accordance with the instructions given you and the ruling handed down to you'.

[2] The root means 'to boil up' and suggests an angry rejection of the decision.

[3] The demand for a king goes back as far as Gideon's day (see Jdg. 8:22, 23).

[4] See 1 Sa. 9:16; 10:1; 13:14; 2 Sa. 6:21; 7:8, *etc.*

ing a picture of Canaanite kings Moses sought to warn Israel about the nature of a monarchy which would assume wide civil powers.[1] There is no reason to think that Moses was less aware of the dangers of secular kingship than Samuel was. Hence it is suggested that the present passage may be regarded as originating basically from Moses himself. This is the only passage in the Pentateuch which deals with the idea of monarchy. No formal law about a king, whether casuistic or apodictic, is quoted anywhere else in the Pentateuch. Moreover, the form of the passage is different from other passages already discussed in which a simple law is quoted and then expounded.

14, 15. These verses assert that Moses had envisaged the monarchy and had declared it to be a possible form of government. However, Yahweh must approve the king, who was to be an Israelite and not a foreigner. It is of interest that in the Near Eastern treaties the suzerain exercised oversight over the king chosen by any vassal state.

16, 17. Various features of the standard monarchy are here depicted, the multiplication of horses, wives and wealth. There is a hint of these irregularities in 1 Samuel 8:11–18. The picture was, however, well known. Military aggrandisement, a large harem, and the amassing of wealth were typical of Eastern potentates long before Moses' day. In Israel the first king to display such features in any significant way was Solomon, but others soon followed him. The reference to *Egypt* as a place where horses were obtained recalls the activities of the Hyksos rulers (1720–1550 BC) well before Moses' day. Solomon obtained horses from Egypt, according to 1 Kings 10:28, 29. Although there is nothing in these verses that would have been beyond the experience of Moses, some modern scholars have argued that the present Deuteronomy represents the work of an editor or editors who re-presented Mosaic material with their own homiletical comments in order to underline the true character of Israel's covenant with Yahweh. According to this view the editor(s), in a piece of free composition, sought to present the instructions of Moses in such a way that they became a severe criticism of the monarchs Israel had known. Such an author, with an intimate knowledge of kings and their ways, but with little respect for them, would take some delight in bringing forward views once expressed by Moses. His plea

[1] I. Mendelsohn, 'Samuel's denunciation of kingship in the light of Akkadian documents from Ugarit', *BASOR*, 143, 1956, pp. 17ff.

would be that Israel's great need was not monarchy but theocracy and a return to the ancient covenant law. Such a demand would have been relevant at almost any time from Solomon onwards. It had as its background a solemn warning once issued by Moses. Such a view, though logically possible, is not absolutely required by the evidence.

18-20. That a copy of the covenant law should be in the hand of the king has an interesting parallel in the secular suzerainty treaties of the ancient Near East. A duplicate of the treaty was provided for the vassal king and was to be read in public periodically. The suzerain also kept a copy which he deposited in the sanctuary of his god. In a similar way Israel's king was required to have a copy of Yahweh's covenant stipulations. It would appear that the Levitical priests had *a copy of this law* at the central sanctuary. In the only detailed description of a coronation ceremony in the Old Testament, the boy king Joash was crowned and presented with 'the testimony' (*'ēḏûṯ*), *i.e.* the covenant stipulations (2 Ki. 11:12). We are not certain about the nature of the document received by the young king, but even if it was only symbolic and in an abbreviated form, it represented the whole law of God.[1] Moses may well have indicated that, when in due course Israel had a monarch, it would be obligatory for him to have a copy of the law for his own private study. Deuteronomy itself represented *the law*. The official copy was in charge of the Levitical priests, and from this the king could have a copy prepared. Only the study of this law could preserve him from the temptations which beset a king. Military aggrandisement, an enlarged harem and the pursuit of wealth would turn his heart away from Yahweh and His commandments and cause him to lift up his heart above his brethren. On the other hand, to follow the law of Yahweh was to follow an austere and holy way, and few kings in Israel were prepared for such a life. The result was that, whereas any one of Israel's kings, by being obedient to God's law, might *continue long in his kingdom, he and his children*, enjoying the blessings of the covenant, most of them suffered the judgment of God either at the hands of foreign kings or through internal rebellions.

Incidentally, the phrase *a copy* (*mišneh*) *of this law* (18) appears incorrectly in the LXX as 'this second law', *to deuteronomion*

---

[1] We may compare with this Old Testament ceremony the presentation of the Bible, described as the 'royal law', to the British monarch at his coronation.

touto. It was this misunderstanding that gave rise to the English name Deuteronomy (see Introduction, p. 12).

v. The priests (18:1–8). An obligation was laid on Israel to support the priestly ministers of Yahweh. The priests, in common with the whole tribe of Levi, had no inheritance in Israel (*cf.* 10:9; 12:12; 14:27, 29), but were to be supported from certain specified portions of the offerings made to God. In this law concerning the priests the writer returns to his special interest in the Levites.

The analysis of this section into a simple law, an explanation of the law, and hortatory comments on the law is not as clear cut as in other parts of Deuteronomy, *e.g.* chapter 15. One possible arrangement is to regard verses 1, 3, 6, 7 and 8 as simple legal formulae and verses 2, 4 and 5 as explanatory.[1]

1, 2. The description of the priests as *the priests the Levites* in AV and RV, or as *the Levitical priests* in RSV, occurs five times (17:9, 18; 18:1; 24:8; 27:9). An alternative expression is *the priests the sons of Levi* (21:5; 31:9). Elsewhere the term used is simply *priests*. In the present verse, three expressions stand side by side, *the priests, the Levites* and *all the tribe of Levi*. Some ambiguity arises as to the exact significance of the total expression. The RSV incorrectly inserts 'that is', suggesting the equivalence of the priests and the Levites. But elsewhere Deuteronomy makes a clear division of the tribe of Levi into priests, who formed a minority group, and the rest of the tribe. To the priests alone belonged the ministry of officiating at the central sanctuary and of offering sacrifices there.[2] But there were many aspects of the total ministry of the tribe of Levi and the offering of sacrifices was only one of them. Other duties were performed by the Levites who did not belong to the priestly family. However, the whole tribe of Levi, priests included, were given the task of instructing Israel in their covenant law (33:10a; Lv. 10:11; 2 Ch. 15:3; 17:8, 9; 30:22; 35:3). Hence the first part of verse 1 might be translated 'the Levitical priests, (indeed) all the tribe of Levi'.

In general the priests had *no portion or inheritance* in Israel. Possibly the expression means that there was no recognized tribal area which could be called Levi in the same way as there were areas called Ephraim, Judah, Benjamin, *etc*. There were, however, Levitical cities (Jos. 21). Sometimes it appears that

---

[1] P. Buis and J. Leclercq, *Le Deutéronome* (1963), p. 136.
[2] R. de Vaux, *Ancient Israel* (1962), pp. 345–405.

members of the priestly families did possess land, *e.g.* Jeremiah (Je. 32:7ff.). Even the present section in Deuteronomy, although somewhat obscure, suggests that a priest could gain some advantage from the sale of ancestral property (8). However, by and large, the priests were dependent for their sustenance on Yahweh's fire offerings and his inheritance (*i.e.* what is rightly his).

The term *offerings by fire* is a technical one which occurs frequently in Leviticus and elsewhere for the burnt offering (Lv. 1:9), the meal offering (Lv. 2:3), the peace offering (Lv. 3:3) and the guilt offering (Lv. 7:5). In all of these, except in the case of the burnt offering, specified portions were allotted to the priests (Lv. 2:3; 7:6–10; Nu. 18:9f.). The other perquisites, 'Yahweh's inheritance (or rightful dues)', possibly comprised first-fruits, tithes, *etc.* (verses 3, 4). All of these were Yahweh's *rightful dues*, but He made them available to the priests (Nu. 18:20).

3, 4. There is a certain ambiguity in verse 3. But it is probably to be regarded as a definition of the 'fire offerings' and the 'rightful dues' of verses 1 and 2. The burnt offering was excluded because all was burnt (Lv. 1:9), but the peace offering was commonly shared between Yahweh, the priest and the people (Lv. 3; *cf.* Lv. 2:3; 7:6, 9, 10, 28–36; 10:14, 15). The regulations in Deuteronomy differ somewhat from those in Leviticus 7:28–36 and Numbers 18:8–19 where the breast and right thigh are prescribed as the priest's portion of the peace offerings, whereas here it is the shoulder, the two cheeks and the stomach. The reason for the difference is not known, but there seem to have been various ways of providing for the priests. From 1 Samuel 2:13, 14 it is evident that there was a special arrangement in use at Shiloh, although it does not seem to have been approved. It is likely that modifications were made in details from time to time and, provided always that there was a portion for the priests, it did not greatly matter about the details. The spirit of Moses' legislation could be observed even if a different portion was set aside. One suggestion is that the items in verse 3 refer to supplementary provisions for the priests set aside from other sacred meals eaten at the sanctuary. However, the real reason for the differences is not known.

The specific reference to the *shoulder*, probably the right shoulder (*cf.* Lv. 7:32–34), is of particular interest, since this was a priestly due in Canaan also. In the Late Bronze temple at Lachish a pit was excavated which contained a great number of right shoulder bones. One significant difference between the Israelite faith and the polytheistic faith of Canaan was that in Israel sacrifices were not regarded as providing for the physical needs of the god, whereas in Canaanite religion offerings were brought to the temples to satisfy the needs of the god and his servants, human and divine, who depended on him for subsistence.

The prescriptions of verse 4 are similar to those in other places in the Old Testament (*cf.* Nu. 18:12; 2 Ch. 31:5). The *fleece*, however, is mentioned only here (*cf.* first-fruits of honey mentioned only in 2 Ch. 31:5, although Lv. 2:11, 12 seems to include honey).

5. The reason for this special treatment of the priest is now given. He is chosen by Yahweh to minister in Yahweh's name to Israel (*cf.* 10:8; 21:5). The singular pronoun *him* refers back to the tribe of Levi.

6-8. An important principle is here stated. The rights of all Levites are guaranteed against any possible restrictions imposed by vested interests at the central sanctuary. Such a principle was no doubt as old as the tabernacle. Not only was all Israel required to show generosity towards the Levites, but the priests also were to treat them generously.

These verses do not refer to the Levitical priests (verse 1), but merely to the non-priestly Levites. There is thus no necessity to link this passage with 2 Kings 23:8, which refers to 'the priests out of the cities of Judah'. The present regulation is concerned with the visit of the Levites to the central sanctuary. Should the Levite wish to participate in the service at the central sanctuary, he had a right to do so. To what extent the Levites ever exercised their rights we do not know. Deuteronomy insists on two things, the centralization of worship as an ideal, and the rights of all the Levites to serve at the central sanctuary if they really desired to do so.[1] In practice such an action would be exceptional. Normally the Levites, along with resident aliens and poor people, were dependent on the charity of their compatriots (12:12, 19; 14:27; 16:11). It was intended that the law should express a principle and an ideal rather than that it should be carried out in detail.

The terminology used to describe the Levitical service, *stand . . . before Yahweh*, occurs also in 10:8; Numbers 16:9;

---

[1] The Hebrew text at verse 6 reads 'with all the desire of his soul', *i.e.* in sincerity, with a determined mind.

2 Chronicles 29:11 and Ezekiel 44:11b. The first half of verse 8 reads, 'They shall eat portion for portion', *i.e.* a similar portion. But an obscurity exists in the latter part of the verse where the translation and meaning are not quite clear. There is probably some reference to a source of income from some ancestral property in addition to the portions allotted from the sacrifices. The phrase may be literally translated 'apart from his sales according to the fathers', *i.e.* apart from the realization of his patrimony. The JPSA translation has *without regard to personal gifts or patrimonies*.

vi. The prophets (18:9-22). The polytheistic nations that surrounded Israel were given to all kinds of magical and superstitious practices designed to discover the will of the gods, or even to compel the gods to action in certain ways. All such practices were forbidden in Israel as being an abomination to Yahweh. However, Yahweh would make His will known through His prophets, whose words would be clearly understandable to the people in contrast with the ambiguous and mysterious 'revelations' of those who worked with magic and divination. The comprehensive law about the prophets is presented in a simple literary arrangement. First of all the forbidden practices are enumerated (9-14). Then the office of a prophet is explained (15-18), and finally reference is made to those who reject the prophetic word or who corrupt the prophetic office (19-22).

9. All occult, superstitions, divination, sorcery, spiritualism, *etc.*, were abominations (9, 12) to Yahweh and invited His judgment (*cf.* 7:1ff.). The practice of consulting unseen powers by these devices was tantamount to acknowledging a power other than Yahweh, and this was rebellion.

10, 11. The first prohibited practice was that of making children walk through the fire. The exact nature of this practice is not known. It may have been merely a kind of trial by ordeal, or a magical test. While this was of no value for divination, its magical value might explain its presence in the list (*cf.* Lv. 18:21; 20:2-5). In some other passages in the Old Testament also the practice is connected with the god Molech[1] (2 Ki. 23:10; Je. 32:35 and perhaps 7:31). How old the practice was is not known, but even though it was common in the days of the monarchy it may have been much older among Israel's neighbours, so that Moses could have referred to it.

[1] See W. F. Albright, *Yahweh and the Gods of Canaan* (1968), pp. 205f., 210.

Next in this list are three terms which describe various practitioners of the art of divination. The first is *one who practises divination*. The expression includes a participle and a noun both derived from the root *q-s-m*. A variety of devices was in use in various lands but all were designed to discern the will of the gods. The same word in Ezekiel 21:21 refers to the practice of whirling arrows in a quiver and deciding the answer to the question by the first arrow thrown out. The second term (*m^{e'}ōnēn*), translated *soothsayer* in RSV, is derived either from the root '-*n-n*, in which case it seems to refer to divination by reading clouds, or from a root which occurs in Arabic meaning 'to make unusual noises', 'croon', 'hum', in which case it may refer to some kind of incantation. The third term, RSV *an augur*, derives from the root *n-ḥ-š*. In Genesis 44:5, 15 the term refers to Joseph's divination by means of a cup, and may point to a kind of hydromancy in which reflections on the water in a cup are observed. The same root in Syriac occurs in a verb meaning 'divine by watching birds, fire, rain, *etc.*', *i.e.* by observing natural phenomena.

Two terms follow which seem to denote different forms of magic. The first, RSV *sorcerer* (*m^ekaššēp*), derived from the root *k-š-p* 'to cut up', may denote one who cuts up herbs and brews them for magical purposes (*cf.* LXX *pharmaka*, drug). The term is used in Micah 5:12 for some such material as drugs or herbs used superstitiously to produce magical effects. The noun, therefore, means enchanter or sorcerer (*cf.* Ex. 7:11; 22:18; 2 Ch. 33:6; Dn. 2:2; Mal. 3:5). The second term means literally 'one who ties knots' (root *ḥ-b-r*), *i.e.* one who binds another by magic knots or magic spells, hence *a charmer*.

The last three terms relate to various forms of consulting the spirit world. The first two refer to those who consult or inquire of the spirits, while the third may be a summarizing term. The three terms occur together quite often but remain somewhat obscure.[1] The first is the Hebrew *'ōḇ*, translated *medium* in RSV. The *'ōḇ* spoke from within a person (Lv. 20:27) with a twittering voice (Is. 29:4).[2] Those who practised this art called up the departed from the realm of the dead, or rather, professed to do so. Greek versions translate the term by

[1] Lv. 19:31; 20:6, 27; 1 Sa. 28:3, 9; 2 Ki. 21:6; 23:24; 2 Ch. 33:6; Is. 8:19; 19:3.

[2] Originally the *'ōḇ* was a ritual pit for communicating with the nether-world. See H. A. Hoffner, 'Second Millennium Antecedents to the Hebrew *'ŌḆ*', *JBL*, LXXXVI, 1967, pp. 385–401.

engastrimuthoi, *i.e.* ventriloquists, while Syriac has *zakkuro*, 'ghost'. The second term (*yiddeʿōnî*), *wizard*, is related to the verb *yādaʿ*, 'know'. Possibly this was some kind of familiar spirit. The difference between the two may have been that those who divine by the former, call up any spirit (1 Sa. 28:11), while those who divine by the latter consult only a familiar spirit.

The third term denotes 'one who enquires of the dead'. In Isaiah 8:19 the term seems to be synonymous with the first two terms in the present passage, so that it may be a typical summing up phrase so characteristic of Deuteronomy. Otherwise it seems to denote *a necromancer*.

12–14. Not only are these practices an abomination to Yahweh, but anyone who practises them is likewise an abomination. Because of such practices Yahweh would dispossess the people of Canaan. Israel, however, must be *blameless* (*tāmîm*) in regard to every form of divination, magic or spiritism.

It may be pertinent to comment that in our own day, when spiritualism, astrology, teacup reading and the like are widely practised, these injunctions given to ancient Israel have a particular relevance. Not only is it impossible to discover the future by such practices, but the practices themselves are forbidden by God to men who count themselves members of the covenant family. God has other ways of making His will known to His people, in which He retains the initiative and is able to speak His word. The classical prophets were men who received a direct message (word) from God – a very different procedure from the reading of the signs of the times in the entrails of beasts, the flight of birds, the falling of leaves, *etc.* God gave His direct personal word to the prophet without ambiguity (18). Hence He disapproved of all the procedures listed in verses 10 and 11 which are described as *abominable practices*.[1]

15–22. By contrast, Yahweh would raise up a line of prophets. The will of God was to be discovered through a prophet and not through a diviner, a magic worker or a spiritist. The terms throughout the section are collectives and represent types of individuals. The sense of the passage is that a succession of prophets would arise to continue the work of Moses who surpassed them all (34:10). In later times, particu-

---

[1] Excellent general treatments on the nature of prophecy may be found in E. J. Young, *My Servants the Prophets* (1952); R. B. Y. Scott, *The Relevance of the Prophets* (1944); G. von Rad, *The Message of the Prophets* (1968).

larly after the cessation of prophecy, an individual interpretation was given to this passage and 'the prophet who should come' became a figure associated with the Messianic age and sometimes identified with the Messiah Himself (*cf.* Jn. 1:21, 45; 6:14; 7:40; Acts 3:20–22; 7:37, *etc.*). This passage is of particular interest as being the only one in the Torah which establishes prophecy as an institution of Yahweh in Israel.

It is not without interest that some of the peoples adjacent to Israel also had prophets who claimed to receive revelations from their deities by dreams or visions or ecstatic experiences or in some other way.[1] Israel, because of her monotheism, would not allow that such prophets were authentic. Their deities were non-existent and the 'prophecies' they declared came from their own minds.

15. The prophet would be an Israelite *from among you* and not a foreigner (Nu. 22:5f.; Is. 2:6). He would be like Moses in the sense that he was Yahweh's spokesman, but not in any sense of equality.

16, 17. The place of the prophet in Israel could be understood in terms of the incident at Horeb (Sinai), when the people pleaded with Moses to meet God on their behalf and to bring the word of God to them from the mountain burning with fire (5:22–31; Ex. 20:18–21).

18. God's method with His prophets was *I will put my words in his mouth* (Je. 1:9; 5:14; 20:8, 9, *etc.*). It is Yahweh who commissions and sends forth the prophet (Is. 6:8). For that reason the prophet could say 'Thus saith the Lord'.

19. An obligation rested on Israel to be obedient to the words of the prophet, for these were Yahweh's words.

20–22. Compare 13:1–5. A true prophet always urged loyalty to the covenant as well as giving reliable predictions. Adherence to what God had revealed was expected of a true prophet. There was no magic in the prophet's words and actions.

But one of the problems associated with the whole prophetic movement was the false prophet, for although the true prophet had a deep sense of divine commission, not all who claimed this were genuine prophets of Yahweh. It was easier for a man to make the claim than to authenticate it. Two answers are provided here. First, the words of the true prophet come to

[1] For an Egyptian example see 'The Journey of Wen-Amon to Phoenicia', *ANET*, p. 26. For examples from Mari see W. L. Moran, 'New Evidence from Mari on the History of Prophecy', *Biblica*, 50, 1, 1969, pp. 15–56.

pass (*cf.* 1 Ki. 22:26–28; Je. 28). But this evidence could sometimes be matched by the false prophet. The difference was that, whereas the true prophet spoke for God, the false prophet spoke presumptuously (Heb. root *z-w-d*, 'to boil up', 'seethe'), *i.e.* he blurted out personal opinions for which there was no backing from Yahweh. Often the desire to please men lay behind such utterances (Is. 30:10, 11; Je. 14:14, 15; 23:16, 21–27, 30–33; 27:9, 10, 14–16; Mi. 2:11; 3:11, *etc.*). A second proof of genuineness was that, whereas the true prophet spoke in the name of Yahweh, the false prophet spoke in the name of other gods, enticing people to idolatry (*cf.* 13:1–5).

For other answers to the problem see Jeremiah 23:9–32; Ezekiel 13. The case of the non-fulfilment of the words of a true prophet was particularly difficult (Ex. 32:14; Je. 18:7–10; 26:19; Joel 2:13f.; Am. 5:15; 7:3, 6; Jon. 3:9f.).

c. Criminal law: homicide and witnesses (19:1–21)

With chapter 19 Deuteronomy commences a section where an orderly arrangement of the laws is not so evident, although smaller pericopes can easily be recognized. In the course of chapters 19–26 a wide variety of topics is covered, most of them merely in outline. Only the questions of homicide (19:1–13) and the Holy War (20:1–20) have a more extended treatment.

The present chapter is concerned with homicide (1–13) and witnesses (15–21), with a brief unrelated law about landmarks (14).

i. Homicide (19:1–13). The basic regulations are first given (1–3) and then interpreted (4–7). An extension of the basic law follows (8–9) and a warning against shedding innocent blood (10). Finally the case of deliberate manslaughter is discussed (11, 12) and the section concludes with a general exhortation (13).

1–3. It is not difficult to think of Moses the lawgiver paying some attention to the question of blood revenge, which was so common in nomadic society. Since immediate blood revenge carried out by the next of kin would prevent a proper trial, Israel was instructed to appoint certain cities which would provide refuge or asylum pending trial. At first cities were appointed in Transjordan (Nu. 35; Jos. 20). The concept was an ancient one in Israel. According to Exodus 21:13, 14 Moses enunciated the principle which is expounded in Deuteronomy. After the conquest of the land three cities were to be set apart on the western side of the Jordan. The towns are not here specified. The expression *prepare the roads* (3) is not clear, unless it indicates that certain recognized ways of access to these cities were agreed upon. The term *manslayer* is the participle of the verb *rāṣaḥ*, which seems to denote anti-social killing rather than killing in war or in the administration of justice. The word 'murder' is hardly an accurate translation, since *rāṣaḥ* covers both cases of murder and of accidental killing.

4. The legal interpretation (*cf.* 15:2) is now introduced by the words *This is the provision* (*dāḇār*, translated in 15:2 as *manner*). The case of the man who kills unintentionally (lit. 'without knowledge or intention') and without prior hatred is first discussed.

5–7. A typical case of unintentional killing is given – death caused by an axehead which flies from the handle. Even this case was, for some societies, one for blood vengeance. Presumably in earlier periods Israel's forbears had practised blood revenge in such cases. It was important to prevent the avenger of blood from acting in hot anger (lit. 'while his heart was hot'), lest the killing had been accidental. It was not that the next of kin was deprived of his right of blood revenge, but only that restraints were placed on the indiscriminate exercise of the right.

8–10. This seems to mean that there were to be three such cities on the western side in addition to those in Transjordan. The point is made that possession of the land across the Jordan was dependent on Israel's *loving Yahweh* and *walking ever in his ways*. However, the shedding of innocent blood was to be avoided by all means, for it would involve the people in the guilt of bloodshed. It has been conjectured[1] that an ancient apodictic law may lie behind this verse in the form 'Thou shalt not shed innocent blood in your land'.

11–13. The case of deliberate slaying is different. The elders of the city to which the dead man belonged were responsible to bring the slayer from the city of refuge and hand him over to the kinsman who would exact blood revenge. The elders were in a position to decide the guilt of the man without being influenced by any sense of personal loss. Finally, the instrument designated to carry out the death penalty was *the avenger of blood, i.e.* the next of kin of the murdered man.

[1] G. von Rad, *Deuteronomy* (1966), p. 127.

An interesting question arises if Deuteronomy in its final form did not appear till some centuries after Moses. In that case the legal requirements stated here would seem to be irrelevant, since processes of law were available to deal with such cases. It might be argued that ancient laws were often left unaltered, not because they were to be obeyed, but because the principle involved was clear enough to allow of some re-application. However, the law would have had had more relevance in an earlier age, in the days of Moses. It is to be noted, incidentally, that this law is in no way dependent on the law of the central sanctuary.[1] The law of Exodus 21:12–14 seems to suggest that refuge was sought at a sanctuary ('my altar'), as in other parts of the ancient Near East. This was, no doubt, always a possibility (1 Ki. 1:50f.; 2:28ff.). But even in such a case some form of trial and some place of refuge was necessary. The view that places of asylum had to be established after Josiah had abolished the local shrines ought to be rejected. Places of refuge were much more ancient in the secular world than Josiah, or even Moses.[2] With the rise of the monarchy and the state, however, independent action would be replaced by standard legal procedures. The *elders of his city* may be compared with the 'judges and officers' of 16:18 who were responsible for local justice.

ii. Encroachment on a man's property (19:14).

In many societies still, the limits of a man's land are marked by a boundary stone or a heap of stones. Boundary stones were removed by those who sought to defraud their neighbours (Jb. 24:2; Is. 5:8; Ho. 5:10). There is abundant evidence that other peoples had the same problem. Large stones (Akk. *kudurru*) which defined the boundaries of royal grants in Mesopotamia carried lists of curses directed against those who removed them (*cf.* 27:17).[3] In Israel, where every man held

---

[1] Adam C. Welch, *The Code of Deuteronomy* (1924), pp. 136–144.

[2] The right of asylum is an ancient one. References in classical writers show that it was common in Greek and Roman times. See W. Robertson Smith, *The Religion of the Semites* (1907), pp. 148f. It continued throughout the Middle Ages. These biblical references suggest that it was much older than the Greeks and Romans. The system of asylum that was in practice in the ancient Near East is now becoming clear (G. von Rad, *Deuteronomy* (1966), p. 128), so that there is no reason to deny that a prescription like this might have been made in Moses' day.

[3] The *kudurru*, however, merely listed the boundaries but was not set up on them.

his piece of land as an inheritance from Yahweh, the removal of the landmark was an offence against Yahweh Himself. There was a close connection between a man's possessions as his means of support and the very life of the man.

The law is here given in an apodictic form, *you shall not remove your neighbour's landmark*. Comparison with 27:17 and with the context in which this latter verse lies indicates that this was one of a list of crimes laid under a curse. Crimes in this list were committed in secret in the hope that the offender might never appear before a human court. But such people were committed to the judgment of Yahweh, who would carry out the curse. It is a solemn reflection and not without its modern relevance that God knows the secret sins of men and it lies within His prerogative to visit offenders with judgment.

The failure of men to observe this law led to great troubles in later centuries. Encroachments on the land of Israelites may have taken place very early, but the practice grew apace after the ninth and eighth centuries BC (1 Ki. 21; Is. 5:8; Mi. 2:2). Prophets condemned the avaricious practices of the great land owners.

iii. False witnesses (19:15-21).

The practice of false witness is forbidden in the decalogue (5:20). However, in order to discourage false witnesses, certain judicial measures were devised. This brief section deals with the whole question of witnesses and in particular with the false witness who has been a menace to society in every age and among many peoples.

15. That Moses should formulate a simple apodictic law in reference to false witnesses is altogether likely. We may postulate some such law as *A single witness shall not prevail* (lit. 'stand') *against a man in respect of any crime*. In explanation of this simple law there follows the proviso that two or three witnesses are necessary before a charge can be sustained.

16-20. The case of the malicious witness (lit. 'witness of violence', *i.e.* his testimony would lead to violence) is now discussed. When such a witness declares that the accused is guilty of wrongdoing (lit. 'turning aside', *i.e.* religious or moral, apostasy, defection or misconduct), the two parties to the dispute were called to appear *before Yahweh* to answer the priests and judges who were in office at the time. The tribunal at the central sanctuary seems to be in view here (*cf.* 17:8-13). After careful enquiry the judges (probably the whole 'bench' of priests and judges) give the verdict. If the witness is false he must suffer the punishment intended for the accused. In that way evil would be 'burnt out' (*purged*) from Israel and false witness discouraged.

21. The penalty for perjury was to be in accordance with the *lex talionis*, or law of retaliation (*cf.* Ex. 21:23ff.; Lv. 24:17ff.), *i.e. eye for eye, tooth for tooth, etc.*[1] This principle is often misunderstood. Far from encouraging vengeance it limits vengeance and stands as a guide for a judge as he fixes a penalty suited to the crime. The principle was thus not licence or vengeance, but a guarantee of justice. A similar law was known elsewhere in the Semitic world.[2] Some societies made use of monetary compensations in certain cases.[3] Basically, the *lex talionis* expresses a view of a man's life as something sacred without a material equivalent (*cf.* 12:23, 24; 15:9; 21:8; 22:6, 7; 25:11, 12). Jesus' criticism of this law (Mt. 5:38f.) arose from its use to regulate conduct between individuals. He did not reject it as a principle of justice which should operate in the courts of the land. For private relationships He proposed the ideal of brotherhood, a strong principle throughout the book of Deuteronomy. To extend the *lex talionis* to this inter-personal domain was to destroy the law of God.

d. Regulations for the Holy War (20:1-20)

The book of Deuteronomy shows a good deal of interest in war, not just any war, but the Holy War. Not every recourse to arms was a Holy War. The Holy War was not undertaken without consulting Yahweh (1 Sa. 28:5, 6; 30:7, 8; 2 Sa. 5:19, 22, 23). The men of Israel were 'consecrated' to such a task (1 Sa. 21:5; 2 Sa. 11:11; Is. 13:3) and put away from their midst all that would offend Yahweh (23:9–14). Yahweh dwelt in the camp (Dt. 23:14; Jdg. 4:14). He invested His leader with special powers, although finally it was Yahweh Himself who was the Captain of the hosts of Israel and could deliver His people by many or by few (Jdg. 7:2ff.; 1 Sa. 13:15ff.; 14:6, 17). At the climax of the battle He sent terror or panic into the midst of the enemy and this brought about their overthrow

---

[1] See R. de Vaux, *Ancient Israel* (1962), pp. 149, 159f.
[2] See Hammurabi Code, Laws 196, 197, 200, 210, 230 in *ANET*, p. 175; the Middle Assyrian Laws 50, 52, *ANET*, pp. 184, 185.
[3] See Hammurabi Code, Laws 206–216, *ANET*, p. 175. It is presumed that the earlier Sumerian law codes on which the Hammurabi Code was based had similar laws.

(Jos. 10:10; Jdg. 4:15; 1 Sa. 5:11; 7:10, *etc.*). The spoils of war were under the ban of sacred consecration (*ḥērem*) and were the exclusive property of Yahweh, whose right alone it was to dispose of the spoils.[1]

Deuteronomy, of all the books of the Old Testament, contains a great deal of information about the discharge of the Holy War, but notably in chapters 20; 21:10–14; 23:9–14; 24:5; 25:17–19, although other passages touch on the topic, *e.g.* 7:16–26; 9:1–6; 31:3–8. But an atmosphere of war permeates the whole book. It is a pressing concern of the writer that Israel should maintain her existence in the face of foreign nations.

The present chapter is concerned with three aspects of the Holy War, the proclamation before the battle (1–9), the siege of a city (10–18) and the treatment of trees (19, 20).

The form in which this material is presented is not in terms of an older apodictic or casuistic law or laws, but rather in the form of a freely composed sermon based, no doubt, on more formal regulations. It is not difficult to conceive of Moses formulating regulations for a Holy War. Such regulations could have been transmitted either in written or in oral tradition over many years, so that they were available for publication along with other Mosaic material at a later time.

i. Preliminaries to the battle (20:1–9). 1. It is not clear whether the *enemies* were invaders of Israel's territory or enemies which Israel might meet in the prosecution of the Holy War beyond her borders. But in either case Israel is exhorted not to fear. Chariots and horses, despite the feebleness of their armament which was no more than that of foot soldiers, had a powerful psychological effect in the Near East, especially on nomads. Israel is urged to recall the mighty deeds of Yahweh in times past when He delivered the people from Egypt. Had not He in those days cast Pharaoh's chariots and horsemen into the sea (Ex. 14:26–28; 15:3, 4, 18, 21. *Cf.* Jdg. 4:13–16; 2 Sa. 8:4; 10:18)? With this in mind the presence of hostile chariots and horses might serve to arouse a greater faith. Israel's first encounters in the land of Canaan were with Canaanites who made use of war chariots (Jos. 11:4; 17:16; Jdg. 1:19; 4:3; *cf.* 1 Ki. 20:23ff.). It was a continuing concern for Israel's religious leaders lest Israel should put her trust in chariots rather than in Yahweh (Is. 30:16; 31:1ff.; Ho. 14:3).

[1] For a useful discussion of the Holy War see Gerhard von Rad, *Studies in Deuteronomy* (1953), chapter 4, pp. 45–59.

A question that arises here is whether Israel herself had horses and chariots. In the desert period and for some time after the conquest it would appear from the biblical material that horses and chariots were not part of Israel's military equipment. It was not till Solomon's day that chariots were added to Israel's defence forces (1 Ki. 4:26; 10:26). Hence such a law as this would be irrelevant from Solomon's time onwards. The inference here is clearly that Israel had no horses and chariots.

2-4. Before Israel entered battle the priest first addressed them, urging them not to fear. We may discern degrees of fear in this brief summary. A man might have a soft heart. He might be afraid, or worse still, he might show trepidation or be terrified. In every case the man of Israel should recall that in the Holy War Yahweh went with His people to fight for them and to bring deliverance to them. The story of Gideon in Judges 7 provides an excellent illustration of the kind of attitude that is here encouraged (*cf.* Nu. 14:7, 8). It is not without interest that one of the Dead Sea Scrolls is entitled 'The War of the Sons of Light against the Sons of Darkness'. It deals with the great battle that is to take place in the days when God will finally overthrow all the enemies of Israel. In this document the priest's address to the army at the beginning of the battle is given. The motif of the Holy War was revived in the first century BC.

5-9. The *officers* (*šōṭēr*) were to deal with two classes of men who were to be exempted from service. Originally these officers may have been tribal officials who organized the tribal militia. In later times they were royal officials (*cf.* 16:18, where the 'officer' is an associate of the judge). These men were to cull out from the army both those who were excused on humanitarian grounds and those who, because of their fearfulness, would weaken the general morale.

5-7. Beginnings were important in the Semitic mind and hence also in Israel. Since death in battle would deprive certain groups of men from commencing particular enterprises, exemptions were made. Three cases are given. The first is the man who had built a new house but had not *dedicated* it (*ḥānaḵ*). The second consisted of men who had planted a vineyard but had not *enjoyed* its fruit. The verb is common in ritual language (*ḥillēl*). It connotes 'to treat as common or profane'. The concept behind the verb is that the first produce of a new vineyard belonged to Yahweh. Only after some lapse of time could the owner bring the vineyard into common use. In fact, only after four years could a man claim access to the fruit (Lv. 19:23–25; Je. 31:5). The third case is that of the man who has recently *betrothed a wife*. It is proper that he should take his wife and raise up a family rather than be slain in battle and have another man take his wife.

In these cases the Deuteronomic law has replaced ancient beliefs in the operation of sinister powers wherever something was being inaugurated, by humanitarian considerations. The fear of these powers in such cases is widely attested in other Near Eastern societies. This humanitarian spirit is a feature of Deuteronomy. Generous treatment of the slave (15:12–18), the stranger, the fatherless and the widow (10:18; 24:17, 19, 20, 21; 27:19), the Levite (12:19; 16:11, 14; 26:12, 13) is required of Israel. The gleanings of the field are to be left to the poor (24:19ff.). The law referring to loans and pledges is generous (24:10–13). Hired servants are to be generously treated (24:14f.). Fruit trees are to be spared during siege warfare (20:19f.); roofs are to be protected by a balustrade (22:8); family millstones are never to be taken in pledge (24:6); excessive beating is forbidden (25:1–3); kindness is to be shown to animals (5:14; 22:6f.; 25:4), *e.g.* the ox is to go unmuzzled (25:4); camps are to be kept clean (23:9–14); reckless assault is forbidden (25:11f.). Such a picture is a noble one and portrays an attitude to life which finds echoes in the New Testament (Mt. 5:43–45; Lk. 6:27–30; Rom. 12:20; Jas. 2:1–13). It is altogether according to the Spirit of Christ.

8. Exemptions were made for another group comprised of men who were fearful or 'soft of heart'. Such attitudes were not merely personal but were a threat to a whole army (*cf.* Jdg. 7:2, 3) psychologically, for they might cause the heart of their comrades in arms to *melt* (*māsas*) as their own hearts had melted. Some commentators vocalize the Hebrew verb form as a causative and translate 'so that he does not cause the heart of his comrades in arms to melt as his own heart'. Clearly, men who were fearful lacked faith, and faith in God's power is necessary for all who fight God's wars.

9. The final act of preparation was the appointment of *commanders* (*śar*) of the army to lead the people.

It may seem that these procedures would reduce the army to too small a size. But then Yahweh could save by many or by few. The size of the army was less important than the faith of those who composed it.

ii. Besieging a city (20:10-18). Two cases of siege are here described, that of a distant city (10-15), and that of a city in the land (16-18). Israel would not be so much concerned with distant cities during her wanderings, although she might become so in coming years. Her first concern would naturally be with the towns in the land of promise. The towns she had encountered on the way (chapters 2, 3) might be classified as distant cities once she was in the land.

10. The city in question here is one that is *very far* away (15). The first approach is to make an offer of peace. The term *peace* in such a context suggests a treaty (Jos. 9:15; Jdg. 4:17; 1 Sa. 7:14; 1 Ki. 5:12; Is. 27:5). In non-biblical texts we have the expression 'to establish peace' in contexts where the Bible would use the expression 'make a covenant'.[1] The present passage may, therefore, be translated 'you shall invite it to make a treaty'.

11. Where the city was prepared to enter into a treaty the usual practice of putting its inhabitants to death is not followed (7:22ff.; *cf*. Jos. 9:11-23). The inhabitants of the city became vassals of Israel and were put under forced labour (*mas*). The verb *serve* and the noun *forced labour* both suggest this.

12, 13. If the city refused to surrender it was to be besieged and its *males* put to death. The expression *to the sword* is literally *to the mouth of the sword*, which has a strange exactness about it. Ancient swords discovered in excavations often have the blade emerging from the haft as the tongue of a wild beast whose head forms a feature at the end of the handle. Thus the expression suggests that the sword was inserted up to the hilt.[2]

14. The women, children, animals and general booty were to be taken by the Israelites for their own private use (*cf*. the treatment meted out to Jericho, Jos. 6:17-21). Even captive women were accorded some rights (21:10-14).

15. It is evident from this proviso that there were differences in practice in regard to the treatment of peoples defeated in war. Certainly a difference is here allowed for peoples outside the confines of the promised land. Only Amalek was excepted (25:17-19). In general, therefore, the carrying out of the ban

---

[1] Several examples come from the Mari texts, dating back to the eighteenth century BC, *e.g. Archives royales de Mari*, I, 60:21; II, 16:16; 40:6; III, 50:15; IV, 24:11, 18; 29:39; 40:8.

[2] T. J. Meek, 'Archaeology and a Point of Hebrew Syntax', *BASOR*, 122, Apr. 1951, pp. 31-33.

(*ḥērem*) was not invariable, although theoretically it was always likely to be carried out. In later centuries Israel laid siege to towns outside the boundaries of the promised land (*e.g.* 2 Sa. 12:26ff.; 2 Ki. 3:25f.). In some cases it is specifically stated that the occupants were spared but were put to work as slaves (*e.g.* 2 Sa. 12:31). This may have happened, at least in part, in every such case. However, the cities within the bounds of the promised land were a greater danger both to Israel's political freedom and to her religious independence, so that there was more reason to apply the practice of sacred dedication (*ḥērem*).

16, 17. Cities within the land were to be placed under the ban or sacred dedication. The verb *utterly destroy* is related to the noun *ban* (*ḥērem*). The injunction of 7:1–5 is applied in this case. None of the inhabitants was to be kept alive. There are examples in the books of Joshua, Judges and 1 Samuel to show that the injunction of these verses was carried out (Jos. 7:21–26; 11:10–15; Jdg. 7:25; 1 Sa. 15), in at least a number of cases.

18. The reason offered for such treatment is *that they may not teach you to do according to all their abominable practices . . . and so to sin against Yahweh.* The instruction to put to the ban men, women and children reads strangely to Christian ears. The instruction in the New Testament is rather to love one's enemies (Mt. 5:43–48). However, if the manner of expression appears unusual, the underlying principle is valid, namely, that anything that tends to undermine Israel's total allegiance to Yahweh is anathema and must be put away. The principle remained through the ages and obtains today in reference to a Christian's loyalty to Christ. The expression of the principle has altered greatly. A Christian can be unswerving in his allegiance to Christ without resorting to the measures advocated in Deuteronomy. But in those far-off centuries it would seem that if Israel had been dominated by any less tolerant attitude towards her pagan neighbours, she might well have been swallowed up by them. The expression of her rejection of paganism must be understood in the light of God's final purpose for Israel and of the conditions that obtained in those days. God always bring His truth to people as He finds them. New truth introduced into a situation has its way of bringing refinements over the centuries. God's revelation does one thing at a time. It implants a truth, constitutes a relation and establishes a principle which may have a rich content implicit in it. Many centuries may elapse before the full implications of the principle become clear.[1]

iii. The treatment of trees (20:19, 20).

Siege warfare was older than Moses. Excavations reveal that there were walled cities in Palestine many hundreds of years before the arrival of the Israelites. Hence there was need for protection from invaders in those days. In times of siege invading armies denuded the hills of trees for fuel and for siege works. Moses undoubtedly knew of siege warfare and of the destruction of trees involved.[2] Cities were captured in Transjordan in Moses' time (Nu. 21:25, 32), as well as during the early conquest (Jos. 10:11, 12). Nor were the Israelites themselves above such destruction (Jdg. 9:46–49; 2 Ki. 3:19, 25). The present law forbids, in the name of common sense and out of a certain respect for life, the kind of total warfare which was later practised by the Assyrians.[3]

19. The latter part of this verse is difficult to translate. Following the statement that Israel may eat the fruit of the trees is a peculiar phrase which reads literally, 'for man is a tree of the field to come before thee into a state of siege'. It does not help greatly to vocalize the first word so as to ask the question, 'Is man a tree of the field . . . ?' The sense seems to be, 'Are the trees of the field men, that they should be placed under siege?' In that case 'trees of the field' is the subject of the sentence and the general sense of the sentence is that warfare is conducted against men, not trees.

20. In order to avoid wanton destruction of all trees the instruction is given that only non-fruit trees are to be used in building *siege works against the city*. Had this law been observed by invaders throughout the centuries Palestine today would not be so denuded of trees.

e. Miscellaneous laws (21:1 – 25:19)

From the beginning of chapter 21 it becomes almost impossible

---

[1] James Orr, *The Problem of the Old Testament* (1909), pp. 465–477; see also J. W. Wenham, *The Goodness of God* (1974), pp. 119ff.

[2] An excellent description of an ancient siege occurs in the annals of Thothmes III, where he describes the siege of Megiddo in northern Palestine *c.* 1468 BC. See *ANET*, pp. 234–238.

[3] The Annals of Tiglath Pileser III (744–727 BC) bear witness to the practice. See *ANET*, pp. 282–284. The practice of cutting down trees without consent was forbidden in Hammurabi's Law, No. 59. See *ANET*, p. 169.

to discern an orderly plan in the arrangement of material. Here and there we find some blocks that are reasonably homogeneous. But these are surrounded by unrelated laws, *e.g.* 21:1–21 is concerned chiefly with family affairs and 23:2–11 with the purity of the assembly of Israel. The associated materials are, however, quite unrelated. Further, the laws are largely impersonal in character. There is a minimum of commentary and laws whose age need not be doubted are simply set side by side, even where they concern different topics. Some order might be obtained if the material were re-arranged. But that were to alter the book and give it another shape than it had originally. It may be that the methods that were followed earlier in the book were never carried through to a conclusion. Despite this, it is significant that laws of heterogeneous origin were taken up and given their setting and their motivation within Israel's covenant faith.

i. Compensation for anonymous murder (21:1–9).

This law would fit very naturally with the material of chapter 19. The procedures to be followed when the body of a murdered man is discovered in the open country without any knowledge of the circumstances of his death are now discussed. Such a murder involved the whole community in blood guilt. Both the people and the land were defiled and some kind of ceremonial execution was required to satisfy the demands of justice.

1. Such a contingency as this belongs to every society, ancient or modern. But whereas modern societies are not troubled by questions such as defilement or expiation, ancient societies often were. The problem is an ancient one. So too is the ritual which was used, although its exact significance is not now clear.

2. The civil authorities, *elders* (*zāqēn*) and *judges* (*šōp̄ēṭ*), were responsible to take action. It would appear that the judges were to be present with the elders to ensure that the task of measuring the distance from the corpse to the nearest village was done justly. The judges do not appear thereafter. We may have evidence here of a slight adaptation of a primitive law to a new society. In ancient times the elders sat in the gate of a village to control village affairs after the traditions of the fathers. In later years judges, whose jurisdiction covered a wider area, were added (*cf.* 16:18–20). It is not inconceivable that Moses might suggest that, once the people settled in the land, there should be a modification in the simple procedures that had obtained in the desert. With the rise of the monarchy and the consequent centralization of many judicial procedures, judges would become common although many local issues were still decided by the elders, as here. It is not without interest that the principle of corporate responsibility exemplified here was known widely in the ancient world. Thus the Laws of Hammurabi require the nearest city to make restitution in cases of robbery and to compensate with a mina of silver the family of a man who was murdered.[1] A similar law obtained among the Hittites.[2]

3, 4. The elders of the village nearest to the corpse were then charged with the responsibility of taking a heifer that had never been used in the service of men, in order to perform the necessary rite. It is not entirely clear whether this was a rite of expiation associated with the cult or a symbolic judicial execution. The expression introducing the formal declaration (7) is the same as that used in the ritual of chapter 26, *i.e.* 'They shall answer and say.' Perhaps the ritual served a double function and was both cultic and judicial, although the mode of execution was not normal for a sacrifice (*cf.* Ex. 13:13). It was therefore something apart from a normal sacrifice. The ritual was, in any case, an old one. The unworked heifer was taken to a stream of running water in an area where men had never ploughed or sown, and there its neck was broken. The heifer, the valley and the water were undefiled, because they had never been contaminated by common use.

5. At this point *the priests the sons of Levi*, known elsewhere in Deuteronomy as *the priests the Levites*, enter the picture. These were the Levites who normally officiated at cultic sacrifices. Their function was, no doubt, to supply the liturgy which must be repeated by the elders over the slaughtered animal. They are described as the ones whom God chose to minister to Him to declare the blessing in His name, and to exercise final judicial authority. By their *word* (decision) every legal dispute and every charge of assault was settled.

6, 7. The elders of the city nearest to the slain man first washed their hands over the beast that had been killed,

---

[1] Laws of Hammurabi, Laws 23, 24, *ANET*, p. 167.
[2] The Hittite Laws, Tablet I, Later version of No. 6, *ANET*, p. 189. See discussion of H. A. Hoffner, 'Some Contributions of Hittitology to Old Testament Study', *TB*, 20, 1969, pp. 39f.

expressing, symbolically, that the city was innocent of the crime (Pss. 26:6; 73:13; *cf.* Mt. 27:24). Then they were to *testify* (lit. 'answer and say'), '*Our hands did not shed this blood, neither did our eyes see it shed.*' The elders swore as though giving testimony before a court that they and the people of the city were guiltless.

8. An appeal to Yahweh to forgive His people follows. The word translated *forgive* derives from the root *k-p-r* which denotes 'cover' in Hebrew and Arabic, and 'wipe off' in Syriac. In any case it signified an obliterating or cancelling of sin. Yahweh is reminded of His deliverance of His people from Egypt. The verb *redeem* (*pāḍâ*) occurs several times in reference to the deliverance of Israel from Egypt (7:8; 9:26; 13:5; 15:15). Thus the appeal is addressed to God in the name of those who had a special relationship with Him. The plea was that the responsibility for shedding the blood of the slain man, of which the city was innocent, might not be charged to this city, but rather that it might be covered over.

9. In this way Israel would clear herself from the responsibility and the stain of murder (*cf.* 19:19.) To do this was *right* (*yāšār*) in the eyes of Yahweh. The formula used, *you shall purge* . . . , occurs often in Deuteronomy (13:5; 17:7; 19:13, *etc.*).

There is much about this ritual that is tantalizing. It could hardly have been an expiatory sacrifice, for the blood was not sprinkled according to the standard rituals. Possibly the meaning of the ritual was that, since the murderer could not be found, an animal was put to death in place of the murderer (*cf.* Ex. 13:13), *i.e.* a kind of ceremonial judicial execution took place in which the heifer served as a substitute for the unknown murderer. Since the procedure was merely a compromise solution, it must be assumed that, if the murderer were subsequently found, he would bear his own guilt. But if not, any evil consequences which might follow upon the shedding of a man's blood were averted. Further, inter-city strife was thus avoided, because the avenger of blood could not rashly demand satisfaction from men of another city.

This ritual raises the whole question of corporate guilt. There is a sense in which a whole nation is corporately responsible for some sins. In modern times one may quote examples such as racial discrimination, neglect of the under-privileged, and a variety of social evils that bring widespread tragic consequences. National indifference or neglect involves the whole nation in responsibility.

ii. Female prisoners of war (21:10-14). The first verse in this section takes up the formulation of laws for the Holy War which commenced in 20:1. The opening words are exactly the same: *When you go forth to war against your enemies.* But the present concern is for women taken in war.

10, 11. Women are listed among the items of war booty in 20:10 15. If the introductory words of verse 10 place this law in the same general context as 20:1, then the reference here is to captive women taken from a nation outside Israel, *i.e.* to one who was not a Canaanite (7:3). It was permissible for an Israelite man to take such a woman as his wife.

12, 13. In fine humanitarian fashion the law required that the woman be given a month to mourn the loss of her parents (*cf.* 34:8; Nu. 20:29). At the worst, her father was slain in the war (20:13) and her mother, if she survived, would belong to another master. The woman in question was to shave her head, cut her nails, and put aside her foreign garments. It is not clear whether these activities were part of the mourning rites (*cf.* 14:1) or symbols of her purification and transfer to another life (Lv. 14:8; Nu. 8:7; *cf.* 2 Sa. 19:24). Certainly the change of garments suggests a change of status. At the conclusion of a month of mourning the man might claim the captive woman as his wife. The prescription of verse 13 can be paralleled in part in some of the texts from the royal archives of Mari[1] dating to the eighteenth century BC. Such kindly consideration is in marked contrast with the cruel treatment meted out to women captured in war among the neighbouring nations, or according to the rules of the Holy War (which may have been an idealized picture. See 7:1-4).

It is strange that this legislation does not envisage the dangers attendant on the presence in the family of foreign women with a pagan background. But it must have been felt that the faith of Israel was strong enough to outweigh any such influence. In some cases the foreigner would embrace the faith of Israel, for she would probably enter by marriage into a similar position to that of a daughter of Israel sold by her father (Ex. 21:7ff.).

14. If subsequently the man of Israel lost his delight in the woman, she was protected from misuse. The relationship rested on a legal basis. If it were dissolved, the woman's social status was not to be impaired. She was not a slave to be sold, but was free to go where she wished.

---

[1] *Archives royales de Mari*, I, Nos. 8 and 75.

iii. The rights of the first-born (21:15–17). The previous law was designed to protect the woman slave taken in war against a capricious Israelite husband. Another law protected the rights of the eldest son of a man in the case where there was more than one wife. Wherever polygamy was practised there was the danger of favouritism. A father's personal preference did not justify his setting aside his eldest son in favour of a younger son. Even so there are cases, both in the Old Testament and outside it, where the father exercised a choice in the matter, but no doubt on good grounds.

The present law differs from the previous law in that it is couched in an impersonal legal style throughout, whereas the law in verses 10 to 14 is in the second singular. Moreover, what has been termed the typical Deuteronomic style is lacking in these verses.

15. The terms *love* and *hate* (*dislike*) in the context of polygamous marriage may not connote the clear distinction that is implied in English. The difference may range from the extremes 'love' and 'hate' to the contrast between 'more loved' and 'less loved' (though not 'hated'), *i.e.* one wife was preferred to the other (*cf.* Rachel was preferred to Leah, Gn. 29:30, 31; 1 Sa. 1:5). If, in such circumstances, the first-born son happened to be the son of the less loved woman, he was not to be at any disadvantage. Indeed, the first-born son of a man, whoever may have been the mother, was regarded as representing the first strength of the father's loins (17).

16, 17. The rights of the first-born (primogeniture) included a share in the property inheritance of double that of the other sons. A father did not have the legal right to treat as first-born the son of the favourite wife in preference to his true first-born. The phrase translated here *in preference to* (*ʿal pᵉnē*) occurs in the second commandment in 5:7, meaning 'in preference to'. This strong preference for the first-born was an ancient custom in Israel (Gn. 27; 48:14). It is, though, one of the themes of the Old Testament that the elder son could be replaced by a younger in special circumstances, *e.g.* Jacob and Esau, Isaac and Ishmael, Ephraim and Manasseh, David and his elder brothers, Solomon and his elder brothers.[1] But these

---

[1] The custom is known at Alalakh in the fifteenth century BC. See D. J. Wiseman, *The Alalakh Tablets* (1953), pp. 54f. Babylonian and Assyrian laws forbade a father to disinherit his son without legal reason. See *ANET*, Lipit Ishtar Code, Law 24, p. 160; Hammurabi Code, Laws 167, 170, p. 173; Middle Assyrian Laws, B1, p. 185.

are exceptions to the normal law and merely stress the tension which always existed between the legal custom and a father's love. The first-born, as the first-fruits of a marriage, belonged to God and had to be redeemed (Ex. 13:11–15; 34:20). Levites were consecrated to God as substitutes for the first-born sons (Nu. 3:12, 13; 8:16–18). In those examples in the Old Testament where a younger son was chosen in preference to an elder son, the fact is stressed that God's choice was absolutely unmerited and completely gratuitous.

The expression *by giving him a double portion* is a strange one. Literally it reads: 'by giving him a mouth or two of all that he has'. The same idiom occurs in 2 Kings 2:9 in reference to the endowment of Elisha, who asked Elijah 'Let there be a mouth or two in thy spirit upon me' (lit.), *i.e.* Elisha asked for a share of the spirit that possessed Elijah twice as large as the other followers of Elijah.[1]

iv. The stubborn and rebellious son (21:18–21). While

it was necessary to protect the first-born from a capricious father, it was also necessary to fortify the authority of the father in certain cases. A stable family was fundamental for a stable community and respect for parents was vital to the whole community of Israel (5:16). A child who struck or cursed his parents was liable to the death penalty, according to Exodus 21:15, 17; Leviticus 20:9. The book of Deuteronomy follows the same precept and here describes in outline the procedures to be followed. The case is set out in a conditional sentence, a kind of casuistic law.[2]

18. The son is described as *stubborn* (*sôrēr*) and *rebellious* (*môreh*) and unwilling to obey his parents. The limits of parental authority were the chastisement of the boy. Beyond that the case was one for the elders of the city. The complaint had to be decided by impartial judges. Whether, in fact, parents went to this extreme is not known. We may have here another example of a penalty stated in an extreme form in order to underline the serious nature of the crime.

19. Both the father and the mother were to take the boy to

[1] The Middle Assyrian Laws, Tablet O, law 3 (*ANET*, p. 188) refers to the allocation of two portions to the eldest son. *Cf.* also Laws of Hammurabi, No. 170 (*ANET*, p. 173).
[2] There is a reference to a rebellious son in the Laws of Hammurabi, Nos. 168, 169 (*ANET*, p. 173). The penalty in this case is not so severe as in the biblical case.

the elders, whose duty it was to deal with offences against the social order and family rights (19:12). These elders assembled at the city gate, the usual place for the administration of law (22:15; 25:7; Ru. 4:1, 2, 11; Jb. 31:21; Ps. 127:5; Is. 29:21; Am. 5:10, 12, 15). It is of interest that both parents were required to act in agreement in such a drastic move, which could easily end in the boy's death. But the judicial decision was one for the elders, since the offence was more than a family concern. It was a community offence.

20. The charge was laid. *This our son is stubborn and rebellious, he will not obey our voice; he is a glutton and a drunkard.* The reason for this behaviour may be inferred from the latter part of the charge (*cf*. Pr. 23:21; 28:7). Perhaps these formulae are quoted merely as examples of the kind of thing to be said on such occasions, since other offences besides gluttony and drunkenness might lead a man to become a community danger. It is noteworthy that only the witness of the parents was sought (*cf*. 19:15–21 for criminals). In the nature of the case the danger of false witnesses resulting from personal hatred was excluded.

21. If the elders found the man guilty, the sentence was death by stoning. The parents were not required to participate, perhaps out of a sense of delicacy, although more likely in order to stress the point that the power of life and death over their children was not theirs. Only the community could deal with refractory conduct which was a danger to the family order.

While no example of the carrying out of this sentence occurs in the pages of the Old Testament, the prescriptions underlined the seriousness of the offence.

The law seems to lie behind the words of Jesus in Mark 7:10. The context of the reference is concerned with the obligation of children towards parents. Not even a vow to present a gift to the Temple should prevent a man from supporting his parents. If there was any oral tradition to the effect that vows absolved children from caring for parents, then the oral law was, in Jesus' view, a making void of the word of God. In Jesus' view such an attitude was a breach of the commandment 'Honour your father and your mother' and called forth the judgment, 'He who speaks evil of father or mother, let him surely die.' This exposition of the obligation of a child to his parents is striking indeed. In the New Testament parents are exhorted not to provoke their children to wrath (Eph. 6:4).

But conversely, the book of Proverbs affirms that 'he who spares the rod hates his son' (13:24). There is, in biblical thinking, a delicate balance in relationships between parents and children.

v. The body of an executed criminal (21:22, 23). It was customary in Semitic societies to expose the corpses of men condemned to death by attaching them to a pole or even impaling them. There are several examples in the Old Testament (Jos. 8:29; 10:26, 27; 2 Sa. 4:12; 21:8f.). The practice was known among the Philistines (1 Sa. 31:10) and was very common among the Assyrians, especially in time of war. The present law, expressed largely in the second person singular, limits the period of exposure. In any case, a corpse was an impure object which defiled the land and should be disposed of quickly.

22. The verse expresses in a very succinct form that a proven capital charge has resulted in the death of a criminal, whose corpse was then hung up for all to see.[1] The language of the verse is extremely terse in Hebrew and is reminiscent of the legal phrases in the Mishnah.

23. The corpse of the executed criminal had to be buried the selfsame day at all costs. The Hebrew syntax is strongly emphatic.[2] The reason was that the corpse of an executed man was an object accursed of God and would defile the land (*cf.* Nu. 35:33f.; Lv. 18:24–27). The presence of the corpse hanging up to the public gaze, with crime, as it were, clinging to it and God's curse resting on it, might result in untold calamities. Hence as soon as the necessary amount of publicity had been achieved and other likely offenders had been warned, the corpse was buried, and that before sunset.

In a later day Paul was to draw from this brief section an analogy (Gal. 3:13). Just as the corpse of a condemned criminal carried the curse of God, so Christ hanging on the cross as a condemned and executed criminal was publicly exhibited as one who bore the judgment of God. He bore the same shame as every executed criminal and was publicly exhibited as one who was accursed of God. To free us from the curse of the law Jesus Himself had to become accursed.

---

[1] The practice is not unknown in Arab lands today.
[2] It comprises the so-called infinitive absolute plus the regular finite verb.

vi. Nine laws for various occasions (22:1–12). While several of the laws grouped here refer to a man's relationships with his neighbours, there are also laws about the care of animals and birds. The impression remains that the systematic discussion of laws, which appears in the early part of Deuteronomy, is left aside. Even so, the present group of nine laws makes it clear that the scope of God's concern for proper behaviour in the covenant family was very wide. There was to be a whole-hearted and comprehensive application of His law. The section is cast in the second singular form of address. Much of it is concerned with brotherly love (*cf.* 15:1–11, 12–18; Lv. 19). While the succinct statement of Leviticus 19:18b, 'You shall love your neighbour as yourself', does not occur in Deuteronomy, it is implied here and in many parts of the book. The covenant law was comprehensive in its demand for love, love for God and love for one's fellows.

1–3. Restoration of lost property. Laws which are observed between members of the same clan are here extended to the whole covenant people. The law of Exodus 23:4, 5 even extended to obligation to one's enemies.

1. A man is exhorted not to 'hide himself' (RSV *withhold your help*) from his neighbour's beasts which had strayed, but to restore them to him, *i.e.* positive action is demanded beyond legal requirements. Such a response could only come from an attitude of heart. The parallel law in Exodus 23:4, 5 has the word 'enemy' in place of 'brother' in Deuteronomy. It is reminiscent of the exhortation of Jesus in Matthew 5:44 and of the teaching in the parable of the Good Samaritan (Lk. 10:30–37). A man's neighbour is anyone in need, whether brother or enemy.

2. Even if a neighbour was at a distance or was unknown, the obligation was to care for the beast until its owner could claim it.

3. In every circumstance of loss to one's neighbour, whether of beasts or property, a man is to render every assistance to restore the item to its owner. The law of Exodus 23:4, 5 is one element in a group of laws dealing with legal proceedings, and in that setting it required the man of Israel to render assistance even to the man with whom he was in legal conflict. The law of Deuteronomy is stated in the most general terms. A man is bound to help all his countrymen, indeed he must help even his enemies. *Cf.* verse 1.

4. The obligation to lift up fallen beasts. The present law is more comprehensive and simpler than that in Exodus 23:5.

5. Prohibition of wearing the clothes of the other sex. This law is probably not merely a prohibition of unseemly dress, although the people of Israel abhorred everything that was unnatural (*cf.* verses 9-11; 14:1, 2). It has been suggested that some association with the religion of Canaan made this practice *an abomination to Yahweh*. Later writers, such as Lucian of Samosata and Eusebius, speak of the practice of masquerading in the worship of Astarte. Apparently women appeared in male garments and men in women's garments. Even this reversal of the natural order was offensive, for a distinction between male and female in the matter of dress is universal. Not even the cloak of religion could make it acceptable. While this law in its original setting has no direct implication for modern life, there are some indirect implications. There are positive values in preserving the difference between the sexes in matters of dress. The New Testament instruction in Galatians 3:28, that there is neither male nor female, but that Christians are all one in Christ Jesus, applies rather to status in God's sight than to such things as dress. Without being legalistic some attempt to recognize the relative difference of the sexes, within their common unity as persons, is a principle worth safeguarding.[1]

6, 7. Sparing the mother bird. The humanitarian attitude of Deuteronomy is reflected here. The regulation is peculiar to Deuteronomy. Perhaps reverence for motherhood in general gave rise to the law.

8. The making of a parapet. There was always a danger in houses with flat roofs that someone might fall and blood might be shed, thus bringing blood-guilt upon the household. The builder of a new house was therefore obliged by this building regulation to provide a protective parapet around the roof of his house. The Laws of Hammurabi (*c.* 1700 BC) had a section designed to hold legally and morally responsible those who did not take all necessary steps to prevent accidents.[2]

---

[1] See H. A. Hoffner, *TB*, 20, 1969, pp. 48-51. Hoffner proposes that the interchange of clothes was a magical practice to cure infertility. The biblical cure was not magic, but prayer and God's power.

[2] Laws 229-240. See *ANET*, p. 176.

9-11. Three laws against unnatural combinations. In several places in the Old Testament the mixing of dissimilar things is forbidden (verse 5; Lv. 19:19). Unnatural combinations violate the purity of the species, whether of seeds for sowing, of beasts for ploughing, or of fibres for weaving cloth. In Arab lands today one can still see combinations of oxen and asses, or asses and camels, *etc.* used for ploughing.[1] The prohibition seems to have been peculiar to Israel. In view of the provision that in the case of the planting of a vineyard (*i.e.* between the rows of grapes) with mixed crops the farmer would be required to forfeit (lit. 'consecrate') his crop to the sanctuary, it would seem that some religious reason may lie behind the law (*cf.* verse 5).

12. The law of knots or tassels. The command to wear tassels on the four corners of one's garment was designed to give Israel something distinctive in her dress. We may compare this with the distinctive dress of the Syrians and Canaanites.[2] A symbolic meaning is given to these tassels in Numbers 15:37-41, namely that they are a reminder to Israel to keep God's law.

vii. Offences against marriage and sexual purity (22:13-30). Six laws touching on the question of chastity are now given. Here is a section of some seventeen verses, where the subject-matter is homogeneous. The laws touch on matters that are basic to family integrity. Most of them are in casuistic form, 'If . . . then . . .'. The conditional particle is *kî* in verses 13, 22, 23 and *'im* in verses 20, 25. The law in verse 30 is apodictic, 'A man shall not . . .'.

13-21. The virginity of a betrothed woman. A woman was betrothed at some time after the onset of puberty, but remained in her parents' house till the wedding ceremonies. This law envisages the case where the husband had taken his wife and the marriage had been consummated, and he rejected (13) her because he *did not find in her the tokens of virginity* (*bᵉtûlîm*, 14). Precisely what this means has been interpreted in different ways. Some commentators have taken it to mean that

---

[1] The practice is dying out with the advent of the tractor and modern farming machinery.

[2] J. B. Pritchard, *ANEP*, pictures 45-54, 58, 62; 'Syrians as pictured in the paintings of the Theban Tomb', *BASOR*, 122, Apr. 1951, pp. 36-41.

the girl's hymen was broken when she was handed over to her husband. Others have held that it was the blood-stained sheets covering the marriage bed resulting from the first cohabitation. Others still have suggested that it was some sort of chastity belt. None of these, however, would be an infallible proof of the girl's virginity, and in any case the husband would know whether the parents could produce clear evidence. The risk of whipping and the 100 shekels fine were too great (18, 19).

An alternative explanation which has much to commend it has recently been proposed.[1] The Hebrew word *bᵉṯûlîm* is of a form which is regularly used for certain abstract nouns denoting age-groups. It could thus denote 'female adolescence' as well as 'virginity'. In that case 'tokens of virginity' may be translated 'tokens of adolescence', which could have denoted that the girl was menstruating regularly. A man who married such a girl would expect to have evidence of this after his marriage unless, of course, she became pregnant to him at once. What was needed was evidence that at the time of marriage the girl was not pregnant and was menstruating. If she had been guilty of sexual misconduct after betrothal, any pregnancy before marriage would eventually show up and a child would be born before nine months had elapsed. The law of verses 13–21 might therefore be concerned with the bride's conduct during her betrothal period prior to marriage and the 'tokens of adolescence' might have been a pregnancy test.

20, 21. If the wife were proved guilty by the absence of *the tokens of virginity* (see on 13–21 above), she was stoned to death because she had wrought folly in Israel by playing the harlot. *Folly* (*nᵉḇālâ*) denotes a breach of the laws of the ancient sacral tribal confederacy and is used elsewhere of sexual offences (Gn. 34:7; Jdg. 19:23; 20:6–10; 2 Sa. 13:12). It is of interest to observe that the root which occurs in *folly* (*n-b-l*) occurs also in the word *fool* (*nāḇāl*) in the expression 'The fool says in his heart, "There is no God" ' (Pss. 14:1; 53:1).

22. Adultery. In Israel, adultery, *i.e.* unchastity with a married woman, carried the death penalty (*cf.* the decalogue, 5:18). It was not only a question of making amends to an injured husband, but it was also destructive of the social order in which the family was sacrosanct.

Israelite legislation in this regard is not unlike Mesopotamian

[1] G. J. Wenham, 'bᵉṯulah, "a girl of marriageable age" ', *VT*, XXII.3, 1972, pp. 326–348, especially pp. 331–336.

law. Thus in Hammurabi Law 129 both the wife and the offending man were to be bound and thrown into the water.[1] Although, if the husband agreed to spare his wife, then the king spared the man. A similar law applied in the Assyrian Code.[2]

According to verse 22 adultery was punishable by death for both parties. By such drastic action it was hoped to *purge the evil* from Israel (*cf.* verses 21, 24). However, Proverbs 6:26–35 seems to suggest that the death penalty was not always mandatory in Israel.

23–27. Seduction of a betrothed woman. Two different cases of the seduction of a betrothed woman are listed. In the first case, when the seduction took place in a city the woman's consent to the act was assumed, since she might have called for help. Both parties were to be stoned. This act was tanta-mount to adultery, since the woman was betrothed, the legal business preceding the marriage was in process or even complete, and the bride-price (*mōhar*) had been paid over.

Where the seduction took place in the open country it was presumed that the woman had been raped and that her cry for help was not heard.[3]

28, 29. Seduction of a young girl. Where the girl was not betrothed and no legal obligations had been entered into, the man was forced to pay the normal bride-price (*mōhar*) and marry the girl.[4] He was not allowed, subsequently, to send her away.

30. Intercourse with a stepmother. There were areas of family relationships in which sexual intercourse was forbidden. These are defined in other parts of the Old Testament (Lv. 18; *cf.* Dt. 27:20–23). In the present passage only one is mentioned, namely relationship with the wife of a man's father. This was regarded as an incestuous union and a particularly dangerous one, since it struck deeply at the maintenance of family life (*cf.* 27:20; Lv. 18:8; 20:10). The expression *uncover her who is his father's* is a euphemism. 'To cover with the skirt' means to

---

[1] *ANET*, p. 171.
[2] *ANET*, p. 181, Laws 12–15.
[3] Compare Code of Hammurabi, Law 130, *ANET*, p. 171; Middle Assyrian Laws, A12, *ANET*, p. 181; Hittite, No. 197, *ANET*, p. 196.
[4] *Cf.* Ex. 22:16f.; Assyrian Laws, A55, *ANET*, p. 185.

take in marriage. 'To uncover' means to encroach on his father's marital rights (*cf.* Ru. 3:9; Ezk. 16:8). The present law is apodictic in form as distinct from the earlier laws in the section. It is evidently ancient and was designed to regulate a particular kind of community life. Incestuous marriage was practised among the Hittites and certain Africans where the son took over the wives of his dead father. The Semites disapproved the practice.[1] Even so, there were breaches of the law (Ezk. 22:10).

These laws on sexual standards have an important relevance for the modern man. In their day they were designed to stress the importance of monogamy in a polygamous world. While in the modern world we would not follow all the penalties for breach of the laws, we need to recognize that purity and fidelity are essential to the well-being of society. If in the modern world we find it difficult to provide a simple solution to its many sexual problems, we do well to remember that the margin of permissiveness is not unlimited. Great nations in centuries past lost their nationhood in considerable measure because of their unrestrained licence in sexual matters. For the Christian, at any rate, nothing less than the standard set by Jesus can be regarded as the norm. 'I say to you that every one who looks at a woman lustfully has already committed adultery with her in his heart' (Mt. 5:28). In this connection Jesus added, 'If your right eye causes you to sin, pluck it out and throw it away; it is better that you lose one of your members than that your whole body be thrown into hell' (Mt. 5:29).

viii. Those excluded from the congregation of Israel (23:1–8).

The assembly (*qāhāl*) *of Yahweh* was called together for a variety of purposes, for war, for annual feasts, *etc.* In their assembly the religious community undertook various sacred rites, particularly worship (4:10; 9:10; 10:4; 18:16, *etc.*). Membership of such an assembly was confined to those who were physically perfect and were not the offspring of any unnatural union. Ammonites and Moabites were likewise excluded. Von Rad[2] has isolated a block of apodictic laws in verses 1–8 and has proposed that these were designed to set limits to the assembly of citizens in Israel and to define their relation to neighbouring peoples.

1. Men who were mutilated in their reproductive organs,

---

[1] Hammurabi Code, Law 158, *ANET*, pp. 172, 173; *Koran*, IV, 26.
[2] G. von Rad, *Studies in Deuteronomy* (1953), p. 20.

i.e. eunuchs, were excluded because they were blemished. Comparison with Leviticus 21:6-8 suggests that this criterion for admission to or exclusion from the assembly was originally religious in character (*cf.* Dt. 14:1), although respect for nature and for life was also important (22:6, 7). Possibly also, because castration was imposed on certain personnel in the Canaanite sanctuary (*cf.* verses 17, 18), the practice was forbidden in Israel. In a later age Israel was to learn that eunuchs who were faithful to the covenant might find an honoured place in God's family, before those who were sound in body but were covenant breakers (Is. 56:3ff.; *cf.* Acts 8:27, 38).

2. The *bastard* (*mamzēr*) was likewise excluded. In the typical language of the ancient Near East this exclusion is extended to the tenth generation of his descendants. The exact definition of the *bastard* is not clear. Some later Jewish exegetes[1] used the term for the children of an incestuous marriage between Jews, while others connected the bastard with the offspring of mixed marriages between the people of Israel and the Philistines (Zc. 9:6), Ammonites or Moabites (Ne. 13:23).

3. Hostility against Moab and Ammon was traditional in Israel (Gn. 19:30-38; Jdg. 11:4-33; 1 Sa. 11:1-11; 2 Sa. 10 and many passages in the prophets). These two nations were thus ranked with eunuchs and bastards.

4-6. These verses are not legal in style but are woven in among the ancient apodictic series to explain the reason for the exclusion of Ammon and Moab. They hark back to the experiences in the wilderness when Ammon and Moab not only refused passage to Israel, but Moab hired Balaam to curse Israel (Nu. 22-24). The three verses demonstrate once more one of the characteristics of Deuteronomy, namely, that the simple law is first stated and then elucidated by expository and hortatory material. Not merely were Moab and Ammon excluded from the assembly of Israel, but Israel was never to undertake anything for their welfare, *peace* (*šālôm*), or for their benefit, *prosperity* (*tôḇâ*), as long as she lived. Israel is here addressed in the second singular. The prohibition was *for ever*. The point is made again that it was because Yahweh *loved* Israel that He turned aside the curse of Balaam and replaced it by a blessing.

7, 8. Israel's attitude to the Edomites and the Egyptians was to be more lenient. The third generation of such people

---

[1] Mishna Yebamoth, IV:13. See H. Danby, *The Mishnah* (1933), p. 225.

who lived as resident aliens in the land might be admitted to the assembly of Israel. Such a view about Edom is certainly older than the Exile, when Edom was condemned most bitterly (Ps. 137:7–9; Is. 63; Je. 49:7–22; Ezk. 25:12–14; Ob.). The verb *abhor* (*tiʿēḇ*) is from the same root as the noun 'abomination' (*tôʿēḇâ*) and is generally used of ritual uncleanness. The verb form here means 'to treat as ritually unclean' (*cf.* 7:26). The reason given for such preferential treatment of Edom is that Edom is Israel's brother, a reference to Genesis 25:30; 36:1, 8, 19, where Esau is known as Edom. Despite many occasions of ill will between Israel and Edom, Israel always remembered her ties of consanguinity with them (Dt. 2:4).

Similarly Israel was not to *abhor* an Egyptian, despite her former time of oppression, since Israel had once been a resident alien (*gēr*) in Egypt, and a guest of the Egyptians. Some prophets later entertained great hopes for the future of Egypt (Is. 19:18–25; 45:14).

ix. The cleanliness of the camp (23:9–14).

The material in this section belongs with chapter 20 and other sections dealing with the Holy War. Certain cultic requirements were associated with the discharge of the Holy War. Yahweh, who was present in the camp with His people (14) and went forth to war with them to overthrow His enemies and theirs, would require that every unclean thing should be put away, lest He depart from the camp.

9. The noun, *evil thing* (*raʿ*), refers not so much to something that is morally evil as to something that is unclean or unbecoming. The term has a wide usage in the Old Testament and a wide connotation. Two particular cases, typical of others, are given.[1]

10, 11. A nocturnal emission made by a man is ritually unclean. He was required to remain outside the camp till evening. Then he bathed and returned to camp (*cf.* Lv. 15:16). The law is, no doubt, motivated by the religious significance attaching to life and reproduction. It is expressed in the casuistic form '*if . . . then . . .*'.

12, 13. Great care had to be taken to cover human excrement. This was both a prescription of hygiene and also a

---

[1] The verse contains an interesting case of the reflexive use of the Niphal in *you shall keep yourself*.

cultic or religious requirement. A place was reserved outside the camp to which a man went taking with him, from his standard equipment, a special digging tool (*yāṭēḏ*),[1] with which to dig a hole where the excrement might be buried.

14. The reason for such ritual cleanness is now given. Yahweh walked in the midst of the camp to protect His people and to deliver their enemies into their hands. The camp was therefore to be kept *holy* (*qāḏôš*), lest Yahweh depart. The symbol of Yahweh's presence in the camp was the ark, in the presence of which no unholy thing could be tolerated. In the days before the ark had a permanent resting-place it was the visible sign of the presence of God. When it arrived in the Israelite camp the Philistines said 'God has come into the camp' (1 Sa. 4:7). The capture of the ark was regarded as the loss of God's presence (1 Sa. 4:22; *cf.* Nu. 10:33–36; 1 Sa. 4–7; 2 Sa. 11:11). Hence its presence in the camp signified that Yahweh was present.[2]

x. Various cultic and social laws (23:15–25). Five unrelated laws comprise this section, all presented in the second person singular. It would seem that the plan followed earlier in Deuteronomy of collecting together laws with a common theme and of adding hortatory comments to them has been abandoned.

15, 16. The refugee slave. The refugee slave referred to had evidently come from a foreign land. Otherwise there would have been legal complications, since slaves were a valued possession. Such a man was to be allowed to dwell *in your midst* in whatever place he chose. Such escapees were not to be oppressed or reduced again to slavery (for the verb *oppress, yānâ, cf.* Ex. 22:21; Lv. 19:33). This was a humane law and protected such people from exploitation. Non-Israelite law codes prescribed stricter measures. In the Hammurabi Code a man who harboured a runaway slave was to be put to death.[3] Such a man in Israel could not of course be a member of the assembly. At times such slaves became a problem in Israel (1 Sa. 22:2; 25:10).

17, 18. Religious prostitution. While prostitution of any

---

[1] The term means, literally, 'tent peg' (see Jdg. 4:21, 22; 5:26).
[2] R. de Vaux, *Ancient Israel* (1962), pp. 299–301.
[3] *ANET*, pp. 166, 167, Laws 15–19.

kind was an abomination in Israel, sacral prostitution, widely practised among the peoples outside Israel, was particularly condemned. Both the female *cult prostitute* (*qᵉḏēšâ*) and the male *cult prostitute* (*qāḏēš*) are referred to here. These were employed in the fertility rites of the Ishtar-Astarte cult. The practice is widely attested in the Canaanite cult (Nu. 25:1–9; 1 Ki. 15:12; 2 Ki. 23:7; Ho. 4:14, *etc.*).

The practice of bringing money to the sanctuary to pay for the hire of such prostitutes was forbidden. The female prostitute is described in verse 18 as a *harlot* (*zônâ*) and the male a *dog*. This usage of the term *dog* is known outside the Old Testament.[1]

19, 20. Money loaned at interest. The rate of interest in the ancient Near East was exorbitant, *e.g.* some contracts in Northern Assyria at Nuzi in the fifteenth century BC show that the interest was fifty per cent. The Laws of Eshnunna from the nineteenth century BC in Lower Mesopotamia limit the interest rate.[2] In this respect Israel was quite superior to her neighbours. Many voices were raised through the centuries against the practice (Ex. 22:25; Lv. 25:36, 37; Ps. 15:5; Pr. 28:8; Ezk. 18:8, *etc.*).

19. It was forbidden in Israel to take interest from a fellow Israelite who was also a member of the covenant family (Lv. 25:35ff.). In any case, loans were normally for the relief of distress, and the need of one's fellow should not become an opportunity for profit among God's people.

20. The *foreigner* (*noḵrî*) stood in a different position. He was a trader and merchant, not a farmer as were most of the Israelites. No objection was raised to charging such foreigners interest. The prohibition was thus confined to the family of Israel.

21–23. Vows. Any man is free to make a special *vow* (*neḏer*) to God, just as he is free not to. But if a vow is made, a man is bound to fulfil it without delay. The present law stresses the need for complete honesty before God. It is no sin if a man

---

[1] D. Winton Thomas, '*Kelebh*, "Dog": Its origin and some usages in the Old Testament', *VT*, X, 1960, pp. 424ff.

[2] *ANET*, p. 162, Laws 20, 22. It ought to be noted that these ancient interest rates were high because there does not seem to have been security. There is thus a different concept of 'interest' – which is still a factor in the modern Middle East.

does not choose to make a vow. But what passes a man's lips voluntarily must be performed. Vows feature among the list of sacrifices in 12:6, 11, 17, 26.

24, 25. Treatment of a neighbour's crops. This law prescribes reasonable limits to an ancient practice which has continued up to modern times. It was, and still is, a duty for peoples of the Near East to show hospitality towards the passer-by. In Israel the visitor was to be allowed to satisfy his appetite from his neighbour's vines or from his grain, but not to carry away either grapes or grain, *i.e.* to take advantage of hospitality to rob his neighbour (*cf.* 22:1–12; 24:19–22). In later Judaism this law was given definition which nullified its true meaning. Jesus came into conflict with the authorities when His disciples plucked ears of grain on the sabbath, which according to the Pharisees was not lawful. The example of David's men who took the bread of the presence from the house of God when they were hungry was then quoted by Jesus (Mk. 2:23–28; Mt. 12:1–8; Lk. 6:1–5).

xi. Divorce and re-marriage (24:1–4). The case under discussion is a special one. It does not deal with divorce in general but merely with re-marriage after divorce. If a man divorces his wife, and she marries another who either dies or in turn divorces her, her former husband is forbidden to re-marry her. The legal definition of the case is set out in the form of several conditions so that the protasis of the conditional sentence takes up three verses (*cf.* Ex. 21:1–6 where a similar lengthy protasis occurs). The law is thus a casuistic one.

1. The first condition was that following his marriage the man found some *indecency* (lit. 'nakedness of a thing') in his wife. The meaning of this noun is not clear, but we may conjecture that some immodest exposure or unwomanly conduct is meant. It cannot mean adultery, for this carried the death penalty. The procedure for divorce is outlined. The husband wrote *a bill of divorce* (lit. 'a document of cutting off'), placed it in the woman's hand and sent her away.

The story of Hosea (1–3) is the story of a man who refused to divorce his wife, despite her unfaithfulness. He was thus in a position to take her back when he had found her. So God was faithful to Israel despite her unfaithfulness and did not put her away irrevocably (*cf.* Je. 3:1–8).

2, 3. The second condition was that the woman should go

to another man and become his wife, and the third, either that the other man hated her, *i.e.* lost his affection, or that he died.

4. The protasis is now given as the conclusion to the casuistic law 'if . . . then . . .'. *Her former husband, who sent her away, may not take her again to be his wife.* The reason given is that she had been defiled and to take her back would be an abomination to Yahweh. The use of the term *abomination* (*tôʿēḇâ*) suggests that the law rests on some ancient religious (cultic) idea (*cf.* 22:5, where the same word is used). A further reason is that such an act would *bring guilt upon the land.* The idea that unchastity defiled the land is found in several other passages in the Old Testament (*e.g.* Lv. 18:25, 28; 19:29; Nu. 5:3; Je. 3:2, 9; Ho. 4:3).

What, then, was the purpose of the laws in 24:1–4? Some have proposed that they were designed to prevent hasty divorce. Others have regarded them as a discouragement of adultery. Yet others think they were concerned with natural revulsion against such a reunion. But there is some value in the proposal that these laws were intended to preserve the second marriage. Once the divorcee has entered a second marriage there is no possibility of the husband reclaiming her. Reunion is forbidden and the second marriage is guaranteed.[1]

Despite these observations probably the strongest deterrent to divorce in Israel and all over the ancient Near East was financial, since the husband had to forfeit the dowry and may even have been involved also in other payments to his former wife.

This ordinance provoked discussion in later times. The rabbinic schools of Shammai and Hillel debated the nature of the original cause of divorce. The prophets debated the question of whether or not Yahweh had put away Israel His wife and whether she would be taken back. The various points of the present law may be discerned in Jeremiah 3:1–3. The case of Hosea and his wife poses the same problem. It would seem that in Hosea's case the law was suspended (Ho. 3).

Reviewing the law it must be said that no actual cause for the divorce is stated, even though it may have been clear at the time. In the world outside Israel, divorce was common and was easily obtained. The present law provides guideposts. A man could divorce his wife if a. there were adequate grounds, and if b. a legal document was prepared and placed

---

[1] R. Yaron, 'Restoration of Marriage', *JJS*, XVII, 1966, pp. 1–12.

in his wife's hands. Although not stated, presumably the case had to be brought before a public official. Such formalities might act as a deterrent. It is possible that the present law represents a disapproval of divorce (*cf.* Mal. 2:14–16), for the offence in question could result in an *abomination* in much the same way as adultery (Lv. 18:20; Nu. 5:12–29). In fact, no Old Testament law or oracle institutes divorce, perhaps because it was taken for granted in view of its widespread practice in the Semitic world. The present law would have had the effect of making divorce a more serious affair, since it reduced the possibility of a man taking his wife back again. Moreover, it would discourage the easy transfer of a woman from one man to another which resulted in the defilement of the woman. The net result would be the elevation of the status of women.

In the New Testament Jesus taught the complete equality of men and women in the marriage bond. In His view the possibility of divorce came about only as a concession to the hardness of men's hearts. Nevertheless the aim of marriage set out in Genesis 1:27 and 2:24 as lifelong fidelity between one man and one woman was God's intention. This union has claims which surpass all other claims, even those of parents (Mk. 10:1–12; Mt. 5:31, 32; 19:1–12; Lk. 16:18). Jesus' picture of the nature and possibilities of marriage is one which the Christian world cannot afford to compromise.

xii. Various social laws (24:5 – 25:4).

5. Exemption from military service. This law belongs with others concerned with the Holy War. Such a law would be out of place in a modern state, but in Deuteronomy it is of far greater importance that the man of Israel should be guaranteed descendants than that he should participate in a Holy War. He was granted a year's leave of absence to be with his wife (*cf.* 20:7), to ensure her happiness and to commence a family.[1]

6. Millstones not to be taken in pledge. This is an isolated law, apodictic in character, designed for the protection of the poor man. The ancient mill consisted of two stones, the top one moving over the bottom one which was stationary.

[1] Until very recently marriage was a ground for deferring call-up for the army in the USA.

The Hebrew word for *mill* is *rēḥayîm*, a dual, while the word for the *upper millstone* is *reḵeḇ*, lit. 'rider'. To take the whole mill or even a part of it as a pledge in the case where a man borrowed from his neighbour, was to deprive a man of his daily bread (*cf.* verses 10–14), and thus to take his life as a pledge.[1]

7. Against the kidnapping of a person. The law of Exodus 21:16 and possibly also of Deuteronomy 5:19 is restated here. It prescribes the death penalty for anyone who seizes a fellow citizen whom he ill-treats or sells into slavery, probably into a foreign land. The offence must have been common in the ancient Near East, to judge from other law codes which legislate against the practice.[2] The law is here stated in a casuistic form, 'If . . . then . . .'. The verb *treat as a slave* means 'to deal harshly or cruelly' (*cf.* 21:14). But whether the kidnapper possessed his fellow or sold him abroad, he was to be put to death. Thus will Israel *purge the evil from the midst.* This latter formula, as we have seen, is associated with capital punishment in several places in Deuteronomy (17:12; 19:11–13; 21:18–21; 22:21, 22–24). The law should be compared with that in 15:12–18, where voluntary slavery is permitted.

8, 9. Leprosy. Comparison should be made with Numbers 12:10–15 for the Miriam allusion, and with Leviticus 13 and 14 for the priestly laws on leprosy. These verses are not couched in legal form but in expository form, introduced by the expression *Take heed.* They are, moreover, in direct speech and show a change from the second singular in *Take heed* to the second plural in the latter part of the sentence. Obedience to the prescriptions of the Levitical priests is here enjoined. The term for *leprosy* (*ṣāra'aṭ*) is a wide one and covers a variety of skin diseases. Indeed, the term is also applied to clothes and houses (Lv. 14:55) and seems to have been used to describe things that were ceremonially unclean.[3]

10–13. Laws about loans. While loans to a fellow Israelite

---

[1] The idea of a pledge was not peculiar to Israel in the ancient Near East. See Hammurabi's Laws 114–116 (*ANET*, p. 170), where a human being was held as a pledge.

[2] Hammurabi Code, Law 14, *ANET*, p. 166; Hittite Code, Law I. 19 A, B, *ANET*, p. 190.

[3] See R. G. Cochrane, *Leprosy in the Bible*[2] (1974).

at interest were forbidden (23:19, 20), it was permitted to take some kind of security. However, the liberty of the borrower was guaranteed. The owner of the item borrowed was forbidden to enter the borrower's house to take a pledge. The debtor had to bring his own pledge, often a piece of clothing, but the sanctity of his home was preserved. The lot of the poor man was of special concern to the author of Deuteronomy. The one who took a pledge from him must return it at sundown so that the poor man may sleep in comfort (*cf.* Ex. 22:26, 27). Such consideration for the poor man would evoke gratitude in him and result in blessing to the creditor, whose generosity was right (*ṣᵉdāqâ*) in God's eyes.

14, 15. Protection for hired servants. Yahweh is concerned that men should receive their wages. A needy and destitute labourer, whether a fellow Israelite *brother* (*'āḥ*) or a resident alien (*gēr*), should not be oppressed, *i.e.* deprived of his rights, but each day his wages should be paid before the sun sets. Being poor, he had no resources and needed (*sets his heart upon*) the money. Since his case was the concern of Yahweh, failure to meet his needs would result in his crying to Yahweh who would hold the employer guilty (lit. 'it will be sin against you'). (*Cf.* Lv. 19:13; Mal. 3:5; Jas. 5:4.)

The humanitarian motive is strong throughout this section (6, 7, 10–13, 17, 18, 19–22). It was fundamental to Israel's understanding of the covenant family that He who delivered Israel from Egypt had a special concern for the underprivileged and the weak.

16. Personal responsibility. The judicial principle affirmed here is important. Family solidarity was a characteristic of Semitic society, especially in patriarchal and semi-nomadic society (Jos. 7:24ff.; 2 Sa. 3:29; 21:1ff.). Special praise was given in a later day to Amaziah, because he broke with prevailing custom when he executed his father's murderers (2 Ki. 14:6), *every man . . . for his own sin*, but spared the children of the murderers. The view held by some scholars, that individual responsibility was a late concept in Israel, cannot be accepted. The principle of personal responsibility is probably very ancient. It is clearly recognized in many of the ancient Near Eastern lands, as a study of the Laws of Hammurabi and others will show. Yet in some areas of Hammurabi's Laws there is a recognition that a son may be punished for a father's sins in some cases, that is, vicarious punishment was permitted in certain cases. Thus in the case where a careless builder caused the death of the son of the owner of the house when the house collapsed, the son of the builder was put to death.[1]

This verse explicitly contradicts this principle in Mesopotamian law. It is of some interest, also, to compare the laws about oxen who gore in Hammurabi's Laws 250–251 and Exodus 21:28, 29. In Hammurabi's Law 250, in the case where an ox gored someone to death unexpectedly, no claim could be made. In Exodus 21:28 the ox was to be slain, evidently because it had shed human blood and was held accountable for being objectively guilty of a criminal act, even when the owner was not legally accountable or responsible. In the case where an ox was known to be a gorer but the owner did not take protective measures and a man was killed, Hammurabi Law 251 prescribed a fine, whereas Exodus 21:29 prescribes the death of the negligent man. However, since the man did not commit the crime himself he was permitted to redeem his own life, if the slain person's family permitted it, by paying a ransom to them. This was not an economic compensation, as in Hammurabi's Laws, but a ransom for his own life which was otherwise forfeit.[2]

17, 18. Protection of the weak and defenceless. The law is first expressed in a simple apodictic form. Justice towards defenceless people, such as the resident alien, the fatherless and the widow, is a classical theme of all ancient moralists whether in Egypt, Canaan or Israel. The Old Testament insists that the protection of the weak is a duty not only for kings (Ps. 72:12–14) but also for the whole of society (Dt. 10:18; 27:19; Ex. 22:22; 23:6–9; Lv. 19:33; Pr. 22:22). Specific reference is made to the confiscation of the widow's garment given as a pledge. Once again the reason given for such a concern for the weak and defenceless is that Israel was a defenceless slave in Egypt, and Yahweh *redeemed* (*pādâ*) her. In other passages the Levite is included (14:29; 16:11–14).

---

[1] Hammurabi Law 230; *ANET*, p. 176.
[2] *ANET*, p. 165; Shalom M. Paul, *Studies in the Book of the Covenant in the Light of Cuneiform and Biblical Law* (Suppl. to *VT*, XVIII, 1920), pp. 79–82; M. Greenberg, 'Some Postulates of Biblical Criminal Law', *T. Kaufmann Volume* (1960), pp. 5ff.

19–22. The law of gleaning. 19. The passage as it is here preserved refers to the people *forgetting* a sheaf in the field at harvest time. But it was obligatory to leave some portion of the crop for the landless in Israel to glean. This was to help the resident alien, the orphan and the widow, *i.e.* the poor in Israel, to eke out their meagre existence. The principle lies behind Ruth's gleaning (Ru. 2). It is probable that in ancient times an offering was thereby made to the deity or spirits of the field. In Israel, such gifts offered to the poor of the land were really offerings to Yahweh (Lv. 19:9f.; 23:22), who would bestow His blessing on all Israel's undertakings (lit. 'the work of your hands').

20, 21. A similar law is applied to both the olive harvest and the grape harvest.

22. *Cf.* verse 18. Those who were children at the time of the exodus and who were now nearly forty years older would remember the days of slavery. But while the injunction had special significance for these, it must be remembered that Israel in every age was called on to identify herself in vivid imagination with her forefathers and to experience their redemption.

25:1–3. Limits to corporal punishment. There was a noble concept of human dignity in Israel. In matters which involved corporal punishment there was a proper penalty for each crime. To give a man the punishment due for his crime did not dishonour him, but to go beyond this was to insult him as an Israelite and degrade him.

In the present law, which is casuistic in form, *a dispute (rîb)* is envisaged between two men of Israel which leads them to law. Judgment is given and one man is declared to be in the right[1] while the other is declared in the wrong.[2] If the guilty man is sentenced to flogging, then the judgment must be carried out in the presence of the judges according to the deserts of the offender. This procedure prevented any hasty beating of an offender without a proper trial. But there was a further restriction. Excessive beating would humiliate a man to the level of a beast and thus his dignity would be offended. The verb *be degraded (niqlâ)* means literally 'be made light', *i.e.* 'humiliated'. The maximum number of stripes was fixed

---

[1] The verb form is the Hiphil of the verb *ṣādaq*, whose root *ṣ-d-q* connotes 'right'.

[2] The verb form is the Hiphil of *rāšaʿ*, whose root *r-š-ʿ* connotes 'wrong'.

at *forty*, a figure which occurs also in the Assyrian Code and suggests a custom that was widespread.[1] In later Jewish law the maximum was thirty-nine.[2]

4. The labouring ox not to be muzzled. In the agricultural society of the ancient Near East the grain was released from its stalk by driving an ox drawing a threshing-sledge, to which sharp stones were attached, round and round over the grain stalks. The threshed material was then thrown up on broad flat forks into the air so that the wind might carry away the chaff and leave the grain. Just as no man was permitted to exercise his proprietary rights over his crops so that no gleanings were left for the poor (24:19–21), so no man was to muzzle his ox. Love and kindness were to be shown to all God's creatures (22:6, 7; Pr. 12:10). This verse is quoted in the New Testament to support the contention that 'the labourer is worthy of his hire' (1 Cor. 9:9; 1 Tim. 5:18).

There was a well-known principle in rabbinic interpretation, that of *a fortiori*. It was argued that if one legislated for a lesser matter, then in a matter of the same general type, but which concerned bigger and more important issues, the legislation for the greater could be deduced from that for the lesser. We appear to have an application of the *a fortiori* principle in 1 Corinthians 9:9ff. Arguing from the legislation in Deuteronomy 25:4 Paul pointed out that the ox that trampled out the grain, which was part of the farmer's staple diet, was not to be muzzled but was allowed, as some compensation for his toil, some share in the grain. Similarly, argued Paul, those who toil to produce spiritual food for Christian believers should receive adequate compensation for their labours, represented in terms of a share in the material benefits enjoyed by those they had helped.

Another explanation is that the rabbis, like later Christians, distinguished a spiritual as well as a literal sense in much of Scripture. Paul may be doing something rather like that here and is making an application in the spiritual sphere of a principle that applied originally in the material sphere.

xiii. Levirate marriage (25:5–10). 5, 6. The practice of levirate marriage (Lat. *levir*, brother-in-law or husband's

---

[1] Middle Assyrian Laws, A18 (forty), A19 (fifty) (*ANET*, p. 181).
[2] 2 Cor. 11:24; *cf.* Mishna Makkoth, III, 13, 14. See H. Danby, *The Mishnah* (1933), pp. 407, 408.

brother) was not peculiar to Israel, for it was practised among the Hittites and Assyrians as well as in countries such as India, Africa and South America. Among the Assyrians it was extended also to one who was betrothed. The purpose of the custom was to ensure that a man who died before he had produced a male heir might nevertheless have an heir. The widow of the dead man was taken by one of his brothers who would *perform the duty of a husband's brother* to her. The first son born from this union became the dead man's heir. In this way the marriage of the dead man's widow to a *stranger (gēr)* was prevented and the dead man's name was not *blotted out of Israel*.

The practice was common in the patriarchal period. The story of Onan in Genesis 38:1–10 suggests that the custom was an old one. Presumably the prohibition of sexual union with a brother's wife in Leviticus 18:16 and 20:21 refers to such an act while the brother is still living. An alternative solution to the problem of inheritance was to allow a woman to inherit (Nu. 27).

In Jesus' day the Sadducees used this law in their attempt to prove the absurdity of the belief in the resurrection (Mt. 22:23–33; Mk. 12:18–27). On that occasion Jesus stated that the resurrection was not to be viewed as simply a prolongation of human marriage arrangements, but the entering upon a new order of life. 'In the resurrection they neither marry nor are given in marriage, but are like angels in heaven' (Mt. 22:30).

7–10. Provision was made for a brother to escape from this obligation, although it would seem that this was discouraged. The legal procedure was undertaken before the elders in the city gate. This consisted essentially of a renunciation of the heritage by a symbolic act. The widow of the man's brother removed his shoe and then spat in his face and declared *So shall it be done to the man who does not build up his brother's house*.[1] The story in Ruth 4:7, 8 is based on this law, although Boaz was not Ruth's brother-in-law (*levir*) but the next of kin who acted as the redeemer (*gō'ēl*) of her husband's property. The law in Deuteronomy implies that the brothers were living together, a state of affairs that did not always obtain. Moreover, a degree of choice in the matter was possible (7). The present passage

---

[1] See H. A. Hoffner, 'Some Contributions of Hittitology to Old Testament Study', *TB*, 20, 1969, pp. 43f.

seems to imply a certain weakening of the ancient practice (*cf.* Gn. 38).

Some commentators have seen a link between the surrender of the sandal in this case and the surrender of an item of clothing at ancient Nuzi in Northern Mesopotamia in the fifteenth century BC when land, regarded as inalienable, was surrendered to another through the fiction of adoption.[1]

xiv. Various laws (25:11-19). Three distinct and unrelated laws follow.

11, 12. A case of extreme immodesty in women who interfere in a brawl is discussed briefly. There are several unusual features about this law. One might ask why Deuteronomy should publish specifically this law forbidding a woman to aid her husband in a fight by grasping the sex organs of his opponent. Possibly it was representative of similar offences and provided a standard for judgment in all such cases. Perhaps also, the law arose from the desire to protect the reproductive organs and thus obviate anything that might prevent a man leaving descendants. The penalty is severe, involving mutilation of a part of the body (*cf.* 19:21, the *lex talionis*). Only here in the Old Testament is mutilation prescribed. By contrast mutilation of human limbs and organs was provided for in both the Code of Hammurabi[2] and in the Assyrian Code.[3]

13-16. Weights and measures.[4] Two apodictic laws, both prohibitions, provide a link with traditional common law of the ancient Near East. In Israel, strict honesty in business dealings was incumbent on every man of the covenant. The weights and volume measures were to be completely honest (lit. 'whole', *šelēmâ*) and right (*ṣedeq*). A similar law occurs in Leviticus 19:35f. It is evident, however, from Amos 8:5 that such honesty was not always observed in Israel. In verses 15b and 16 two covenant sanctions are expressed, one directly, and one by implication. Obedience to the covenant law resulted in blessing, disobedience in cursing. All who acted dishonestly

[1] E. A. Speiser, 'Of Shoes and Shekels', *BASOR*, 77, Feb. 1940, pp. 15-20.
[2] Code of Hammurabi, Laws 195-200, *ANET*, p. 175.
[3] Middle Assyrian Code, Law A8, which is very similar to the law in Deuteronomy, *ANET*, p. 181.
[4] As a result of archaeological excavations in the mounds of Palestine it is now possible to give a remarkably complete picture of the weights and measures of the Old Testament. See art. 'Weights and Measures', *NBD*, pp. 1319-1325; R. B. Y. Scott, 'Weights and Measures of the Bible', *BA*, XXII, 1951, pp. 22-40; R. de Vaux, *Ancient Israel* (1962), pp. 195-209.

were an abomination to Yahweh, and by implication would fall into judgment.

17–19. The Amalekites to be exterminated. This passage is not expressed in the legal phraseology of other parts of Deuteronomy, although something of an apodictic instruction is finally given, *You shall blot out the remembrance of Amalek from under heaven*. The background to the present injunction is the hostility displayed when the Amalekites cut off stragglers in the rear of the Israelites coming from Egypt (Ex. 17:8–16). This was inhuman and barbarous. Nomads from the desert would normally display some fear of God in such cases (*cf.* Am. 1:3 – 2:3). Amalek's failure to show mercy to the weak merited divine judgment, for God judged nations for crimes against natural law. Israel would be used as an instrument of divine chastisement in later days (Ps. 149:7; Is. 41:14, 15). Through the centuries there was continuous conflict between Israel and Amalek (1 Sa. 14:48; 15; 27:8, 9; 28:18; 30:1–20; 2 Sa. 8:12; 1 Ch. 4:43). In terms of the conduct of the Holy War these foes were to be exterminated along with those from whom Israel wrested the promised land (Dt. 20:10–15, 16 18). This law would have been particularly relevant in the early days of the kingdom. In the days of the kings it was irrelevant, since the Amalekites had ceased to be significant.

f. Two rituals and concluding exhortation (26:1–19)

With chapter 26 Deuteronomy concludes the purely legal material. Its final regulations concern two important rituals, namely, the presentation of first-fruits (1–11) and the presentation of the tithe of the third year (12–15). These two rituals were in continual danger of being influenced by the practices of the Canaanites, since they were originally agricultural rituals.

i. Liturgy for the presentation of the first-fruits (26:1–11). As the narrative is presented here, the entry into the promised land was still in the future. It is not difficult to conceive of Moses requiring the people of Israel to undertake some such act of worship.

2. It was only a sample of the first-fruits that was to be taken,[1] but it may be inferred that it was a widely distributed

[1] The *min* in Hebrew is partitive.

sample, for it was *the first of all the fruit of the ground*. The point is made that it was Yahweh who had given the increase to His people. By inference, therefore, it was not Baal. The first-fruits were taken in a basket to the sanctuary approved by God (*cf.* 12:5 and the discussion there). On the law of the first-fruits see 18:4; Exodus 23:19; Numbers 18:12ff., *etc.*

3. *The priest who is in office at that time* refers to the chief priest at the central sanctuary (*cf.* Eli at Shiloh is called 'the priest', 1 Sa. 1:9; 2:13–16). The first of the solemn declarations is to the effect that the worshipper acknowledges that he has come, not to any land, but precisely to the land which Yahweh promised to the fathers. It was an acknowledgment that the divine promise had been fulfilled. Each succeeding generation would take up that affirmation anew and identify itself with those first arrivals for whom the wonder of the divine faithfulness was so overwhelming. The people of Israel were thus to make continual thankful acknowledgment to Yahweh for His goodness by offering their first-fruits (2, 10).

4. The priest was to take the basket and set it before the altar of Yahweh. Some have imagined a contradiction between verse 4, which seems to imply that the basket is handed to the priest at the start of the ceremony, and verse 10, which seems to suggest that the basket was not handed over till the end of the ceremony.[1] But the literary methods of the ancient world were not as systematic as are those of the twentieth century AD. It is more likely that verse 4 simply defines the sense of verse 10. Any apparent contradiction arises from the fact that verse 4 precedes verses 5 to 10. But verses 3 and 4 might be taken as an explanatory note. It is reasonable to think that the declaration was made as the offering was presented.

5–10. These verses constitute something of a crux in modern Old Testament discussion. They comprise a confession of faith which refers to the patriarchs, the descent into Egypt, the oppression in Egypt, the exodus, and the entry into Canaan. In this enumeration of events there is no reference to what took place at Sinai. This confession, together with that in 6:20–25, represents 'the small historical credo' proposed by G. von Rad in 1938.[2] According to von Rad there are reflections of the same credo in other Old Testament passages, such

---

[1] G. von Rad, *Deuteronomy* (1966), p. 157.
[2] First published in German but now available in English in *The Problem of the Hexateuch and other essays* (1966), pp. 1–78. See also his *Deuteronomy* (1966), pp. 155ff.

as Joshua 24:2b-13; 1 Samuel 12:8; Psalm 136, *etc*. The absence of reference to Sinai in these passages led von Rad to propose that the most ancient form of Israel's confession did not contain a reference to Sinai and that it was only later that this tradition was woven in with the simpler credo. It was, on this view, a quite different religious tradition. Now, that there was a confession of faith like that in 26:5-10 need not be denied. But that the absence from it of the Sinai tradition points to a quite independent tradition is open to question.[1] It is not unlikely that for a particular purpose, namely, at the time of the bringing of the first-fruits, Israel may have wished merely to recall that long ago God had promised a land to the fathers and that now, after a long period of dependence on other peoples and of suffering at the hands of others, God had fulfilled His promise. There may have been other significant features in the story of the past, but these, like the Sinai story, were irrelevant for the present purpose. No credo ever contains all that a body of believers would wish to confess. Indeed, some branches of the Christian church reject formal creeds, arguing that the faith of Christians is wider than any creed.[2]

5. The AV *A Syrian ready to perish* and the RSV *A wandering Aramean* are alternative translations. The reference is probably to Jacob, although it might refer further back to Abraham. The association of the patriarchs with the Aramaeans is quite strongly suggested in Genesis. Abraham, Isaac and Jacob all had links with Aram-naharaim[3] where the tribe of Terah lived (Gn. 11:31). The term Aram features several times in the Genesis narrative in connection with the patriarchs (Gn. 25:20; 28:5, 7; 31:20, 24). In Genesis 22:21 a certain Aram is mentioned as the grandson of Nahor, Abraham's brother. Whatever the character of the Aramaeans in this connection it is evident that the biblical tradition places the patriarchal origins in the area from which the later Aramaeans came. Perhaps they were, in fact, one group of the widespread proto-Aramaeans.[4] The term *wandering* ('*ōḇēḏ*) is ambiguous, since it can denote 'wander' or 'perish'. The reference is a subtle one as Jacob was both a wanderer and, as such, a man whose life was in jeopardy. From such a wanderer, whose chances of

[1] See J. A. Thompson, 'The Cultic Credo and the Sinai Tradition', *RTR*, XXVII, May/August 1968, pp. 53–64.
[2] For example, Baptists, Churches of Christ, Quakers, Christian Brethren.
[3] See *NBD*, p. 56.
[4] See Martin Noth, *The Old Testament World* (1964), pp. 237–239.

survival seemed so slender, there came a great people. He went to Egypt *few in number*, actually seventy (Ex. 1:5), he lived there as a resident alien (*gēr*; *cf*. Gn. 47:4), and finally became *a nation, great, mighty, and populous* (Ex. 1:9). The latter expression is perhaps to be translated, with the JPSA, 'a great and very populous nation'.

6. The harshness of the Egyptian oppression with its hard labour was an important element in the total theme, for it was from such a plight that Yahweh delivered His people (Ex. 1:14).

7. The response of Yahweh to the call of His people is an oft-repeated theme of the Old Testament (Ex. 3:9; 4:31; Jdg. 3:9; 6:7f., *etc*.). The identification of Yahweh with the God of the fathers is an important aspect of the period of the oppression in Egypt (Ex. 3:6, 13–16). It was a new name but not a new God. The severity of their plight is expressed by the strong nouns *affliction* (*ʿŏnî*), *toil* (*ʿāmāl*) and *oppression* (*laḥaṣ*).

8. The deliverance wrought by Yahweh is often described in the vigorous terms used in this verse, *with a mighty hand and an outstretched arm, with great terror, with signs and wonders*. The expression *great terror* might be translated 'awesome power' (4:34; 6:22; 7:8. *Cf*. Ex. 6:6; 7:3–5, *etc*.).

9. For the expression *a land flowing with milk and honey*, *cf*. 6:1–3.

10. See comments on verse 4. The verb *worship* has a significant basic root and usage. The root *ḥ-w-y* is used both in Hebrew and in Canaanite and connotes 'prostrate oneself'. In usage the verb occurs in contexts where an inferior prostrates himself before a superior (Gn. 37:9; 1 Sa. 24:8; 2 Sa. 9:8), or where a man worships Yahweh or another deity (Jos. 23:16; 1 Ki. 9:6; 2 Ki. 5:18; 19:37). Hence *worship* involves obedience to the sovereign commandments of Yahweh and personal surrender to Him. In the present passage a more personal note is struck, in that the worshipper offers fruits from *the ground, which thou, O Yahweh, hast given me*, *i.e*. the man who brought his first-fruits has taken his own place in the story of God's saving activity and acknowledged himself to be the personal recipient of the gift promised centuries beforehand to the patriarchs.

11. There is a joyous note in the worship of Yahweh (*cf*. 12:6f., 11f., 17f.; 16:11, 14, *etc*.). The association of a man's *house* with the Levite and the resident alien, in his rejoicing in all the *good* which God gave him, suggests some kind of sacred meal. Elements of the first-fruits were associated with each of the great annual feasts. At the feast of unleavened bread a sheaf of first-fruits was taken (Lv. 23:10ff.). The feast of weeks was called 'the day of the first-fruits' (Nu. 28:26; *cf.* Ex. 23:16; 34:22). The first-fruits of wine could not be offered till the feast of tabernacles, when the vintage had ripened. All these were occasions for happy festive activity. Perhaps we might translate here with JPSA, *You shall enjoy, together with the Levite and the stranger in your midst, all the bounty that the Lord your God has bestowed upon you and your household.*

ii. Liturgy for use at the presentation of the third year tithe (26:12–15). Every third year the tithe was kept in the villages for the relief of the poor (14:28, 29) and was thus outside the control of the priests. To prevent irregularities in its distribution, and at the same time to preserve the religious character of the obligation, the man of Israel was required to make a solemn declaration at the central sanctuary that he had used the tithe according to the divine law.

12. The underprivileged in society, *the Levite, the sojourner* (*gēr*), *the fatherless, and the widow*, were to be given the benefit of the tithe on this occasion. They were to eat their fill.

13. Since the distribution was not made *before Yahweh, i.e.* as a rite performed at the central sanctuary (*cf.* 12:7, 12, 18; 14:23, 26; 15:20; 16:11, 16), the man of Israel was required to go to the central sanctuary to declare that he had fulfilled all the requirements of the law. The time at which this was done is not given here or anywhere else in the Old Testament, although it may have been at the feast of booths. The man declared that he had *removed the sacred portion* (*qōdeš*, 'holy thing') from his house. The verb *remove* (*biʿēr*) is used elsewhere for the total removal of something evil from Israel (13:5; 17:7; 19:19; 24:7, *etc.*). The connotation in the present context would seem to be that the man confessed that he had utterly and completely removed the tithe from his house and given it to Yahweh for the relief of the needy. The confession goes on, *I have not transgressed any of thy commandments, neither have I forgotten them.*

14. There are some negative aspects to the confession. The worshipper denies that he has been involved in three specific practices: *I have not eaten of the tithe while I was mourning, or removed any of it while I was unclean, or offered any of it to the dead.* It has been suggested that the background of these practices is probably Canaanite.[1] Each year at the time of harvest there were festivals in which the vegetation gods Baal and Tammuz featured (*cf.* Ezk. 8:14). The offering of the first-fruits was incorporated into these rites. The theory is without actual support, but it would not be unlikely that Israel should be forbidden to engage in practices which owed something to Canaanite influence. All festivals related to the harvest were to have only one focal point, Yahweh Himself.

15. The confession closes with a prayer that God would bless Israel and her land as He looked down upon them from His holy habitation (*cf.* 1 Ki. 8:30; 2 Ch. 30:27; Je. 25:30; Zc. 2:13).

iii. Covenant ratification (26:16–19). If we regard the long section 5:1 – 26:15 as containing the heart of the covenant law, both in terms of the general principles and of the specific stipulations (even allowing that in the present setting the material is 'law preached' rather than 'codified law'), we may regard this small pericope[2] as in the nature of an oath of allegiance (*cf.* 29:10–15; Ex. 24:7). In form, the pericope looks like a contract in which the two parties bind themselves by means of a solemn declaration. Moses acts as a covenant mediator between Israel, who declares that she will be Yahweh's people, and Yahweh, who declares that He will be Israel's God (*cf.* Ex. 6:7; Je. 31:33; Ezk. 36:28). In fact the wording of the pericope makes it clear that both declarations refer to the obligations which must be fulfilled by Israel alone. Yahweh has no obligations to keep, but in grace He has blessings to bestow.

16. A hortatory conclusion to the whole block of obligations set out in chapters 5 to 26. Israel is commanded to perform all the statutes and judicial decisions (*mišpāṭîm*) with all their heart and soul, *i.e.* whole-heartedly.

17. The verb form is causative, meaning literally 'you have caused (Yahweh) to say'. The picture is based on a secular parallel in which the two contracting parties to a covenant each required the other to recite the terms of the agreement between them, *i.e.* 'the one causes the other to say (declare)'. This secular metaphor is put to a religious use. Israel is

---

[1] By H. Cazelles, 'Sur un rituel du Deutéronome (Deut. xxvi:14)', *RB*, 55, 1948, pp. 54-71.
[2] The term means 'a literary unit'. It is widely used in literary studies where the smaller units of a larger block of literature are identified.

pictured as requiring Yahweh to say that He was their God, which is equivalent to their own acceptance of the fact. The verb has evidently changed its connotation somewhat and now bears the sense of 'affirm'. The verse may be translated: 'You have affirmed this day that Yahweh is your God, that you will walk in his ways, that you will observe his laws and his commandments and his ordinances and obey him.' As the verse now stands the final emphasis is on the obligation of Israel to obey the covenant stipulations.

18. The same verb, 'cause to say', occurs here also. Yahweh 'caused Israel to say (declare)' that she was His people, which is tantamount to saying that He accepted the fact Himself, and could affirm 'You are my people'. They were, moreover, His prized *possession* (*s*ᵉ*gullâ*), according to His promise to the patriarchs.[1] Again, the divine intention was that Israel should keep the commandments.

19. Yahweh guaranteed the blessings of His covenant to Israel. The blessing was promised to the people as a whole, even though particular individuals may suffer on particular occasions. In broad terms Yahweh promised to set His people *high* ('*elyôn*) *above all nations* which He had made, in fame (lit. *praise, t*ᵉ*hillâ, i.e.* as an object of praise), in renown (*fame*, lit. 'name'), and in glory (*honour, tip̄*'*eret̠*, an object of pride). It is a noble picture, although stated in very general terms. The final promise was that Israel would be *a people holy to Yahweh*. The term *holy* (*qāḏōš*), often applied to Israel in the Old Testament (7:6; 14:2, 21; 28:9; Ex. 19:5, 6, *etc.*), denotes something that is set apart completely for the sole use and enjoyment of its possessor. This character was conferred by Yahweh on Israel and was not something that Israel could achieve herself. In practice the adjective has the double connotation of something set apart by God and something which Israel could become by separating herself from all evil.

IV. COVENANT RENEWAL IN THE PROMISED LAND (27:1–26)[2]

Chapter 27 poses a number of problems for the commentator. Moses is introduced in the third person. Not since 5:1 has he

---

[1] See Introduction, p. 74, for discussion about the meaning of the word.
[2] This section has been called the Document Clause. See p. 19.

been referred to in this way, for chapters 5–26 are presented as a single hortatory speech of Moses to Israel. In chapter 27 Moses is presented again in narrative in the third person (1, 9, 11).[1]

One's first impression is that chapter 27 appears to be an interruption to a smooth sequence which flows easily from 26:19 to 28:1. The chapter consists of at least three fragmentary and apparently unconnected sections, each introduced by a reference to Moses. Thus verses 1 to 8 are concerned with the summons by Moses and the elders to the people to set up plastered stones in Mount Ebal after the crossing of the Jordan and to build an altar where peace offerings are to be offered. Some covenant renewal ceremony seems to be envisaged. Verses 9 and 10 refer to a proclamation by Moses and the Levitical priests that Israel had become the people of God and was therefore bound to keep Yahweh's covenant stipulations. Such a statement might be connected with 26:16–19. Finally verses 11–26 contain Moses' instructions to Israel to draw up representatives from the tribes in two groups, one on Mount Gerizim and one on Mount Ebal, for the recitation of the curses of the covenant.

Another feature of this chapter is that verses 1–8 and 11–26, unlike the rest of Deuteronomy, in which the general and specific stipulations of the covenant are given and expounded, are concerned with two different cultic ceremonies, which, once performed, did not need to be repeated.

Again, it might be asked what was the connection between the altar on Mount Ebal (4–7) and the place in one of the tribes where Yahweh would meet Israel and where He would place His name, *i.e.* which He would claim as His own. (See p. 41.) Certainly on the theory that Deuteronomy was written in the seventh century BC, long after Moses' day, with the intention of centralizing worship in Jerusalem, this injunction would make strange reading, for it seems to contradict the centrality of Jerusalem. A book written with the intention of centralizing worship in Jerusalem would not be expected to include a command to set up an altar on Mount Ebal. To be sure, Mount Ebal did not feature as a sacred place in the days of the kings, but in the same general area stood Shechem where the central sanctuary stood in early Israel (Jos. 24:1).

---

[1] Moses' name occurs very seldom in the whole of Deuteronomy. In 4:44 – 30:20 it occurs only in 4:44–46; 5:1; 27:1, 9, 11 and 29:1, 2.

How, then, should chapter 27 be understood, since it seems to interrupt the sequence between 26:19 and 28:1 ?

One suggestion is that, when the later editor had completed 26:16–19 with its reference to a covenant renewal ceremony, he considered this to be a convenient place to introduce material about the ceremony on Mount Ebal and on Mount Gerizim, probably associated with Shechem (*cf.* Jos. 8:30–35; 24:1ff.). Another proposal is that chapter 27 represents one aspect of the covenant renewal ceremony on the plains of Moab. In the standard Near Eastern treaty, once the covenant stipulations had been given, the oath was taken and the curses and blessings were proclaimed as part of the ratification ceremony. It is possible that the second stage of the ratification ceremony is given in chapter 27, while the initial stage occurs in chapters 28 to 30. The second stage was concerned with the offering of sacrifices in the covenant ratification ceremony (*cf.* Ex. 24:1–8).[1]

A recent proposal by G. J. Wenham[2] allows chapter 27 to follow quite naturally after chapter 28. The requirement in 27:1–8, that Israel should build an altar on Mount Ebal and write the law on a plastered monument, is taken to be the last of the covenant stipulations. After the response of the people in 26:16–19 Moses and the elders gave one further piece of instruction, which concerned the reiteration of the covenant demands and the renewal of the covenant once Israel had crossed the Jordan. The small pericope 27:9, 10 points to some kind of covenant ceremony in which the covenant demands were stated and the people charged to be obedient. Finally, 27:11–26 may be regarded as a detailed explanation of the ceremony to be carried out on Mount Ebal. While it might be objected that the blessings are omitted here, it should be noted that it was not necessary to include references to every aspect of a covenant ceremony in every reference to it. However, the two groups, which stood one on Mount Gerizim and one on Mount Ebal, symbolized both the blessings that were implicit if the covenant were kept and the curses which would follow if the covenant were broken. Details of these curses and blessings follow in chapter 28.

---

[1] Meredith G. Kline, *Treaty of the Great King* (1963), p. 122.
[2] In a paper given in July 1967 to the Old Testament Study Group of the Tyndale Fellowship at Tyndale House, Cambridge. The idea was later developed in his unpublished thesis, *The Structure and Date of Deuteronomy*, pp. 206–208, 210–212.

Another general point may be made. In 27:11–26 the people are pictured as answering *Amen* to each utterance of the Levites. G. J. Wenham proposes that responses may be inferred also after 26:19, 27:8 and 27:10. We are comparatively ignorant of the details of covenant-making ceremonies either in the Old Testament or in the secular world of the day, although some aspects of these ceremonies are clear. That responses were given is clear from Exodus 19:8; 24:7; Joshua 24:16, 21, 24; 1 Samuel 12:19. There are hints also of responses in the Hittite and Assyrian treaties.[1] It is clear also from Mari, Alalakh and from Assyrian and Aramaean documents that animals were slain as part of the ceremony for the ratification of a treaty (or covenant). Indeed, at Mari in the eighteenth century BC the expression 'to kill an ass' denoted 'to make a covenant'.[2] At Alalakh a formula was recited which indicates that the killing of the beast symbolized the punishment that would follow the breach of the treaty.[3] Thus the three small sections introduced as separate utterances of Moses in 27:1, 9 and 11 may well represent stages in a covenant ceremony.

a. The final stipulation of the covenant (27:1–8)

1. Direct references to Moses are rare in the 'legal' sections of Deuteronomy (*cf.* 4:44, 45; 5:1). This verse, like 5:1, introduces a significant section. Moses here associates himself with the elders in commanding the continuity of the covenant when Israel crosses the Jordan.

2–8. The crossing of the Jordan is pictured as yet in the future. A number of specific instructions are given for the ceremony of covenant renewal in that day. Moses and the elders commanded the erection of plastered stones on which the law was to be written. Also, an altar was to be built on which peace offerings were to be offered and a ritual meal eaten. Comparison with Exodus 24:3–8 reveals a close similarity in the rites described and the sequence of events.

2, 3. The practice of writing laws on a plastered surface was known in other lands, notably Egypt, where the texts were painted rather than engraved. This public exhibition of the

---

[1] D. J. Wiseman, 'The Vassal Treaties of Esarhaddon', *Iraq*, 20, 1958, p. 26; E. F. Weidner, 'Politische Dokumente aus Kleinasien', *Boghazköi Studien*, 1923, p. 53 in the treaty of Mattiuaza and Suppiluliuma.

[2] See *Archives Royales de Mari*, vol. II, document 37, line 6.

[3] D. J. Wiseman, *JCS*, XII, 4, 1958, lines 40ff. on pages 126, 129.

law in the new land was part of the covenant renewal. The point is made that the final entry to the *land flowing with milk and honey* was the fulfilment of the promise made to the fathers.

The statement that this monument should be set up *on the day you pass over the Jordan* might suggest that stones were set up in proximity to the Jordan, *e.g.* at Gilgal (Jos. 4:20), much earlier than the arrival of Israel at Mount Ebal. It is not impossible that such a ceremony took place more than once. On the other hand the expresssion *on the day you pass over the Jordan* may simply mean 'once you have crossed the Jordan' without any reference to time.

4. This is largely a repetition of verse 2 and seems to interrupt the sequence of verses 3 to 5. That would be quite in the manner of Hebrew writing. Rather than regard it as a gloss (in which case verse 3 would also be a gloss, since it is a repetition of verse 8), it might be regarded as the beginning of a separate ancient fragment from which verses 2 and 3 arose. It is characteristic of Hebrew to be repetitious. The facts of the case are reported in outline in verses 2 and 3. There follows, as though to provide substantiation for the action described, a quotation derived from an earlier utterance of Moses.

5, 6a. The erection of an altar on Mount Ebal raises the question of the central sanctuary (see commentary on chapter 12). The facts of the biblical record indicate that even where there was a central sanctuary, *e.g.* at Shiloh in Samuel's day, there might be an altar elsewhere (*cf.* 1 Sa. 9:12) in a place where Yahweh chose to place His name.

The *altar of stones*, on which no iron tool was to be wielded and which was to be made of 'whole' (*šālēm*), *i.e. unhewn* stone pieces, is reminiscent of the altar in Exodus 20:25.

6b, 7. Two types of offering are mentioned, *burnt offerings* (*'ôlâ*), and *peace offerings* (*šelem*, pl. *šelāmîm*). The whole burnt offerings were for Yahweh, since they were completely consumed in the fire (Lv. 1:1–17). The peace offerings were largely consumed by the worshippers (Lv. 3:1–17), who ate and rejoiced in Yahweh's presence. Burnt offerings and peace offerings are often associated in the historical books (Ex. 24:5; Jdg. 20:26; 21:4; 1 Sa. 10:8; 2 Sa. 6:17; 1 Ki. 3:15). In Exodus 24:5 they are offered, as here, in connection with a covenant ceremony.

8. The words of the law were to be written *very plainly* (lit. 'engraving well'). The expression is a strong one and consists grammatically of two infinitives used adverbially. The first derives from the root *b-'-r*, 'dig' or 'hew', and is used in Habakkuk 2:2 of writing on a tablet. Metaphorically it signifies engraving on the minds of people, *i.e.* explaining or expounding (*cf.* Dt. 1:5). The other infinitive derives from the root *y-ṭ-b*, denoting 'be good', 'do good', 'do well'. Hence the whole expression connotes 'do well in engraving', *i.e. very plainly*.

b. Covenant challenge (27:9, 10)

This brief section appears to be the conclusion of a challenge to enter into the covenant and to obey the covenant stipulations (*cf.* 26:16–19). We have already proposed that the context of these words may have been a covenant ceremony. Some response to these words of Moses and the Levitical priests would be expected, even though it has been omitted. It would be said on the day when the covenant was renewed on the western side of the Jordan, *This day you have become the people of Yahweh your God*. To this we would expect some such response as 'All that Yahweh has spoken we will do' (Ex. 19:8).

The exhortation to *keep silence* (*sāḵaṯ*) is common at the climax of some religious ceremony or liturgy (Ne. 8:11; Zp. 1:7; Zc. 2:13; *cf.* Hab. 2:20).

The term *Levitical priests* (lit. 'the priests, the Levites') simply stresses the tribal association of the priests. Not all Levites were priests, but all priests were Levites. The Levitical priests were the guardians of Moses' words (*cf.* 17:9, 18; 21:5; 24:8).

These verses underline with beautiful clarity the relationship between the covenant and obedience. The covenant was established first and obedience followed. The covenant was thus Yahweh's free gift and was not determined by any prior obedience of 'good works' on Israel's part. Obedience was not a condition of the covenant but the outcome of it. Obedience was to be motivated by gratitude to Yahweh for all He had done for His people and for His acceptance of them as His people (*cf.* 8:1ff.; 9:1ff.). The motif of gratitude is writ large in Deuteronomy.

c. Details about the ceremony on Mount Ebal (27:11–26)

11–14. Six of the tribes, descendants of Jacob's wives Leah and Rachel, namely, Simeon, Levi, Judah, Issachar, Joseph and Benjamin, were commanded to stand on Mount Gerizim, the southern hill of the twin peaks between which the highway passed to the north, *to bless the people*, while the other six tribes, Reuben, son of Leah who had forfeited his birthright through incest (Gn. 49:4; *cf.* Dt. 27:20), Zebulun, Leah's youngest son, and the four descendants of the handmaidens Bilhah and Zilpah, namely, Dan, Naphtali, Gad and Asher, were to stand on the northern peak Mount Ebal, *for the curse* (*q*ᵉ*lālâ*). The nature of the ceremony is not at all clear. It ought not to be assumed that the groups on the two mountains spoke at all. Their action in standing on the two mountains may have been symbolic. *Mount Gerizim* in the south may have symbolized the place of good omen, being on the right-hand side of a man looking East (*cf.* Gn. 48:8 ff.; Mt. 25:31ff.), while the northern peak, *Mount Ebal*, may have symbolized the curse of the broken covenant. It would seem that selected members of the tribes (there is no contradiction between verses 11 and 14, since only representatives of the Levites are concerned in each case and not the whole tribe) stood facing the Levitical priests who read out the curses of verses 15–26. Then *all the people*, presumably the people in these groups, representing the whole of the twelve tribes, replied *Amen*. The absence of a list of blessings may simply mean that they were omitted, since they would have corresponded with the curses except that they negatived every one in turn. Those who were blessed did not offend in the areas in which those who were cursed did.

There is not here a list of the actual curses, but only a statement that those who offend in a certain way will be cursed. The specific curses and blessings are given in chapter 28.

15–26. Twelve formulae, each introduced by the word *Cursed* (*'ārûr*), form the basis of the declaration made by the Levites, *i.e.* the Levitical priests.[1] These twelve formulae have been referred to as the Dodecalogue of Shechem,[2] since they have been thought to refer to twelve laws, the breach of which is envisaged in this passage. The laws implied in these formulae can be paralleled elsewhere in the Old Testament. The general reply *Amen* is the customary formula of assent (Nu. 5:22; 1 Ki. 1:36; Ne. 5:13; 8:6; Ps. 72:19; Je. 11:5). By affirming *Amen* the

---

[1] Albrecht Alt in his important discussion on the origins of Israelite law saw in this list a group of laws that was closely related to apodictic laws. See A. Alt, *Essays on Old Testament History and Religion* (ET, 1966), pp. 114f., 130.

[2] G. von Rad, *Deuteronomy* (1966), pp. 166, 167.

representatives of the two groups agreed to a kind of self-malediction, calling upon themselves and their tribe a curse if they offended in reference to the particular law that was implied in the formula. The twelve laws were, no doubt, symbolic of all Yahweh's laws. This whole literary form suggests a liturgical dialogue which was common enough in covenant ceremonies (Jos. 24:14–24; 1 Sa. 12:3–5). It is not impossible that something that Moses devised became the pattern for later liturgies used in covenant renewal ceremonies.

15. The underlying offence here is the making of an *image*. This is the longest of the twelve formulae. In its present form it may represent an expansion of some simpler formula such as 'Cursed be the man who makes a graven or a molten image and sets it up in secret'. The reference could be to either a representation of Yahweh or to a pagan deity. Both were *an abomination to Yahweh*. An image *made by the hands of a craftsman* was not to be worshipped. The contrast with Yahweh is made in a number of references in the Old Testament (Is. 44:9ff.; Je. 10:1ff.; Ps. 115:3–7). One of the more offensive aspects of this practice is that it was done *in secret*. The same feature may be noted in several of the offences listed in this chapter. Hidden from human view and hence not open to human justice, they can be exposed only to a man's conscience. Comparison should be made with 4:16; 5:8; Exodus 20:23; Leviticus 19:4; 26:1 for a similar prohibition.

16. The dishonouring of parents is referred to in 21:18–21; Exodus 21:15; Leviticus 20:9; Ezekiel 22:7. The verb *dishonour* derives from the root *q-l-l*, which connotes 'light', 'small', 'despised'. The sense here is 'to regard as small or insignificant'. Once a man thinks in such a way, his parents become insignificant as far as he is concerned and he treats them thus. The derivative *qᵉlālâ* came to mean 'curse' (28:15).

17. *Cf.* 19:14. The *landmark* defined the limits of a man's divinely allotted portion, his inheritance. To remove this was to encroach on something God had appointed.

18. *Cf.* Leviticus 19:14. Less fortunate members of society were under God's special care.

19. *Cf.* 10:18; 24:17; Exodus 22:21; Leviticus 19:33; Proverbs 28:10; Ezekiel 22:7. The resident alien, the orphan and the widow were likewise the special concern of God. To *pervert the justice* of such people would result in divine judgment.

20. *Cf.* 22:30; Leviticus 18:8; 20:11; Hammurabi Law 158.[1]

[1] See *ANET*, pp. 172, 173.

The text reads literally 'he has uncovered his father's skirt'. With this verse we are introduced to a small group of four laws dealing with illicit sexual relationships. *Cf.* Leviticus 18:6-23. The central law is Leviticus 18:6, the others being extensions and explanations of the basic law. Such a 'code' certainly reaches back to very early times of nomadic or semi-nomadic life, when tribal peoples lived together in very large family units.

21. *Cf.* Exodus 22:19; Leviticus 18:23; 20:15; also Hittite Laws 188, 199.[1]

22. This law should be taken with verse 20. *Cf.* Leviticus 18:9; 20:17.

23. *Cf.* Leviticus 18:17; 20:14.

24. *Cf.* Exodus 21:12; Psalms 10:8; 64:2-5.

25. *Cf.* 1:17; 16:19; Exodus 23:8; Leviticus 19:15, 35; Proverbs 17:23.

26. A curse is proclaimed against any man who *does not confirm the words of this law*. The term *law* (*tôrâ*) means more generally 'teaching'. Its use here should not be taken to indicate that the list in verses 15 to 26 is 'law' in the narrow sense. In any case, the reference here is probably to all the instruction of the book of Deuteronomy.

Reviewing the present list, it is clear that it was designed to provide a terse list of items similarly worded and easily remembered. It is to be compared to the decalogue (Ex. 20; Dt. 5)[2] and to the list of laws in Leviticus 18:7-18 referring to illicit sexual relationships, as well as to numerous other carefully collected legal maxims which must have been compiled for didactic and pedagogical purposes.[3] The present list consists of a prohibition of images (15), four breaches of filial or social duty (16-19), four cases of sexual irregularity (20-23), two cases of bodily injury (24, 25), and a concluding comprehensive demand that *this law* (instruction) should be kept.

[1] *ANET*, p. 196.
[2] There are a number of direct parallels between the dodecalogue in chapter 27 and the decalogue in chapter 5. Compare 27:15 with 5:7-10; 27:16 with 5:16; 27:17 with 5:19; 27:20-23 with 5:18; 27:24, 25 with 5:17.
[3] For an interesting discussion of some of the smaller legal series in Deuteronomy see Gerhard von Rad, *Studies in Deuteronomy* (1953), chapters 1 and 2.

V. DECLARATION OF THE COVENANT SANCTIONS: BLESSINGS AND CURSES (28:1–68)

Chapter 28 takes its place quite appropriately now as the declaration of the covenant sanctions in a standard Near Eastern treaty pattern following the completion of the treaty stipulations.[1] It would appear from the list of curses and blessings that follows that there is a disproportionate space allowed to the curses. But this is quite normal in the Near Eastern treaties.[2] In the present chapter the blessings are declared in verses 1–14 and the curses in verses 15–68. The space allotted to the curses is about four times that given to the blessings. This is probably due to the fact that, human nature being what it is, the threat of a severe judgment on the covenant breaker seems to act as a stronger stimulus to correct behaviour than any promise of blessing.[3]

The chapter divides neatly into two sections, the blessings and the curses. Broadly speaking, both the curses and the blessings have to do with security, material prosperity and abundance in the land God is giving to His people. The principle that obedience to the covenant will result in blessing, while disobedience will result in judgment, is quite characteristic of Deuteronomy as a whole. It was, indeed, an important principle in Israel's theology. The idea is not unique to Israel, for the secular treaties express much the same idea.

An important aspect of this doctrine should be noted. It might appear that there was something almost mechanical in the operation of this so-called Deuteronomic principle, so that blessings were rewards for moral goodness and curses were punishment for evil-doing and rebellion. Such a view is too shallow. There is a deeper note. Israel was God's covenant people. God, in sheer grace, displayed many mighty acts of

[1] See *ANET*, pp. 205f., for two sets of curses and blessings in Hittite treaties. The first of these gives a good idea of the structure of a Near Eastern treaty.

[2] In the treaty of Esarhaddon with his vassals, out of a total of 674 lines in the treaty over 250 lines are given to curses. See D. J. Wiseman, 'The Vassal Treaties of Esarhaddon', *Iraq*, 20, 1958, pp. 1–99.

[3] See M. Noth, 'For all who rely on works of the law are under a curse', in *The Laws in the Pentateuch and other Essays* (1966), p. 131. Noth's conclusion is that there is no place for the view that the blessing is earned for meritorious works. The blessing is freely promised. If, however, men act independently, transgression and defection result. The curse and judgment follow. Thus the blessing is freely promised but the curse follows on transgression.

deliverance on her behalf and took her into covenant. In gratitude Israel accepted His invitation. It was her covenant with Yahweh which created, sustained and gave meaning to her nationhood. To disobey Yahweh was to betray and to reject the very source of her life. The only way for Israel to live her peculiar life was to remain in fellowship with Yahweh. In that fellowship lay her whole 'peace' (*šālôm*), *i.e.* the totality of her well-being.[1] Out of fellowship with Yahweh she was cut off from life. Her choice was essentially one between the blessing of life and the curse of death (30:15-20). The primary concern of chapter 28 is not, therefore, with rewards. In the secular treaties, the blessings and curses were mere sanctions. It was quite different with Yahweh's covenant. If Israel asked how life may be lived full of hope, in the enjoyment of God's blessing and with promise for a wonderful future, the answer was that only in fellowship with Yahweh and in obedience to His commandments could life like that be found. There was no other way. If His sovereignty were denied and His law rejected, Israel would depart into the way of death. But that would be to reject all Yahweh's love toward Israel. He would then enter into controversy with His people and would bring His judgment upon them so that they might be purged, refined and restored. His judgment would be with a view to their repentance.

a. The blessings (28:1-14)

1, 2. In a simple conditional sentence Moses addressed the people: *If you obey . . . Yahweh will . . . .* It was the divine promise inside the covenant setting. At no point was the covenant conditional on Israel's doing anything at all, since the covenant was a gift of divine grace. But to accept the covenant was to come into a noble status and to be in the way of enjoying Yahweh's blessing.

3-6. The list of blessings in these verses provides a striking piece of Hebrew rhythmic prose with its succession of phrases without co-ordinates between them. The sense of rhythm is supported by the repetition of *Blessed* (*bārûk*). The six blessings, which form a complete unit in themselves and suggest some kind of liturgical use, have not been expanded by any hortatory comments. Of the six phrases five consist of only three short

---

[1] The point is argued in a theological setting in John Murray, *The Covenant of Grace* (1954).

words in Hebrew. Only the third (4) is longer, although in Hebrew it may be read as a single line consisting of two parts each with three beats. These blessings are very similar to the curses in 16–19, although there is a slight difference in the order and the wording.

The blessings cover life in the city and in the field (3), the increase of man's progeny and of his crops, his herds and his flocks (4), the vessels used to collect and utilize the products of the field (5) and finally the whole range of a man's undertakings. The expression *come in . . . go out* is often used in the Old Testament to denote a man's ability to come and go in the affairs of life (31:2; Jos. 14:11; 1 Ki. 3:7; Ps. 121:8; Is. 37:28). The blessings of Yahweh touch the whole range of a man's life and depict a comprehensive fullness of divine favour.

7–14. What is concisely presented in a liturgical form in verses 3–6 is now elaborated in some detail in a general commentary, in language which one finds in other areas of Deuteronomy.[1] The arrangement of the material is chiastic, *i.e.* the various items are mentioned in a given order which is then reversed. Thus foreign relations are mentioned first and last (7, 12b, 13a), domestic affairs next (8, 11, 12a) and finally Israel's relationship to Yahweh comprises the centre feature (9, 10).

7, 12b, 13a. Israel will overthrow all her enemies. She will lend to them and not borrow from them and will assume the leadership (*head*) and will not be subject (*tail*).

8, 11, 12a. All Israel's undertakings (lit. 'the sending forth of the hand') will be blessed, so that her barns will be full and she will enjoy prosperity in every way as He sends the rain to bless her labours.

9, 10. The central piece in this literary form is a reiteration of the divine promise to establish Israel according to His oath, as a holy people, obedient to Him. In that happy relationship all the peoples of the earth will take note of His favour toward them and will stand in awe of them (2:25; 11:25).

13b, 14. The way of obedience is the way of blessing, but to turn aside from Yahweh to *serve* other gods is to destroy the basis of blessing, fellowship and loyalty.

b. The curses (28:15–68)

We may divide this lengthy list of curses into three groups:

[1] See Introduction, p. 30.

a. those in verses 15-44 which conclude with the warning of verses 45, 46; b. those in verses 47-57 which refer to dangers from Israel's enemies; and c. those in verses 58-68 which give warning of Israel's banishment and despair. At first reading there appears to be a great deal of repetition in these curses. This is consistent with the literary methods of the ancient Near East, where it was important to build up a total picture to impress upon the audience that the matter was serious. A good illustration may be found in the piling up of vivid pictures of judgment against a city like Babylon in Jeremiah 50, 51. To ensure that the message was understood the preacher needed to indulge in what seems to us unnecessary repetition and detailed itemization. The list of curses in the present chapter is of this character. Actually, a logical analysis of the chapter is almost impossible, since the final aim was not to be logical but to build up a vivid impression by presenting picture after picture until the hearer could see and feel the import of the preacher's words.

Many attempts have been made to see in this chapter evidence of expansion by exilic or post-exilic editors in view of the references to siege and exile. While expansion should not be ruled out, we ought not to conclude too readily that references to exile must be post-exilic. The threat of siege followed by exile is quite in the manner of the Near Eastern treaties. The curses of verses 47-57 could have been written into a Hittite treaty long before Moses' day. In any case, the people of Israel understood the nature of siege from an early date. In pre-exilic times there are a number of sieges reported in the pages of the Old Testament (1 Ki. 14:25; 2 Ki. 6:24; 16:5; 17:5; 18:9; 24:10). Egyptians, Syrians, Assyrians and Babylonians all besieged towns in Judah or Israel in pre-exilic times.

15-19. Verse 15 defines the people upon whom the curses will fall, namely, those who will not obey Yahweh and keep His commandments. Six curses follow in verses 16-19. These correspond with the blessings of verses 3-6. The writer indicates thereby that, just as God's blessings will reach out to the whole range of the life of an obedient man in Israel, so the curses of the covenant will touch the whole life of the man who is disobedient and breaks the covenant.

Ideas that are parallel to those in verses 3-6 occur here with the same rhythmic arrangement. The curses take up word by word the areas of blessing in order to stress the contrast. Thus verse 16 corresponds to verse 3, verse 17 to verse 5, verse 18 to verse 4, verse 19 to verse 6, verse 25 to verse 7 and verse 20 to verse 8. It will be seen that the order is changed slightly. The fourth blessing (4) corresponds to the third cursing (18), which lacks the phrase 'and the fruit of your beasts'. But this phrase is lacking in the main MSS of the LXX and seems to be redundant alongside *the increase of your cattle*, so that it may not have formed part of the original formula.

The noun *curse* (*qᵉlālâ*, 15) derives from the root *q-l-l* meaning 'be small' (*cf.* 27:16), while the verb *cursed* ('*ārûr*, 16–19) derives from the root '*-r-r*,, which is related to an Akkadian root meaning 'bind (by magical means)' or 'exorcize'.[1] In Israel it was God's word that bound a man, for once uttered the word of Yahweh had power to come to fulfilment.

The expression *all these curses shall come upon you and overtake you* introduces this series, which concludes at verse 45.

20–24. These verses contain a group of curses illustrative of the kind of calamity that might befall the covenant breaker.[2]

20. Under broad comprehensive terms the extent of the cursing is described: *curses* (or calamity, *mᵉʾērâ*, from the root '*-r-r*), *confusion* (or panic, *mᵉhûmâ*), and *frustration* (*migʾeret*). The term *confusion* is significant. Normally the climax of the Holy War was the panic sent by God into the enemy.[3] The same root occurs in the verb 'discomfit' in the AV in Joshua 10:10; Judges 4:15; 1 Samuel 5:11; 7:10, *etc.* The contrast is striking. In the day of cursing it will be Israel that is overtaken by panic and not her enemies. Cursing, panic and confusion will attend all they undertake to do (lit. 'the stretching forth of the hand') until they *are destroyed and perish quickly* (*cf.* 24, 45, 51, 61). It is repeatedly stated that the final issue of the various types of curse will be nothing short of Israel's destruction (20, 21, 22, 24, 26). The cause of all this and the essence of Israel's rebellion was that she had forsaken Yahweh.

21. This verse commences a short series (21–25a) which roughly matches the curses in 7–13a. *Pestilence* (*deber*) is a very

---

[1] E. A. Speiser, 'An Angelic "Curse": Exodus 14:20', *JAOS*, 80, No. 3, 1960, pp. 198–200.
[2] For an interesting list of the parallels between the Vassal treaties of Esarhaddon and Deuteronomy 28 see R. Frankena, 'The Vassal Treaties of Esarhaddon and The Dating of Deuteronomy', *Oudtestamentische Studiën*, 14, 1965, pp. 152–154; M. Weinfeld, 'Traces of Assyrian Treaty Formulation in Deuteronomy', *Biblica*, 46, 1965, pp. 417–427.
[3] See helpful discussion in Gerhard von Rad, *Studies in Deuteronomy* (1953), pp. 47, 48.

general term denoting perhaps an epidemic of some kind (*cf.*
1 Ki. 8:37; Am. 4:10; often in Jeremiah in the combination
'sword, famine, pestilence').

22. Seven plagues are listed, four for men and three for
crops: *consumption* (*šaḥep̄eṯ*) is a wasting disease like tuberculosis
or a wasting fever; *fever* (*qaddaḥaṯ*) may denote malaria;
inflammation (*dalleqeṯ*, lit. 'burning') may be an ague or typhoid;
fiery heat (*ḥarḥûr*, lit. 'burning') may be some kind of irritation,
or possibly the word should be taken with the next word to
give a pair, 'scorching heat and drought' (JPSA). *Drought* (*ḥōrēḇ*)
is to be preferred here to *ḥereḇ*, *sword*, since the word is linked
with other plagues that affect the crops, *blasting* (or blight,
šiddāp̄ôn), the effect of the hot sirocco winds, and *mildew*
(yellowness, *yērāqôn*).

23. *Cf.* Leviticus 26:19, a vivid picture of the searing heat of
summer with no relief from clouds or rain. *Cf.* Esarhaddon's
treaty, lines 530-533, which read:

'Just as rain does not fall from a brazen heaven
So may rain and dew not come upon your fields
And your meadows; may it rain burning
coals instead of dew on your land.'

The comparison between Deuteronomy and Esarhaddon's
treaties suggests that there were widely current cursing
formulae in the ancient Near East. Curses not unlike these
occur in a variety of documents which come from several lands
during both the second millennium and the first centuries of
the first millennium BC.

24. In consequence of the drought, dust and sand in the air
descend in fierce dust-storms in place of rain. The rain of
dust accompanies the sirocco.

25-37. There is a chiastic arrangement in these verses, *i.e.*
ideas are mentioned one after another up to a certain point
and then mentioned again in the reverse order. We have the
following items listed: *a.* defeat before enemies, 25a; *b.* Israel
will become a horror and her corpses will be unburnt, 25b, 26;
c. incurable diseases, 27; *d.* madness, 28; *e.* continual oppression, 29; *f.* frustration, 30–32; e^1. continual oppression, 33;
d^1. madness, 34; c^1. incurable disease, 35; a^1. Israel defeated
by an enemy, 36; b^1. Israel becomes a horror, 37. There is, in
fact, a slight breakdown in the chiasmus at the end, for the
elements *a* and *b* are reversed.

25a. The reversal of verse 7 (*cf.* Lv. 26:17). The defeat of

Israel, however, will be more severe than that of her foes. *You shall march out against them by a single road, but flee by many roads* (JPSA); *and you shall be a horror to all the kingdoms of the earth.* The term *horror* (*za'ăwâ*; lit. 'shuddering') denotes something that causes men to shudder, an awe-inspiring spectacle (Je. 15:4; 24:9; 29:18; 34:17).

26. The inglorious end of the Israelite dead will be that they will remain unburied and become food for carrion birds, the ultimate dishonour. Nor will anyone *frighten* (AV *fray*) the birds away. Denial of burial in the ancient Near East was a misfortune more fearful even than death (Je. 7:33; 16:4 which quotes this verse; 19:7; 34:20).

27. A series of curses in the shape of diseases of the body is given here: the *boil* (*šᵉḥîn*) *of Egypt, ulcers, scurvy, itch*. The first of these terms derives from a root which in cognate languages means 'be hot or inflamed'. The term has been variously identified with smallpox, elephantiasis, bubonic plague (*cf.* Ex. 9:9–11; Lv. 13:18–20, 23; Jb. 2:7). *Ulcers* (*'ᵒpālîm*), or swellings, are possibly haemorrhoids (*cf.* 1 Sa. 5:6). *Scurvy* (*gārāḇ*) may be a skin eruption, mange or scab (Arab. *jarab*, 'scale'). *Itch* (*ḥeres*) is common all over the East (Arab. verb *harasa*, 'scratch').

28. Diseases of the mind are now given, *madness, blindness* and *confusion* (lit. 'terror or dismay of heart'). The same three words occur in Zechariah 12:4 referring to the panic that seizes horses and horsemen in battle and makes them powerless. Here all the terms refer to the heart or mind.

29. Israel will be reduced to a condition of blindness at noonday when all should be clear before them. The verbs are in the second singular but the sense must be collective. Their *ways* will not prosper, *i.e.* the lines of political action will result in disaster and lead to oppression and continual plundering by the enemy with no-one to help. This was a theme to which prophets such as Isaiah, Amos and Jeremiah returned again and again.

30–33. Various ways in which an enemy might oppress and plunder *continually* (lit. 'all the days') are now listed: the ravishing of Israel's wives, the seizing of their houses and vineyards so that they have no use of them, the slaying of their oxen, the removal of their asses and sheep, the deportation of their children before their eyes while they were powerless to help.

34–37. The curses mentioned in verses 28–33 are now

mentioned in the reverse order. The end result will be that Israel will become a *horror* (*šammâ*), a *proverb* (*māšāl*), and a *byword* (*šᵉnînâ*) among the pagans, *i.e.* the tremendous decline and the unprecedented calamities that would befall Israel would become talking-points for the nations who would take them captive. There is no necessary·reference here to the days of the Babylonian exile. Captivity was a regular feature of warfare in the ancient Near East. Israel had suffered deportation from Egyptians, Syrians and Assyrians before the Babylonians had even appeared. In any case, the Hittite treaties of the fourteenth century BC include deportation among the curses.

38–44. A further series of curses concentrates on the economy of the country. Both in her agriculture and in her commerce Israel would fail. Locusts would devour her crops. Worms would devour her wines. The olive trees would drop their fruit. Children, normally used for work on the farms, would be taken into captivity. Locusts would destroy all trees and the products of the ground. The resident alien would prosper and Israel would become more and more impoverished. Just who the resident alien was, is not clear, but possibly the reference is to the Canaanites who had been formerly dispossessed (contrast to verses 12, 13), but who could now enjoy the benefits of the land once again.

45, 46. This brief conclusion to the block of curses just completed takes up expressions from verse 15 and underlines the theological significance of the curses and their educative value for future generations. Disobedience to the voice of Yahweh brought judgment and the curses would remain as a *sign* (*'ôṯ*) and a *wonder* (*môp̄ēṯ*) to warn the descendants of those who disobeyed for the centuries to come.

47–57. Several times in earlier verses reference has been made to Israel's enemies and their part in the bringing of the curse on those who rejected Yahweh's covenant (25, 32, 33, 36). Now the activity of the enemies is taken up in some detail. With great vividness the writer portrays the appalling distress and degradation to which Israel, once the head of the nations, will be reduced in the curse of siege warfare.

47. Israel had failed to serve Yahweh, a benevolent and kindly sovereign who had given them *abundance of all things*. She might have lived in a beautiful relationship of loving fellowship with *joyfulness and gladness of heart*. But when she rejected Yahweh's sovereignty, she placed herself in a position where she would serve another, and that without abundant provision or joy or gladness of heart.

48. The service which Israel will have to render to her enemies will be a hard one. She will experience lack of food and water and the necessities of life. She will return to the status of slavery from which she was once rescued and from which God called her in covenant love (*cf.* Lv. 26:13). This is expressed in the vivid metaphor of the *yoke of iron* upon the neck (*cf.* Je. 28:14).

49, 50a. These verses are sometimes taken as applying to the Babylonians (*cf.* Je. 5:15) and therefore to represent an exilic or post-exilic addition to the original form of the curses. While later editorial additions are possible, there is no real necessity to identify the foe here. Assyrians came *from afar* (Is. 5:26) as well as the Babylonians. But an enemy like this generally did. He came swiftly like an *eagle* for plunder and destruction. The picture is used of the Assyrians in Hosea 8:1 and of the Chaldeans in Habakkuk 1:8; Jeremiah 48:40; 49:22. Such a foe naturally spoke an unintelligible language (Is. 28:11; Je. 5:15). Several of the expressions in these verses are stereotyped ones that seem to have been used of any conqueror, Assyrian, Babylonian or Greek (*cf.* Dn. 8:23).

50b, 51. A detailed description of the activities of such invaders follows. They respect neither young nor old. They devour the cattle and the crops, leaving nothing behind for Israel's sustenance.

52–57. A vivid description of the horrors of the siege is now given. Sieges were known at various times in Israel's history and similar horrors might well have been perpetrated, so that these verses do not necessarily come from the days following the fall of Jerusalem.

A vivid contrast is drawn between the natural appetites of the invaders (51) and the unnatural lust of the Israelites under siege who eat their children (53) and in whom every vestige of mercy and tenderness seems to have been cast aside. The picture in these verses is blood-curdling in the extreme. There are few more degrading pictures in the Bible than that of a mother who, even during a siege, ought to have put away the after-birth of her child and to have cherished her new-born baby, but in her desperate need eats both, secretly denying to her own husband any share in the ghastly meal. From such horrors there will be no refuge anywhere in the land (53, 57). Similar pictures of such horrors at a time of siege occur in

Leviticus 26:29; 2 Kings 6:28, 29; Jeremiah 19:9; Lamentations 2:20; 4:10; Ezekiel 5:10.

58–68. The idea developed in these verses is that, since Israel has broken the covenant, Yahweh will abolish all the benefits about which she had boasted (6:21–23; 26:5–9). She will no longer be preserved from the ills that befell her neighbours (59–61). She will diminish in numbers (62; *cf.* 1:10; 10:22). She will no longer serve Yahweh but idols (64; *cf.* 4:28; 6:14). She will be torn from her own country and lose all security (65; *cf.* 3:20; 12:10; 25:19, *etc.*), and finally she will find herself as a slave in Egypt (68; *cf.* Ho. 8:13). Her history will thus be quite annulled. Such will be the end of Israel if she fails to observe *all the words of this law which are written in this book* (58) and to reverence the honoured and awesome name of Yahweh. It will be Yahweh Himself who will initiate all these curses (59–65, 68), and deliver Israel back to Egypt *in ships*. The ships may have been Phoenician, engaged in slave traffic (Ezk. 27:13; Joel 3:6; Am. 1:9). But even in Egypt no man would buy such slaves. It is a vivid climax to a sustained picture of unspeakable suffering.

C. Third address of Moses: recapitulation of the covenant demand (29:1 - 30:20)

The opening verse of chapter 29 in the English Bible poses a problem. In the Hebrew Bible it is the last verse of chapter 28. The question thus arises whether this verse is the subscription to chapters 5–28 or the superscription to the third address of Moses. It is, in any case, an editorial comment. If the verse concludes chapter 28 then *the words of the covenant* would refer to the body of material in chapters 5–28 where the covenant stipulations are set out. On the other hand the verse may introduce chapters 29–30. A close link appears to exist between verses 1 and 9, both of which refer to *the words of the (this) covenant.* Again, the connection between verses 1 and 2 is similar to that between 4:45 and 5:1, where a statement concerning the law which Moses spoke to Israel 'in the valley opposite Beth-peor' (4:45f.) provides a transition to 5:1 which commences 'And Moses summoned all Israel, and said to them'. Here in chapter 29 Moses is spoken about in the third person (as in 4:45 – 5:1). The address which follows in verse 2 is Moses' third address as far as the literary form of Deuteronomy is concerned. These chapters are clearly concerned with the covenant in the land of Moab as distinct from the covenant at Sinai (Horeb), although the covenant in Moab may be interpreted as a covenant renewal which both extended and adapted the Sinai covenant.

These two chapters seem to be a summary of Deuteronomy 1–28 and may be interpreted as a duplicate of earlier chapters, albeit abbreviated. Duplicate copies of treaty texts were quite usual in the ancient world and it may be that this was in the mind of the original writer here. Alternatively, chapter 29 may be seen as a summons to the covenant oath which is finally taken in 30:11–20. In that case chapter 29 reflects the over-all pattern of the Near Eastern treaty with a review of the Lord's past works of deliverance (2–9), a call to enter into covenant (10–15), a warning that the curses of the covenant will fall on rebels (16–29), although ultimate restoration is intended (30:1–10), and finally a call to the firm decision to accept the covenant (30:11–20). Hence 29:1 – 30:20 constitutes a kind of recapitulation of the total covenant demand. (See p. 19.)

I. ISRAEL EXHORTED TO ACCEPT THE COVENANT (29:1-15)

a. A historical review (29:1-9)

1. The third address of Moses is introduced at this point (*cf.* 1:1; 4:44). Moses is the covenant mediator. *Yahweh commanded Moses to make* (the covenant) *with the people of Israel*. The Hebrew for 'make a covenant' is literally 'cut a covenant'. The expression has ancient associations with the Near Eastern non-biblical treaty (covenant), which was ratified in a ceremony where beasts were slain. The covenant *in the land of Moab* (*cf.* 1:5; 5:2, 3) is contrasted with the covenant at Horeb (1:2). To judge from a comparison of the contents of Deuteronomy 5-26 and those of Exodus 19-24, the two were closely related, although the covenant of Deuteronomy contains many new regulations.

The rest of chapter 29 contains many reminiscences of the Near Eastern treaty pattern. It is not presented in a systematic manner but in narrative form. However, elements of the pattern are clearly discernible, making it extremely likely that some kind of covenant ceremony underlies the events here reported.

2-9. The first element of the covenant pattern discernible is the historical review (2-8). It commences *You have seen all that Yahweh did before your eyes in the land of Egypt, to Pharaoh and to all his servants and to all his land* (*cf.* Ex. 19:4). What Yahweh did is described as *great trials* (*wondrous feats*, JPSA), *signs*, and *great wonders* (*prodigious signs and marvels*, JPSA). The nouns here are reminiscent of the nouns in the Exodus narrative (Ex. 4:8, 9, 17, 28, 30; 10:1, 2 refer to *signs*, *'ôṭ*, and Ex. 4:21; 7:9; 11:9, 10 to *miracles* or *wonders*, *môp̄ēṭ*).

4. Alas, Israel, so signally favoured as to have lived in the midst of many evidences of divine favour and power, lacked the deeper understanding and insight to discern behind the external events a deeper significance. They needed the enlightenment that Yahweh could give but which, by reason of their disobedience, He had not given to them. Such blindness on the part of those who reject God's revelation is not uncommon. Men may hear but not understand, because of a hardness of heart. It was the problem of several of the prophets of the Old Testament who preached to audiences who would not hearken (Is. 6:9f.; Je. 1:17-19; Ezk. 3:4-11, *etc.*). It prevented the Jews believing in the Lord Jesus (2 Cor. 3:12-15).

5, 6. The manner of the speech changes at this point and Yahweh speaks in the first person singular. In typical Near Eastern hyperbolic language the wonder of the Lord's providential care is described: *I have led you forty years in the wilderness, etc.* For similar language see 8:2-4. Strictly, very few of those who stood that day in Moab had known the experiences of the exodus and only some had lived through the wilderness events, for the old generation had died (Nu. 14:28-35). Hence the *you* must be the corporate Israel. But the Israel of any age was always a part of the corporate Israel and might share the experiences of the past by seeking to identify herself with that former Israel. Hence in the corporate sense Yahweh could say: *I have led you forty years . . . you have not eaten bread . . . that you may know that I am Yahweh your God.* But rebellion and disobedience would prevent Israel in any age from discerning the providential hand of God in her national life. In those wilderness years Israel was not sustained by *bread* made by human hands, but by manna. Nor did she drink *wine or strong drink,* the product of human endeavour, but water from the rock (*cf.* 8:3). God's providential care was designed to demonstrate that He was indeed God. The expression *that you may know* occurs frequently in the Old Testament (Ex. 6:7; 7:5; 14:4; 16:12; 29:46; some fifty times in Ezekiel, *etc.*). For the obedient man there was abundant evidence of God's care for Israel. For the disobedient the very facts of the divine activity would make plain the power of God.

7, 8. The speech of Moses is now resumed. He quotes further evidence of Yahweh's help in past years. The reference is to the conquest of areas to the east of Jordan (2:32ff.; 3:1, 3, 8, 12f.; *cf.* Nu. 21:21-35).

9. Following the recitation of the historical review, in which the saving acts of Yahweh are recalled, there comes the appeal to enter into the covenant with the words: *Be careful to do the words of this covenant, i.e.* 'observe faithfully all the terms of this covenant' (JPSA). The latter part of verse 9 might be regarded as an abbreviated statement of the covenant blessings (*cf.* 30:16-18).

b. Exhortation to commitment (29:10-15)

These verses remind us of the final stages of the covenant

ceremony before the oath is taken. The covenant community is assembled and the nature of the event is explained.

10, 11. The expression *stand before Yahweh* is a significant one. In Hebrew the verb has a reflexive sense, 'You have taken your stand'.[1] In a number of other Old Testament passages it is used in a similar way (Jos. 24:1; 1 Sa. 10:19). The covenant assembly is described accurately according to its tribal heads, elders, officials, men of Israel, children, women, resident aliens (*i.e.* non-Israelites; *cf.* Ex. 12:38; Nu. 10:29; 11:4) and servants (*cf.* Jos. 9:21). The expression *he who hews your wood and he who draws your water* seems to have been a descriptive way of denoting the servile group in the land (*cf.* Jos. 9:21, 23, 27). The verb translated *hew* (*ḥāṭaḇ*) may be related to the Arabic *ḥaṭaba*, 'gather'.

12, 13. The purpose of the assembly is now declared: *that you may enter into the sworn covenant of Yahweh your God . . . that he may be your God.* There are two aspects of this intention. The first was that Israel might enter into the covenant of Yahweh. This expression is found only here in this form and means literally 'that you may pass over into the covenant of Yahweh' (*cf.* Gn. 15:17, 18). A further feature of this entry into the covenant is that Israel was also required to enter into the curse (*'ālâ*). The text reads literally 'for your crossing over into the covenant of Yahweh your God and into his curse'. The noun 'curse' refers to the curses of the covenant. When one enters a covenant he places himself in the position where the curses will fall upon him if he violates the covenant obligations. The sense is neatly captured in the JPSA translation 'the covenant . . . with its sanctions'.

The second purpose of the covenant was that Yahweh might establish Israel as His people and Himself as their God, in accordance with the promise made to the patriarchs (13). The covenant correlate 'my people . . . your God' is a continuing theme of the Old Testament (26:17, 18; 28:9, *etc. Cf.* Ex. 19:5).

14, 15. The covenant demand is here extended to those who were yet to be born. Future generations were one with that early Israel who took the oath at Sinai. There is a genealogical continuity to the covenant, not because God's covenant mercies are an inalienable family right, but because God is faithful to His promise to extend His blessing to all who love Him and obey His commandments. Each new generation must

[1] Hebrew Niphal is often used in a reflexive sense. The same root is used in similar contexts in the Hithpael stem.

renew the covenant for itself and take its stand before Yahweh as did Israel of old. Then, having learnt again of God's saving actions on their behalf and of His covenant stipulations, they accept the covenant for themselves in their own *this day*. This latter expression occurs six times in verses 2–15. In later years, by means of a ceremony of this kind, the concept of covenant was kept alive and was for ever contemporary (*cf.* 2 Cor. 6:2; Heb. 2:3).

II. PUNISHMENT FOR DISOBEDIENCE (29:16–28)

a. Warning against hypocrisy (29:16–21)

This short section contains several of the elements of the Near Eastern treaty pattern, namely, the historical prologue (16, 17), the statement of a general principle (18), and the threat of the curse falling on the disobedient man (19–21).

16, 17. The sojourn in Egypt, the exodus and the wandering in the wilderness, which brought the people into contact with the gods of the nations (*their detestable things*), are here recalled. Such a recall would remind Israel both of God's saving acts and also of the danger of falling into idol worship (*cf.* Nu. 25).

18. Idolatry is here described as a plant which takes root and issues in a harvest of poison weed and wormwood. It is a classical kind of imagery which is found also in 32:32; Hosea 10:4; Amos 6:12, *etc.*

19. The root which bears such evil fruit is now described as a person who hears the covenant sanctions (lit. 'words of the curse') and *blesses himself in his heart*, *i.e.* he fancies himself immune, thinking, *I shall be safe, though I walk in the stubbornness of my heart*. The result of such rebellion would be the utter ruin of *moist and dry alike*, *i.e.* of all plants, whether watered or thirsty. The meaning of the picture is that, if idolatry were to take root in Israel, its ultimate issue would be the utter ruin of the nation.

20, 21. The serious nature of disobedience is here expressed in terms of God's refusal to pardon the offender (although this was presumably for deliberate disobedience), and of His *anger* and *jealousy* (passion, zeal) which would *smoke against that man*. Every sanction (*curse*, '*ālâ*) written in this book would *settle* (lit. 'crouch') upon the man and Yahweh would blot out his name. This latter possibility was dreaded by every man in Israel who desired his name to be remembered in his posterity. Such a man Yahweh would *single . . . out from all the tribes of Israel for calamity* and put upon him all the curses which he had idly invoked upon himself (19). We are reminded of the striking case of Ananias and Sapphira in the New Testament (Acts 5:1–11).

b. A lesson for posterity (29:22–28)

The writer now takes his stand in the future and describes in a vivid way the final result of the curse. A coming generation, as well as foreigners from afar, seeing the plagues and diseases inflicted on the land, its soil ruined by sulphur and salt making the land unproductive like the area of Sodom and Gomorrah (Gn. 19), will ask why Yahweh had acted so violently. The answer will be simple: *They forsook the covenant of Yahweh . . . and went and served other gods.* Such language is very general and does not necessarily refer to the exile. The dramatic dialogue between Israel and foreigners, standing amid the charred ruins of the land where once Yahweh ruled His people and which was formerly the land flowing with milk and honey but was now a barren waste, makes striking reading. A similar picture occurs in the annals of Ashurbanipal.[1] The motif was evidently a well-known one in the Near East. Even verse 28 need not refer specifically to the exile that followed the fall of Jerusalem, for the threat of exile was ever present in the ancient Near East.

The modern reader of these verses who knows something of the intense suffering of the Jews (sometimes, alas, at the hands of Christendom) over the many centuries since these words were first uttered may well ask again: *Why has Yahweh done thus to this land? What means the heat of this great anger?* (24). In terms of Deuteronomy the reply would be: *It is because they forsook the covenant of Yahweh, the God of their fathers, which he made with them when he brought them out of the land of Egypt* (25).

III. SECRET THINGS AND REVEALED THINGS (29:29)

An exhortation for Israel to carry out the will of Yahweh as it

---

[1] *ANET*, p. 300. The text reads: 'Whenever the inhabitants of Arabia asked each other "On account of what have these calamities befallen Arabia?" they answered themselves "Because we offended the friendliness of Ashurbanipal, the king, beloved by Enlil".'

has been revealed is now given. *The secret things (nistārôt), i.e.* things beyond man's knowledge, such as the future, are God's concern. *Revealed* things, such as God's law and Yahweh's will expressed through it, are within the range of man's knowledge now. For these Israel is accountable. Sufficient is revealed in Yahweh's covenant with Israel to provide her with a sure guide for living in the present and to this she is called. This is a salutary observation which is as relevant for the Christian community as it was for Israel.

IV. REPENTANCE AND FORGIVENESS (30:1–10)

Beyond the curse of exile lay the promise of restoration. God's redemptive programme did not fail finally even if historical Israel failed. If in exile the people turned to Yahweh again, He would have compassion on them and they would be restored to enjoy yet greater blessings.

1, 2. The hopeless condition of Israel in exile has already been described in 28:64ff. But beyond all the promise of the blessings (*bᵉrākâ*) and the curses (*qᵉlālâ*) set forth in the formal covenant document there was the hope of a new covenant and wonderful restoration. In exile Israel would take to heart the covenant sanctions, the blessings and the curses, and would return to Yahweh to obey His voice with all their heart, *i.e.* completely. The verb *return (šûḇ)* is a significant element in Israel's covenant vocabulary. It represents on the one hand 'turn away' from Yahweh, and on the other hand 'turn back' to Yahweh.[1] The verb defines the direction in which Israel's obedience is directed.

3–5. Israel will be restored to her land when she turns to Yahweh with all her heart, for He will *restore your fortunes, and have compassion upon you*. The expression *restore your fortunes* (lit. 'turn thy turning') has generally been translated as in RSV. However, some translators have taken the noun in the phrase to be 'captivity' and have translated *turn thy captivity, i.e.* to bring to an end the captivity, which, of course, amounts to a change of fortune. The reference is to a radical change in Israel's conditions, whatever the exact translation may be. In His *compassion (raḥᵃmîm)* Yahweh will gather His people from

---

[1] It is also used of other deities with the same range of meaning, so that it has a wide significance in the covenant idea. See W. L. Holladay, *The root ŠÛBH in the Old Testament* (1958).

the lands to which they have been driven. The total picture is of a repentant people being restored to their homeland, a very different picture from that which obtains in modern Israel, where there is little evidence of repentance and where great numbers of people are agnostic. Comparison with Ezekiel 36:24–36; 37:23–28 is of interest. *Cf.* Romans 11:25–27. In these passages God seems to be taking the initiative in restoring His people and in cleansing them for His name's sake, apparently before they repent. However, no contradiction need be suggested. The Old Testament writers were not always concerned with exact chronological sequence. The one thing that seems clear is that a new heart and a new spirit would characterize a restored people. Deuteronomy does not mention the everlasting covenant of Jeremiah 32:40 and Ezekiel 37:26. In glowing terms the passage describes the final state of blessing. Yahweh *will make you more prosperous and numerous than your fathers.*

6. God Himself will carry out the inward renewal of Israel (*circumcise your heart*), so that Israel will love Yahweh with all their heart. By His own gracious activity He will reconstitute Israel. Repentance in itself will not suffice. Perhaps, indeed, the origin of repentance itself lies in the divine activity. Certainly, the origin of heart-love for Yahweh lies in Yahweh Himself. The end result will be *that you may live* (lit. 'for thy life's sake', a variation of the common expression 'that you may live', 19; 4:1; 5:33; 8:1; 16:20; *cf.* Je. 31:31ff.; 32:39–41; Ezk. 36:24ff.).

7. The *curses* (*'ālâ*) which formerly rested on Israel will be transferred to those nations who brought about Israel's destruction and exile. Even the wicked agent of Yahweh will not escape the justice of God (*cf.* Is. 10:5–23).

8. Thus renewed, Israel would obey her sovereign Lord and keep His commandments.

9. The outcome of obedience is blessing. This verse recalls the areas of blessing set out in 28:3–6. Commentators who want to see in this verse a post-exilic expansion have overlooked the fact that blessings not unlike these are written into the secular treaties of the second millennium BC.[1] The fact of Yahweh's *delight* in prospering Israel is reminiscent of Jeremiah 32:41. The broad picture of the blessing and healing of the people in a coming day has a strong parallel in the whole of Jeremiah 32.

[1] See *ANET*, p. 206, for a typical Hittite treaty.

10. A succinct summary of the prerequisites for divine blessing, repentance and obedience.

V. THE SOLEMN APPEAL TO CHOOSE LIFE (30:11–20)

The point is now reached where the people are called upon to make a decision in the matter of the covenant. After making clear to the people that what they are asked to do is neither 'too hard' nor 'far off', but something that is evident and comprehensible (11–14), the appeal for acceptance and commitment is made (15–20).

a. God's covenant accessible to all (30:11–14)

11. Yahweh's commandment, *i.e.* the whole revelation of the divine will as set forth in Deuteronomy, was not incomprehensible (*too hard*), nor unattainable (*far off*).

12, 13. Israel's duty was not hidden in some inaccessible place (*in heaven*), nor beyond some insuperable barrier (*beyond the sea*). The expression *go up to heaven* was evidently in general use in the ancient Near East. It occurs in the Amarna letters written by Egyptian vassals in Palestine to their overlords in Egypt in the fourteenth century BC.[1] The statement that the divine command was 'near' or 'far off' may also have had an idiomatic usage in the Near East over many centuries (*cf.* Eph. 2:13).

14. Some biblical references represent Wisdom as being inaccessible (Jb. 28:12 ff.), but the Law lay at everyone's door. In this Israel saw a special evidence of God's love for her (4:6–8; Pss. 19:7–11; 119). The Law could be in the mouth of every man as he repeated it over and allowed it thus to enter his heart and flow out into his life. God's will expressed in the covenant did not require deep searching among the mysteries of the universe, for it was as near as hearing and seeing and had been revealed plainly to Israel (29:29). Hence, being in Israel's *mouth* and understanding (*heart*), it was something that could be acted upon: *you can do it* (*cf.* Is. 45:19). Even if there were secrets yet to be revealed, Israel could now enjoy life by loving God and by loyally obeying His covenant. They need not wait to comprehend the universe in order to begin to live.

[1] J. A. Knudtzon, *Die El-Amarna Tafeln* (1915), No. 264, lines 14–19. *Cf. A Pessimistic Dialogue between Master and Servant*, XII, *ANET*, p. 438.

This passage is used by Paul in Romans 10:6–8. Moses said to Israel, 'You know the commandment. God has revealed it to you and has drawn near to you to point you to the way of obedience. You are called on to receive with humble hearts the word of His grace which has come to you in the shape of His Law.' For Paul there was a new situation. God now approached men in Christ and as the living Lord He asked not for some superhuman effort but only for a glad acceptance of His grace in Christ.

b. The call to commitment (30:15-20)

The covenant which was set before Israel opened up two possibilities, *life and good* and *death and evil*. The present brief section calls Israel to choose. Despite its brevity it contains several of the standard elements of the treaty or covenant pattern – stipulations, covenant sanctions, witnesses and the call to commitment.

15. The phrase *I have set before you* in the present context means 'I have set before you for choice'. In 11:26–28 the alternatives are blessing and cursing. Hence the full alternatives are life, good and blessing, or death, evil and cursing. The term *good* (*tôb*) denotes 'prosperity', while the term *evil* (*ra'*) denotes 'misfortune'.

16-18. An explanation is now given of what is meant by the two alternatives. In regular Deuteronomic language the positive alternative is given first. The man who *obeys the commandments of Yahweh, walks in his ways,* and keeps all His statutes and laws *shall live and multiply* and Yahweh will *bless* him (*cf.* 10:12–22). The man whose heart turns away, who will not obey, but who worships and serves other gods, will perish and will be denied long life in the land of promise.

19. The calling of witnesses was a regular feature of the secular treaty. The gods of the two parties to the treaty were normally invoked as witnesses. In Israel such an appeal to the gods was rejected, but in a symbolic way *heaven and earth* were called to witness (4:26; Mi. 6:1, 2).[1] In the presence of witnesses the choice before Israel is declared, life or death, blessing or cursing. The final decision was Israel's to make. It was one for the free choice of the people. The covenant mediator speaking

---

[1] It was quite regular in the ancient Near Eastern treaties to include heaven and earth among the witnesses to a treaty. See *ANET*, p. 206, para. 2, col. 1; p. 205, col. 2; Treaty of Esarhaddon, lines 472–475; *etc.*

on Yahweh's behalf could only make the alternatives clear and then appeal to Israel to *choose life, that you and your descendants may live*.

20. Life consists in *loving Yahweh, obeying his voice, cleaving* (clinging) *to him*. With life came length of days and the happy occupation of the land Yahweh had sworn to the fathers, Abraham, Isaac and Jacob. The appeal to choose between life and death is common in the Old Testament (Jos. 24:14–24; Je. 8:3; 21:8, *etc.*). In the book of Proverbs this appeal has a strong individual sense (Pr. 8:35; 11:19; 12:28; 13:14), whereas in Deuteronomy the appeal is to the whole nation. Even so, the individual was not so swallowed up in the community that he could avoid personal responsibility. Indeed, these final verses (15–20) are expressed in the second singular. In the general context this may not carry the purely personal connotation, but it is incorrect to say that the idea of individual responsibility came late in Israel. From early times individuals had personal dealings with God and were challenged to respond.

The emphasis on free choice associated with love and obedience towards God is not peculiar to Deuteronomy (*cf.* Jos. 24:14–16), nor indeed is it unique for Israel. Ready comparison may be made with the New Testament. We have noticed that Paul quotes from verses 11–14 in Romans 10:6–8. But the call to choose (believe, follow) and to obey comes in a variety of contexts in the New Testament (*e.g.* Mt. 19:17; Jn. 3:36; 6:35; Rom. 6:12–18; 15:18; *cf.* Rom. 12:1, 2).

D. The last acts of Moses and his death
(31:1 – 34:12)

The three discourses of Moses conclude at chapter 30. With chapter 31 there commences a brief account of the concluding stages of Moses' life. A significant feature of these closing chapters is that they too exhibit some traces of the treaty pattern. Thus there is an instruction to lodge the covenant document in the ark (31:24–29), a reference to the appointment of Joshua as the visible head of the covenant community (31:1–8, 14–23), a promise of the blessings to be enjoyed by the tribes (chapter 33), and a fascinating chapter which is strongly reminiscent of the standard indictment document issued to an erring vassal (chapter 32). The book concludes with a touching account of the death of Moses (34).

I. MOSES' PARTING WORDS AND THE PRESENTATION OF JOSHUA (31:1–8)

As Moses approached his death he gave a series of charges to the people (1–6), to Joshua (7, 8), and to the priests (9–13), each concerned in some way with the maintenance of the covenant. The first of these was a charge to Joshua. This section (1–8) reveals several elements of the standard treaty pattern.

1. The verse reads literally 'Moses went and spoke these words (things) to Israel'. The LXX and one ancient Hebrew MS interpret this as meaning that Moses 'finished speaking'. AV and RSV regard *these words* as a continuation of Moses' former address and thus they refer to what follows. The LXX regards 'these words' as a reference to what has preceded. Commentators are thus divided, some of them regarding the last chapters as appendices which are not directly related to what has preceded, while others regard these last chapters as a continuation of Moses' address in chapter 30.[1] In fact, the possibility of a transfer of authority to Joshua after the death of Moses was already hinted at in 1:38 and 3:28, so that it is arguable in terms of the total literary structure that what was

---

[1] Meredith G. Kline, *Treaty of the Great King* (1963), p. 135.

given merely as a hint at the beginning of the book is now brought to fulfilment.

2. The age of Moses is given as *a hundred and twenty years* (34:7; *cf.* Ex. 7:7). The significance of the figure is not clear. In Egyptian literature 110 years was the life-span of a wise man and numerous examples are known.[1] The fact that Moses' life was ten years longer may be a device to express Moses' superiority over the wise man of Egypt. Again, the age 120 is three times forty (*cf.* the time spent in the wilderness, 2:7) and may well denote three generations. In any case Moses was an old man who had seen his grandchildren grow to maturity. At such an advanced age Moses confessed that he was no longer active (*able to go out and come in*; *cf.* 28:6; Jos. 14:11). Moreover, Yahweh had forbidden him to cross over the Jordan (3:23-29; 32:50-52; Nu. 20:11, 12).

3-6. Israel's leader would continue to be Yahweh. The motif of the Holy War is clearly present here (*cf.* 1:30). In practice Yahweh's deputy was to be Joshua (1:37, 38; 3:28; 31:7f., 23). But in the conquest of the land of promise, Yahweh would overthrow the inhabitants as He had overthrown Sihon and Og. In the light of this promise and of Yahweh's final leadership, Joshua was bidden to be strong and resolute (7, 23; Jos. 1:6-9, 18). *Yahweh your God marches with you. He will not fail you or forsake you* (JPSA).

7, 8. Joshua had already been set apart by Moses before Eleazar and the congregation to assume the leadership after his death (1:38; *cf.* Nu. 27:18-23). Repeating the promise of the divine presence already given to the people, Moses now charged Joshua publicly to lead Israel to the land of promise. The concept of the Holy War lies very close to the surface in these verses. Yahweh will be with Joshua and will not forsake him in the conflicts of coming days. Hence there is no need for him to fear or be dismayed.

II. THE SEVENTH-YEAR COVENANT RENEWAL CEREMONY (31:9-13)

Moses is here pictured as handing over the law of God in written form to the priests and elders so that Yahweh's revelation might be preserved for posterity.

9. It was normal practice at the conclusion of a secular

[1] J. Vergot. *Joseph en Égypte* (1959), pp. 200f.

treaty for the suzerain to hand a copy of the treaty to the vassal to be lodged in the sanctuary of the vassal under the care of the priests and under the eye of the gods. Again, on the death of the vassal, his successor was approved by the suzerain but was required to ratify the treaty himself. There need be no problem in the statement that Moses handed over a document of some kind to Joshua, even if this was not Deuteronomy as we now have it.[1] Writing had been in common use in the ancient Near East for at least a thousand years before Moses. Even the use of the alphabet was known for perhaps three centuries before Moses' day.

The written law was then committed to the care of the Levitical priests who carried the ark, here referred to as *the ark of the covenant of Yahweh, i.e.* the ark was the receptacle for the tables of the law.

10–13. Instructions are given for a solemn ceremony of covenant renewal every seventh year, *at the set time of the year of release, at the feast of booths*. The *set time* (*mô'ēd*) was one of the regular appointed times of festivals. For *the year of release*, see 15:1ff., and for *the feast of booths*, see 16:13–15. These verses make explicit reference to a festival of covenant renewal at the time of the feast of booths, or tabernacles. It was an occasion *when all Israel comes to appear before Yahweh . . . at the place which he will choose*. Precisely what is meant here is not clear. It may be argued that Israel was required to appear at the central sanctuary every seven years to renew the covenant. That *all Israel . . . men, women, and little ones, and the sojourner* should assemble at one place would mean that the whole land would be bereft of people. Possibly *all Israel* was represented at the place which Yahweh chose, by a symbolic group of people. Some commentators have even suggested that a variety of centres were approved for the occasion as places which Yahweh might choose. Whatever the truth of the matter, it is clear that in one way or another Israel was required to *hear and learn*

---

[1] The exact connotation of *this law* (*tôrâ*) is not certain. In the context it appears to refer to the covenant document which might be interpreted as including chapters 1 to 30. The expression occurs in 1:5; 4:8; 17:18, 19; 27:3, 8, 26. In the present chapter (here and at verse 24) the claim is made that Moses wrote *this law*. Some writers take the expression to refer to the central section of the book, chapters 12 to 26. It would seem that a much smaller amount of writing is intended in 27:3, where *this law* is to be written on two large stones. In 4:8 *this law* is equated to *statutes and judgments*. It would seem difficult, therefore, to specify exactly what is meant by the expression in the present verse.

to fear (reverence) *Yahweh your God, and be careful to do all the words of this law.* In secular suzerainty treaties too, directions were given for the reading of the treaty to the vassal people at regular intervals. This was as frequent as from one to three times annually. In Israel, of course, apart from the ceremony described here, the regular services of the cult and the ministry of prophets both served to ensure that a constant proclamation of the will of Yahweh was made. The reading of *this law before all Israel* every seven years at the feast of tabernacles, in the year of release, was a special occasion to remind Israel of her covenant obligations. One other value of such a covenant renewal ceremony was that the children, at least once during childhood years, and possibly twice, could stand with a considerable congregation and share in a great act of covenant renewal. The participation of *all Israel* in such a ceremony would be facilitated if there were several places besides the central sanctuary where such a ceremony could be conducted on the appointed day. In our own day a nation at prayer may be represented by congregations all over the land. If, however, specifically the central sanctuary is meant here, it would seem that there must have been only representative attendance in view of the very considerable practical difficulties in bringing a whole nation together at one time.

III. THE DIVINE CHARGE TO MOSES AND JOSHUA (31:14-23)

There are two themes in this section. Part of the section is devoted to the formal commissioning of Joshua by God at the tent of meeting (14, 15, 23) and is thus a continuation of the narrative in verses 6–8, and part of it (16–22) is in the nature of an introduction to the song of Moses in the next chapter. Such a weaving together of themes is not uncommon in the Old Testament. It is to be regarded as a characteristic of the literary methods of the people of Israel.

a. The investiture of Joshua (31:14, 15, 23)

A brief narrative referring to the formal commissioning of Joshua by God acts as a framework for the introduction to Moses' song. Joshua, like Moses, was personally commissioned by Yahweh Himself. Moses was allowed to fall into the background and Yahweh alone gave the commission to Joshua.

14, 15. The Lord often met people at *the tent of meeting* (*'ôhel mô'ēḏ*; Ex. 25:22; 27:21; 29:42; 33:7; Nu. 11:16; 12:4) in order to make an important announcement. In such circumstances *Yahweh appeared . . . in a pillar of cloud* (Ex. 33:9, 10; 40:34-38; Nu. 12:5).

23. This verse appears to follow logically after verse 15, with verses 16-22 enclosed between them. The introduction to Moses' song is thus framed between the beginning and the end of the narrative of Joshua's commissioning. Moses' song is basically a warning against disloyalty on Israel's part in the years to come. One way to display disloyalty would be to reject the leadership of Joshua. From Joshua's point of view the divine promise *I will be with you* was reassuring. It was a promise Yahweh had made and would make to many of His servants through the centuries (*cf.* Gn. 28:15; 31:3; Ex. 3:12; Jos. 1:5; 3:7; Jdg. 6:16; Je. 1:8, 19; Mt. 28:20).

b. Introduction to the song of Moses (31:16-22)

The narrative in these verses records how Moses at God's command wrote a song which, in a coming day when an ungrateful Israel had forsaken Yahweh, would remain as a testimony against them.

16. The sad possibility is now declared that after the death of Moses Israel would turn aside to worship other gods, forsaking the covenant of Yahweh. The expression *play the harlot* is used in a variety of places in the Old Testament for such an act of unfaithfulness (Ex. 34:15, 16; Lv. 17:7; 20:5; Nu. 15:39; Jdg. 2:17; 8:27, 33; Ho. 1:2; 4:12; 9:1, *etc.*). It is not clear whether the physical act is intended here or whether the usage is figurative. However, since religious prostitution accompanied by the physical act was common among the Canaanites, this may be part of the total picture here. It was certainly so in the mind of Hosea. The expression *break . . . covenant* (*hēḇēr bᵉrîṯ*) occurs rarely in the Pentateuch (Gn. 17:14; Lv. 26:15, 44), but occurs a number of times in the rest of the Old Testament (Jdg. 2:1; 1 Ki. 15:19; Je. 11:10, *etc.*).

17, 18. The outcome of a breach of the covenant is the operation of the curses. Once Yahweh forsook His people they would fall victim to many evils as the various curses began to operate.

19–22. The song that appears in chapter 32 was to be written as a witness against Israel. It would place in a proper perspective the promise of blessings made to the fathers and the curses of the broken covenant. Already a purpose (*yēṣer*) was forming in the people's hearts. The word *purpose* might be translated 'tendency', 'impulse', 'disposition'. It is reminiscent of the later Jewish concept of the 'evil impulse'. This 'disposition' would lead to Israel's breaking the covenant and she would turn to other gods. The song which would *live unforgotten in the mouths of their descendants* would make clear the elementary fact that covenant rejection results in the operation of the curses of the covenant and would confront them as a witness. In fact, the song of chapter 32 is strongly reminiscent in its structure and content of a well-known secular political form, namely, the formulation of a complaint against a rebel vassal by his overlord with its threat of punishment.[1] It is not impossible that some, at least, in Israel would have understood such a pattern and Moses would certainly have met it in the pharaoh's court.

IV. THE LAW TO BE DEPOSITED IN THE ARK
(31:24–29)

24–27. The instructions in these verses bear some relation to those in verses 9–13. In the earlier verses Moses is seen writing down *this law* (or instruction) and giving it to the Levitical priests, instructing them to produce it for public reading every seventh year. Now the specific instruction is that the record (or document, *sēp̄er*) containing Moses' teaching (*tôrâ*) was to be placed *by the side of the ark of the covenant of Yahweh*, where it was to remain as a witness against Israel. Only the decalogue was to be placed within the ark (Ex. 25:16; 1 Ki. 8:9). Moses argued that if, while he was still alive in Israel's midst, they were defiant towards Yahweh, how much more would they be when he was dead (27). Some commentators, in an attempt to preserve the unity of verses 24–29, have argued that the word *law* (*tôrâ*) in verse 24 is a scribal error for *šîrâ*, 'song'. In that case verse 24 would read: 'When Moses had made an end of writing the words of this song in a book (document)'. A similar change would be made in verse 26, substituting the words 'the book (document) of this song'

[1] See footnote on verse 28, p. 295, below.

for the Massoretic reading. Following these changes the whole passage would become a unity and form a good introduction to the song in chapter 32. There is no textual evidence for any such change here. Moreover it would seem from the whole context that the editor wished to establish the song of Moses as one of the *witnesses* against Israel alongside the *law*. It may be that he adapted for this purpose a form of words which was normally used for the writing down of the law. But that he wanted a reference to the recording of the song seems clear. If it be objected that the present passage seems confused because of the association of two different topics in one section, then it must be observed that such a weaving together of motifs is extremely common in the Old Testament (*e.g.* Nu. 16). Editors in possession of data, and unwilling to reject any of it, evidently held it all together in a manner which seems strange to twentieth-century readers but was evidently acceptable in their day. Apparently, heterogeneous material could be held together by ancient editors in ways which we moderns reject. Even so, the idea of witnesses against Israel in case of her rejection of the covenant does provide a unifying theme.[1]

28. The elders and officials of the tribes are here bidden to assemble to hear the indictment of God as plaintiff against Israel as defendant. To that assembly the heavens and the earth are called as witnesses. There are interesting parallels between the picture here and that in other areas of the Old Testament (Ps. 51; Je. 2; Mi. 6:1-8). The picture also has its secular parallels. Great suzerains might call a vassal to hear an indictment against him. The term used in the Old Testament for indictment is 'controversy' or 'legal suit' (*rîḇ*). Nowadays scholars have isolated the particular literary pattern which was used to depict such legal proceedings and, following the Hebrew term, have called it the *RÎḄ*-pattern.[2] We shall describe the nature of this literary form in the exegesis of chapter 32.

29. The need for Yahweh's legal proceedings against Israel would arise from Israel's misdeeds following her rejection of the covenant. Moses declared: *I know that after my death you will surely act corruptly, and turn aside from the way which I have commanded.* The case would be serious enough to warrant God's

---

[1] N. Lohfink, *BZ* (NF), 6, 1962, pp. 32-56, finds no need to suppose that the law and the song are confused.

[2] H. B. Huffmon, 'The Covenant Lawsuit in the Prophets', *JBL*, LXVIII, 1959, pp. 285-295; J. Harvey, 'Le RÎḄ-pattern réquisitorie prophétique sur la rupture de l'alliance', *Biblica*, 43, 1962, pp. 172-196.

judgment on Israel. The song that Moses composed was in the nature of an indictment. Its contents were so generally applicable that it could have been read to the congregation of Israel at almost any time in her long history and found to be relevant to her condition.

V. MOSES' SONG OF WITNESS (31:30 – 32:47)

The song of Moses, which occupies the major part of chapter 32, has been the subject of a great deal of discussion over the years. One of the major problems has been its literary genre. Another question has been the place it occupies in Deuteronomy as a whole. More recently the antiquity of the poem has been recognized because of a number of archaic linguistic features, and several noted scholars now date it as early as the eleventh century BC, *i.e.* in the time of Samuel, in its original form. Some help in the interpretation of the poem has come from the study of a literary form which was used by suzerains in dealing with their vassals in the ancient Near East, *i.e.* in the area of international law. Two literary forms which differ only in their conclusions were commonly used when a suzerain confronted an erring vassal. In the one the document concludes with a declaration of war, and in the other with an ultimatum to the vassal who had shown signs of breaking his treaty. Examples of these forms are known from the second millennium BC, even as far back as the time of the Mari documents in the late eighteenth and early seventeenth centuries BC. The pattern has become known as the *RÎB*-pattern (Heb. *rîḇ*, lawsuit). It commences with an appeal to the accused to give heed to what is being announced. Heaven and earth are summoned as witnesses to hear the indictment. Then follows a section of interrogation in which the plaintiff (or his representative) poses questions in which an accusation is implicit. Next comes a declaration of the past benefits bestowed on the rebel vassal by his overlord and of the ingratitude of the vassal. Some reference to the futility of other alliances in the face of rebellion is now made. Finally, the declaration of guilt is made and the vassal is either warned of coming judgment or is warned to amend his ways.

Something of this pattern can be discerned in Deuteronomy 32, which may be analysed as follows: a. Introduction, the calling of heaven and earth and the declaration of the character of God (1–4); b. Interrogation and implied accusation (5, 6); c. Recollection of the mighty acts of God on Israel's behalf in years past (7–14). d. Direct indictment (15–18); e. The sentence (19–25). At this point a new theme is introduced which is not found in the secular *RÎB*-pattern, namely, a word of hope. The analysis of the chapter then proceeds with f. The assurance of Israel's deliverance (26–38); g. Yahweh's own word promising deliverance (39–42); and finally, h. A call for Israel to worship God (43). The chapter concludes with narrative material referring to Moses' ascent of Mount Nebo to view the land he would never enter.

The recognition that this chapter is in the literary form of a covenant law-suit makes it possible to link it closely with the rest of Deuteronomy, where the covenant motif is so strong. The fact that the chapter is not completely parallel to the standard covenant law-suit calls for some explanation. The poem is described in verse 2 as *my teaching* (*leqaḥ*, a rare word). Hence it is not strictly a covenant law-suit document, but a didactic poem based on the covenant law-suit pictures. Further, verses 30–43, which give expression to hope and trust in God's salvation, do not correspond to any element in the secular covenant. The deliverance depicted is one which Israel came to expect in their Holy Wars so that we should, perhaps, look to this idea as the source of such an expression. Thus we gain the impression that chapter 32 is based on the covenant law-suit as a primary theme, but some expansion has taken place to produce a poem which is really an adaptation of a secular picture to serve a religious purpose. Did such a poem derive from Moses? According to the text as we have it today, it did. There is no reason to deny that Moses knew about these literary forms, since they were well-known in political life before and after his day. Nor need we deny that Moses, out of his intimate knowledge of the weakness of his people, might anticipate that they would one day break their covenant with Yahweh and warrant the issue of an indictment from God by the mouth of one of His servants, which would resemble in some ways the indictment an erring vassal might receive from his overlord. It is possible, therefore, to argue that Moses could have spoken in terms not unlike those represented here.

The fact that several recent writers date this poem no later than the eleventh century BC has led to a search for some historical catastrophe when Israel suffered a severe setback at the hands of some non-Israelite group (the *no people* of verse 21).[1] Thus O. Eissfeldt has dated the poem to the early Philistine era.[2] W. F. Albright dates the poem from about 1025 BC, some time after the fall of Shiloh.[3]

Whatever the facts were, we may agree in broad terms that Moses envisaged such a contingency and wrote a warning for posterity to read. Such a warning was preserved and at the appropriate time was suitably expanded and re-applied. Detailed comments on the chapter may be made in the absence of an exact knowledge of the date of the final composition.

1–4. The summoning of heaven and earth to hear God's indictment of His people is known elsewhere in Deuteronomy (4:26; 31:28) as well as in the prophets (Is. 1:2; Mi. 6:1, 2). These, which must have seemed the most permanent aspects of God's creation, were bidden to attend to Moses' *teaching* (the word derives from the verb *lāqaḥ*, 'take', and may denote something which he had received from God). This instruction is like *dew*, or *the gentle rain upon the tender grass*, or *the showers upon the herb*, bringing life and refreshing to a people in need. The words *teaching* (*leqaḥ*) and *speech* (*'imrâ*) are common in wisdom literature, although they occur elsewhere also (Pss. 17:6; 78:1f.; Pr. 4:2; 16:21, 23; Is. 28:23; 29:24). These verses, with their use of a 3:3 stress pattern, set the style for the whole poem.[4] The declared intention of the poem is to *proclaim the name* (character) *of Yahweh* and to *ascribe greatness to our God*. Yahweh is further described as *the Rock*, whose deeds are perfect, all of whose ways are *justice* (*mišpāṭ*), and who is *a God of faithfulness* (*'emûnâ*), *without iniquity*, *just* (*ṣaddîq*) and upright (*yāšār*).

5, 6. A direct accusation is given in verse 5, followed by questions in verse 6. This is the normal sequence in this literary form. The interrogation by which the accusation begins is extremely brief, but its vigour is undoubted. In the normal *RÎB*-pattern the interrogation was put by the king's messenger, who transmitted the accusation. The same person made the opening appeal to the heavens and the earth and recalled the past benefits of the great king. The parallel is very close in these verses, where Yahweh is King and Moses is His

---

[1] Gerhard von Rad, *Deuteronomy* (1966), p. 198.
[2] O. Eissfeldt, 'The Hebrew Kingdom', *CAH*[2], Fasc. 32, p. 77, n. 13.
[3] W. F. Albright, *Yahweh and the Gods of Canaan* (1968), p. 15.
[4] Even those who do not read Hebrew will observe the neatly balanced phrases in the Hebrew Bible.

messenger. The corruption of Israel, who is described as *a perverse and crooked generation* and a *foolish and senseless people*, is in sharp contrast with Yahweh's own character. It was shameful ingratitude that a *foolish* (*nāḇāl*) and *senseless* (lit. 'not wise') people should thus requite Yahweh their Father, their Creator and their Maker.

7-14. It was a regular part of the *RÎB*-pattern to list the kingly acts of the suzerain performed on behalf of his vassal. So, too, Yahweh's providential care of His people was displayed in many gracious acts which were performed during Israel's past history, in *the days of old* and through *the years of many generations*. Fathers and elders could bear witness (7). Three great facts are stated: the election of Israel (8, 9), their deliverance at the time of the exodus (10-12), and Yahweh's gift of Canaan to His people (13, 14).

8, 9. At the beginning of history *the Most High* (*'elyôn*) allotted to the nations their own portion of the earth as their home (Gn. 10) and fixed the boundaries of peoples in relation to Israel's numbers. There is disagreement among the textual traditions at this point. The LXX reads *according to the number of the sons of God*, whereas the MT has *the sons of Israel*. A fragment from cave four at Qumran agrees with the LXX against the MT, which seems to have modified the original so as to make it mean that God ordained a plan whereby the number of nations corresponded to the number of the sons of Israel.[1] However, if the LXX reading be followed, there may be some idea of a supervising heavenly being, a kind of guardian angel, in view. In any case, Israel received special treatment, for Yahweh chose her for Himself. His portion was His people and His allotted heritage was Jacob, *i.e.* Israel.

10-12. Having arranged for Israel's inheritance to be placed in Canaan, Yahweh set about bringing His people there. The exodus is implied. His care during the wilderness wanderings is depicted under three metaphors: an encircling protector who guarded Israel as He would the very pupil of His eye, a mother eagle that stirs up her young to fly but hovers beneath them to support them in their first faltering attempts at flight, and a kindly shepherd or leader who guided His people without any other to help Him. Stress is placed on the fact that *Yahweh alone* led Israel. There was no alien deity

---

[1] *Cf.* R. Meyer, 'Die Bedeutung von Dt. 32:8f., 43 (IV Q) für die Auslegung des Moseliedes', in *Verbannung und Heimkehr, Festschrift für W Rudolph* (1961), pp. 197ff.

at His side. It was all the more shameful, therefore, that Israel turned towards other gods.

13, 14. Israel moved on through Transjordan until she reached *the high places of the earth*. Here she feasted on all the choicest products of the field and flock, honey, (olive) oil, curds and milk, fat beasts, the finest of the wheat and choice wine.

15-18. A specific indictment of Israel is now given. Despite all Yahweh's goodness, *Jeshurun* (a title for Israel, lit. 'the upright one'; *cf.* 33:5, 26; Is. 44:2) behaved like an unruly beast fattened up on rich pasture. Bountifully fed on Yahweh's rich provisions so that he had grown fat and gross and coarse (or *sleek*), he refused to give undivided allegiance and exclusive loyalty to Yahweh and like an intractable beast turned against his Master and spurned *the Rock of his salvation* (15). In all her well-being Israel forsook God her Creator and the ground of her salvation. 'A full stomach does not promote piety, for it stands secure and neglects God' (Luther). The picture of God as a *Rock* (*ṣûr*) occurs also in verses 4, 18, 30 and 31 in this chapter. In verses 31 and 37 the gods of other people are called *rock* also. But the same picture is to be found several times in the Psalms (18:2, 31, 46; 31:3; 61:2; 62:2; 71:3; 89:26; 95:1, *etc.*) and also in 2 Samuel 22:3. It seems to have represented the divine unchangeableness and security, to whom men might come for refuge in a world which was filled with many foes, both physical and spiritual. The imagery has found its way into the hymns of the Christian church in such hymns as 'Rock of ages, cleft for me', and 'O safe to the Rock that is higher than I'.

The next step in Israel's decline was to provoke the Lord to anger by her worship of alien gods and she vexed Him with abominable practices. *They sacrificed to demons* (*šēḏîm*, a rare word in the Old Testament, occurring only here and in Ps. 106:37) *which were no gods*, and to gods which were recent arrivals in the land, gods whom the fathers had not *dreaded*, *i.e.* reverenced or worshipped. An alternative rendering of the last line of verse 17, *with whom your fathers were never acquainted*, preserves parallelism with verse 17b. So unspeakable was Israel's ingratitude that she preferred such new deities to the *Rock* that bore her and the God who gave her birth. God is here pictured both as father (*begot you*) and as mother (*who gave you birth*).

19-25. The judicial sentence is now pronounced. The

passage deals with the curses that fall on those who break their covenant. Observing Israel's rebellion (19), Yahweh determined to hide His face, *i.e.* to withhold His favour and to send punishment.

21. There is a play here on *no god* (*lo' 'ēl*) and *no people* (*lō' 'am*). We are reminded at once of Hosea (1:9; 2:23). Poetically there is a strict parallelism:

> *They have stirred me to jealousy with what is no god;*
> *they have provoked me with their idols.*
> *So I will stir them to jealousy with those who are no people;*
> *I will provoke them with a foolish nation.*

The identification of *no people* or *foolish nation* is not certain, but it can remain symbolic without any loss. Commentators have sought identification in the light of the date they give to Deuteronomy.

22. There will be no escape from the fire of divine wrath, which will *burn to the depths of Sheol*, the place of the dead, and will *devour the earth and its increase, and set on fire the foundations of the mountains*.

23–25. The curses listed here, hunger, pestilence, wild beasts, sword, siege, death, are reminiscent of chapter 28.

26–38. The assurance of deliverance. The section commences with the statement *I said*. Some new deliberation has taken place in the heart of God. The introductory words may be translated *Then I said* or *Then I thought*. The following verses express the hope of deliverance or redemption. We are lifted out of the turmoil of historical events to hear a soliloquy in the heart of God.

26, 27. While a note of hope appears in verse 26, what has preceded should not be forgotten. Israel merits annihilation by being scattered afar so that all memory of her would be lost. This, however, would not be carried out. God would refrain from scattering His people lest her enemies should say *Our hand is triumphant, Yahweh has not wrought all this*. This argument is known elsewhere in the Old Testament (9:28; Is. 48:9–11; Ezk. 20:9, 14, 22; 36:21, *etc.*).

28, 29. Israel, alas, is a nation void of understanding. The events of their history spoke aloud of the activity of Yahweh, Israel's *Rock*, who had delivered them into the hands of their enemies. Some commentators take these two verses as referring to Israel's enemies who are unable to understand God's purposes in allowing His people to fall into their hands. This is possible in the context.

30. The point is made that, if a comparatively small invading force could overthrow a whole nation, the conclusion must be drawn that Yahweh, the Rock of Israel, had delivered over His people to the enemy.

31. A parenthetical note stresses the cogency of verse 30 by eliminating the possibility that the gods of the enemy could achieve victory for their people. In any case, the nations themselves, *being judges (pālîl)*, are obliged to acknowledge that this was the work of Israel's God (*cf.* Ex. 14:25; Nu. 23; 24; Jos. 2:9, 10; 1 Sa. 4:8; 5:7ff.; 1 Ki. 20:23–30; Dn. 4:34ff.).

32, 33. The character of the enemy is portrayed in vivid metaphors. Their nation is deep-rooted in evil (depicted as comparable with Sodom and Gomorrah), hence their products are venomous and poisonous.

34, 35. The end of Israel's enemies will be divine judgment. The bad fruit produced from evil lives is known to God and is stored up in His storehouses. At the proper time God will be the avenger. The term *vengeance (nāqām)* denotes the zeal of God in the discharge of justice. To the repentant, God's zeal issues in forgiveness and salvation. To the unrepentant and the rebel, God's zeal issues in judgment. In Isaiah 61:2 the noun *nāqām* should probably be translated 'salvation'. This involves both judgment and grace (as also the word 'righteousness', *ṣedeq* or *ṣᵉdāqâ*, which should sometimes be translated 'salvation' or 'deliverance', as in rsv in Is. 46:13; 51:5, 6; 54:17; 56:1, *etc.*). Verse 35 is quoted in the New Testament in Romans 12:19 and Hebrews 10:30. In the former verse, Deuteronomy is quoted to support Paul's contention that Christians ought to live at peace with all men and under no circumstances should they seek revenge. There may be occasions when God's wrath is carried into effect by human agency (Rom. 13:4), but even then it is by divine appointment (Rom. 13:1). No individual should assume that he can carry out the divine sentence by the exercise of his own vengeful feelings. In Hebrews 10:30 the writer's application of Deuteronomy 32:35 is not out of keeping with the original context, once it is realized that a principle enunciated in Deuteronomy is given a new application. In the original context the *vengeance* (judgment) of God was directed against Israel's enemies, who reaped what they had sown. But God's own people were not exempt from this law and should expect to reap judgment where they had 'profaned the blood of the covenant by which (they were) sanctified, and outraged the Spirit of grace' (Heb. 10:29).

36–38. By contrast, the just judgment of God upon the wicked enemies of Israel will prepare the way for the forgiveness of God's people.

36. An interesting parallelism occurs in this verse. The verb *vindicate* (*dîn*) is set parallel to *have compassion* (*nāḥam*). A legal act brings about deliverance, which is a display of compassion.

37, 38. Although Yahweh turns in favour to His people, He exposes to them the foolishness of their former trust in idols to whom they offered sacrifices and drink offerings.

39–42. The word of Yahweh Himself is now given to confirm the word of the poet. Speaking in the first person Yahweh now announces His sole deity, *I, even I, am he, and there is no god beside me*. The false gods are impotent. Only Yahweh can kill and make alive, wound and heal, and no power in heaven or earth can deliver out of His hand.

40. Lifting the hand was the gesture of a man taking an oath. It was probably intended to imply that he appealed to God as a witness. The common oath formula was 'As Yahweh lives'. Yahweh swore by His own name, *As I live for ever*.

41, 42. The terrible nature of God's zeal is now set out in vivid detail. The expression *my glittering sword* means literally 'the lightning of my sword' and may be translated 'my flashing blade' (*cf.* Na. 3:3; Hab. 3:11; Ezk. 21:9f.). Yahweh is pictured as a warrior arming himself for battle (Ex. 15:3; Is. 42:13; 59:17). He seizes *judgment* as though it were a weapon, in order to bring judgment on His adversaries. The figures of *arrows drunk with blood* and of a *sword devouring flesh* suggest scenes of carnage (*cf.* Is. 34:5ff.; 49:26; 63:3–6; Je. 12:12; 25:30–33; 46:10; 50:25–32). *The long-haired heads of the enemy* may be a poetic expression either for the great strength of the enemy displayed by long hair (*cf.* Samson), or for the fact that they were consecrated to battle. However, the term translated *long-haired* (*pera'*) means either 'hair' or 'leader', and the phrase may mean 'from the head of the leaders of the enemy'.

43. The poet's final exhortation, addressed to the nations of the world, bids them sing the praise of the God of Israel who avenges the blood of His servants and brings judgment on His enemies and 'covers' His land and His people. The verb 'cover' (*kippēr*), often translated 'make atonement', is taken up from the vocabulary of sacrificial worship and refers to God's act by means of which atonement or expiation is effected. God is here pictured as clearing away and covering over the guilt of His people and His land. He not only forgives His people but covers over their offence. Both the presence of unclean enemies and the moral and cultic evils of Israel had polluted the land, making such a covering necessary.

44–47. With verse 44 we return to prose narrative. Moses and Joshua recited the words of this poem to the people and then charged them personally to *lay to heart all the words which I enjoin upon you* and to see to it that their children should observe the law of God. The song and the law seem to be joined together in these final instructions. The most significant feature was the law. Even an important item like the song needed to be brought into conjunction with the law of God. Finally, Moses declared that the law was no trifling thing but the very life of Israel, through which she might enjoy long life in the land which God had given her to possess.

VI. MOSES PREPARES FOR DEATH AND BLESSES THE PEOPLE (32:48 – 33:29)

The time for Moses' death was at hand. He ascended Mount Nebo to view the land of promise from afar and then delivered his final blessing to the people before his death.

a. Moses commanded to ascend Mount Nebo (32:48–52)

48. Moses delivered his final address and *that very day* Yahweh spoke to him (*cf.* 3:27; Nu. 27:12–14).

49. At the command of God Moses went up the *mountain* (heights) *of Abarim, Mount Nebo*, where he would die (Nu. 27:12). The heights of Abarim are to be identified with one of the mountain spurs overlooking the north end of the Dead Sea. Probably Mount Nebo was one of the more prominent peaks. The modern Mount Nebo provides a fine view over the Jordan valley and is traditionally identified with the site.

50. Moses was to die on a mountain top in the same way as did Aaron his brother, on Mount Hor (Nu. 20:22–29; 33:37–39).

51. Yahweh recalls the fact that Moses *broke faith* (*māʿal*) with him among the people at Meribath-kadesh (1:37; 3:26; 4:21; Nu. 20:10ff.; 27:14b) by failing to uphold Yahweh's sanctity (RSV *You did not revere me as holy*). The exact offence of

Moses is not easy to discover. Several suggestions have been
made, *e.g.* Moses struck the rock twice, thus displaying anger·
or, Moses made arrogant personal claims in asserting 'Shall we
bring forth water for you out of this rock?'; or, following
Psalm 106:32, 33, the people provoked Moses to speak rash
words; or, Moses and Aaron failed to lead the people after the
report of the spies. Whatever the offence was, it resulted in a
lessening of Yahweh's authority. This verse makes it difficult
to accept the view that Moses' suffering was vicarious.

52. Moses was granted to *see the land* from a distance. The
RSV rendering *before you* means literally 'away from opposite'
(*minneḡeḏ*). It is translated in JPSA *from a distance*, which is a
happy turn of phrase.

b. The blessing of Moses (33:1–29)

This lengthy psalm introduced into Deuteronomy at this point
has some unusual features. Literary critics have not found it
easy to attach it to one of the usually defined sources of the
Pentateuch. Moreover, it appears abruptly without any
evident link with chapters 32 or 34, unless it be interpreted as
the blessing of a patriarchal figure at the threshold of death.
It has certain features that are reminiscent of a hymn of war
such as is found in Judges 5, Psalm 68 or Habakkuk 3.
Linguistically it has a number of archaic grammatical and
vocabulary usages.

The poem itself commences with a section in which the
majesty of Yahweh is described (2–5). The description here is
reminiscent of the theophany in Habakkuk 3. This section
concludes with a reference to an assembly of tribes (5). There
follows a lengthy section in which a sequence of blessings on the
various tribes is given (6–25). The poem closes with a section
of praise to Yahweh accompanied by reflections on the favour
bestowed on Israel (26–29). The interpretation of the poem is
difficult. The tribe of Simeon is not mentioned. Reuben seems
to be in peril. Dan is situated in the north of the land in the
region of Bashan. The extensive blessing of Joseph and his
sons Ephraim and Manasseh points to a day when these tribes
occupied a pre-eminent place in the confederacy in the high-
land areas. Such features as these would point to a period in
Israel's history when the tribes had settled and when Dan had
migrated from the south to the north (Jdg. 18). Studies in the
orthography and grammatical forms of the poem suggest a

date not later than the tenth century BC for its final writing down, although it may have originated from an earlier period, perhaps the eleventh century, which would agree with the historical[1] allusions to be inferred from the poem itself. At such a time Judah was pressed by the Philistines, Reuben had suffered greatly at the hands of the Ammonites (6), Ephraim and Manasseh had emerged into prominence (13–21), Gad had migrated (22), while Phoenician activity had hardly begun in the area of Asher (24, 25).

This all poses the question of the exact nature of any final blessing that Moses might have given to the tribes. It is not inconceivable that one who had led the tribes for so long should make some final depositions about them before his death, and he might even have given a characterization of them in terms of what he knew of them. On the view that Moses was the prophet *par excellence* (18:15; 34:10), Moses might have predicted the future and so have seen what Israel might have become in due course, although in not a very distant future from Moses' day. Alternatively, it is not impossible that a sympathetic collector and editor of Moses' utterances, who was true to the general spirit of Moses' blessings, might well have actualized Moses' words. The poem could thus partake of the general character of Deuteronomy as a whole, namely, that it represents a mature reflection on, and re-presentation of, earlier words of Moses.

1. This verse represents the introductory note of the final editor. Moses is called *the man of God* (*cf.* Jos. 14:6), a title used elsewhere in the Old Testament for a prophet (*cf.* 1 Sa. 9:6, 10; 1 Ki. 13:1, 8; 17:18; 2 Ki. 4:7, 9, 16, *etc.*). He is pictured as giving a *blessing* (*bᵉrāḵâ*) before his death, rather like the patriarchs (Gn. 27:7; 49:1; 50:16). Such blessings were more than empty wishes and, once uttered, they carried the promise of fulfilment. The expression *the children of Israel* is more common elsewhere in the Old Testament than in Deuteronomy, where the regular description for Yahweh's people is 'all Israel' (see commentary on 1:1).

2–5. These verses, along with 26–29, are concerned with the praise of Yahweh who had delivered His people. The intervening verses (6–25) refer to blessings on the tribes. Even if the blessings were omitted, verses 2–5 and 26–29 make a meaningful poem. It has been conjectured that the blessings were

[1] F. M. Cross, *Studies in ancient Yahwistic poetry* (1950), p. 186. I. L. Seeligmann, 'A Psalm from pre-regal times', *VT*, XIV.1, Jan. 1964, p. 90.

inserted into an earlier psalm of praise and are now enclosed between the first and last sections of the hymn. Such a proposal is difficult to prove. The methods of ancient writers were different from our own and it is not unlikely that a writer might begin with praise to Yahweh, switch to blessings, and then return to praise.

2, 3. The activity of Yahweh as He led His people from Sinai is here recalled. The theme of verse 2 appears in almost identical terms in the song of Deborah (Jdg. 5:4, 5) and in the psalm of Habakkuk (3:3). Yahweh is depicted as coming from Sinai and rising like the sun upon Israel from Seir, shining forth from Mount Paran, approaching from Ribeboth-Kodesh (Heb.; *cf.* Meribath-kadesh in 32:51), possibly the desert of Kadesh, with a flaming fire at His right hand. Slight changes in the vocalization of the Hebrew text and one emendation in the last clause of verse 2 give a translation:[1]

> *With him were myriads of holy ones,*[2]
> *At his right hand proceeded the mighty ones.*[3]
> *Yea, the guardians of the peoples,*
> *All the holy ones are at thy hand.*
> *They prostrate themselves at thy feet,*
> *They carry out thy decisions.*

Such a proposal represents Yahweh coming to Israel's aid accompanied by the heavenly host of holy ones and mighty ones who have the care of the nations in their hands (32:8, 9). However, variant readings in Greek, Syriac, the Vulgate and the Targum in these verses suggest that the text has been badly preserved and there are alternative approaches to the text.[4] Thus the JPSA translates:

> *The Lord came from Sinai; He shone upon them from Seir;*
> *He appeared from Mount Paran, And approached from*
> *Ribeboth-kadesh,*

[1] F. M. Cross, *Studies in ancient Yahwistic poetry* (1950), p. 189.

[2] This translation follows the Targum, Vulgate, and in part the LXX. The Hebrew vocalization is *'ittô-m ribᵉbôt qᵉdōšîm*. The *h* in the first word is taken as the 3rd singular masculine suffix, and the *m* as an enclitic. See F. M. Cross, *ibid.*, p. 203.

[3] This translation involves some changes in an obscure text from *'šdt lmw* to *'šr 'lm*. In terms of tenth-century orthography the final *waw* is omitted, but more fully the reading proposed is *'ašᵉrû 'ēlîm*. F. M. Cross, *ibid.*, p. 205.

[4] Bigger commentaries need to be consulted for other suggestions about this difficult text.

> *Lightning flashing at them from His right.*
> *Lover, indeed, of the people,*
> *Their hallowed are all in Your hand.*
> *They followed in Your steps,*
> *Accepting Your pronouncements.*

4, 5. Here too, interpretation is extremely difficult. Various attempts have been made to reconstruct the text. Some commentators have observed that verse 21b, revised on the basis of the LXX, is very like a phrase in verse 5, suggesting that 21b may once have belonged here in some earlier poem. So far as we can reconstruct the picture, these verses seem to refer to the organization of Israel in the wilderness when Moses gave the law of God to the assembled tribes of Jacob (Israel), and when Yahweh became king in Israel. The description of Israel as *Jeshurun* is an honorific title (32:15).[1] The designation of God as *king* is not common in the Old Testament, although the idea of God's kingship, *i.e.* His rule and His dominion, is quite common (Nu. 23:21; Jdg. 8:23; Is. 33:22).[2] The present passage may be understood as referring to Yahweh's theocratic kingship over Israel for whom Moses, as Yahweh's earthly representative, mediated the covenant. Some specific historical reference seems to be in view, probably the Sinai event. The verse is translated in RSV as *Thus the Lord became king in Jeshurun.* But the text does not demand such a translation and NEB translates *Then a king arose in Jeshurun, when the chiefs of the people were assembled together with all the tribes of Israel.* In that case the reference is not to Yahweh's kingship. Indeed the name Yahweh does not occur in the passage and is only inferred as the subject of the third masculine singular form of the verb.

6-25. The blessings now follow without interruption. The interpretation of the various blessings is not always easy, so that a certain amount of conjecture is unavoidable. The tribes are generally introduced by a short phrase in prose which is not part of the poetic structure, *e.g. And of Levi he said* (8). In each case the actual blessing is in poetry.

---

[1] The root *y-š-r* suggests a meaning something like 'upright one'. *Cf.* verse 26; Is. 44:2.

[2] The representation of Yahweh's covenant with Israel in the literary form of a Near Eastern treaty is a tacit recognition of His kingship. The whole of Deuteronomy bears witness to this literary form and this underlying concept.

6. Reuben. The introductory phrase is omitted. The blessing is expressed as a wish, *Let Reuben live, and not die*. Some translators render the second phrase *although his men be few*. This would make it appear that the tribe at the time was in danger of extinction. The census lists in Numbers 1 and 26 show that Reuben was still numerous at the time the census of Numbers 26 was taken and far from being extinct. Later in the eleventh century, when Reuben suffered repeatedly from Ammonite incursions, such a statement would have had some meaning. It is tempting, therefore, to regard the verse as representing the state of affairs in the eleventh century. Moses may have made some such utterance as 'and may Reuben, despite his size, never be diminished'. Was there a characteristic in Reuben which made the possibility of his diminution a likelihood? He is described in Genesis 49:4, 'Unstable as water, you shall not have pre-eminence'. It would seem that a wise leader like Moses might have discerned in Reuben some weakness and referred to it in his final depositions. What actually happened found expression in this poem.

7. Judah. The saying about *Judah* is a prayer of intercession for Yahweh's help in a time of need. There are translation problems in the third line. The Hebrew text reads literally *with his hands he contended*. Proposed translations are *His strength, O Yahweh, increase for him*[1] or *Though his own hands strive for him*. Others omit the line as untranslatable. To what period might such a prayer refer? It is to be noted that nowhere in the poem is Simeon, who lay south-west of Judah, mentioned. It may be argued that Simeon is thus not recognized as one of the tribal groups, so that a date after the disappearance of an independent Simeon and his absorption into Judah seems possible. Again, the expression *bring him in to his people* may have reference to the division of the kingdom, or, if the second phrase is translated *And to his people come Thou*,[2] the situation described may reflect the Philistine encroachments of the twelfth-eleventh centuries. This gains support from the fourth line, *and be a help against his adversaries*. The lack of any reference to the monarchy may also be significant. None of these interpretations is certain, but all suggest a date no later than the tenth and perhaps as early as the twelfth or eleventh century. What then of Moses in this case? He could have made

[1] F. M. Cross, *op. cit.*, p. 219.
[2] F. M. Cross, *op. cit.*, pp. 190, 218 n. 25.

a very general utterance such as *O Yahweh, give heed to Judah and come to his aid in any time of need.*

8–11. Levi. The blessing is introduced by the standard formula and is likewise in the form of a prayer. A close study of the Hebrew text reveals that verses 8–10 differ from verse 11 both in orthography and in metre. Whereas verse 11 contains many archaisms, verses 8–10 are marked by an absence of the tenth-century spellings and archaic forms and by the presence of more regular features such as the relative *'ªšer*, the article and the sign of the definite accusative. Indeed, these three verses stand isolated amid the surrounding verses in these respects. Some scholars have suggested that they represent either a revision of earlier material, or, perhaps, a later editorial addition to make clear the function of Levi. The point is difficult to prove. If verse 11 alone represents the original blessing it is in fairly general terms, being a prayer to Yahweh to accept the work of Levi's hands and overthrow his enemies.

8. The Hebrew text lacks *Give to Levi* which appears in RSV. The first part of the verse reads *Let your Thummim and your Urim be with your faithful one.* The Urim and the Thummim were probably two flat stones.[1] One conjecture is that each was inscribed on each side with the words *Urim* (derived from *'ārar*, 'to curse') and *Thummim* (derived from *tāmam*, 'to be perfect'). When the stones were taken from the high priest's breastplate (Ex. 28:30; Lv. 8:8) and thrown, if both sides showed *Urim* the answer was No, and if *Thummim* the answer was Yes. The present reference is to the possession of these stones by the high priest of the tribe of Levi. If the Massoretic text be allowed to stand, we have here a request that the use of the Urim and the Thummim be granted to Levi, which implies a claim to the office of priest. The historical allusions to *Massah* and *Meribah* are not entirely clear (*cf.* 6:16; 9:22; 32:51). The narratives in Exodus 17:1–7 and Numbers 20:1–13 refer to acts of rebellion by Israel when they murmured and God gave them water from the rock. But these narratives contain no reference to Levi, so that the precise meaning of the historical reference is not clear unless it be that in Moses and Aaron, leaders of the tribe of Levi, the whole tribe was on trial. The present verse suggests that the tribe of Levi may have been approved on these occasions and some writers have conjectured

---

[1] See article by J. A. Motyer, *NBD*, p. 1306.

that they may have acted as they did at Horeb (Ex. 32:25–29) or at Shittim in reference to Baal of Peor (Nu. 25:1–9).[1]

9. The tribe of Levi set their duty to Yahweh above all the claims of kindred (Mt. 10:37, 38; Lk. 14:26). This led them to devote themselves to the service of Yahweh so that in times of national crisis, when people turned aside to other gods, they administered swift and severe punishment to evil-doers whoever they were, whether members of their family or not. Thus in the incident of the golden calf in Exodus 32:25–29 they drew their swords against their brethren (*cf.* Nu. 25:8). On these occasions the Levites manifested a spirit which is here predicated of the whole tribe. *Your precepts alone they observed and kept your covenant* (JPSA).

10. Such devotion led to Levi's appointment to a dual office, firstly to guard the law and teach it (9b), and secondly, to undertake the various duties associated with the offering of sacrifices. The area of teaching is defined as the *ordinances* (*mišpāṭîm*, 'norms', 'judicial decisions') and the *law* (*tôrâ*, 'teaching', 'instruction'). In the area of cultic observances they were to bring incense before Yahweh (lit. 'they shall place incense in your nostrils'), and to offer *whole burnt offerings* (*qālîl*) on His altar. The functions outlined in verses 9 and 10 were normal for the priestly Levites in days when the temple services were organized.

11. The prayer for blessing on Levi is accompanied by a prayer for the overthrow of his foes. The *work of his hands* denotes his 'undertakings'. What occasions might have called forth such a prayer is not clear, although Genesis 49:5–7 refers to an early occasion when Levi was a warlike tribe. The story of the rebellions of Korah against Moses and Aaron (Nu. 16:1–11) may give a reference point. As we have seen, verse 11 is marked by ancient orthography and archaic forms and is regarded by F. M. Cross as the only genuinely ancient element in this section on Levi.[2]

12. Benjamin. Following the introductory words there is a simple statement about Benjamin which is neither a blessing nor a prayer. Benjamin, the *beloved* (*yādîd*) of Yahweh, is pictured as dwelling in safety beside Yahweh. The expression *he encompasses him all the day long* (RSV) has been translated *The*

---

[1] P. Buis and J. Leclercq, *Le Deutéronome* (1963), p. 208.
[2] F. M. Cross, *op. cit.*, pp. 191, 220 n. 29.

Exalted one hovers over him, following a slight emendation.[1] The final phrase *and makes his dwelling between his shoulders* may mean that Benjamin rests between Yahweh's shoulders, *i.e.* in the place of affection and protection. The JPSA translates:

> *Beloved of the Lord, He rests securely beside Him;*
> *Ever does He protect him, as he rests between His shoulders.*

If the reference is to Benjamin resting between Yahweh's shoulders (or *dwelling amid his slopes*), there is no suggestion here that the central sanctuary where Yahweh dwells is situated in the Benjamin area, either at Nob (during the reign of Saul) or at Jerusalem (the tabernacle of David or the temple of Solomon).[2] Alternatively the picture may be of a child sitting on the shoulders of its parent, *i.e.* between his shoulders. There is nothing that requires a date even as late as Saul, so that the passage could go back to some original, utterance of Moses.

13–17. Joseph. This is the longest of the blessings. The first part (13–16) is really a blessing and is expressed in noble language. The term 'bounty' or 'abundance' (*meḡeḏ*) occurs five times in this section. It is translated by RSV in a variety of ways, *choicest gifts, choicest fruits, rich yield, abundance, best gifts,* to give a variety of nuances in connotation. The parts of the poem are constructed in symmetrical units. The blessing is related to Genesis 49:25, 26, both poems being full of imagery which is known in Canaanite poetry. The areas of nature which are specified are virtually personified, although this is merely a poetic device. Joseph is presented as the two tribes Ephraim and Manasseh (17).

13. The verse is represented in Hebrew by three-stress elements (colons). Joseph's land is blessed with the bounty of heaven from above and with the bounty of earth from beneath. The term 'bounty' (*meḡeḏ*) is parallel to 'blessing' (*berāḵâ*) in Genesis 49:25, 26. The noun *deep* (*tehôm*) appears elsewhere in the Old Testament (Gn. 49:25; Ex. 15:5, 8; Hab. 3:10) and frequently in Ugaritic (Canaanite) in a personified sense. No article appears here, so that the sense is *Tehom crouching beneath*, rather like a great monster. It is a vivid symbol and although the term may go back to ancient Near Eastern mythology, it has lost any such significance here.

---

[1] F. M. Cross, *op. cit.*, p. 223 n. 38, where *'elî hôp̄ēp̄ 'ālāyw* replaces *ālāyw hôp̄ēp̄ 'ālāyw*.
[2] The view is expressed by S. R. Driver, *Deuteronomy* (ICC, 1902), p. 404.

14. Two three-stress colons form the second phrase with a contrast between the abundance of the harvests of the sun and the rich yields of the *months* (moon). The sun and the moon are connected with the seasons and so are thought of as influencing the seasonal crops. Both words appear without the article in a personified form.

15. Next we have a three-stress, two-colon section which provides a parallelism between the ancient mountains and the eternal hills, both sources of Joseph's abundance (Gn. 49:26).

16. Reference is now made to the bounty of the earth and its fullness, and the favour of the One who dwelt in the bush, *i.e.* Yahweh. AV, RSV read *him that dwelt in the bush*, which is in keeping with Exodus. However, since in the tenth-century orthography the only consonants to appear would be *sn*, the present *snh*, now vocalized to mean 'bush', could have been Sinai, which was a much more significant term in Israel's thought than the bush where Moses met Yahweh. Hence verse 16b may have read *the favour of him that dwelt in Sinai*. The prayer is that such blessings as these might descend on Joseph's head and on the crown of the head of him who was the leader of his brethren. Joseph is thus described as the dominant figure in the tribal confederacy. The tribes of Ephraim and Manasseh[1] occupied such a position more or less continuously, since they were the largest of the northern tribes. But this would have become evident very early in Israel's history following the conquest. In the present passage no attempt is made to treat Ephraim and Manesseh separately. Historically they remained together as the central core of the Northern Kingdom of Israel and between them they occupied a considerable area of the promised land. It might be argued that in Moses' day the tribe was recognized merely under the name of its great progenitor Joseph, because the later division of the tribe into two large sub-tribes was not relevant (*cf.* Gn. 49). Later events made the division of Joseph into the tribes of Ephraim and Manasseh more significant. The division helped to maintain the tribal strength at twelve after Levi was withdrawn from land occupation. Did Moses discern features in Ephraim and Manasseh which would lead him to declare such

---

[1] According to Gn. 41:51f. the name Manesseh (*menaššeh*, root *našâ*, 'to forget') was chosen by Joseph because 'God has made me forget all my hardship and all my father's house', while the name Ephraim (*'eprayim*, from the root *perî*, 'fruit') was chosen because 'God has made me fruitful in the land of my affliction'.

pre-eminence in general terms, or was the area allotted to them such as to suggest the idea? Most of the language in verses 13–16 is perfectly general and does not point specifically to any particular historical period. Incidentally, Joshua, who was to succeed Moses in due course, belonged to the tribe of Ephraim (Nu. 13:8).

17. This is a long verse and contains six lines each carrying three stresses and arranged in pairs. The general symbolism is military. Joseph is described as Yahweh's *first-born bull* who possesses majesty and the horns of a *wild ox* or buffalo (*r⁰ēm*).[1] With his horns he gores the nations and pushes the peoples to the ends of the earth. (The phrase *all of them* in RSV can be taken as deriving from the root *d-ḥ-y* denoting *thrust* or *push violently* by a simple transposition of letters.[2]) Finally, Joseph the attacker of the nations is defined in terms of the *myriads* (*rib⁰bōt*) *of Ephraim* and the *thousands* (*ᵃlāpîm*) of Manasseh. The term *thousand* (*'elep*) here, as in many places in the Old Testament, denotes a military grouping (*cf.* Nu. 1).

18, 19. Zebulun and Issachar. 18. Zebulun in his *going out* ('journeying') and Issachar in his *tents* are both called upon to rejoice.

19. This verse is a difficult one for translators and interpreters alike. The first part of the verse seems to suggest some kind of cultic observance. The two tribes are depicted as calling *peoples* (JPSA *their kin*, vocalizing the Hebrew as *'ummām*) to the mountain where they offer *right sacrifices*, *i.e.* offered in a right attitude of mind (JPSA *sacrifices of success*). The last reference is obscure. Once the tribes had settled, Mount Tabor, which lay between them, became a place for unauthorized worship (Ho. 5:1).

The last phrase in this verse suggests a connection with the sea. According to Joshua 19:10–16 Zebulun did not touch the sea, but Genesis 49:13 seems to indicate that at one time Zebulun was a maritime tribe with access to the sea (Galilee or the Mediterranean). Issachar, too, may have had access to Galilee. The *affluence of the seas* and the *hidden treasures of the sand* refer to the results of fishing and commerce (Gn. 49:13, 14). It is not impossible that Zebulun and Issachar provided transit

---

[1] The Hebrew term possibly derives from Akk. *rimu*, which denoted a large species of ox referred to in Assyrian documents.

[2] F. M. Cross, *op. cit.*, pp. 231, 232, reads *yidḥê* from the root *d-ḥ-y* instead of *yaḥdāw*. The line is then translated *He attacks the ends of the earth.*

areas for the products of the sea without being actually on the seashore.

20, 21. Gad. The area of Gad lay in Transjordan (Dt. 2; 3; Nu. 32) in the central area controlling the tablelands east of the lower half of the Jordan, here described as *the best of the land*.

20. The expression *he who enlarges Gad* is not clear. It may refer to Yahweh, in which case we have a call to bless Yahweh rather than a tribe. Alternatively, it may be a general statement that all who help Gad to prosper are to be blessed. An alternative translation, based on a revocalization of the participle *enlarges* (*marḥîḇ*) so as to read the noun *merḥāḇ*, 'broad areas', would be *Blessed be the broad lands of Gad*.[1] Gad is then described as a lioness (RSV *lion*) who tears the arm and the scalp.

21. Another feature of Gad is that he 'looked out' (RSV *chose*) the best portion for himself. The second phrase in this verse is obscure. The word translated *reserved* in RSV, *sāp̄ûn*, in post-biblical Hebrew means 'esteemed'. Hence JPSA translates *He saw the best choice for himself, for there was the portion of an honoured leader*. Another translation is *For he pants after a commander's share*, thus pressing a parallelism. In order to do this there must be an emendation which seems probable enough.[2]

The latter part of the verse is composed of three phrases. Some commentators would transfer this section to the introduction to the whole poem, perhaps following verses 4, 5 where the activities of Yahweh are described in more general terms. But it may still be possible to leave the text as it is and understand the words as applying to Gad who *was in the van of his people to fulfil the Lord's design and his decisions for Israel* (JPSA). The LXX reads *And the leaders of the people (Israel) gathered themselves together*. The Hebrew of the last two phrases reads literally 'Righteous deeds has Yahweh done, his judgments with Israel' which might be rendered 'Deeds of salvation performed by Yahweh, His acts of salvation on behalf of Israel'. Such a range of translations suggests that the real sense of the passage remains obscure.

22. Dan. Dan was one of three northern tribes situated in the Galilee area. The saying here is a mere statement, a sort of aphorism with little content. Dan is described as *a lion's*

---

[1] F. M. Cross, *op. cit.*, pp. 194, 234 n. 66.
[2] F. M. Cross, *op. cit.*, pp. 194, 235 n. 71, reading *kî yiśśōm* for MT *kî šām*. The root *n-š-m* denotes 'pant' or 'breathe'.

whelp. The second line as translated in AV, RSV and elsewhere raises a question. There is no original association of Dan and Bashan. Only later did Dan move to the north (Jdg. 18). If the link between Dan and Bashan can be established, the verse points to a date in the twelfth or eleventh century. But a clue to an alternative translation comes from Genesis 49:17, where Dan is described as a viper. If we see in the word *bāšan* a cognate of the ancient Ugaritic or proto-Sinaitic word *b-ṭ-n*, 'serpent', we might translate,

> *Who leaps forth (shies away) from a viper.*[1]

The point is not, however, beyond dispute. Verses 22-25 seem to link Dan, Naphtali and Asher together in the Galilee area.

23. Naphtali. This tribe, also situated near Galilee, is described as *sated with favour and full of Yahweh's blessing*. The final descriptive phrase is more difficult. The term translated *lake* in RSV, *yām*, sometimes means 'west', so that the line might read *west and south will he inherit*. In that case the meaning is obscure. If the word means *lake, i.e.* Galilee, the expression is easier to understand. Naphtali will inherit the lake. It is not clear what is meant by *south*.

24, 25. Asher. The saying about Asher is in the form of a wish. As in Genesis 49:20 the fertility of his territory is noted. He is *blessed above* (the other) *sons, i.e.* he is most blessed. The expression *let him be the favourite of his brothers* seems to indicate that he was to be held in special esteem by them. The last phrase in verse 24, *He dips* (or, may he dip) *his feet in oil* is to be understood as a wish that Asher may enjoy prosperity. The Galilean highlands were famous for olives and both Josephus[2] and one of the Jewish Midrashim refer to this fact.[3] The latter contains the saying, 'It is easier to raise a legion of olives in Galilee than to bring up a child in Palestine.' Asher stretched along the coast from Acre to Tyre. It was also on the highway by which invaders entered Palestine. Hence it was natural to wish strong fortifications for Asher. The link between the two wishes may turn on a play on words, since Hebrew *min'āl* means both 'sandal' and 'lock' or 'bolt'.

26-29. Concluding song of praise. The closing verses of

---

[1] F. M. Cross, *op. cit.*, pp. 194, 236, 237.
[2] Wars, II.21.2.   [3] *Midrash Bereshith Rabba*, 20.

this long poem revert to the praise of Yahweh with which the whole poem began. The rare appellation for Israel, *Jeshurun*, appears in both verses 5 and 26. Attempts have been made to provide a link between verses 5 and 26 and this has been found by some commentators in verse 21b. But the point is not clear and must remain for the present as a conjecture. What seems fairly evident is that the earlier verses depict Yahweh coming to the help of His people accompanied by His heavenly hosts and in due course being acknowledged as Israel's King in the assembly of the tribes. The latter verses (26–29) depict Yahweh, Jeshurun's God, driving out Israel's foes and enabling her to occupy the land of promise.

26. Israel's God (*El*) is here described as the one

> *who rides through the heavens to your help,*
> *and in his majesty through the skies.*

An alternative translation is:

> *Who rides the heavens mightily,*
> *Who rides gloriously the clouds.*[1]

The figure of deity riding on a chariot through the heavens is an ancient Near Eastern motif known to the Canaanites, but occurring also in the Old Testament (Pss. 18:10; 68:33; Is. 19:1; Ezk. 1).

27. The description of God as a refuge and a support for His people has been a source of strength to many:

> *The eternal God is your dwelling place* (AV *refuge*),
> *and underneath are the everlasting arms.*

Following ancient orthography[2] this verse has been translated:

> *His (Jeshurun's) refuge is the God of old*
> *Under him are the arms of the Eternal One.*

The latter part of this verse seems to be defective, since the regular 3:3 beat is destroyed. However, the main thrust of the phrase is clear. It was Yahweh who drove out Israel's enemies.

[1] Following the translation of F. M. Cross and D. N. Freedman, *BASOR*, 108, 1947, pp. 6, 7.
[2] The Hebrew word *me'ōnâ*, translated in RSV as *your dwelling place*, should more accurately be translated simply *a dwelling place*. But the consonants of this word m-'-n-h may be revocalized to read *me'ōnō* where the final *h* is equivalent to the normal third singular masculine suffix for 'his' and is a consonant carrying the vowel o. See F. M. Cross, *op. cit.*, pp. 196, 239, 240.

28. As the result of Yahweh's action Israel was able to dwell securely in her land. The second phrase *the fountain of Jacob alone* may be rendered *Jacob dwells apart*, if we substitute for the present noun 'spring' or 'fountain' the verb 'dwell'.[1] The bounty of Israel's land is marked by the divine provision of *grain*, *wine* and *dew*. The language resembles that of Genesis 27:28. It was doubtless a stereotyped formula more ancient than Israel itself.

29. The good fortune of Israel is now declared. She is *a people saved* (found safety) *by* (in) *Yahweh*, whose shield was their help and whose sword was their glory. In the presence of such people her enemies will come cringing to her. In the style of the ancient Near East Israel will place her foot on the neck of the conquered foes. The picture is preserved in the LXX (*cf.* Jos. 10:24; 2 Sa. 22:41). The Hebrew word *bāmôṯ* remains ambiguous. It could refer to the high mountains of the land (32:13), but also to the *backs* of the enemies named in the previous line. Assyrian and Persian sculptures have made familiar to us this picture of a conqueror treading upon the backs of his conquered enemies.[2]

VII. THE DEATH OF MOSES (34:1–12)

The final chapter is a brief prose narrative which forms an easy sequel to 32:48–52, although the connection is interrupted by chapter 33. The story of Moses' last days is recounted elsewhere in 3:23–28; 32:48–52 and in Numbers 27:12–14.

1–3. From the *plains of Moab*, *i.e.* the eastern plain of the Jordan Valley immediately to the north of the Dead Sea (1:1–5), Moses went up to *Mount Nebo*. The traditional Jebel Neba, rising some 2,600 feet above sea level, is possibly the mountain referred to. The highest peak in the mountain range was *Pisgah*, generally identified with Ras es-Siaghah to the west of Mount Nebo. The mention of both mountains seems strange. One suggestion is to regard the two as alternative names. Alternatively, the general range may have been known as Mount Nebo with Pisgah as one specific peak in the range. If Pisgah was indeed Ras es-Siaghah the view to the north and

---

[1] F. M. Cross, *op. cit.*, pp. 196, 241 n. 87. The change is a minor one. The noun *'ayin* is replaced by the verb *'an*.

[2] *ANET*, picture 249; J. Finegan, *Light from the Ancient Past* (1947), illustrations 89, 90.

west is superb. Even so, the view does not extend beyond Mount Gilboa, the highlands of Gilead on the east, and the Judaean hills to the west. But the portion that was visible symbolized the whole. The enumeration given in verses 1a–3 follows a large anti-clockwise circle from north to south – Gilead, Dan, Naphtali, Ephraim, Manasseh, Judah as far as the Mediterranean Sea, the Negeb and finally the Plain (*kikkār*) or Valley of Jericho, the city of palm trees (Jdg. 1:16; 3:12, 13).

4. This land was the land of promise, the land which Yahweh swore to give the patriarchs. The words here are identical with those in Exodus 33:1. The invitation to Moses to view the land (*cf.* 3:27) was not merely a kindly provision of God to allow His servant to view Israel's inheritance. It may have had some legal significance. There is some evidence that this was part of a legal process. A man 'viewed' what he was to possess.[1]

5, 6. Either there were companions with Moses at his death or they came soon after, because he was buried on the mountain. The expression *he buried him* might be translated 'one buried him', *i.e.* he was buried. The context suggests that it was Yahweh who buried Moses, although, no doubt, He had agents. Perhaps the second phrase *no man knows the place of his burial to this day* was intended to surround his burial place with an air of mystery, although it seems to be defined in general terms in the expression *in the valley in the land of Moab opposite Beth-peor.* The place is evidently the same valley in which Israel assembled to hear the final addresses of Moses (3:29; 4:46).

7. Moses' age of *a hundred and twenty years* is three times forty years. His life divides into three periods of forty years. There may be some symbolic meaning here. Forty years was the length of a generation, so that Moses lived for three generations. The state of Moses' health at the time of his death is variously described. Thus in 31:2 he is reported as saying, 'I am a hundred and twenty years old this day; I am no longer able to go out and come in.' Here the expression used is *his eye was not dim, nor his natural force abated, i.e.* his vision was sound and his physical strength (*lēaḥ*) unimpaired. This latter term (*lēaḥ*) and the parallel term *laḥ* is used variously of green wood (Gn. 30:37; Nu. 6:3; Ezk. 17:24) and of newly made green cords (Jdg. 16:7, 8). The cognate terms in related Semitic languages connote 'fresh', 'moist'. In Ugaritic (Canaanite) the

---

[1] D. Daube, *Studies in Biblical Law* (1947), pp. 28–31.

noun means 'life force' in contrast with the weakness shown in death. Hence the term seems to denote, in a metaphorical sense, 'vigour', 'life force', 'energy'. The picture would seem to be a typical Eastern expression where the facts are idealized. No doubt Moses in old age was a man of some vigour.

These remarks in 34:7 and 31:2 should not be regarded as standing in any sort of contradiction. There are numerous expressions in the Old Testament which have a metaphorical sense, *e.g.* 'a land flowing with milk and honey' (6:3; 11:9; 26:9, 15; 27:3; 31:20), which seems to have meant that the land had adequate resources of food. Similarly 'cities great and fortified up to heaven' (1:28) was an expression denoting cities with high walls. So here the expression *his eye was not dim, nor his natural force abated*, whatever its literal meaning may be, should be taken as a figure of speech, the exact meaning of which may not be entirely clear to us. Perhaps it meant that for a man of his age he had retained his powers in a remarkable way, even if he was no longer able 'to go out and come in' (even this latter expression is a figure of speech). Alternatively it may have meant something like 'he met death triumphantly and in full possession of his faculties'.

8. The people wept for him thirty days in the plains of Moab where he was buried (*cf.* Nu. 20:29 for Aaron).

9. The task was now to be taken up by Joshua, who was filled with the charismatic gift, the spirit of wisdom (*cf.* Ex. 28:3; Is. 11:2). It was the divine gift of wisdom required by every one of Israel's great leaders, wisdom to be able to govern and lead a whole nation. Moses *had laid his hands upon him* when he set him apart for the office of leadership (Nu. 27:18–23). But it was God who gave him the gift.

10–12. A final evaluation is now given of the character of Moses. He was the greatest of Israel's prophets (18:15–22; Nu. 12:6–8). He possessed an intimacy of fellowship with God unknown to others, for *Yahweh knew* (him) *face to face*. He was unequalled in the performance of the *signs* ('*ôt*) and *wonders* (*mōpēt*) which Yahweh sent him to perform in Egypt. He was unequalled, too, in the display of great and awesome power among the people of Israel. In short, he was God's chosen charismatic leader in Israel, God's spokesman, God's agent. In him were concentrated all the great offices of Israel – prophet, ruler, judge and priest. If some who held these offices were great, Moses was the greatest of them all.